THE SECRET OF THE CREATIVE VACUUM

The cycles of creation and dissolution represent the in-breathings and out-breathings of the universal mind. The universal mind is also known as Brahm and these rhythmic fluctuations or cycles are called *a Day of Brahm* and a *night of Brahm.*

THE SECRET OF THE CREATIVE VACUUM

Man and the Energy Dance

JOHN DAVIDSON
M.A. (Cantab)

New Age Books

ISBN: 978-81-7822-337-7

First Indian Edition: Delhi, 2009

First published in Great Britain 1989, by
The C.W. Daniel Company Limited, England

Published by
NEW AGE BOOKS
A-44 Naraina Phase-I
New Delhi-110 028(INDIA)
Email: nab@vsnl.in
Website: www.newagebooksindia.com

Printed in India
at Shri Jainendra Press
A-45 Naraina Phase-I, New Delhi-110 028

Dedication

To All Torchbearers

All creation is made of cosmic dream-texture . . .
All dream-bubbles must eventually burst at a final, wakeful touch.

Sri Yukteswar

What we see doesn't exist.
What we don't see really does exist.

Maharaj Charan Singh Ji

We are such stuff as dreams are made on;
And our little life is (sur)rounded with a sleep.

William Shakespeare (Prospero, The Tempest)

I have transcended space and time . . .
I am even smaller than the atom,
But I have expanded to the outer limits of space.

Tukaram (1598-1650)

Men occasionally stumble over the truth,
But most pick themselves up and hurry off
As if nothing had happened.

Winston Churchill

Words are at best an honest lie.

Mikhail Naimy, The Book of Mirdad

Acknowledgements

I would like to acknowledge the many friends and associates who have provided help in so many ways to make this book possible. In particular, I have quoted from or mentioned the work of the those listed below. I am grateful to the authors, originators and publishers for the use of this material:

Autobiography of a Yogi, Paramhamsa Yogananda.
Bhagavad Gita, translated by Juan Mascaro.
The Book of Mirdad, Mikhail Naimy.
The Ether of Space, Sir Oliver Lodge.
Ether Technology, Rolf Schaffranke.
Generation of Electric Power by Magnetic Force, Kohei Minato, translated by Mitsuo Nakada.
Ghost Mass and the Unseen Energy World as Revealed by the Anomalies of the Gyroscope, Harold Aspden.
Ideas and Opinions and *Out of My Later Years*, Albert Einstein.
Kinship With All Life, J. Allen Boone.
Letter to the U.S. President, Chief Sealth.
Life Beyond the Veil, Rev. G. Vale Owen.
Living Water, Olof Alexandersson.
Mathnawi, Jalalu'ddin Rumi, Translated by R.A. Nicholson.
Max Planck, lecture in Florence, Italy.
Mystic Experiences of Medieval Saints, R.P. Aug. Ponlain.
Psychotronics and *Paradigm of New Science*, Dr Shiuji Inomata.
Radha Soami Satsang Beas for translations from *Tukaram, Saint of Maharastra*, Chandravati Rajwade and quotations from *Heaven on Earth*, Daryai Lal Kapur.
The Rhythm of Living Form, Dr Peter Guy Manners.
The Seed of Truth, Silver Birch.
Through the Looking Glass, Lewis Carroll.

Towards a New Electromagnetics and *The New Tesla Electromagnetics and the Secrets of Electrical Free Energy*, T.E. Bearden. Also other stimulating ideas presented by T.E. Bearden.

The work of *Thomas Townsend Brown*. Article in *Science and Invention*, 1926 and *Interavia*, 1956, and letters to Rolf Schaffranke, 1973.

Also: *St. Francis Xavier, St. Ignatius, Dr Arthur Cam, Dr Marcel Pages, Dr Jean-Pierre Petit, Don Kelly, Christopher Seebach, Keith Tutt, Vita de Waal, Scott Strachan, Andrew and Monique Michrowski, Moray King, P. Tewari, Bruce DePalma, Adam Trombly, Leonard Holihan, Sandy Kidd, Lao Tse, Francis Thompson, William Blake, William Shakespeare, Howard Johnson, Dr T. Henry Moray, Viktor Schauberger, P.L. Barrett, Joseph Newman, John Searl, Nikola Tesla, Fritjof Capra, Stephen Hawking and Albert Einstein.*

Special mention must also be made of the Masters of Beas, India. They are the first succession of Perfect Mystics, in recent history, who have fearlessly taught the full, universal and ageless, mystic path and practice in unveiled, non-symbolic language – freedom of speech being tolerated by law in India and many other counties during the nineteeth and twentieth centuries. They are: Swami Shiv Dayal Singh Ji (1818–1878), Baba Jaimal Singh Ji (1839–1903), Maharaj Sawan Singh Ji (1858–1948), Sardar Bahadar Jagat Singh Ji (1884–1951) and my own Satguru, Maharaj Charan Singh Ji (1916–). My small understanding of things mystical has sprung from this bountiful source.

My thanks are also due to physicist and avant-garde engineer, Dr Gunnar Sandberg for checking the manuscript and writing the one of the two forewords, to Dr Shiuji Inomata for writing the other and to Dennis Halls for almost all the drawings and diagrams.

Permission to use copyright has been obtained where applicable. In a few instances, short passages or letters have been quoted where I have been unable to trace either the source or the individual concerned. For these few lapses, I trust I may be forgiven. A full bibliography is to found at the rear of the book.

Contents

Foreword from the East

by Dr Shiuji Inomata

Dr Inomata was born in Niigata-Pref., in 1933. Graduating from university in electro-communications (1956), he immediately joined MITI's Electrotechnical Laboratory (ETL), later obtaining his doctorate from the Tokyo Institute of Technology. He is presently the senior scientist at ETL, has been a visiting scientist at America's M.I.T. and is president of the Japan Psychotronics Institute (JPI).

To the eyes of a non-physicist, physics seems to have been in great trouble these last fifteen years or so. First came public demonstrations of paranormal phenomena such as Uri Geller's metal-bending, which could not be explained by the known paradigms of contemporary physics. In Japan, as elsewhere, repeated TV showings of these phenomena induced a number of metal-bending instances amongst the general public and an increasing number of people began to realize that they were genuine phenomena.

Then came the Chernobyl nuclear disaster in the USSR. Radioactive clouds contaminated not only the entire Europe, but even reached Japan, more than 8000 kilometres from the disaster site.

An ETL colleague, whose background is in electrical engineering, commented to me, "What a crazy technology the physicists have brought about! When something happens to an ordinary electrical power plant, the influences are limited only to that region!"

Bearing this in mind, John Davidson has devoted a number of chapters in this book to unorthodox and clean energy technologies which aim to tap energy directly from a 'creative vacuum' or from a 'sea of non-material aether.' I think it is very timely.

Is the vacuum creative or non-creative? Conventional physicists normally consider that the vacuum is non-creative. So John Davidson's book has come to challenge openly the general belief of contemporary physics that, "there is no aether," that vacuum is both void and inert. Additionally, he has made an important point that the assumed constancy of the speed of light to all observers, a sacred cow for Einstein's relativity, special and general, might be against the experimental facts. But these experimental results are being witheld by the orthodox physics journals.

This principle, regarding the constancy of light speed, was used by Einstein, against experimental findings such as Bradley's aberration, to expel the 'ghost' of the aether from the scientific scene. After that, the vacuum was considered to be 'non-creative'.

But during my recent visit to Europe, Swiss colleagues told me that Einstein himself had begun to think quite differently during his latter years. Everybody makes mistakes when he or she is young, even when we are old, but in Einstein's case it has caused science to drift for 80 years in the wrong direction. The Chernobyl disaster is one result. However, we should not blame Einstein too much. In reality, he was a true follower of Sir Isaac Newton, former Lucasian professor of Cambridge University, who, in his *Principia* published in the seventeeth century, put forward a mechanistic world-view.

In *The Secret of The Creative Vacuum*, John Davidson – also from Cambridge University – points out that, as Newton himself admitted, his understanding of gravity was superficial. Newton, for example, could not have known that the electrical force obeys an inverse square law, just like the gravitational force. Surely this alone points to a direct connection between electricity and gravity? It is also quite clear from the *Principia* that Newton knew of the existence of paranormal phenomena. However, he put aside such phenomena from legitimate science, saying that the experimental findings were still not enough at that time.

But by ignoring crucial evidence, science has thus set itself upon a totally material path. Anything which challenges this world-view is ignored or ridiculed by the materialistic scientist, wishing to see not so much his science as his inner world-view, remain unchallenged.

Science, for the human race, is a 'radar signal', an early warning of present and future directions. Our present situation is as if a radar device were to be found malfunctioning on a jet airliner cruising on the north pole route between Japan and Europe.

It is really a dangerous situation.

In this book, you will find many such 'radar signals', many such anomalies which cannot be understood by conventional physics. One of these is the Biefield-Brown Effect. The present paradigm of electromagnetism does not predict or explain this phenomenon. If it is real, it would mean that our understanding of electromagnetic (EM) phenomena is inadequate. And, you see, the conventional theories of EM lie at the central core of theoretical physics, our scientific understanding of the physical world.

I have repeated the Biefield-Brown experiment at ETL and, to our surprise, have confirmed it. Any suspicious physicist should perform this experiment for himself. And the Biefield-Brown Effect points to a connection between EM and gravity.

As described by John Davidson, one of the founders of present day EM understanding, Michael Faraday, believed that EM and gravity were connected. But he failed to demonstrate the connection experimentally. It is ironical, in this age of EM, that the other 'important half' of EM has neither been examined scientifically nor explored technologically.

However, it seems that in seeking for new energy sources, some unconventional inventors are already invading this new field of research.

John Davidson is kind enough to describe me as one of the originators of 'Japanese New Science'. My own experiences of metal-bending, more than ten years ago, made me believe that present mass-energy physics is not enough to describe man and our universe. And these experiences awoke in me the role of consciousness in science, just as a falling apple awoke Professor Newton to the role of gravity. More than ten years struggle to seek for a new paradigm of science has turned out to be a success. In the the autumn of 1987, I published the book, *Paradigm of New Science, Principia for the 21st Century.* Unfortunately, it has not yet been translated into English.

It has been said that my 'New Principia' is the product of the Japanese mind and western 'know-how'. Until recently, the Japanese mind was deeply influenced by the influx of eastern philosophies from mainland China. Now, it is increasingly affected by the world-view of western science and technology.

So, in the midst of our planetary crisis, it has been the role of a Japanese to help reorganize ailing western science along the lines of eastern philosophies. That is what I have been doing in Japanese New Science. And I feel that in the West, John Davidson has done the same thing in his *The Secret of the Creative Vacuum.*

Dr Shiuji Inomata
Tsukuba-shi, Japan.
September 1988

Foreword from the West

by Gunnar Sandberg

Born and educated in Sweden, where he worked for some years in an industrial and technological environment, Gunnar Sandberg is presently an electronics research engineer at the University of Sussex.

Observational and experimental research carried out during the last fifty years has revealed that the vacuum is filled with the continuous creation and destruction of the tiniest pairs of subatomic particles. Additionally, on the almost inconceivably smallest of scales (smaller than the nucleus of the tiniest atom), the vacuum is also in violent motion: the so-called quantum fluctuations, or oscillations in the electromagnetic field filling all of space – whether between the stars or within the atom. Theoretical work suggests that the geometry of space-time is also subjected to violent quantum fluctuations, giving rise to gravitational interactions.

Although the energy density of these vacuum oscillations is immensely high, fundamental obstacles are raised when trying to convert this form of energy into useful work. However, it is conceivable that the energy contained in the quantum fluctuations of the vacuum gives rise to some form of interactive 'space particles', generating an ordered, dynamic vacuum structure containing both electromagnetic as well as gravitational aspects, also integrally associated with the creation, support and patterning of biological life forms.

Based upon this hypothesis, John Davidson shows how the physical vacuum could serve as an interface between biological life and higher planes of existence. He also shows how the human mind, through meditation, could reach and possibly enter a state of conscious and sustained presence in the vacuum field, allowing the mind to connect with the higher planes of being.

This is a new approach to an immensely important issue that could be a very fertile ground for new discoveries concerning the spiritual development of the individual. Equally, it could significantly contribute to new fundamental physical discoveries. There are claims made by various individuals that the energy contained in the vacuum has been successfully converted into electricity and motion. These claims, although controversial, nevertheless deserve a closer examination. They are discussed in this book. If just one of them proves to be a real and practically usable phenomenon, man's energy problems will be solved for all time. He could take energy from the space around him whenever he so desired.

More important still, the concept of the vacuum field as an interface between physical life and an afterlife could supply us with a new tool to gain a more direct access to precise, factual knowledge concerning the survival of bodily death. Such knowledge would have a profound impact on our western society by removing the paralysing effects of the fear of bodily death.

Few people have had the benefit of mystical experience, convincing them that life is sacred and eternal. For the rest of us, no such convincing knowledge has yet come our way. However, it is my conviction that John Davidson's approach to this question will serve as a source of inspiration to all those men and women who possess the spiritual awareness required to explore new avenues in search of the innermost secrets of life itself.

Gunnar Sandberg
University of Sussex
Falmer, England.
November 1988

Introduction

My perception of the Universe is primarily a mystical one. This is what I have spent my adult life developing, through specific meditational practices of the mind and consciousness, and after a childhood and youth in which intimations of the mystical were frequent companions. However, I have been raised in a modern world and have a scientific bent of mind, too. This has also been my nature since birth. But my essential interest is in personal evolution of the mystical and this implies discipline of thought, of mind – not wooliness, but an ever-increasing clarity, lucidity and ability to concentrate within oneself.

There are many ways of communication, but all are essentially an utter-ance – an attempt to 'utter' or 'outer' what we understand or experience within *ourselves*. Language is only one such mode, and is a limited one at that.

But if one is going to use thought and word as a means of expression, the mystic path requires that one does so with considered mental application. This I have attempted to do. Most modern writers, who have attempted to show the unity in all expressed or outward scientific knowledge, have been scientists first and only secondarily may have attempted to demonstrate parallels to mystical understanding. For myself, I hardly read a single book of science for seventeen or eighteen years after I graduated from Cambridge University, other than was required for my work as a computer scientist. So I am working the other way around, looking at science and life from the point of view of mysticism.

One does, of course, pick up a lot by osmosis, especially working in a university, and in this respect I can endorse Rupert Sheldrake's idea that there is a universal field in which all our minds are connected. For when, after the lapse of all these years, I came once again to read recent scientific material, almost like a new university student, it was mostly quite clear and familiar to me. Much of it was already expected and anticipated, as a reflection of the social context and the mode of expression and being of the present times.

It was like arriving in a town for the first time, but with a feeling that you have been there before and know its basic street structure. Getting to grips with the physics without wanting to understand the mathematics has been the most difficult task – I was always more biologically oriented. But I believe I have grasped the essentials of what goes on in the minds of physicists (regarding physics, that is!) and I hope I have not done them any serious injustice in my discussions. No doubt, someone will let me know if I have been successful or not! And it always impossible to please everybody.

Modern physics is on the edge of an abyss. On the one hand, there are those scientists who feel that the answers to all of life's mysteries will be revealed if we can just get the mathematics to work out right. On the other, there are those who intuitively feel that life and consciousness extend beyond material substance. But they cannot find the link between what we perceive outwardly or conceive of as scientific theory (e.g. subatomic structure etc.) and their intuitive understanding or acknowledgement of the soul and mind within.

In this hopefully simple book, I would like to propose one possibility and then see how it affects both the human, the mystical and scientific idioms of expression and perception.

This simple idea is that vacuum or 'nothing with spacial dimensions' is actually a real energy field, or state of subtle material substance, out of which all perceivable matter is formed and within which are found, in even finer levels of manifestation, the energy fields in which our thoughts and instincts have their existence.

This idea is not, of course, a completely new one, but many of the implications of such a simple suggestion have been largely ignored or, at least, they have not been clearly expressed in the language of our present times. They have certainly not been linked into current and conventional scientific paradigms.

Some of the detailed expression of this kind of thinking is already to be found in my two books, *Subtle Energy* and *The Web of Life*. In Part I (chapters one to five) of *The Secret Of The Creative Vacuum*, therefore, I have by design used a simple manner of expression. In some respects, these first five chapters can be read as a prologue to both *Subtle Energy* and, especially, *The Web of Life*. In Part II, the first nine chapters (six to fourteen) are scientifically more complex, but contain important material concerning the continuation of our present technologically-based civilization. I have also had a go at showing where modern physics fits within the full mystic appreciation of the universe and at pointing out where it seems to me that theoretical physics is going wrong. I trust that this will not be considered too presumptuous.

Chapter fifteen suggests a simple experiment by which certain things may be verified.

After raising a myriad points which for some may have only served to confuse the mind, rather than to clarify, the final section – the epilogue – attempts to put all these pieces back into Pandora's box once again within the overall context of the mystic reality.

Ideally, the pursuit of knowledge should be inwardly edifying and/or have some good practical value in any of a variety of ways. Above all, it should be a source of both enlightenment and enjoyment. So I hope you have fun with this book and find it to be of value in your life.

John Davidson M.A. (Cantab)
Cambridge, England
February 1988

PART I

The Magician's Dance

The Vacuum and Subtle States, The Energy Paradigm and Life

All that you see is a magician's show.
The world is like a dream.
Baba Jaimal Singh Ji

—— CHAPTER I ——

The Mysterious Vacuum

Many folk, myself included, have a tendency to read books of non-fiction by dipping in here and there. There are good reasons for doing this, but if you try it with this one, you may get hopelessly lost. I would even suggest that if, like myself, you often totally ignore the introduction until later (if ever), that in this case you do glance backward at it, because it will give you my plan and purpose in writing what follows. I will start, therefore, without further preamble.

What is the Vacuum?

Mostly, we think of vacuum as being 'nothing'. If you suck all the air out of a bottle, and prevent the ingress of any electromagnetic or other radiation, you have 'nothing' left inside and we say that it is a vacuum.

Similarly, outside the envelope of gas which surrounds our planet, there is 'empty space'. Well, nearly empty. It does contain light from the sun and stars, a few (relatively speaking) cosmic particles, comprised of atoms, bits of atoms and other subatomic particles, plus some other forms of radiant energy akin to light, but outside the range of our senses. And there is not much, if anything, else out there. Or so they say.

But it is not just inside empty bottles and in outer space that there is 'nothing' or vacuum. In fact, modern science has known for a long time that all the apparently solid, liquid or gaseous material that surrounds us is comprised mostly of 'nothing' with a comparatively small number of molecules, atoms and so on, moving about in it.

Solid objects are only solid because other solid objects cannot get through them. This is due to the *forces* between the atoms and molecules. In fact, some solid objects do let other smaller molecules get through. This is how some stone, for example, can be porous to water or the atmosphere. Or how light can pass through glass, whereas you or I cannot. Light is not molecular in composition, of course, but is thought to be comprised of subatomic *particles* called *photons*.

However, even such subatomic particles are seen by modern physics more as smears of existential probability with wave-like and vibrational properties than as little solid blobs of something.

In other words, what looks to us as solid is actually a dance of tiny particles in a vacuum. In fact, if all the space were compressed out of our planet earth, it would end up the size of a tennis ball, or some say, even a pea. The exact final dimension is irrelevant because firstly it is not likely to happen and secondly the point is made either way.

In summary, then, according to modern physics: *physical material substance is mostly nothing or vacuum*. This is expressed simplistically and graphically in figure 1-1.

Where Did (or Do) the Particles Come From?

So modern physicists find themselves trying to explain how it is possible that something appeared out of nothing in a Big Bang, long, long ago. How we got something for nothing. But these kind of explanations and theories do not really add up. In fact, this approach to understanding the mysteries of existence is clearly missing some essential factor. Primarily, that factor can only be our own life force and consciousness. We are asking a question of the puzzle when we ourselves are an integral and dynamic part of that puzzle. To find the answer, we have to know what the real question is – and that will not be couched in words or even thoughts. We need to know what we *are*, within ourselves – what is our life, our consciousness – before we can really expect a valid answer to the question, "What is the nature of the world that *we* perceive?"

So the neo-Darwinian concept that life and consciousness have evolved out of a soup of subatomic particles just doesn't make sense. It presupposes that the substance of nature exists independently of us. Moreover, the theory

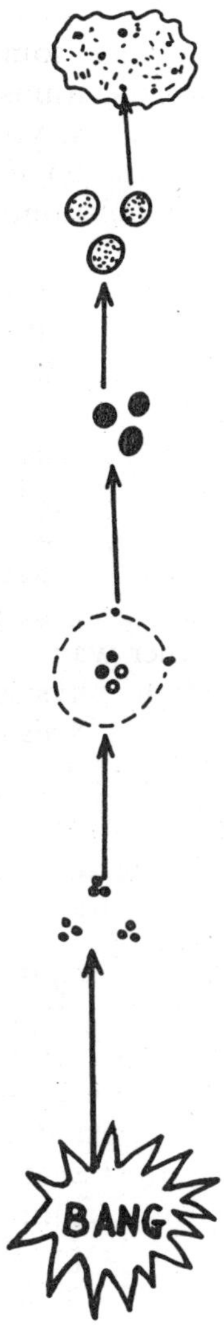

Forces and interactions between the particles or objects are said to be due to other particles (described by quantum theory) or stresses in their geometrical arrangement within space and time (relativity).

Gravitation *is the attraction of objects at a distance.*

Electromagnetism *is represented in the force of electrical charge and magnetic polarity.*

The Strong Force *holds subatomic particles together and forms them into atoms.*

The Weak Force *provides the energy required to convert one subatomic particle into another.*

Figure 1-1. The 'conventional' understanding of material substance, according to modern physics.

completely ignores a host of our everyday experiences and some highly valid, but not such everyday ones, too, called mystical experiences. Our emotions, our thoughts, as well as beauty, meditation, inner aspirations, intuition, health, healing, disease, psychology, psychic experiences, religion – in fact, the whole of our life as we *experience* it – is safely ignored and has no real place in this kind of mechanistic theory.

And if a theory is spun out in *thought* and we do not know what thought actually *is*, then how valid is it as a *total* answer to the puzzle of life?

Science, therefore, has its place, but it cannot presume to answer the fundamental questions. And to be fair, one must acknowledge that many scientists do not expect it to. They are not the popular archetype of bleak, hard-hearted individuals, but are just as sensitive as all the rest of us with as wide a spectrum of opinion and experience as you will find in any group of humans.

Where's the Link?

We have, therefore, an image of subatomic particles or vibrational smears of energy bouncing about in a medium of 'nothing', but obeying very precise laws all the same. Laws and relationships which we do not fully understand. But let us now rearrange our visual picture of what is actually happening. We know that you cannot get something for nothing. There is no 'cosmic free lunch', as the saying is. For something to exist it must be *coming* from somewhere. Note the use of the present tense. Creation is not something that happened long ago and then God (or whatever name you call that central organizing Power) went off on holiday. Creation is continuous. The Indian mystical tradition, for example, says that the universe is the *play* or *projection* of the Creator, of the Universal Life Force or Consciousness, and that He (or It) is continuously maintaining it from within.

It is one of the greatest fallacies of both science and religion alike, that creation happened a long, long time ago. In the most real of senses, it did no such thing. Creation is a *continuous* show. It is happening all around us and within us, right now. Ebb and flow there may have been and will be. Things, including universes, come and go. But the Creator is beyond time. He is infinite and eternal. The Eternal Now. Everything is continuously contained within Him, and is continuously being manifested or projected out of Him. What we see is just the dance, the puppet show. We may not see the strings being pulled. We may not see just how the magic is performed: how spirit, mind and matter are woven out of one Source. But the magic of the Creative Power is constantly present, vibrating within all things. It is, indeed, the very motion and vibration itself. And it is also the stillness of the One, beyond all motion.

Science, then, is able to follow that inwardness only until it disappears beyond the ken of external, physical observation. But we will understand the little that we do observe so much more clearly if we realize that it is being constantly manifested, constantly being expressed, constantly being projected, constantly being brought into existence from a Source deep within.

Then we know that we can relax our grip upon the search for the final, indivisible blob of something in our material world. For that ultimate something exists no more than the shifting images upon a movie screen. It is all just a show, patterns in energy, patterns of movement, held in their mesmeric dance by the inward power of the Creative Current.

And as to the obvious query, "Where then did the Creator come from?", there are a number of possible responses, but ultimately the answer is, "Develop your own spiritual consciousness until you become a part of Him, then you automatically understand the answer." But that is an experience, not an intellectual concept or thought. And the answer is, of course, associated with Infinity, the Eternal Now, that He is *beyond time and space*, that in fact He *created* them. So the question of *where* did He come from or *when* did He do it, becomes meaningless.

Moreover, the one who at our human level asks the question, that is our *ego* or sense of identity and individuality, has undergone some radical changes through expansion of consciousness, even upon the very earliest stages of our approach to the Universal, so the nature of the question automatically changes with inward progress. It is, like many other such questions, more dissolved than resolved.

But we are dealing with the domain of physical substance and where the subatomic particles *are coming from.* Note once again the use of the present tense, for the show of creation is *continuous.*

The answer, however, as is often the case, is staring us in the face all along. We cannot see the wood for the trees. Very clearly, *the particles are coming out of the 'nothing', out of the vacuum.* There is nowhere else for them to arise. *So 'nothing' must, in fact, be a 'something'.*

The Enigmatic Vacuum

We had better, therefore, have another close look at the vacuum and see if it really is nothing! Why do we think that is is nothing, anyway? Mostly because we cannot perceive it with our five physical senses – sight, hearing, smell, taste and touch – or with any instrumental extension of these. But is that a very good criterion for such an assumption? We cannot perceive thoughts or feelings with our senses, but do we believe that they exist? Do we for that matter believe in atoms and subatomic particles without seeing them? Or radio waves or X-rays? We believe in these things because of their effects, not because of direct sensory perception.

So maybe we just do not have a physical sense that perceives the vacuum. It might be pretty confusing if we did perceive not only the somethings, but also the nothing! One can also suppose that we are not *meant* to see the nothing. If we could automatically perceive that nothing were something, then the charade of life in this world would be to some extent exposed.

In a sense, the vacuum is a wall to our earthly prison, so that we cannot see our way out of this world before our time is up. At least, not unless we develop a different kind of more inward perception that also requires purification of our human mind, with all its weaknesses, as well as its strengths. So that perception is linked to our spiritual development. It is a sort of built-in mechanism for ensuring that the 'bad' guys (that's us) stay in jail.

So if the vacuum were a real something, a real energy

field within which exist forces, vibrations and movement and on the 'surface' of which are formed bubbles and waves, then we can ask the question, how do these bubbles (or subatomic particles) and waves actually come into physically observable manifestation?

In scientific detail, this is a matter for mathematics and the concepts of physics, but it can be described in simple terms, as follows.

The Zero Point of Vacuum

First of all, why does the vacuum appear as nothing or, mathematically, as zero? The answer is because it *is* at zero. It is a *zero point*. Consider, for instance, two equal teams of people playing tug-of-war on a long rope.

If we assume for the sake of the example that all the people had exactly equal strengths, then *however many were playing,* the rope would remain in the same place, *unmoved.* Mathematically, it would always be identical in terms of its position. It would always be at zero. Yet it is very clear to us that the *full* situation is always *different,* but always 'summing to zero'. And the people pulling on the rope, the forces that all sum to zero, we may call the *substructure* of the zero condition.

Not only that, for although the total energy of the forces on the rope may *sum* to zero, that does not *make* them *actually* equal to zero. The rope is actually 'full' of *potential* energy. Potential energy means energy which *exists* but awaits expression.

Now supposing that the rope spanned a street with the two teams hidden from our view down two side alleys, (see figure 1-2). We would then be only able to see the *rope* and not the *people* and we would actually see nothing moving, *because we only perceive differences.* We certainly would not perceive or even suspect the state of tension, or potential energy, within the rope due to the forces applied by the people we could not see.

Similarly, the vacuum state or state of zero energy is all pervasive and as long as it remains in a zero-summed condition we do not perceive it. It is rather as if our rope were everywhere, simultaneously, but because it shows no outward signs of movement or difference, we fail to see it.

Figure 1-2. Two equally matched teams of people play tug of war from two side alleys with a rope stretched across the street. From our view in the street, the rope appears motionless. In fact, as long as the teams are equally matched in strength – as long as their net effects sum to zero – then the number of possible variations in the numbers of people comprising each team will be infinite. There can be one strong man and two weak ones, five strong ones and ten half-as-strong ones, and so on. This is known as the substructure.

What we do perceive, however, are changes or inequalities. Suppose one of the people stops pulling. We then have a movement. The rope is no longer at apparent rest or zero and we immediately notice the difference. Similarly, it is forces within the zero point or *locked-in potential energy* of vacuum which result in movement and change which we perceive as subatomic particles, electromagnetic radiation and forces – the phenomena which comprise our physical world.

And more than that. For as all physicists agree, the quality of movement in subatomic particles is of paramount importance to their existence. There is no such thing as a *still* particle. Movement is an intrinsic aspect of its being. They spin, vibrate, possess electrical charge and possess other more abstruse properties. And whenever there is a property of one kind (eg. charge or spin), there has to be an equal and opposite property for the continued balanced manifestation of the whole. This is the intrinsic law of duality, polarity or cause and effect, by which all manifestation occurs. And it is these qualities which amount to their existence, not so much as little, solid, indivisible blobs of matter, but as vibrating, spinning vortices of energy. This can be understood by way of example.

The Blip and Bud Model of Manifestation

Space (or vacuum, or 'nothing') is (observably) three-dimensional, but let us look at it for a moment as two-dimensional, for ease of visualization. Vacuum can then be conceived of as being like a plain white, featureless sheet, stretched tight and all-pervasive[1]. Within the substructure of this sheet (which we do not perceive with our gross physical senses or instrumentation) arise waves, oscillations or vibrations which result in a manifestation of substructural inequality upon the surface of vacuum. The result might be a *blip*, (see figure 1-3a). If this blip were to begin to spin, it might *appear to bud off*, or become independent of the sheet, or vacuum, which is continuously giving rise to its existence, (see figure 1-3b).

In effect, it would appear as a *spinning particle* in the world of our physical perceivable 'reality.' *Mass then becomes understandable as a vacuum wave, vibration, oscillation*

[1]Actually, it is not like that at all, but let us temporarily think of it in that way and expand the perception later on. Really, it is the very structure of vibrational relationships comprising the energy patterns of the vacuum, wherein lie the secrets of manifested things and their interrelationships.

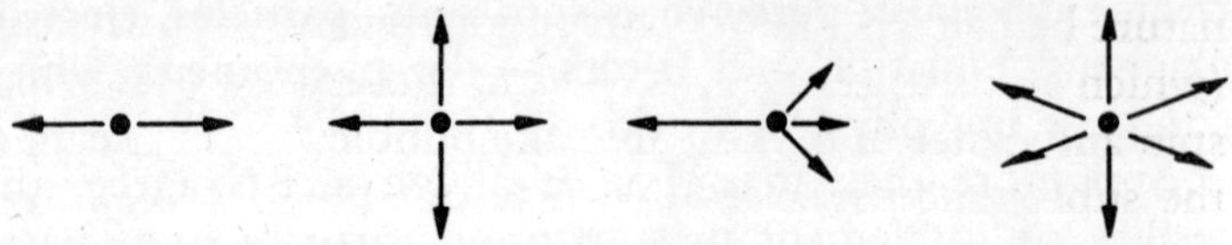

Figure 1-3a

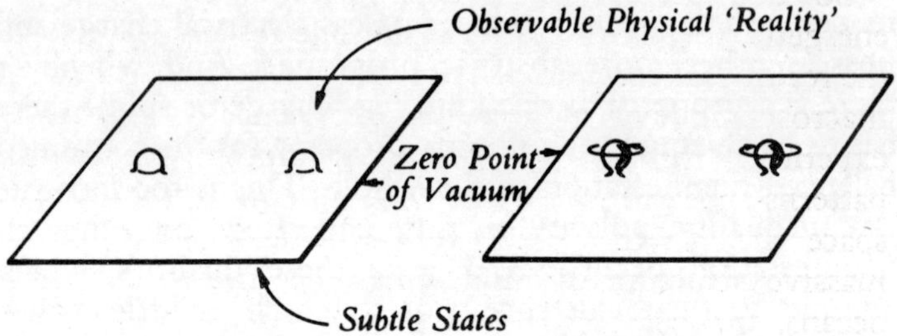

Figure 1-3b

Figure 1-3. The Blip and Bud Model of Manifestation

or rhythmic movement trapped by spin into appearing as a particle. Similarly, all the four basic forces of nature – gravity, electromagnetic and the two intra-atomic forces can be seen as manifestations of stresses or energetic interactions within the fabric, tapestry or matrix of the *vacuum state.*

Our entire physical reality is comprised of these subatomic particles and forces, but in an all-pervasive three dimensions, not two.

In fact, at the high energy physics research laboratories at CERN in Switzerland, physicists routinely orchestrate the transmutation of one kind of subatomic particle into a host of others. Clearly, the fundamental energy of vacuum can be configured in a variety of different ways. And it is these different configurations which we call subatomic particles – formations or patterns of energy conjured up out of the vacuum. Unfortunately, the concepts by which physicists are constrained or conditioned does not presently permit the majority of them to realize the significance of what is taking place.

Notice that the concept of the vacuum state as a matrix, a lattice-work or tapestry, has been introduced. For if vacuum is a real energy field, then it must by its very nature be patterned both in its (unobservable) substructure (which sums to zero), as well as in those parts of it which spin and dance into existence, like bubbles on an ocean, as the subatomic particles known to our present day physicists, and in composite form, to our everyday sensory experience.

So this perception of the vacuum state as a real energetic, formative matrix is not one reserved purely for the realm of theoretical physics, but can be seen even at the macroscopic level of everyday experience. For what we experience through our senses are nothing more than patterns appearing and disappearing upon the fabric of the space within which we are embedded. Whether it is the massive structure of mountains, the immensity of the oceans, the details of a woodland brook, the forms of natural organisms, our own bodies or the everyday objects around us – all of these are just patterns upon and within space, the vacuum.

I remember recently while at a friend's house being given the tea-time role of slicing up an extremely rich and moist fruit cake into about twenty slices. Nuts, dried fruit, glutenous wheat flour, and a generous topping of icing and marzipan clung to the knife with a thousand tiny fingers. "Ah", I said, "I can see that the vacuum matrix of this cake is demonstrating a state of dense manifestation." And even despite such dubious humour and suspect science, the cake was delicious.

So this matrix is around and surrounding us, if we can but tune in to its scintillating, vibrant, natural, awesome, yet delicate symphony. And direct experience of *that* is of far greater value than all the scientific theorizing in the world.

Vertical Energy Spectrum

This understanding, then, of how the energy patterns of the physical universe are created from within the vacuum state leads us to perceive that this is a vertically or inwardly continuous process. That is, the vacuum state is itself not the primary energy field, but is also 'created' from within in a vertical spectrum of energies that ultimately reaches back to the timeless, spaceless, infinite and all-encompassing Source.

The concept of a vertical energy spectrum requires a caveat, however. As has been indicated, everything comes from within. And the process intimately involves our own life or *consciousness* of what appears to be 'out there'. In fact, there is no 'out there', at all, it is all 'in here'. The lack of a full understanding of this reality is why quantum physics, while being almost reluctantly forced to admit that the 'outer' is related to the 'inner', gets itself into such a tangle, mathematically and philsophically. The the objects of our senses are not separate from the senses themselves. Perception is not objective, but subjective.

What this means, therefore, is that the vertical energy spectrum lies within ourselves, *including the apparently outward world*. You cannot, for example, find subtle or thought energies by examining apparently physically objective substance, because they – like the physical substance – are within us.

But even this model or manner of explanation is inadequate, for the apparently external universe seems to have a reality independent of the perceiver. Things do not cease to exist, for example, when we are no longer perceiving them, as some philosophers have tried to argue. Or put in another way, if you and I are both 'dreaming' our physical existence, then why are we having such similar dreams? In inward thought, feeling and interpretation, of course, we may not be, but all the same there is an apparent concreteness associated with physical existence that we *both* acknowledge and experience.

Expressed in another fashion, this paradox again appears when we consider that although the life force, energizing the mind and subtle physical energies, is primarily responsible for patterning the energetic blueprint of our physical bodies, yet when we die, the physical body remains behind to decay, as does the external world which that soul and mind once perceived. So it means that the 'outside' world does have a measure of differentiation from our sensory perception and inward life. Everything – inert or animate – is created from within, but the life force weaves the inanimate states of material substance into a physical body by patterning the vacuum matrix into the complex biochemical and bioelectronic processes which we perceive as a living body.

This differentiation is a built-in part of the mechanism of creation, under the law of *karma* (causality and relationship), because when souls are incarnate in human or other physical bodies, they constantly relate to each other through the medium of inert material substance, giving and taking in the endless karmic cycle of birth, death and rebirth.

But true understanding lies in mystic experience within oneself, so the best one can do is to say that under the law of karma we are all shareholders or co-creators, we are all an integral part of the mechanism by which our physical universe is created and within which the Universal is ever present in His sustaining power. But we will return to the nature of this mechanism, later.

The physical universe, then, is comprised of a spatial, vacuum matrix upon the three dimensional 'surface' of which appears a dance of what physicists *describe* as interreacting subatomic particles. So let us for a moment have a look at the nature of scientific descriptions.

Oranges, Electrons and Theoretical Models

When we describe an orange, or any object, in scientific terms, we analyze its weight, colour, dimensions, texture, molecular and atomic content and so on. This analysis defines the way we perceive the orange. The Zen Buddhist, however, would perhaps take the orange and banging us on the head with it exclaim, "THAT is the orange!' – NOT the word 'orange' or our mental and verbal description of it. It is thus important to understand the difference between our direct experience of a thing, the meaning or concept we have in our mind concerning that thing, and the words we use to express that mental appreciation. In science, these mental concepts and verbal/mathematical descriptions are called *models*, or *theoretical models*. All scientific 'explanations' are such models – they do not constitute the reality of the thing itself.

In subatomic physics, the implications of this process become clear when, for instance, we attempt to describe or devise a theoretical model of an electron. We can array its properties in terms of mass, spin, charge, speed, particle-like nature, wave-like nature – and so on. There is, however, a fundamental difference between our knowledge of an orange and our understanding of an electron. For in physics, it is only our verbal/mathematical *description* and *mental imaginings* of an electron's properties which define its existence to us. We have no direct sensory perception or experience of an electron. An electron is specified by its properties, which are known only by an intellectual process, augmented by laboratory experiment. The possibility of our experiencing the THAT-ness of an electron is precluded.

That is to say that our understanding of an electron is not of 'a something with properties', but that – for us – it *is itself the sum of all those properties*. Unlike our orange, which remains – in itself – steadfastly the same, whatever we may say about it. In fact, if we change our description of our electron's properties, we actually change our understanding of what our electron is. Emphasizing this point, is the fact that physicists have no all-inclusive theoretical model of an electron or any other subatomic particle or force. In other words, no physicist understands (through his physics) how the physical universe is put together or how it came (or comes) into being.

So even with all our best (though incomplete) descriptions of reality according to physics, whatever we may say, we remain without any personal experience of the reality we are describing.

The mystic approach, however, is fundamentally different, though not incompatible. Here, the mystic approaches an understanding of reality purely through experience – inward experience – perceiving things from within-out, rather than from without-in. And this inwardness is not in his thoughts, but in real and genuine inward *vision and perception*, a state of *consciousness*. And though unusual at this present moment in the cycle's of man's existence, this experience is nevertheless completely valid.

Our description, therefore, of an electron – or any subatomic particle or force – as a pattern or a collection of properties upon the surface of this vast sea of vacuum energy is quite in accord with the fundamental thinking of 'conventional' modern physics. It just takes the matter a little more deeply and links it through to our subjective experience of sensory perception, giving us an inkling of the mechanisms by which the illusion of creation is spun out before us. It is an ever-shifting dance or tapestry of energy in manifestation: a matrix of polarity and pattern in which the observer is inextricably bound up, through experience and perception, into the cosmic mystery of existence.

This analogy, however – this description – does itself break down when we consider that our orange is itself comprised of 'particles' and 'forces', spun out upon the vacuum matrix and has its apparent reality only through the experiential mechanisms of our five senses and their inward-outward linkage. For although the orange may appear to be a 'something', in the subatomic realm of which it is comprised we can find no 'somethings' at all – just properties and relationships to both ourselves and other 'particles'. Suddenly, the mat is pulled out from beneath our feet and we are left with a delightful feeling of the dream-like nature of the physical world we once considered so concrete.

Alice In Wonderland

Physicists do of course acknowledge that the properties they ascribe to electrons (or any subatomic particle or force) do not constitute a complete and integrated model of that electron (let alone that of the complete subatomic world). So it is quite safe to say that science does not know what an electron or anything else in the subatomic domain really is. That is, since everything is comprised of this unknown subatomic structure, science does not comprehend the *essential* nature of anything in this world at all.

For this reason, physicist and writer John Gribbin, in his book, *In Search of Schrodinger's Cat*, and many other scientists too, have turned to Lewis Carrol's, *Alice's Adventures In Wonderland*, for their inspiration on the nature of reality. *Alice In Wonderland* has become a constant reference in popular science journals such as *New Scientist*, for the realm of subatomic physics throws up so many bizarre mathematical, philosophical and experimental conundrums.

Quotations from the *Jabberwocky*[1] are favourites:

The slithy toves
Did gyre and gimble in the wabe

Gribbin, pointing out that subatomic particles appear to behave in ways that have no parallel in our macroscopic world, declares them to be more appropriately christened 'slithy toves' than particles or waves, with their activities more accurately described as 'gyring' and 'gimbling', than 'spinning', 'rotating', and so on.

I would add that within the basic constraints of energy in manifestation, of polarity and duality, and of an *extended, non-linear understanding of the law of causality*, this must be quite true.

For the law which governs the vertical manifestation of energy from within, as well as the horizontal patterning and changes with which we are familiar, is also a part of this extended law of cause and effect, causality or karma. All karma takes place within the realm of duality or polarity. This is intrinsic. Duality and karma are thus both part and parcel of the same creative mechanism and lie at the base of all the phenomena of life.

For what we are dealing with is energy movement, potential, polarity and relationship. Linear mathematics will not be sufficient to model the integrated relatedness of complex energy patterns. I suspect that a return to geometry as a basis for mathematical expression, may provide a better modelling technique, because geometry is capable of expressing simultaneous and non-local relationships far more readily than pure, linear mathematics.

This, indeed, is the basis of Einstein's model of gravitational attraction being due to the curvature of a geometrically-conceived space-time. But as a model, Einstein's ideas have been limited to conceptions of a three-dimensional space and the modelling of the gravitational force alone. More of this, however, in later chapters. For the present, I am trying to keep things simple and relatively straightforward.

[1] From *Through The Looking Glass*.

Antimatter, the Vacuum State and Perception

I am intending now to lead into a discussion of energy, duality and the extended, non-linear understanding of causality, but will begin obliquely with a discussion of antimatter. Many people are fascinated by the concept of antimatter and it comes as a surprise to not a few that antimatter is not simply an invention of science fiction writers, but really does exist. Antimatter is, of course, comprised of antiparticles – that is, subatomic particles with some of their properties being the polar opposite of their normal matter counterparts. Thus, an anti-electron or positron, for example, has identical mass but opposite electrical charge to an electron. Similarly with protons and anti-protons.

The concept of antimatter is not a new one. The British physicist, Arthur Schuster, first suggested the possibility back in 1898, nearly 100 years ago, though he did point out that the idea was purely speculative. This was excellent thinking for his time, for the atomic nucleus was yet to be discovered and Einstein's famous equation relating mass and energy was still some years away. It was Paul Dirac, however, who first predicted the existence of antiparticles in the early 1930's, and although physicists were at first sceptical, Carl Anderson in California and Patrick Blackett at the University of Manchester in England, independently, but almost simultaneously, helped to clinch matters by discovering positrons in cosmic rays during 1932. Twenty years later, a group at the University of California discovered the anti-proton and the theory became even more firmly established.

When antiparticles and normal particles come into contact, the mass content of the particles is transformed into a huge quantity of electromagnetic energy. In the case of positrons and electrons, this is in the form of gamma rays. For this reason, it is presumed that any parts of the universe which are comprised of antimatter are separated from those parts comprised of matter, for the one would interact with the other producing an incredible quantity of rapidly radiating electromagnetic energy. Realising this, scientists are in fact seriously considering ways of making anti-hydrogen[1] to use as a fuel for space vehicles. The problem, of course, is how – and in *what* – to store it, because it would have an inherent tendency to interact with any container made of normal matter.

Looked at from the point of view of vacuum manifestation, one can visualize how two subatomic particles, one of matter and the other of antimatter, whose highly energetic spinning vortices of energy are oppositely polarised electrically, meet. The result is a spontaneous 'unravelling' of the particles into an ultra-high-speed, linear radiation of electromagnetic energy. That is to say that one set of highly local effects upon the vacuum 'surface' (a particle) is replaced with another rapidly expanding set of effects, the total energy or activity remaining the same. And it presents us with an intriguing image regarding the possible nature of electrical *charge*.

I can remember driving my school physics teacher to despair with my enquiry as to, "What is gravity?". He could only present me with an equation, which was clearly different from the experience of an apple dropping upon my head. But which holds the greater reality – the experience or the concept? And the same question has to be asked of all phenomena. What are weight, electrical charge, even movement and time? Each one is defined in terms of the others, in terms of its *effects*, not in terms of what it *is*. This results in a closely-knit tapestry of scientific concepts, each defining the other in terms of each other, but still without our having understood what things actually *are*.

Even with a full comprehension of all the science known to man, one can still look with wonder at the panorama of 'ordinary', everyday objects and events presented to us by our senses and can still – indeed should – ask the basic questions – what is it all, fundamentally? And what, too, am I? Without an answer to that question, any answers which come from that 'I' regarding any other questions, must be intrinsically suspect. Any if you want to get perhaps too tortuously philosophical, the very *questions* asked by the 'I' are suspect as well. It means that the intellectual method of seeking reality is inherently flawed.

[1] A hydrogen atom is the smallest possible atom consisting of a proton plus an electron, so anti-hydrogen is an anti-proton plus a positron.

From our understanding of the vacuum matrix, we can see how all manifestation is a pattern, a dance, an effect given specific 'reality' and linked to our consciousness *through our sensory perception.*

Different species have different perceptions. They are linked into this patterning in different ways, according to their own inward subtle or 'mental' structure. Thus, some insects perceive infrared radiation, the radiations due to temperature, and so they see things where we humans see the 'nothing' which we call darkness. Air, indeed all objects, have a temperature whose infrared radiation can thus be visible to such species, by day or by night. They can even 'see' the specific infrared emissions of certain molecules, which we humans would experience as scents. Insect antennae are actually highly tuned aerials or receivers for modulated infrared signals. Such molecules are known as pheromones and are used for communication – sex and food-plant attraction and identification, warning signals to other members of the species and other necessary communication requirements of their social and environmental circumstances.

Indeed, what one creature smells, another may feel as heat, while another may see it. Presumably, this applies when moths fly into a candle and are burnt to death. They cannot have known what was going to happen to them. They see the heat of the candle which looks like something to which they are instinctively attracted – perhaps a food plant, or a flower, or a member of the opposite sex. And too late do they discover that the flame burns and is lethal.

So which is the 'real reality'? What *we* perceive or what another species perceives? Even amongst humans we all react differently to sensory, social, intellectual and other experiences. So which is 'real', or do none of them possess an absolute 'reality'?

We are thus always drawn back to our *experience* as somehow being involved intimately with what we may think is objective. Experience is subjective, whether sensory, conceptual or otherwise and our confusion only arises when we think we are *separate* from what we perceive. In fact, in a gloriously mystical way, we are an integral part of this cosmic energy dance and can only really understand it all by mystic superconsciousness, from within.

Energy and Causality

When matter and antimatter meet, physicists actually talk of *annihilation* with the release of energy. But that is not actually annihilation, it is just *transformation*. The content of material substance and forces is and always was *energy*. *Energy is all that is*. Things do not *contain* energy – they *are* energy. This is, of course, at variance with the classical scientific definition of energy which states that energy is the capacity to perform work, if and when we arrange for work to be done. But that is a very limited point of view.

Energy is the dance of life and form. Everything that is manifested, whether gross or subtle, is energy. It is the movement and differentiation that constitutes the panorama of existence, both within and without. In mystic terms, its patterning is Maya – the ever-shifting play of change and illusion. Energy is the primal creative outpouring of the One, the Creation Song of the American Hopi Indians, the Word of the Bible. It forms the Universal Mind, which itself responds to the theme by an endless splitting, shifting and reflection of itself within itself until we are bamboozled and bewitched by the scintillating, magician's show. It is the one egg of Humpty Dumpty broken into a myriad fragments, which dance and glisten before us, beckoning our human minds with an irresistable beguilement.

Energy is both the pattern and the thing itself. Between the two there lies no difference. It is the movement that makes up the illusory show of reality. It is the vibration that makes every subatomic particle exist. It is the motion of the stars and galaxies. To the mind, it is causality and matter; to the soul it contains the essence of the Creator's Love. The Lord plays the game of Love within himself through the energy dance of his creation. Energy is the essence of our thoughts and our emotions, it is the fabric of our bodies. Energy relates and weaves, it appears as separations and polarities, yet it never forgets its connection with its one inward source. Its patterns are the bubbles on His Ocean, the froth on His Wave. It is His *Leela*, His play, His game.

Energy is a snowflake, a flower, a leaf. It is atoms and molecules, DNA and all the rest. It is the giant redwood and the gentle violet. It is ice-crystals on the window pane, the wonderfully intricate tapestry of tissues and cells in living creatures. It is the cycle of the seasons, the span of a life, the rhythm of the planets. It is the hazy calmness of a summer's day, the power of the hurricane, the crush of a great ocean breaker. It is the gentle flame of a candle, the explosion of a supernova.

We cannot escape from energy. Our soul is surrounded by its multifarious forms. Our mind is energy, the physical world is energy. We communicate 'our' energy to 'its' energy by means of energy. It is both the information content and the carrier wave. We are embedded in energy. Its law is of causality, though extended beyond our linear, intellectual comprehension. It always relates within itself, all parts to the whole. It is legion and yet it is one.

It is this intrinsic oneness within the many which is the essence of causality, the cause of causality, one could say. Causality means relationship, pattern, association and it might be astute to ask: 'What *is* causality, in itself? Why are things not random? Why are they connected?" Here we have the answer, for within the One Source, there is only one. Without two or more, there can be no causality, for who is to cause what, when all is one? But the One creates the many and yet remains both undivided within Himself and present within the myriad energy patterns and forms of His creation. The presence of the One within the many thus gives rise to connection and relationship between the many 'parts' – that is, to causality.

So causality, or karma, is the natural outcome of the creative process from within-out. It is an expression of the fact that the One is still present within the many. Connection and relationship is an expression of His presence within the creation.

BUT – and this is a very big 'but' – the nature of those relationships becomes increasingly close, holistic, holographic, or integrated, as one moves within on the vertical energy spectrum. Physics currently addresses itself entirely to the horizontal nature of causes and effects and is consequently confused by apparently 'non-local' relationships, which it then describes as an outcome of 'quantum indeterminacy'.

Diagramatically, it appears as we can see in figure 1-4.

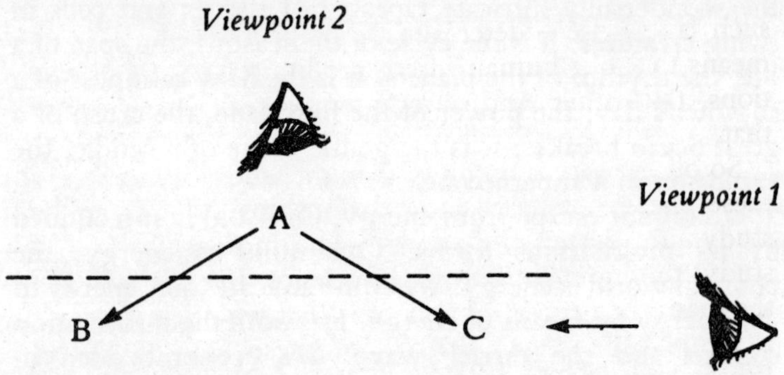

Figure 1-4. Generalized view of hidden relationships.

If we view only from point 1, we may see B and C as possessing no causal relationship. But if we can look from point 2, then the relationship between B and C becomes clear to us. Viewpoint 1 is our normal human mental/sensory perceptive mechanism, but viewpoint 2 is a mystic, experiential point of consciousness. Quite a different kind of experience.

In the terminology of physics, Schrodinger's probability wave function never actually sets out. It is 'collapsed' at every point by the extended law of inward causality. But more of this in later chapters.

Let us be very clear that absolute determinism is a basic fundamental of the true mystical perception of 'life, the universe and everything'. It is experienced and expressed by all mystics. Christ says, "The hairs of your head are all numbered." The Indian mystic, Nanak, wrote, "Not a leaf stirs but by His Order." Not a subatomic particle vibrates but by the law of the inner Omniwill. We are all a part of just the one 'Great Huge' going on. When, with our minds, we perceive the One as many, we unknowingly interpret the oneness of the One as our familiar causality. When we cannot see what we consider to be causal connections, we revert to a statistical way of handling the data, but that does not mean that the universe is run on probabilistic lines. For both statistical and more obviously deterministic descriptions of physical reality are based upon observation of order and continuity. Without this there could be no 'law' of chance! If we do not see how such laws arise – deterministic or probabilistic – it only means that our human minds are limited in their perceptions, that is all. And no-one would really disagree with that.

So our science is no more than the study of just some of these energy patterns and relationships. The deeper the study, the deeper the science. The more superficial the study, the more superficial the science. In fact, the deeper the man, the deeper his science. What we do in this world is simply the rearrangement of these energy patterns. What a fuss we make about such a small matter! We play king of the castle with the cosmic sand. We "Strut and fret our hour upon the stage."

Let me also quote a rather beautiful passage from Dr Peter Guy Manners, a greatly respected natural physician from England, who sums it up quite succinctly. Dr Manners has for many years pioneered the use of finely tuned sound vibrations and resonance as a means of re-harmonizing and amplifying the energy patterns that comprise our physical bodies, as well as our minds, emotions and subtle energy fields. In a lyrical article, *The Rhythm of Living Form*, he writes:

> The most apparent thing about energy is that there is nothing else. Its rhythms are not only outside and within us, but they are us, from the oscillating particle comprising the atoms of our bones and eyelashes, to the rhythms which ebb and flow in our minds. Energy moves in cycles or wave motions: it is never at rest, and it is always everywhere, appearing in countless hierarchical modes – like the waves on an ocean breaker, the ripples on those waves and the flutings on those ripples, each being part of an organic flux, but played in a different key. The difference between blue and orange, F sharp and E flat, even between a circle and a square are differences only in wave motion.
>
> Vibration takes us to the different expressions of energy in our immediate environment, the music of crystals, plants and human beings, the links between vibration and form, the resonance woven through trees, the movement of water, the shedding of colour and sound from the sun into the symphonic mantle of the earth. We examine those points at which the 'subtle environment' are being broached by the new scientists of the invisible. We see how discs of sand vibrated at certain frequencies produce 'mandalas', the sacred shapes

which are at the heart of nature and of human worship. We see how plants have 'aetheric' nervous systems which respond to music and human thought forms, and how the aura itself can be photographed to reveal the colours and moods of the psyche. Even the rhythms monitored in the human mind show that the visions of consciousness are themselves woven with vibration.

Our own bodies as well as the consciousness they contain are seen to be merely force fields – refrains, like all existence, in the harmonic flux of energy. True medicine is merely a retuning of our tapestry of vibration to the over-riding energy from which we spring. 'Dis-ease' either of body or of belief, disappears with realignment to what is already there, but which we are unable to see. The growing adherence to New Age medicines can be seen as a barometer of the shifting cultural awareness which is moving from viewing man and the universe as determinist machines to seeing them in the context of a web of interrelated forces. The human body, like the electromagnetic bodies of the sun or the earth, has, with our present knowledge expanded beyond its physical confines, revealing the subtle human faculties beyond the five senses: the auras of the 'aetheric' body, and its organs, the 'chakras' of religious tradition; the streams of 'ch'i' energy which the acupuncturist traces, all of which emanations parallel and fuse with the energy rhythms of our planet and beyond.

Advances in Modern Physics

I have a strong feeling that modern physics will make great strides forward when it realizes and fully accepts the implications of three factors with which it is currently confused.

Firstly, that the vacuum state is a real, energetic, vibrating matrix – a real, though formative, condition of matter.

Secondly, that the statistical descriptions of quantum theory are underlain by a deterministic, but more subtle order, and one in which the laws of causality and polarity are also intrinsic. In fact, as I have pointed out, *any* descriptions of order, whether more obviously deterministic or statistical, *is an observation of order*, not of chance or randomness. If chance were really chance, surely it could have no laws describing its operation? The 'laws' would themselves be subject to random change!

Thirdly, the suggestion of quantum theory that the observer is implicated in the process of manifestation is, in fact, the primary reality. The mystic perception is that apparently objective substance is, indeed, a part of our consciousness itself. Or stated more simply, God is everywhere and within everything. Yet, He is also 'separate'.

The trouble is that we are attempting to describe the world we perceive through our senses as if we were somehow separate from it. But the very act of perception should tell us that we are not. The fact that we can alter our perception of 'outside' reality by means of meditation, by slowly and slowly changing the direction of our attention from outward to inward, tells us that the outside is integrally connected to the inside. For by changing the state of our mind through meditation, by expanding our consciousness, by focusing our attention within, we fundamentally change our understanding of the nature of the 'reality' perceived through our senses.

The semantic and dualistic aspects of this difficulty become even more apparent when we turn our attention to our own body and, especially, the brain. For having decided that outward material substance is a reflection from within and contained within our own mind, we are faced with the problems not only of brain-mind interface, but also of attempting to observe the processes of observation – both in the operation of the senses, as well as in the brain – *by using the very senses and brain that we wish to understand.*

Words – which are from the mind – fail us, therefore, for we are trying to describe the whole thing using just a small part (our mind and senses) *of* that whole thing. It is like expecting a brick to describe a house, or asking an atom to explain the fundamentals of chemistry. Ultimately, the cry would be, 'But I *am* the house,' or 'I *am* chemistry'. And this is the problem which is inherently recognized by quantum theory, that the observed is integrally connected to the observer, the two cannot be separated. So to really understand what is going on, we have to *become the whole thing*, and that means mystic experience.

In order to talk and speak, therefore, we have to assume and understand these limitations underlying all words and explanations, and work from there. We speak or write as if things were separate from us, when in reality we know that they are not. Hence the Buddhist saying, "He who speaks does not know. He who knows does not speak." Or the Zen way of attempting to flip the mind out of its dualistic obsession by asking such questions as, "What is the sound of one hand clapping?" But mystic enlightenment does not come as a flash of intuitive insight into the meaning of such statements. It is a much deeper experience towards which we may move in an ever-increasing degree.

So all explanations and descriptions, whether scientific, mystic or a mixture of both are only partial truths. The vertical energy spectrum, man as a microcosm reflecting the macrocosm, the brain as a vacuum state computer, the subtle energy interface, quantum theory and relativity theory, mystical descriptions of the universe and so on, are only pointers to a reality which has to be experienced inwardly to be fully comprehended. That is the only way for a brick to understand the house or for a drop to know the Ocean. And this is totally beyond the realm of science.

—— CHAPTER 2 ——

The Human Constitution

In order to complete the framework for what follows in subsequent chapters, I need to give a broad outline of the mystic description of what constitutes a human being. For greater details, the reader may like to consult *Subtle Energy* and *The Web of Life* or any other good books on these topics.

Soul, Mind and Body

A human being is comprised of soul or consciousness, a drop of the Divine Ocean, to which are associated a mind and a physical body. The mind itself is complexly structured[1], but at our human level, mind manifests as our thoughts and mental processes (such as memory, intellect, volition and so on) which we instinctively know are located in our head. In fact, our thinking centre is in our forehead. When we want to concentrate, we automatically put our hand to our forehead, we do not strike our knees or other part of our anatomy!

Our thoughts are vibrations within a real energy field, part of the vertical energy spectrum described in the last chapter. Our human constitution, therefore, is comprised of an inward soul; which is the real life force within us. However, it is knotted together with the energies of our human mind at the thinking centre in our forehead.

From this point, we are usually unconscious of the processes of manifestation until we become aware of the final outcome once again through the medium of our five senses, whose mechanism of operation is itself linked into this same vertical spectrum of energies, so that we may be

[1] For those who have read about or even experienced such things, this also includes the *astral* and *causal* minds and bodies, existing above (or deeper within) the level of human thought and mental function.

actually conscious of our sensory input and motor output. Consequently, we are able to bend a finger, for example, but have no consciousness of the intricate mechanisms by which this is accomplished.

This energy hierarchy is expressed in pictorial and simple form in figure 2-1.

There is thus a direct linkage between mind, emotion and body, providing us with an understanding of the energetic pathways by which psychosomatic phenomena take place and, indeed, of how mind, emotion and body are so integrally wrapped up to make one complete whole. For how else can thought, emotion and personality be betrayed upon the physical face, in the attitude of the body and within its state of health or disease, than by a direct energetic pathway moving both from within-out and from without-in, to complete the circuit?

Indeed, it seems likely that the movement and being of every subatomic particle in our body is influenced from within by the nature of our thoughts and personality, conscious and unconscious, thus providing a unique fingerprint at both the vacuum and subatomic levels.

For most of us, our emotions rule our rationality and we spend much of our life struggling between our higher and lower selves, so to speak, or just caught on the wings of our ever-active mind. Our emotions are most closely linked with our bodily functions as we know from the effects of stress in terms of ill-health, as well as in the more obvious results of things we do or say under the influence of our emotions.

In fact, the word 'emotion' means to 'move out'. And this is exactly what happens. The mind moves out from the centre of consciousness in the forehead. Becoming largely unconscious, it plays against the subtle energies of our inner constitution which lie between the level of thought and the gateway of vacuum. We thus experience emotion in the physical body. The eyes weep, the throat is choked, the heart beats faster, we have a knot or butterflies in our stomach and so on. The more subtle energies directly control the vacuum matrix as it manifests the subatomic particles which make up our physical bodies.

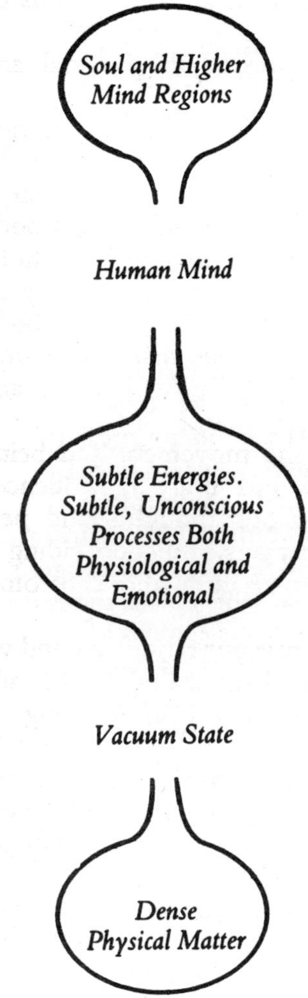

These remain after death of the physical body. The soul is eternal and indestructible. Vast in extent, compared to the physical universe.

Mind energies, a control point. This includes thought energy. The effect of human mental-emotional-physical activity also remain after death of the physical body.

Subtle energies. This includes emotions, instinct and the subtle physical body, also called the etheric body *– the blueprint of the physical body, the energy crossroads from within-out and without-in.*

Vacuum is the hidden gateway between gross and subtle matter. Science is just beginning to approach this energy field.

Dense physical matter – the realm of present day physical science. Includes the physical body.

Figure 2-1. The physical universe and human constitution. The proportions of this sketch have no meaning.

Human Emotion

Many people think of emotions as being those of anger, fear, grief, infatuation and so on. Some people, especially those of an intellectual mien, consider themselves uninfluenced by such feelings, but this is normally incorrect. Mind, when away from its central focus, is automatically under the influence of emotion. This is what the word means. We are away from the focus because of emotions and the primary emotions are those of attachment to physical things, sexual desire, anger, greed or a grasping emotional tendency, and the focal point from which all these arise – egotism, pride or an imbalanced understanding of our own human individuality.

All these qualities are, of course, an instrinsic part of being human, but in most of us, are out of control. Thus, the practical necessity to possess certain physical things such as food, clothing and shelter, when unbalanced, becomes an emotional attachment to these things. Similarly the procreative urge becomes rampant lust, frustrated drive leads to anger, the ability and need to collect together the essentials of life becomes greed, whilst all of these arise out of egotism – the illusory sense of personal identification with both the things around us as well as the emotional and mental energies of our inner beings. A sense of one's role or position within the fabric of life is essential to being human, and this is the naturally balanced ego. It is the building of this into an identification with a false mental image of our position which constitutes the imbalance we call egotism. Clearly, it is this sense of self which underlies the other emotional imbalances or human weaknesses. Remove the inflated sense of self and the natural human faculties of possession, procreation, drive and procurement, all return to a balanced state.

In summary, then, the basic human emotions are:

Balanced Faculty	*Human Weakness*
Possession	Attachment
Procreation	Lust
Drive	Anger
Procurement	Greed
Identity	Egotism

This may seem very simplistic, but actually, it is these five states when mixed into a myriad possibilities, according to circumstances, which give rise to our subconscious mind expressing itself as our personality. It is these subtle energies which are the fundamental basis of all our psychology. So even the apparently cool-headed, rational person will be under the sway of these emotions, whether he thinks he is, or not, because the influence of these emotions upon what we think are our rational thoughts and decisions is largely subconscious. Furthermore, our emotional life will be a mixture of these five primary conditions.

Fear, grief and jealousy, for example, result from their admixture. Jealousy arises from an attachment to what is considered mine or potentially mine, and if it concerns the opposite sex, its origins will contain an element of thwarted sexual desire too. Its expression may well be an explosion of self-justified anger or an icy rebuttal. Its origins may arise from frustrated greed to possess something which has gone to another, whilst underlying it all is an unbalanced view of the individual's position in the pattern of life. He feels that something has happened which should not have occurred in that fashion. Moreover, mind and emotional energies form fixed patterns, as does all energy. We do not have one personality today and another tomorrow. We are creatures of habit, of pattern. We react inwardly and outwardly in predictable ways. This is no doubt essential in order to give us some kind of inner confidence and stability, but it is a conditioning that also prevents us from entertaining alternative ideas, as well as alternative social and emotional responses. Add then, to all this unconscious emotional mayhem, the experiences of a lifetime or more – both mental and emotional – and we have our unique personality and individuality.

Now this is only a brief overview of the basis for a science of psychology founded upon an understanding of energy patterns, and naturally the subject requires greater elucidation. But its relevance here is that all of science is created by individuals in whom these emotional habits and patterns are highly active. And the level of awareness or consciousness of individual scientists concerning their subconscious emotional patterns varies, just as much as it does in all other humans.

So science is *not*, therefore, the result of pure rational thought, but is highly coloured by the emotional life of the scientists themselves. The rejection of a new idea, for example, is the natural, predictable outcome of presenting a new energy pattern to a habituated, grooved, conditional energy field. Then add to this mental-emotional melee – professional jealousies, desire for personal fame and fortune, the fear of being wrong, concern over career prospects, worries about the mortgage and the family, plus a host of similar feelings, and one can readily see how the personal interactions of scientists can lead to the rejection of good ideas in favour of maintaining the status quo.

It is rather like the wife, out shopping with her husband for a new dress. "It doesn't suit you, dear," he says hardly aware of his own dishonesty. For in reality it is his surreptitious glance at the price tag which has not suited him!

So bear all this in mind when approaching the apparently rational pronouncements of 'science'. For it is not science which exists, it is good old mixed-up human beings and our ideas about things which exist. And this is a topic we will return to from time to time as this book progresses.

Flatlanders and The Inner Life Dimension

Much of our problem in understanding life and the physical reality in which we find ourselves is that when we look at the world and living things with our normal sensory perceptions and through the coloured glasses of our unconscious emotions, we see only material forms. We do not see the inward life either of our fellow humans or that of other species. We may be aware to one degree or another of our own thoughts, emotions and consciousness, but most of us are unable to *directly* perceive these essential aspects in others, even in those to whom we are close. Hence people say, "So-and-so does not understand me," or "I do not understand so-and-so."

This we can readily accept. But to assume therefore that what we can perceive in other creatures, human or otherwise, is all that exists of them and to build an entire 'scientific' structure upon that totally mechanistic premise is quite superficial and entirely fallacious, as a means of providing ultimate or even mundane and pragmatic answers.

What we perceive with our five physical senses is only the outer dimension of existence – the skin, the surface or the form. It is like the example often given to physics students to help them understand the concept of additional spatial dimensions. The story that is told goes like this:

There is a world where the inhabitants perceive only two dimensions. It is known as Flatland and the population are the Flatlanders. Take a two-dimensional view through any object and that is all that the Flatlanders would see.

One day an orange passes through Flatland. But all that the inhabitants can see is at first, a point. This becomes an expanding circle, which then diminishes to a point and finally disappears again.

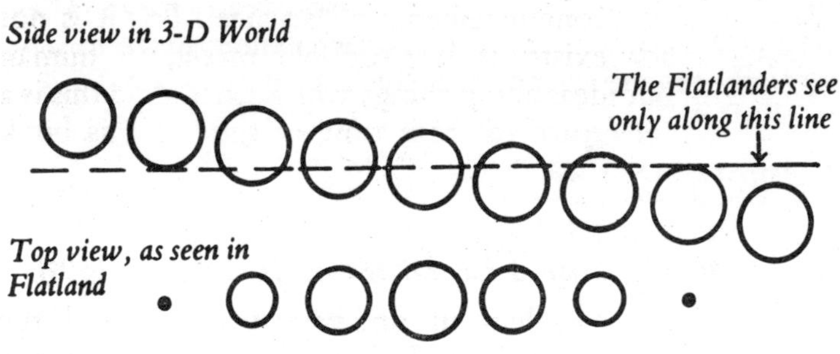

Figure 2-2. The Flatlanders perception of an orange passing through their world.

When we perceive with our physical senses only, all we can see is the external form – Flatland. The inward dimension of life is lost to us. This inward dimension, however, is the reality that gives the outward form its appearance of existence. Just as the orange is the reality and the Flatlanders' perception of it is only partial, similarly, the delicate, inward, subtle life energy patterns within all creatures are perceived by our senses only indirectly as the patterning of their physical form. We thus fail to perceive the inward, subtle dimensions of their life.

And just as the Flatlanders may argue and debate over the nature of expanding and contracting orange circles, so too has our science spun out a mechanistic philosophy that has mostly failed to perceive the inward dimension.

But once the existence of that inward dimension is comprehended through expanding the awareness of one's own personal inwardness, then a quite new picture emerges and things fall into place in a way we never previously imagined was possible. But this is not something which can be taught in our conventional kind of school.

So Darwinian-style, mechanistic theories of the origin and evolution of species are as meaningful as the Flatlanders explanations of an orange, because the essential quality of life – inward consciousness – and all the other subtle paraphernalia, is quite overlooked. And the meaning of life lies within.

Similarly with our scientific comprehension of 'fundamental' particles and forces. Our assumption that they must have arisen out of nowhere is so sweetly naive. They have not, and neither have we, even though we cannot normally remember our past lives.

Memory of The Past

There was a BBC TV documentary shown in 1987 in which a highly intelligent and musically gifted man was interviewed and filmed. This man had had the misfortune to have contracted a rare viral infection of the brain and to have lost parts of the functionality in his temporal and frontal lobes. Consequently, he has lost his memory and his ability to remember events that happened more than just a few minutes previously. But, strangely enough, his ability to talk and express himself is quite unimpaired and moreover he can still read music, play the piano and conduct a choir of which he was once the professional conductor.

But when asked about these skills, he does not remember that he has them. Nor could he remember having conducted his old choir (who had assembled for the purpose) just a few hours later on that same day. When – in the afternoon – he was shown a video of his playing and singing that had been recorded in the morning, he laughed and could not recall that he had ever done so or even that he had such talents.

He continually feels, therefore, that he has just woken up from a condition in which none of his five senses were in operation. "Up to this point, I have been blind and deaf," is one of his frequent comments.

By a natural, protective mechanism, we are all in a similar condition. When we are born, we lose the memory of our past lives, although we carry their impressions or *sanskaras* with us into our present life. This is where all our talents and interests come from and it explains all the incidents of child prodigy - Mozart playing the piano at the age of four, a young child of five or six playing tournament-style tennis shots and so on. Actually Ravi Shankar, the Indian sitar player, comments that it takes more than one lifetime to learn to play the sitar. We carry the already trained mental patterns with us from past lives, which we then instinctively manifest in future lives, although we have lost sight of how we originally came by them.

Sports coaches realize the importance of the mental pattern as a blueprint for the action, when they teach their players to enact their weakest shots *mentally* and with the greatest finesse and skill. Thus, when all hindrances are removed from the mind and the player really believes that he can perform the act superbly, its physical enactment far more readily becomes reality. If an individual is vascillating and has no confidence in their mind, it is unlikely that the game or sport can be played with excellence. This is the same with all of life. However, we digress.

So we only consciously remember the barest outline even of our present life. The details of what happened only a few minutes or hours before are soon lost and when we look back over the years only certain major landmarks stand out. Talents and skills, however, do remain with us, though they may get a little rusty. Or, for example, we may remember how to find our way around a town we have not visited for years – but only when we arrive there. We could not, in advance, have drawn a map of the area.

So, once again, we are forced into the realization that there is more to life than meets the eye and that it is within the grasp of all of us to seek the inwardness of our own life. This, indeed, is the purpose of life.

The Life Force

The physical matter that is woven into the amazing complexity comprising the bodies of living organisms is vastly more detailed in organizational structure than that found in inert substance. Moreover, there is no intermediate condition. Either substance is dead or inert, or it is a part of the body of a living organism. Even the simplest single-celled creatures and bacteria have infinitely complex patternings in their biochemistry and physiology. There are *no half-dead creatures*, contrary to one's more facetious observations! When life departs, the body immediately begins to decompose. The multifarious complex processes immediately cease and the reduction to a more simple and comparatively static condition instantly commences.

This then is the power of the soul or Life Force within. This Life Force is the essence of our being and the primary organizing power that acts upon the vacuum matrix, modified by the content of our mind and emotions, and which patterns and maintains our physical body.

Conventionally, the life force is overlooked in modern science because there is no place for it within conventional, present day scientific conceptual frameworks or paradigms. An understanding, however, of vacuum state manifestation, the vertical energy spectrum and the fact that consciousness is *prior* to matter, not the product of it, leaves us with a clear comprehension of the significance of this supreme force and of how it may be linked to current scientific understanding.

In a very real sense, *the Life Force needs to be 'discovered' by science in the same way that Newton 'discovered' gravity!*

In fact, the 'laws' of energy transformation and interrelationship (the ways in which they behave) are more complex, more intricately woven, in physical substance that is patterned by the Life Force into a living body, than they are in inert matter. This fact needs to be appreciated by mainstream science.

Given, therefore, a mechanism by which energy is created from within both in inert matter as well as in the bodies of living creatures, we are able to describe many previously obscure experiences and phenomena in quite rational terms.

The remaining chapters of this book will provide starting points for a number of these investigations.

— INTERLUDE —

The Barber of Qazwin

Readers have sometimes suggested that in order to reach the more materially-minded thinkers and scientists, I should omit much of the material which would upset them. That means all the mystical aspects. But in the world of what is called *New Science*, there are a number of excellent writers and researchers who do approach things from this angle, because, no doubt, this is the way which feels most appropriate and comfortable for them. So this approach is covered, and no doubt many more scientists will step forward, too, to take part in the re-animation of scientific thought. Science is only a reflection of the thoughts of men. When the humans grow, inwardly, so does their science.

But my feeling for maintaining a whole picture is summed up most succinctly in this short tale from the Persian mystic Jalalu'ddin Rumi.

How the man of Qazwin was tattooing the figure of a lion in blue on his shoulders, and (then) repenting because of the (pain of the) needle-pricks.

Hear from the narrator this story about the way and custom of the people of Qazwin.

They tattoo themselves in blue with the point of a needle on body and hand and shoulders, so as to suffer no injury.

A certain man of Qazwin went to a barber and said, "Tattoo me (and) do it charmingly (artistically)."

"O valiant sir," said he, "what figure shall I tattoo?" He answered, "Prick in the figure of a furious lion.

Leo is my ascendant: tattoo the form of a lion. Exert yourself, prick in plenty of the blue dye."

"On what place," he asked, "shall I tattoo you?" Said he, "Prick the design of the beauty on my shoulder-blade."

As soon as he began to stick in the needle, the pain of it settled in the shoulder,

And the hero fell a-moaning, "O illustrious one, you have killed me: what figure are you tattooing?"

"Why," said he, "you bade me do a lion." "What limb (of the lion)," asked the other, "did you begin with?"

"I have begun at the tail," said he. "O my dear friend," he cried, "leave out the tail!

My breath is stopped by the lion's tail and rump: his rump has tightly closed (choked) my windpipe.

Let the lion be without a tail, O lion-maker, for my heart is faint from the blows of your prong (the tattoer's needle)."

That person commenced to prick in (the blue) on another part (of the man's shoulder) without fear, without favour, without mercy.

He yelled, "Which of his members is this?" "This is his ear, my good man," the barber replied.

"O Doctor," said he, "let him have no ears: omit the ears and cut the frock short."

The barber began to insert (his needle) in another part: once more the man of Qazwin set out to wail,

Saying, "What is the member (you are pricking in) now on this third spot?" He replied, "This is the lion's belly, my dear sir."

"Let the lion have no belly," said he: "what need of a belly for the picture that is (already) sated?"

The barber became distraught and remained in great bewilderment: he stood for a long time with his fingers in his teeth;

Then the master flung the needle to the ground and said, "Has this happened to any one in the world?

Who (ever) saw a lion without tail and head and belly? God himself did not create a lion like this."

Rumi, of course, tells the story to illustrate that:

When thou hast chosen thy Pir (spiritual Master), be not faint-hearted, be not weak as water and crumbly as earth.

If thou art enraged by every blow, then how wilt thou become a clear mirror being polished?

O brother, endure the pain of the lancet (the difficulties of meditation, controlling the mind), that you may escape from the poison of your miscreant self.

Anyone in whose body the miscreant self has died, sun and cloud obey his command.

The thorn becomes entirely beautiful, like the rose, in the sight of the particular (the soul) that is going towards the Universal.

> You have fastened both your hands tight on (are determined not to give up) 'I' and 'we': all this (spiritual) ruin is caused by dualism.

In the more limited sense in which I began in my preamble, one can also take it to mean that appreciation of the whole reality cannot be grasped by missing out essentials simply because the recipient may scream a little!

—— CHAPTER 3 ——

Biological and Healing Implications

Thoughts in a Vacuum – The Brain as a Vacuum State Computer

One of the fundamental and unanswered queries concerning living organisms in general and human beings, in particular, is: how does the brain interface with the mind and consciousness? The subject is discussed at considerable length in *The Web of Life*, but in essence we can only start our speculations with our day to day observations and experiences, both personal and medical or scientific.

It is clear that the electro-biochemical nature of brain function is intimately connected to mental activity and yet it is also evident that memory, knowledge, philosophy, ethics and most aspects of mental function are not specifically related to any particular part of the physical brain itself. And the relationship of the blissful illumination and enlightenment of mystical experience to brain function are quite unclear, when approached scientifically.

The central link to mind and consciousness would appear to be localized in the mid-brain area, for large sections of the outer cerebral cortex can be damaged or removed without loss of life, while a single bullet in the mid-brain will result in instant death. The outer cortex seems to be involved in the integration and interpolation of physical life – movement, speaking, writing, sensory perception and so on – into consciousness, through the intermediary of the mind.

The brain itself consists of over 10^{11} or 10^{12} nerve cells[1], each of which may contain up to 100,000 individual connections to other nerve cells. There is a complex and little understood system of biochemical, electrical and

[1] 10^{11} means 100.000,000,000 or one hundred thousand million.

electromagnetic signalling which operates between these cells and it seems fair to assume that since the vacuum state is part of the energetic pathway between mind energies and molecules, that this complex brain network must effectively be a part of the vacuum state input-output and information processing system.

The brain can thus be thought of as a *Vacuum State Computer*. For if our central nervous and cerebral system was intended as nothing more than an enlarged domestic wiring system, then why are we not endowed with straight wire connectors, (or their biological equivalent)? It is our limited, linear, conceptual mind-functioning which thinks in terms of linear, bumper-to-bumper, causal connections and pathways. Nature is more holographically structured, where the laws of energy relationship reflect the harmony and complete integration within the whole.

Unconscious and instinctive processes are thus comprised of patterns and a complex vibratory network within the vacuum and more subtle energies of our constitution.

Mental Disturbances

Furthermore, it becomes possible to understand not only how psychosomatic phenomena take place, as previously discussed, but also how an infinite variety of both neurotic and psychotic states can occur. The sense of self, personality, identity, direction of attention, memory and all such faculties of mind are lodged in the higher harmonics of energy beyond the realm of biochemical and physiological activity – beyond both the subatomic and vacuum energy domains. The one, however, affects the other, and thus psychotic states, which are to be seen as energetic disturbances and disharmonies within these subtle fields, can both affect the biochemistry and electrical activity at the physical level, as well as being themselves affected by biochemical and bioelectrical changes. This is how drugs can affect the mind and alter the state of consciousness – whether the drug be alcohol, LSD, dopamine or any other substance, naturally occurring or otherwise. In fact, just eating (or not eating) food will affect one's mental and emotional condition. Similarly, it is this mental-physical interfacing which enables us to do anything, even just bending a finger.

The age-old debate, therefore, of whether schizophrenia (for example) has biochemical or psychological origins is resolved. The answer is *both*, because both biochemistry and psychological or mental and emotional energy fields are part and parcel of one integrated energetic complex and reciprocally affect each other, automatically.

As long as one can comprehend the principle of the vertical or creative energy spectrum, as well as the more obvious horizontal energy spectrum, then all facets of human behaviour, manifestation and experience, become understandable.

The Molecule as a Subatomic Energy Dance Spun out of the Fabric of Vacuum

Just as experimental physicists seem to have zeroed in on studying particle behaviour under amazingly synthetic and high energy conditions, so too have the medical fraternity concentrated on the study of linear molecular interactions as their primary approach to understanding the body.

But a molecule is comprised of atoms and the atoms are made up of subatomic particles, so it becomes very clear that a molecule is a vibration spun out of, and dancing into existence from, the complexly organized fabric of the vacuum state. The study of biochemistry and life processes should therefore include a study of the subatomic energy dance, the movement and harmony within which is primary to our experience of health and well-being. We also need to examine our visualization of molecular processes and reconsider them in the light of our knowledge concerning this vibrating, energetic dance of which they, and therefore our entire bodies, are comprised.

In living creatures, the life force maintains a highly intricate degree of integrated order and structure and indeed some scientists have pointed out that even the water in our bodily cells is in a state of 'maximum order'. That is, every subatomic particle and hence every atom and molecule is *deterministically* manoeuvred in an almost infinitely complex and fast moving sea of energy transformations. The primary patterning lies in the vacuum and more subtle states, and it appears to us as the cells of our body with their highly and intelligently organized activities. Full medical understanding and treatment should therefore include an appreciation of these levels, too.

Health, Healing and Disease

Given a conceptual framework in which all aspects of our being are seen in terms of energy, the definition of health automatically becomes a condition of balance and harmonious interaction between and within all the energy levels of our constitution. Blockages in energy flow, disharmonies of whatever nature and from whatever cause, result in a state of dis-harmony or dis-ease, with the result that we do not feel too good and may also experience pain – physical, emotional or mental.

Healing therefore becomes the process of recreating harmony amongst the energy patterns. And it is clear that the mental and emotional cooperation and involvement of the patient is essential even for physical healing to take place. Indeed, any disharmony or dis-ease at the physical level will have its roots in the mental, emotional and more subtle levels of energy within the individual.

In fact, in any healing process there are just three important factors involved:

1. The patient, his attitude, belief system and the patterns with which he was born and which are modified during the course of his life.
2. The therapist or doctor, his attitude, belief systems and the patterns with which he was born and which are modified during the course of his life.
3. The therapy itself.

Clearly, the best form of treatment will include the positive involvement of all three, but amazing and real cures can be achieved even with only one of them active. Especially, if the only one operating is the patient. The patient always holds the key, and any observant doctor or nurse can verify that if the patient really *wants* to get well, then the chances of success in any form of treatment are infinitely higher.

The placebo effect is therefore a real *energetic* phenomenon in which the mental and emotional energies of the patient are mobilized by belief and desire to create a cure.

Consequently, it is of great value to be able to mobilize the psychology of the patient to his own advantage. For otherwise, whatever we attempt to perform at the physical level is promptly re-arranged by the patient's more inward and psychological energy patterns. Conversely, if we feel that the primary source of a physical ailment lies in the patient's mind, then clearly the healing approach adopted needs to take this firmly into consideration. The diagnosis, *just psychological*, should not herald a dismissal of the case, but an identification of the primary area in which energetic disharmonies exist and, hence, where treatment should commence. Ignoring these signs, or worse – making a negative or critical value judgement concerning both them and the patient – will simply bring forward the day when psychology will be translated into pathology.

It should also be clear that the more a physician and his form of treatment are in tune with the complete or whole energy of the patient, then the better will be the result. Those therapies, like acupuncture and radionics which work on the subtle side have an advantage in that they are working on the energetic blueprint of physiological manifestation. But at the same time, the energetic quality of the therapist becomes of primary importance, because there will be an interchange of energy at the subtle level between the patient and the therapist. The therapist, especially, must understand the correct mental attitude to adopt if he is to avoid picking up the patient's condition, by vibrational transference. And there are also particular physical precautions that a therapist or doctor can take.

At the other end of the spectrum, the addition of an energetic vibration at the biochemical level, in the form of a molecule or drug, is most likely to be operating at a purely symptomatic level which may cause other damaging 'side' effects. It may also, by suppressing the symptoms of the disease, drive the energetic disharmony deeper into the system where it can cause deeper and more undermining damage. In practice, there is a time and a place for most forms of treatment – physical, subtle or psychological.

In all the machines created by man, it is possible for someone else to understand the underlying thought that has given it existence. And when the machine malfunctions, we call in such a technician to fix it. The energetic make-up of man, however, is not so clear to us and consequently our attempts at healing are greatly imperfect.

The secret of good therapy is therefore a good understanding of the human energetic constitution and how the subtler aspects of our being manifest themselves as physically observable symptoms through the medium of the vacuum state. We then need to learn how to work with *nature's unknown integrated processes*, so that she may weave her own healing magic.

But since this understanding is so clouded by our social conditioning, by our philosophical outlook, our training, our degree of perception, awareness and consciousness, and by the full range of human emotion – all of which are acting upon us mostly subconsciously – so we find it difficult to comprehend the energetic nature of that which is closest to us – our own beings. And this lack of understanding is reflected in our approach to the healing arts, indeed, to the whole of our life.

—— CHAPTER 4 ——

The Subtle Body

States of Matter – The Elements or Tattwas

The ancient traditions of many cultures have spoken of the five states of matter or the *elements*, the primary octaves in which material substance is manifested. The Greeks knew them and the Indian yogis still know them as the *tattwas*, and we also experience them everyday.

Science also recognizes them, unknowingly, in their gross material forms. These outwardly experienced conditions are: earth or the solid state, water or the liquid state, fire – the expansive state, experienced as heat, light and the plasmic state, air or the gaseous state, and ether, also known to the Indian mystics as *akash*[1] – in the dense physical universe, this refers to the vacuum state which we have been discussing. These five states cover all the material phenomena with which we are familiar.

On the other side of the curtain or wall of vacuum lies what we have loosely called subtle energies. These subtle energies are themselves found in five major states – earth, water, fire, air and another, more subtle, formative vacuum state. It is this subtle vacuum which is linked into our human consciousness, and – being the formative state for the other four subtle states, which are themselves the blueprint for the gross states – this gives us the ability to contemplate the physical universe through the medium of rational and discriminative thought. A faculty denied to lower species.

It is also this inner vacuum which prevents most of us from leaving the physical body during our lifetime and travelling in the higher regions. It is the inner prison wall, just as the outer vacuum with which we are familiar is the wall that prevents us from seeing into the realm of subtle

[1]*Akash* is a sanskrit term meaning space, ether, sky, void.

energies. It is the valve, which readily permits energy to flow downward and outward, but is difficult of ascent in reverse.

Actually, it is more correct to say that these five tattwas do not so much manifest themselves in both subtle and gross forms, but that we *experience* each tattwa in both subtle and gross ways. It is our *experience* which makes the apparent difference.

In fact, the classes of species inhabiting our planet are determined by the number of these subtle elements which are linked in to the constitution and awareness of the creature. Plants, for example, have only one active element within them – that of water. Water is the element or tattwa associated with procreation and plants are indeed mostly concerned with reproducing themselves. It is also their lack of active fire that prevents them moving about. They are indeed rooted to the spot.

Insects have two active tattwas – fire and earth or fire and air, and for their size insects are the fastest movers on the planet, movement and expansion being primary qualities of fire. Birds possess three tattwas – air, fire and water, while animals have four – air, fire, water and earth. Man alone possesses all five, thus making him the 'highest' creature upon the planet. And with the subtle vacuum linked into our mental constitution whilst also being the formative matrix out of which the other elements are manifested, it gives us the apparent ability to choose and exercise *free-will*, to *form* our life around us.

I am aware, of course, that in brief description this may all sound somewhat facile. However, when fully understood, it is not, and there is a considerably more expanded discussion of this subject in *The Web of Life*. After all, if we accept that consciousness is *prior* to matter, that life creates form, that the brain and biochemistry are secondary to the more inward structures of mind and instinct, then why do other species possess a lower degree of intelligence? We cannot say that it is because they have a simpler brain structure, because we know that physical matter, and therefore the brain, are not primary or self-existent. The difference must therefore lie in the more inward, subtle blueprint of the physical body.

Furthermore, why are there missing links between all

the divisions of nature, not just between man and other mammals? There are no half-plant-half-insect or half-bird-half-mammal, neither alive nor in the fossil record. Nor, as we have discussed, are there are any half-alive-half-dead creatures. It is because material substance, both subtle and gross is not homogeneous, but is divided into the five octaves or tattwas, and out of which the physical bodies of all creatures are fashioned. The subject does, however, need considerably fuller discussion.

I must also point out that the division of material matter or energy into these five basic states is one of the most overlooked aspects of present-day science. Scientists felt so happy when they were able to begin their dealings with the atoms of chemical elements, that mention of these five material conditions sounds like a reversion to what is seen as antiquated, Greek natural philosophy. "We have progressed," it is frequently said, "We know now that there are over one hundred elements, not just five." But a chemical element is quite different from a state of material substance.

There are indeed over one hundred chemical elements, but yet each of those chemical elements can manifest in the solid, liquid, gaseous and plasmic states. And they all arise out of the akash, or spatial fabric of vacuum. The word 'element' is used with two quite different meanings, which is why I prefer to call these five by their Sanskrit name of 'tattwa'. Because that term implies a subtle essence or real energetic principle that is experienced through consciousness and unconsciousness in a variety of ways, not just the outwardly obvious material states.

Scientists have largely ignored the amazing fact or 'coincidence' that the energies of our known universe manifest themselves in just these *five* states. Why not two or three? Or six or seven? At the molecular and atomic levels certain mechanisms are known that underlie our physical experience of these *sudden* changes of state. But this level is underlain by a subatomic realm which physicists freely admit they are unable to adequately model or understand. So no physical event or substance is really understood by science at all, including why there are these particular states of material existence. We know as much about them as we do about gravity, light, time or space.

And as we will see, this is not really so very much, despite all the fuss we have made about it!

Actually, it makes an amusing line of thought to imagine how the planet and the universe might be constructed if there were no sharp demarcations between solid, liquid and gaseous. Earth, water and air would become homogeneous – a sort of spectrum of increasing and decreasing stickiness! There would be no earth surface, no well-defined air-space, no rivers, oceans and shore-lines – just an unending cosmic porridge, an awful, sticky mess – or worse! Our bodies, too, would become a kind of uniform goo! It is the different modalities that put tone and character into the system.

If you then consider the separateness of vacuum, or space and think what would happen if it, too, were homogeneous with the other tattwas, then – with the barrier to the subtle realms removed, and with something odd having happened to spacial dimensions, the whole of creation, inward and outward, would turn into nothing more than a homogeneous soup of varying viscosity. And probably not even varying! Then – to be complete – add to your mental image what might be the case if fire (movement, light, the sun, heat etc.) were also to become homogeneously distributed. . . . The whole idea is, of course, plainly absurd. In fact, the remarkable ability of matter to divide into these primary elemental or tattvic states is an essential and integral part of the mechanism by which creation is maintained.

And as we have seen, this is apparent at both the subtle and gross levels.

Instinct

The lower species are creatures of *instinct*. And it is within the realm of the subtle elements that all such formative patterns are primarily encoded. And the less aware or conscious a creature is, the more it is reliant upon its instinctive patterning. It is within these subtle energy fields that the blueprint exists which makes a cow look like a cow, which makes it moo even if raised by humans, that gives it all the characteristics that are identifiable as a cow; that makes an insect, bird or animal know what food it should eat and how it should go about its life; that gives a bird the ability to build its nest or to fly south or north on a migratory journey it has never travelled before. It is also this subtle blueprint that is encoded, through the vacuum state, into every cell of our body as the DNA – a complex and vibrating energetic dance spun out of the fabric of vacuum.

Thus, DNA is *not* the primary energy complex for the patterning of life forms, but only a part of the outworking of the more inward vibrations and patterns within the subtle energy fields, and is present as a kind of holographic, cellular intelligence within every cell of our body.

Every creature, including ourselves, has a blueprint in the subtle energy fields which make it what it is. These fields are linked into the consciousness of the creature and provide, therefore, not only the morphogenic matrix out of which its biochemistry, physiology and anatomy are formed, but also the patterning of behaviour or the curtain through which the inner life force manifests in the physical world. The more complex and complete is this curtain, then the more intelligence and apparent degree of choice or free-will is manifested in the species.

Instinct is therefore that part of the subtle encoding which is linked into the conscious aspect of the life force. For it is as much an aspect of instinct which enables a bird to fly or a man to walk, as it is that guides the young swallow on its southbound flight.

Prana

In all creatures, the inner Life Force of soul or consciousness becomes stepped down in vibration as it enters a physical frame. At this point, modified by the mental and subtle substructures of the creature, it becomes known as *prana*. Prana is the life-giving, organizational energy which patterns first the subtle elements and through them the biochemistry, physiology and anatomical form and function of the living creature.

Consciousness only reaches down to the thinking centre. Below that, it continues its journey and functions as the unconscious pranas.

It is like waves through water which whip it up into a

multitude of patterns. But when the soul departs the body, the pranas 'evaporate' and the material substance becomes comparatively still, maintained in its far simpler atomic and molecular patterns by only a diffuse echo of the primal life force.

Chakras

As the pranas move through the five states of matter, they form points of vibrational organization and administration within the subtle elements. These focal points are known as the *chakras*. There are five located from the neck down to the coccyx and one other, the thinking or *eye centre*, is located in the forehead behind and between the two eyes. This makes six in all. There are further centres located in higher mental and spiritual regions, but although of great importance, they are not our subject here. It is these higher centres or chakras which sometimes give rise, in descriptions by authors, to the mention of a seventh, crown chakra. In reality, this is more correctly understood as relating to the higher centres. It is not a subtle physical centre, as are the other six chakras.

The chakras and pranas are located within the subtle energies of our being and are thus not to be found by dissection or under the microscope, any more than it is possible to find a thought by examining the brain.

There is, however, a representation, a lower harmonic or reflection of their administrative role to be found in the six major endocrine centres of the body. The function of each endocrine centre can be clearly seen as a reflection of the role of the respective element and chakra. This is a subject of considerable discussion in *The Web of Life*.

The universal schema is summarized in figure 4–1.

The Laws of Nature and the Life Force

What we think of as the scientifically discovered 'laws of nature', determined from an analysis of things in the world of *inert* matter, are vastly more intricate and possess more power when the inward life force is directly implicated in the formation of living bodies. From an outward, physical point of view, this also appears as a far greater integration

The Source of everything. Known to different cultures by many names.

The Shabd or Word is the central creative current or power of life, the primal Life Force emanating from God and sustaining the creation. It is the primary vibration, experienced in mystic transport as Sound. And from this Life Stream, or Sound, also comes Light.

This includes the purely spiritual regions as well as the causal realm of Universal Mind, and the astral region.

The human mind is comprised of the Antashkarans. This is the 'organ of thought' or the energy field in which thoughts exist. The pattern of destiny is also built into this centre.

The soul and mind are knotted together at the Eye Centre in the waking condition, but are drawn out into the tattvic fields of the body and inert matter through our senses and motor responses. The area that includes the Eye Centre and the Antashkarans is also known as the 'sky' of the body.

The pranas flow out from the sky of the body as Idà, Pingala and Sushumna, representing the three primary modes of pranic vibration (positive, neutral, negative) in the central spinal axis.

The pranas carry the cohering and patterning power of the Shabd, the life force into the realm of the five subtle and five gross tattwas.

Vibrating with intelligence from above, prana patterns the five subtle tattwas, forming, by its movement, the six chakras and the innumerable nadis. This subtle tattvic tapestry is sometimes known as the etheric body.

Patterned by prana, the subtle tattwas become the immediate blueprint of the grossly observable physical body. The five subtle tattwas precipitate, condense or dance into observable physical existence, through the medium of the gross akashic or vacuum state.

Thus are built up the complex patterns of subatomic and fundamental natural forces, forming molecules and the integrated biochemical and bioelectronic tapestry.

Contrary to modern scientific opinion, life is not the outcome of a self-organizing molecular complexity. In fact, the patterning of physiological and biochemical processes are actually maintained by the life force from within.

Figure 4-1. Schematic representation of the subtle human constitution.

of energetic relationships into the holographically structured 'wholes' we call bodies, though in reality, the entire universe is in a state of complete order and integration, whether inert or animate.

But under the patterning influence of this life force, energies are more readily translated, the one into another, even from the subtle to the gross and vice versa. The French biologist, Kervran, actually showed that chemical elements are transmuted on a day-to-day basis in plants and probably all other living organisms, too. The subatomic structure can quite clearly be readily manipulated by the life force.

Actually, soil bacteria that can transmute elements are an intrinsic part of the natural processes and will be useful in the ecological planetary clean-up that is so urgently required. This is one of the relatively unknown aspects contributing to the success of organic agriculture and gardening, where the soil is full of the bacteria so fundamental to healthy plant functioning, but which are destroyed by modern clinical and chemical farming technology. But a full discussion of this topic is a digression beyond the scope of this book.

Similarly, the material substance woven into the bodies of living creatures by the inward life force and through the medium of a subtle energy patterning matrix, exhibits properties of superconductivity usually associated either with very special materials or with temperatures approaching that of absolute zero (−273.15°C). It also maintains a state of maximum order at the molecular (and hence subatomic) level, with certain Russian research indicating that intracellular water possesses a crystalline structure moving from a liquid-to-solid-to-liquid state many times per second, aiding in the exact control of body temperatures and probably much more besides.

There is also a finely-tuned network of intercellular (between cells) and intracellular (within cells) communication, via continuous electromagnetic emission and absorption (especially microwave, infrared and ultraviolet), right down at the molecular level.

All this is accomplished through the maintainance of a subtle energy body present in all living creatures, possessing a complexity and integration relative to the subtle tattvic constitution of the creature. Man is the most complex and the most complete. Psychic people have observed this energy blueprint and called it the *etheric* body or *subtle* body. It maintains, patterns and integrates every complex molecular structure, every bioelectrical activity, every bodily intercommunication. The whole plan and pattern of bodily existence from the subatomic domain to its overall shape, including all the organs and sytems of the body – those we know a little about and those we have yet to discover – all these take their shape, administration and activity from this subtle body.

It is a complete blueprint, the 'ghost' in the machine, which permits the mind and consciousness to function in this world, through a body of physical, material substance. It is the all-important interface between the mind and the life force, on the one side, and the gross physical, on the other. In addition, it has its own 'laws' of energy relationship which are more closely interwoven than the 'laws' we think we perceive in inert matter.

The best modern parallel from our world of known science by which to understand these relationships is that of a hologram. A hologram is a means of storing an image, like a 35mm photographic slide. It can therefore be used to project an image of the original. But the uniqueness of a hologram is that every part of the image can be used to project an image of the whole.

In more mystic parlance, it is said that man is a microcosm containing the macrocosm. The inward centres at which consciousness can be focused permit access to the entire universe. Hence such comments as Shakespeare's, "This little kingdom, Man". And the chakras and other higher centres are also known as the microcosmic centres. They are focuses through which the true nature of the macrocosmic universe may be glimpsed.

Similarly, in the living and vibrant energy structure of a living body, every part reflects within it, an image of the whole. Every cell contains the same DNA, for example. DNA is a dynamic energy pattern that contains within it a pattern for the entire physical body. It is an indication of the 'mind' or subtle organizational focus within each cell, part of the holographic mechanism linking the body into one whole. It reflects the holographic nature of energy relationships within the subtle body and within the vacuum state, too.

The detailed nature of this energy structuring is not understood at the present time, but there are currently many excellent minds at work upon it throughout the world and their first attempts will be published within the next few years, and probably throughout the next century. Once some of the essential principles are laid down, there will be plenty of scope for scientists to follow the recipes in order to elucidate those many facets of life which puzzle all of us, not just the 'scientists'.

But for more details concerning the present state of this art, I must refer you to *The Web of Life* and to the next book in this series, *Natural Creation*.

Psychic Phenomena

All psychic phenomena are manifestations of activity within the vacuum and more subtle states of matter up to and including that of our human mind and thoughts. Those of our experiences where the major focus of attention is within these subtle fields we call psychic.

It becomes quite clear, therefore, how concentration of our mind's attention upon physical substance can result in apparent miracles, for we have already described the energetic pathway between the two. When these normally unconscious pathways are brought into the consciousness of the individual by specific yogic or meditational exercises, then the manner by which the elements and forces of nature come into gross physical manifestation is revealed within the concentrated mind of the practitioner and can thus be mentally manipulated at will. Then the practitioner can walk on water, fly in the air, understand the language of animals and birds, communicate telepathically, heal the sick, foretell the future (a direct observation of the development of patterns), and so on.

However, these faculties are not to be used, for they result in a loss of spiritual power, which should be used for higher and more inward mystic ascent. Use of psychic abilities is often performed largely for show and as such inflates the ego and instigates an aura of what is known as 'glamour'. Those who claim and constantly 'exhibit' psychic capabilities are usually unreliable in their intuitions, since such 'powers' have been incorporated into an egocentric personality. This does not mean, however, that an awareness of such things is lacking in spiritually developed people, but they just do not make any outward show of something which is as natural as breathing. The general rule is to obey the natural laws of the plane upon which you are operating. And this includes living harmoniously within the social context of the times, and as far as the social laws are in harmony with or at least do not contravene natural law.

The mind itself is a multifaceted structure and all the strange events that one hears of are explicable in terms of its linkage to various parts of our normally unconscious processes or with the so-called outer world of inert energy. Some of these are discussed in greater detail in *Subtle Energy* and *The Web of Life*.

Mind, Matter, Healing and The Life Force

I have suggested that the vacuum energy field is patterned from within by the mind. But is there any outward evidence to support this suggestion? Well, yes, there is. For this is the mechanism by which a concentrated mind is able to control physical matter and manipulate the laws of nature. This is how the miracles associated with yogis and holy men are performed. It is also the means by which paranormal phenomena take place.

All spiritual practices entail concentration of the mind, whether it is prayer, meditation, telling of beads or some other technique. Our minds are mostly scattered into the world through the focusing of our attention upon the senses and the myriad forms which surround us. The mind has thus moved out from its natural centre behind the eyes and become unconscious of itself and its powers, as it plays through the body below the eyes. We thus live emotionally. E-motion means to move out and it signifies the move of the mind out from its centre of attention behind the eyes. And since consciousness does not naturally descend below this eye centre, our life becoms controlled by subconscious emotion. We thus lose sight of the true capabilities of our mind and the part it is constantly playing in our physical life. This subject is described and discussed at length in *The Web of Life* and other mystic literature.

So when the mind is concentrated, it is capable of controlling the lower vibrations of matter with which it is already associated. In certain forms of yoga, these miraculous powers are carefully inculcated and even used. In our western society, we have observed the fire-walking cults in California, 'imported' from the Philippines. Here, the prospective fire-walkers are trained for at least one full day (only!). Their minds are shaped, formed and concentrated in preparation for actually walking on a bed of hot coals. And although some people do burn their feet, the large majority do not. This is a matter of fact, there is no doubt that this fire-walking does take place and that the prepared and concentrated minds of those taking part does provide the required protection against burnt feet. It has been reported on TV and in the media and has been mentioned in a number of books.

I have spoken to people who have walked upon these fiery coals and the general comment is that those who do get their feet burned are those who panic whilst in the middle of their walk. Panic means a loss of mental concentration. The mind power holding the patterning of the feet in an unburnt condition is lost and the normal processes of nature automatically ensue. Often the degree of burning is in relationship to the degree of panic or loss of mental focus. Most people, however, who do attempt the walk reach the other side quite unscathed. Not everyone who goes through the preparation decides to do the walk!

There are many such phenomena and I have described this particular one at length, because media coverage has brought it to the attention of most people. But in the east, the miraculous powers of yogis have been acknowledged as a fact of life for centuries, even millenia.

So levitation, the power to walk on water or fly in the air, to sit on hot coals, to stay naked in the Himalayan snows, to materialize objects – all these are possible by conscious application of the mind to manipulate the way in which physical substance comes into being. The power of levitation demonstrates immediately that the mind can manipulate the force of gravity, creating a gravity-free body.

Similarly with all material phenomena. If the normal mental connection of the mind to material energy patterns is made conscious, or even partially so, then there is little limit to its powers.

Fortunately, such concentration is normally associated with an increase in mental purity and spiritual consciousness, for it is human weakness and emotion that prevents us from being aware of such capabilities and scatters the mind. But black magic is also practised, though the impurity of mind and motive within the practitioners automatically and thankfully limits their 'powers'. Black magic can have no hold over one with a reasonably pure and concentrated mind.

In fact, in all the higher mystic practices, the use of these miraculous powers, whether for good or ill, is strictly advised against, for it requires a downward flow of mental energy which should be used for higher spiritual ascent.

So yogic powers are spoken of as party tricks and one is advised to wait for the boat, rather than waste mental energy, increase one's ego and save a little money by walking on the water or moving lightly through the air.

This discussion highlights one other aspect of the laws of nature. That is that the energy patterns that produce what we experience as inert matter are far less complex than those which are involved in the manifestation of a living organism. The laws of nature, of energy relationships, are far more intricate and complex in matter (energy) that is held specifically by the web of mind and consciousness, than in that of matter not held into the interwoven tapestry of a body.

This fact needs to be far more fully comprehended than it is at present. For the power of the mind and consciousness to form material substance into a body is apparent in every movement of a hand or foot, in every beat of the heart, in every intricate biochemical and physiological activity within the body. The minds and bodies of living creatures operate as one whole, integrated unit – a part of a greater whole – and the overall patterning nature of the mind and the life force is demonstrated there.

If a body operates as a whole, with every subatomic

particle and fundamental force under the highly ordered control of the life force within, it tells us that this life force employs an interwoven structure of energy relationships at the subtle level. This is the subtle matrix already mentioned in this chapter and discussed more fully in *The Web of Life*. As soon as life departs, this intense degree of organization vanishes and the molecular, bioelectrical, biochemical, cellular and overall structure rapidly begins to dis-integrate, to lose its central wholeness or integrity.

Matter, then returns to the inert condition until once again caught up into the bodies of living organisms. Actually, this breakdown process is also achieved through the agency of a myriad organisms – the complexity woven by one life force is of great value to the others in the grand economy of nature. Hence, all creatures except plants live on the bodies of other living creatures, rather than sand, minerals and water. But plants, too are not independent.

In inert matter, the more simple patterning is immediately apparent. The complexities of molecular and biophysical activity simply do not exist.

Modern physics, by and large, studies only inert matter. At least it assumes that the matter comprising the bodies of living organisms behaves in the same way as inert matter. But this is not so. Inert matter is patterned and held together by a diffuse form of the universal creative Shabd, the primal Life Force, and is patterned by our mind under the influence of our pralabdh karma or destiny. But the material substance held within the orbit of a living creature is patterned by a focused life force, manifesting physically through a subtle mind structure. It is infinitely more complex in structure.

One can understand how difficult it is for modern physics to approach matter within living bodies, for as soon as high energy experimentation begins on such a body, to examine its most intricate mechanisms, the life force departs, leaving only inert energy patterns. But the ability of living bodies to transmute elements, communicate between cells and molecules via coded electromagnetic signals, to maintain exact cytoplasmic temperatures, to generate superconductivity and integrate the whole amazing subatomic mosaic is telling us in loud and clear language that the subatomic realm is receiving messages from the life force that are quite absent in inert matter. As soon as a body is dead, these intricate functions cease, so it is difficult to catch them at it, since most experimentation is invasive and life-destroying.

Indeed, at the level of biochemistry and bioelectricity, we can only see the *effects* of the life force, not the life force itself. In fact, effects are all we ever see of anything at the physical level. We do not see the force of gravity or magnetism, we observe only an effect, which we analyze and quantify and use accordingly. But the Primal Cause of all physical manifestation is not available to our normal perception.

Even medical physics apparatus (CAT scanners and so on) is largely based upon an understanding of the way inert, not living, matter behaves. Supremely delicate equipment needs to be developed to be able to really monitor the fine bodily activity at the subatomic and vacuum state levels. We need to understand that we are looking at energy patterns organized by a vastly more complex set of rules and relationships than is apparent in the physics laboratory.

The lack of an appreciation of this knowledge is why we just do not understand how a body functions. This is the rationale behind natural approaches to medicine and the healing arts. When our car goes wrong, we take it to an expert mechanic who we feel confident will be able to diagnose the exact problem and put things right.

But in medicine, we have no such mechanic. No-one can fully understand the detailed mechanisms by which our mind and body are integrated. We can perceive many pathways, but we cannot see the whole interplay in a clear and cogent fashion. This is why there are so many schools of thought in healing.

When I take my car to the garage, there is no real dispute over how to handle its ailments. There is not a choice of different garage-therapies to choose between. Cars are understood and their problems are capable of complete diagnosis and remedy. Man was the one who put cars together, derived from a partial analysis of the way matter behaves at the physical level.

But not so the body of any living creature. Despite all our advances, our science is still ignorant of the fundamentals. We have theoretical models in physics. Although they are known to be inadequate and incomplete, they do help us make and mend our technological artefacts. But, if you think about it, mainstream medicine has absolutely no theoretical model of any living creature. There is only an endless array of bits and pieces. It is rather like an enormous jigsaw puzzle where we have only succeeded in getting a few pieces to fit, here and there. I do not say that the fitting together of these pieces has not proved to be of great value to us, but we still have no understanding of what the entire picture looks like at all. Even our knowledge of the subtle body is not formulated in any really detailed way that interlinks with observable biochemistry and so on. A theoretical model that included mental, emotional, subtle, pranic and tattvic energies and patterns; that took into account the vacuum state, the subatomic realm, the generation of form at both the molecular, electromagnetic and cellular levels as well as that of organs, systems and the shapes comprising the whole body – this would be a theoretical model, but no such detailed concept exists as yet.

For this reason, therefore, the more humble healer takes the natural approach. He says, "I do not know the intricacies of this wonderful body machine. But I do know that there is tremendously detailed organization and method within it. Nature *does* know what it is doing. Therefore, my approach must be to learn how to work *with* nature, how to help these natural processes perform their magic function."

But if the healer or doctor assumes, out of ignorance, that he knows a lot, then the trouble starts. Both for the doctor and the patient! If the healer also sees the situation as an opportunity for making a good profit, then things get even worse. And this is unfortunately the case with much of medicine today. The drug industry could do so much more if the motive was re-aligned to human betterment, instead of profit. The doctors may take the Hippocratic oath to serve humanity and observe a code of ethics, but the drug and medical equipment companies do not.

Their motivation and structure is based upon new products and profit, not human betterment. Imagine the progress that would have been made if the resources of the drug companies had been applied to the study of natural medicine. Towards working *with* nature and understanding her wonderfully intricate patterns and relationships instead of the ungainly and heathen approach that has come into being.

Where on earth did this strange idea arise that we know enough to be able to ignore the most wonderful mechanisms that pervade a living organism and feed it alien molecules (synthetic drugs) as a part of our major approach to healing? Actually, if you analyze medical science you will find that the most effective treatments are those that work with nature and allow her to perform a magic which we do not comprehend. Immunology and the eradication of some infectious diseases are a good example of where man has come to know only enough to adjust the natural balance and stimulate the little understood natural mechanisms involved in the body's defence against disease and attack by other living organisms. It is no discredit to admit to ignorance and to understand that we have to work with nature and with forces we do not understand. This is our human situation.

Consider how much more effective our hospital facilities would be if they were turned into places of healing, rather than clinical offices of disease? A visit to a hospital should be an enriching and nourishing experience, but very few are run along such lines. But there are signs that change is afoot as a higher consciousness and awareness creeps into the minds of the medical profession.

I am digressing, however, and will leave the subject here, for there are many points of view and practicalities that would need to be expressed for a full appreciation of the subject. And it is beyond the limits of this book.

—— CHAPTER 5 ——

Vibration and Atmosphere

Shabd – The Primary Vibration, Energy and Life Force

In chapters two, three and four, we have concentrated attention almost entirely upon the complexly ordered structure of living creatures and, in particular, man. In this chapter, we consider the vibrational aspects of the inert matter which surrounds us.

Relative to the organization of substance within the physical bodies of living creatures, inert matter is simply structured. It is, however, far from random, as physicists can readily tell us. It 'obeys' strict laws and follows repeating patterns. Its molecular, atomic and subatomic structure is highly, though simply, organized. Within every particle of created matter there lies a distant echo of the formative and creative power of the primal energy of life.

In the Christian part of the Bible (the New Testament), this power, this primal Life Force, is called the *Word* or the *Logos*. It has also been called the *Creative Word*. The Indian mystics – both modern and ancient – have called it *Shabd*, which means *Sound*, or *Nam* – which means the *Name* of God. They have also called it *Ajapa Japa* (Unutterable Utterance), whilst in the Vedas it is called *Nad* (Sound) or *Akash Bani* (Song of Heaven). In fact, in Hindi translations of the Bible, Shabd is used to translate "Word" at the beginning of St John's gospel: "In the beginning was the Shabd." The American Hopi Indians have called it the *Creation Song*.

When all is One, there can be no names. A name requires duality, one to whom the name is given by another and which is required for identification. Hence this Creative Power, being the first outflow, differentiation or movement within the One is known as His Word,

His Creative Sound, His Name or His Will. In the Bible it is also known as the Holy Ghost, and to "sin against the Holy Ghost", or to "take the Name of God in vain" means to turn oneself away, inwardly, from one's own inner life force or soul. This is the real "blasphemy", of which we are all culpable, to one degree or another, every day. It is our normal condition whilst being away from the mystic Source. And for this we are "punished" by "death" – by being reborn time and again in this physical universe, the endless wheel of birth and death. The only way back is through the highest kind of meditation, which is inner experience of this Creative Life Stream. And to learn that, as in all other matters, a qualified teacher is required.

Muslim mystics have also experienced this power and have called it *Ism-i-Azam* (the Highest Name) or *Kalam-i-Ilahi* (the Word of Allah). In the Kabbala, the mystical tradition within Judaism, it is known as *Yod-He-Vau-He*, the sacred Name of God. It is known in all traditions and cultures, because it is within everyone of us as our primary place or source of being and consciousness. It is natural within all creatures and in all the creation. Mystics of whatever caste or creed have experienced it and described it as the true source of everything, living and inanimate.

So, in reality, the Universal is present within every particle of the creation. The structure of creation is like that of a vast hologram with both inward and horizontal dimensions. Or in religious terminology: God is everywhere and within everything. And the human body is the true temple, church, mosque, gurdwhara or synagogue in which, by meditation, He is to be worshipped.

Man is the microcosm, the part of this macrocosm through which all parts of the whole can be reached and experienced. So meditation, experience of this Primary Life Force, is the real prayer to Him, not presenting Him with a shopping list, however well-meaning our desires may appear. In a very real sense, prayer – as it is conventionally understood – assumes that God is about to make a mistake and that it is our duty to tell him about it. Real prayer is an inner communion of the soul with the Lord, of the drop with its Ocean. No words are required.

Vibrational Experience

But we digress. It is the experience of many people that places, rooms, houses and so on, carry an atmosphere, a vibration. This can relate to the individual, to the creatures living there, to those who have lived there before, or it may be intrinsic in the place itself – the powerful vibration of the mountains or the forests, for instance.

This vibration is carried within the substructure of the vacuum and more subtle states which gives rise to the material forms themselves. Probably, it is also encoded into the harmony or otherwise, of movement and being within the subatomic realm; as clockwise and anticlockwise particle spin – centripetal and cohering or centrifugal and expanding – or as waveforms or even as scientifically detectable vibration and oscillation.

Mind affects matter, as we have seen. In fact, mind is really just a more refined vibration or higher harmonic of matter. So, quite naturally, wherever we go, we carry our vibration with us, emanating from us in our aura and in our attention, as we perceive and act. And this, quite naturally, becomes encoded into our places of dwelling, creating a vibration or atmosphere in which we feel comfortable and at home.

And as we become aware of these atmospheres, we automatically find ourselves seeking places of good vibration for our more inward nourishment.

We also become appreciative of aesthetics and beauty, of form, colour and shape, for these attributes of material substance do themselves carry a particular vibration which can be harmonizing, or the reverse.

This is the reason why pyramid shapes, for example, possess the characteristics that they do and why arches and some other shapes are more *pleasing* than others. *Pleasure* being a condition of mind and emotion and therefore a state of energy at subtle levels.

Good and truly artistic designers, architects, interior decorators, painters, sculptors and the like are all intuitively aware, to one degree or another, of the impact of structure on atmosphere. Musicians are really sculptors of changing forms and patterns in the air waves, and there is no doubt of the subtlety of atmosphere and mood which can be created by music. There are a number of therapies which use sound and musical vibration for healing purposes, with some considerable success. Music is also used to stimulate growth in plants. Recent experimentation has also shown that the mechanical vibration of sound can induce molecules to emit electromagnetic radiation, even at visible wavelengths (ie. light). This is most probably a natural part of biological processes and animal communication.

In China, the art of design and form has been a science and a knowledge for long ages. It seems a part of the ambience of the land itself. Even Chinese trees have an unmistakable shape and structure. The science is called *Feng Shui* and it encompasses all aspects of energy manipulation and arrangement from interior decoration, landscaping, the siting and location of dwellings and, of course, the energies of money, business and finance. The Orientals would never forget that!

The Chinese call energy, *Ch'i*, and while *acupuncture* is the art of directing and harmonizing body energies, Feng Shui is the art of creating good Ch'i in an environment. It is an art worth studying and a knowledge worth possessing. Our architects, builders and town planners could have created a far more beautiful and energetically nourishing environment for us if only they had cared more for the quality of life they were creating. It would have been just as financially rewarding in the long run, too. For good energy brings in good money and good feeling. Actually, many countries in Europe keep a closer eye on the quality of architecture than we do in the British Isles. And the results are there to be seen.

Of all the influences on our environment, however, the presence of a *diversity* of life forms, living naturally, are amongst the greatest providers of good vibration. But there must be diversity. A London park of mostly trees and grass with comparatively few other species is not nearly as beautiful and nourishing to one's inner being as a more diverse, naturally occurring and abundant ecosystem. It is said that the tropical rain forests, which now cover only seven per cent of the earth's surface, contain more than half of its known species.

Gardens, parks, rivers, woodlands, forests and wild

countryside are amongst our most treasured national and planetary heritage. Without these sources of nourishment, life can become dry and sterile, and although this is not a book on environmental issues, it must be clearly understood that if we attempt to destroy our planet and its biosphere, we will inevitably destroy ourselves. We should nurture and care for our planet and its living creatures – human included – as if it were our own beloved garden, for in truth it is.

Environmental Pollution

Similarly, the *vibration* of pollution can be carried within the vacuum and more subtle states, spreading into the surrounding area and indeed throughout the entire planet. So although chemicals may be tightly sealed, and buried deep underground, their vibration can affect the immediate area and will spread. Our sources of power – nuclear or conventional electricity generating centres – can similarly become centres of vibrational disharmony, explaining why they are frequently at the centre of leukaemia or cancer clusters, quite apart from the more obvious physical causes due to emission of radioactive materials. And it also explains why there are spontaneous and naturally occurring areas of ill-health when there are no obvious physical reasons. For the structure of rock, mineral and water channels within the ground, especially crystalline or piezo-electric formations such as the commonly occurring quartz, can be centres of atomic and molecular stress, creating vibrational or vacuum state ripples of a disharmonious nature. Similarly, harmonious vibration created by these sources adds to the peaceful atmosphere of such places.

Electromagnetic pollution – radio and TV broadcasting, microwave radar and their similars, not to mention radiation from radioactive decay, as well as the intensely powerful electric fields surrounding overhead power cables – these too are sources of vibrational disturbance to the vacuum state. This, in fact, is how electromagnetic energies are formed and is how they affect not only our biochemistry, but also our thoughts and moods. Indeed, research into psychotronic weaponry uses electromagnetic vibration as a means of controlling mood, mind and emotion. Not a very pleasant thought.

So pollution means the destruction of an environment by the disharmonizing of the energetic constituents that comprise it. The killing of species, destruction of ecological niches, the spraying of vast areas of farmland with chemicals designed to favour just one species of plant while destroying countless others including the bacteria which give life and nourishment to the soil, deforestation, reforestation with tree species that support little other life, the contamination of our food, our water, our air and our planet with ill-considered, industrial effluent – all these represent human idiocy at its worst. We are trading short-term gain (for a few) for long-term disaster (for all of us).

Already, we have planetary epidemics and millions dying of starvation. This is the backlash of exploiting nature for egocentric advantage. Nature keeps its own balance.

We must become aware of the delicate equilibrium of manifestation and creation, of the forces and patterns that are at work, and of the balancing energies that automatically come into play when one species gets out of control.

Man is a microcosm. Within him is reflected all the Universe. And the universe correspondingly affects him. What one part of our human family does, affects all of us. This we must understand. It is true that the spiritual goal lies within, beyond the realm of outward strife and struggle, but spiritual development is also worked out by our learning to live correctly while confined to a human existence. What we do and the way we do it, both of these affect our spiritual life.

Memory and the Akashic Record

I am unsure where the term *akashic record* originated. In Sanskrit, it is possibly within the yogic texts, but it is certainly one which the theosophists coined, in the English language, and which has captured the imagination of occult-minded people ever since. So let us see if we can shed some light upon it.

Akash, it has been said – at the dense physical level – is the vacuum state. But in general, this akashic state is found in increasing degrees of subtlety as the energetic gateway or threshold between all the inner regions. In all cases, it is an energetic divider of region from region, upon the vertical, inward energy spectrum. In some writings, akash is also called *gagan*, which means 'sky'. But this is a sky, not in the sense of our earthly sky, but as a barrier in the ascent of the soul, a point requiring a tremendous degree of inward concentration and purity in order to pierce the veil and move into the next higher state.

Now these gateways are points or levels of creative potential. They are manifested from within-out as the reality of the next lower level and they are also impressed from 'without' by the happenings in that lower level. The two are really part and parcel of the same process of creation.

In terms of the gross physical vacuum, what this means is that every event that takes place, together with every thought and mood in the minds of the observers, is impressed upon this vacuum state and remains there afterwards. The degree of intensity of this impression will vary, depending upon the intensity – emotional or physical – of the activity.

It is this that sensitive people, of whom there are many, register as the *atmosphere* of a place. It is the general trend in the thoughts of a myriad worshippers which give a church, a mosque, a synagogue or a temple their characteristic atmosphere of devotion and prayer. It is an energetic aspect of association, but far more than something which is 'just psychological'. It is the mind and manner of living which is impressed upon a home and tells the observant soul a great deal concerning what goes on there.

It reflects the love with which an artist or craftsman imbues his creation and it is the vibration that a loving (or otherwise) cook unconsciously injects into his or her food, and which helps determine its flavour, as well as the mood induced in those who partake of it. It is the difference vibrationally between the pottery we buy direct from the craftsman and the mass-produced pottery we find in the department store. It has more character, we say, though we may be hard put to explain exactly why.

This vibrational record arises, as does all manifestation, from the inward mechanism by which the mind patterns the vacuum or akashic state from within in the process of creating physical reality. It is this which also constitutes the subatomic fingerprint.

Similarly, within our human physical constitution, lies what mystics call the sky of our body, a more subtle inward akash. It is here that a *memory* of our whole life is etched – every thought, emotion, word and deed. It is this very black box which provides the patterning energy for future incarnations. We draw on parts of this as our normally rather poor memory of events. We remember very little concerning the details of our days. But it is this subtle pattern which patterns the more gross vacuum state, with the consequent creation of the physical world we take so seriously as a 'hard' reality.

This creative principle becomes more universal as we progress within and the akash of the astral and causal zones will contain within them an imprint of all that has happened, as well as all that will happen, in the worlds below. This is a part of the creative mechanism. It is, no doubt, these akashic skies that are being referred to as the akashic records. So the atmosphere and vibration of places encoded into the vacuum state, our own memory as well as the more inward skies, are all essentially different levels or reflections of this akashic record.

Homoeopathy, Radionics and the Vacuum State

The understanding that the vacuum state is patterned both by our mind, from within, and by the activities of subatomic particles, atoms and molecules from without underlies many hitherto inexplicable, yet valid, phenomena.

We see this in a general way in all aspects of body-mind function. The currents of mind and pranas 'direct' the vacuum to pattern the subatomic particles comprising the physical substance of our body. It is by such means that our heart beats or that we can waggle our finger, and all else besides.

Conversely, we can affect our mind by ingesting various molecular substances – eating a meal can change our mood, for example, while consuming alcohol, coffee and other mind-affecting drugs clearly reaches into the subtle areas of our mental being. And this dynamic, two-way process is made use of in both homoeopathy and radionics.

In homoeopathy, a chemical substance is increasingly diluted with distilled water until, in the higher potencies, there is no molecular substance remaining.

According to conventional science, there is no physical basis for the phenomenon – and yet millions of people attest to the efficacy of homoeopathy, even the British royal family.

There have also been verifications of the effect from the world of conventional science. In June 1988, Britain's *Nature* magazine published the findings of Dr Jacques Benveniste, a highly respected and well known scientist of impeccable credentials from the French Medical Research Council laboratory at the University of Paris-Sud. He has shown that antibodies, part of the body's immuno-defence system against allergens and microbial invaders, retain their efficacy even when they have been successively diluted in distilled water beyond the point at which any molecules of the antibody might remain. This is the procedure used in the preparation of homoeopathic remedies, a system of medicine even more widely practised in France than in Britain or America.

Jacques Benveniste has thus demonstrated that *the effects of the antibody are still biologically present and active, even when no molecules of the antibody actually remain in the solution.* From an understanding of vacuum state manifestation, it should be clear what is happening.

Molecules are aggregates or specific configurations of intensely active atoms and subatomic particles. They are swirling patterns upon the vacuum surface. But their outward manifestation as what we call molecules is only a surface phenomenon. Like an iceberg, what appears on the surface is only a fraction of what is going on underneath. But unlike an iceberg, when the surface phenomenon is removed, the vibrational patterns which go on beneath the surface, within the formative vacuum itself, would appear to continue.

And since biological organisms take their form and function out of the vacuum and more subtle energy fields, these vibrations still affect living systems. The vacuum, effectively, possesses an inward memory of its outwardly manifested forms.

Dr Benveniste even persuaded colleagues from Israel, Italy, Canada and Paris to repeat the experiments in double-blind trials and the results seem reasonably clear. *Nature* published his paper together with an unprecedented editoral comment inviting readers to share in their "incredulity" and emphasizing that "there is no physical basis for the phenomenon." Without an appreciation of physical substance as a continuously created dance out of the vacuum or spatial state, this would, of necessity, have been their conclusion.

Here then is the long-awaited acknowledgement by the conservative scientific fraternity that homoeopathy really works. Something that millions of patients and practitioners have known for a long time!

But ulterior motives lurk as much in scientific minds, as elsewhere, and it was not long before the rival *New Scientist* magazine pointed out that the publication of such an article by *Nature* (normally a highly conservative journal) may well have been part of a pre-planned publicity stunt aimed at boosting sales. For the article in *Nature* was not only reported in the national and other scientific press, giving them a good dose of free publicity, but within a very short time – clearly indicating that their whole plan had been preconceived – *Nature* had sent in a team of three 'experts', (not one of them an expert in Benveniste's field). The trio consisted of their editor (John Maddox), the magician James Randi – a man dedicated to proving that everything he or the 'known' laws of science cannot explain must be phoney – and Walter Stewart, a single-minded American scientific fraud investigator. Not a team of objective scientists, but men with a mission.

In fact, Maddox himself admits that the investigation was planned and accepted by Benveniste as an unprecedented precondition of publication. Benveniste, however, had had no idea at the time of the original agreement who Maddox had in mind for the 'investigators'. When Benveniste found out, he immediately telephoned Maddox to complain, but it was already too late to manoeuvre. Benveniste had been manipulated.

The question also has to be asked: why was the 'investigation' not carried out *before* publication? *Nature*, apparently, had been refusing publication of the paper for *two years*, so there had been no lack of time and opportunity. Clearly, they wanted to make an issue of it. It certainly generated publicity for them.

However, these three 'investigators' apparently created an extremely unpleasant inquisatorial atmosphere in Benveniste's laboratory, (where they were invited guests), finally pronouncing after only five days 'examination' of five years research and thought, that Benveniste's results were the result of "subconscious selection of data." Given that one could hardly have chosen a more biased team of 'experts' and conditions of examination, their 'conclusions' were already predictable from the moment they set out from home. Their own subconscious mind sets performed the very same trick upon them of which they were later to accuse Benveniste. A clear case of psychological projection, observable by every kindergarten psychologist.

There is another aspect to the psychology of such situations. Since mind energies are so powerful, yet – being so subtle – largely remain undetected below the threshold of awareness, the negative mental vibrations of such hostile, 'independent' inquisitors which kill stone dead the subtle and sensitive vibrations of psychic people or subtle phenomena that they may be 'investigating'.

The subconscious mind and consequently the vibrations or aura of such 'investigators' seethes with insecurity that its illusory sense of ego or false identity will be 'found out'. This is exhibited outwardly as intolerance, criticism, anger, fear, suspicion, even violence, not allowing the other to have their say by trying to talk them down, continuous repetition of conditioned beliefs as if they were self-evident realities, refusal to acknowledge the experience and feelings of others as genuine whilst forcefully promoting their own point of view, justification of such behaviour by stating that, "the truth as everybody knows it to be should be protected from 'charlatans'" – and so on.

In societies where democracy is not protected by law the result can be imprisonment and even death, as an 'enemy of the state.' Socrates, Christ and many others have suffered such a fate. But it arises, always, from a challenge to the unconscious habituation of deeply ingrained mind patterns and the individual's subsonscious *identification* with them. The sense of being and identity is thus unconsciously threatened. It is the automatic response of a mind scattered into subconsciousness, far away from its true inner centre and understanding of its real identity.

No-one, for example, but the man with death in his heart and a gun on his shoulder is surprised that the wild creatures flee his path! But the hunter himself, spreading mental vibrations of killing wherever he goes, may never come to understand it. Negative and destructive mind patterns are themselves the most efficacious screen and blanket to the world of the subtle, as well as to a real awareness of life and consciousness itself.

It is not surprising then, that Benveniste afterwards wrote that the atmosphere in his laboratory during the visit of this trio was:

> A tornado of intense suspicion, fear and psychological and intellectual pressure, unfit for scientific work.

Never again, he declared, would he allow such an inquiry, when – in a spirit of great openness and furtherance of human knowledge – he had made available all his research notebooks to a team who seem to have been insensitive, arrogant and self-opinionated intellectual bullies. No wonder so many of the scientific fraternity, whatever their opinion of the research itself, felt embarrased to be associated with such behaviour. But let us hope that the nett result will be a wider knowledge of homoeopathy and Benveniste's work. After all, since homoeopathy really does help people, why do these 'scientists' want so desperately to knock it?

Regarding their behaviour, Maddox even admitted, "We were certainly rude . . . impolite. We weren't, as most academics would have been, respectful." In particular, the American fraudbuster, Walter Stewart, caused considerable problems. "Stewart has no manners," commented Maddox, "He's a zealot." As the emotional temperature rose, so did the pitch of Stewart's voice. Said Maddox, "He does have a high-pitched voice and when he's tense, his voice sounds like a Dalek. We had to tell him to talk naturally." Tone and quality of voice are deeply indicative of an individual's underlying unconscious emotion.

The significance of this kind of negative atmosphere to Benveniste's case is this: Most practitioners of homoeopathy will know that the quality of the remedy is also related directly to the quality of mind, motive and understanding in the one who prepares it. The care and comprehension of what is being done are all encoded into the vacuum state – a physical akashic record. This is actually true in all areas of life.

So an important aspect of the homoeopathic principle is that the mind itself is capable of creating the same effect within the vacuum energy field as the homoeopathic dilution process itself.

Again, homoeopathic practitioners will note that many of their remedies are related to *psychological* symptoms – and with the individual mind being involved in the patterning of the vacuum state, this is what one would predict. The more subtle the energy field in which the medicine is active, then the more subtle (and therefore the more mental-emotional) will be its effect.

This is again the same phenomenon as the cook who puts her vibration into the food, or the vibrational encoding of the motivation of all who have dealt with the foods and medicines sold in our modern shops and supermarkets. Hence the lack of vibrational, subtle, vacuum state, nourishment from such products. In this manner, we are all connected at a mental level. This is a part of the integrated mechanism for the outworking of all our karmas. The 'homoeopathic' vibration is present in all our foods, clothing, environment – everything.

Indeed, in radionics, homoeopathic remedies are prepared entirely within the vacuum state. A radionics instrument is often used, but I have a strong feeling that the use of the machine is no more than an (important) 'ritual' to enable the practitioner to focus or 'shape' his mind, thus unconsciously creating the desired vibrational impression upon the remedy.

Reinforcing this suggestion is the observation of Dr Edward Bach, also a homoeopath, and discoverer of the subtle flower remedy essences. These remedies capture the vibrational qualities of the flowers and can be an extremely effective form of treatment. But Dr Bach also pointed out that when one mentally understands the nature of this vibration, then the same effect can be created in one's mind *and* body simply by *thinking* of the remedy, by holding in mind its qualities and vibrational nature. This alone re-patterns and re-harmonizes body function.

And this, of course, is the essence of all psychosomatic phenomena. They are real, but as I have commented before, our entire physical existence is psychosomatic – a combination of mind and body.

Interestingly, Benveniste himself observes that there seemed to be 'unknown' factors affecting his results. Trials worked on some days and not on others. Or they only worked after procedures that seemed to bear no relationship to the results – cold overnight storage, vigorous shaking – and so on. With subtle and mental factors known to be involved, this is exactly as one might expect. For all activity, whatever its mechanical effect, engenders the mental focusing of the individuals involved, like a ritual, regardless of the nature of the actual activity itself. This would be especially true of the vigorous shaking, characteristic of homoeopathic preparation.

In fact, I would actually predict that results would vary depending upon *who* performed the experiment, ie. whose mind was actually directly involved. This phenomenon is well known in highly delicate experimentation and is related to more than just skilful fingers. It is especially apparent in all biological experiments, particularly in the world of human healing and medicine as well as in research dealing with other living creatures, from plants to chimpanzees. The mental content and atmosphere or aura of the experimenter, doctor or therapist is also of considerable importance.

Bearing this out is the fact that during the visit of the three inquisitors, seven additional trials were conducted for their benefit. The first four were completely successful, embarrassingly so for the *Nature* team, since they had insisted on somewhat puerile additional 'anti-fraud' checking procedures. "They were white with shock," Benveniste recalled. "They kept saying, 'extraordinary, flabbergasting, impossible'."

But by this time, Benveniste and his team were tired from lack of sleep and emotional strain. The emotional atmosphere was supercharged. It is not surprising therefore that the remaining three tests failed. Tiredness, leading to less than perfect technique, the anxious desire to succeed though mentally out of tune with what they were doing, plus the overall disturbed and negative mental vibration would naturally influence such subtle tests.

Indeed, the *Nature* team remarked (though as a criticism!) on the dedication and team spirit of the laboratory staff. They said it led to a loss of objectivity. Perhaps they would have the same complaint of dedicated and caring doctors and nurses. Atmosphere and the quality of mind brought to bear on any task is of paramount importance in achieving good results in any sphere of life. And where one is attempting to measure the subtle vibration of atmosphere itself, how much more important it is.

So it is not surprising that psychic investigator and magician, James Randi, finds that the world of the subtle evapourates whenever he comes on the scene. But it is – at least in genuine cases – his own subtle mental atmosphere which is responsible, not fraudulent psychics! In the world of the mind, *all* minds are involved. There is no such thing as objectivity.

Captain James T. Kirk's Life-Form Monitor

All creatures put out vibrations at many levels – this we call their aura. Vibrations or oscillations at the vacuum state level are no exception and it is quite conceivable that a purely mechanistic piece of equipment could be devised which would recognize such vacuum state waves, even perhaps identifying the kind of creature from which such waves emanated and whether or not it was friendly, or in a good mood. So the life-form monitor of Captain Kirk and his Star Trek crew may ultimately be a realizable reality!

Morphogenic Fields

It is said that within a space of five to seven years, every atom in our body is replaced by new atoms. That is to say that our nose and our brain, for example, are comprised of different material to that of seven years ago. Our face, hands, liver, all our organs, even our DNA – these all contain different molecules and atoms, as the years roll by. Yet the *form* remains the same. The same nose, face, body structure, organs and DNA. Even scar tissue can remain. Broken bones knit; regeneration of tissues and, in some species, even organs regularly takes place. Can one say, therefore, that form is more fundamental than substance?

The world of formative blueprints, lies in the vacuum state and in more subtle, inward fields of energy. The vacuum state has a memory, as we have said. This is the atmosphere and vibration within all places and things, which is present even in the absence of the living creatures who have made the original impressions. And atmosphere is something we experience in our mind.

Rupert Sheldrake, and others before him, noting especially the phenomenon of embryonic growth, have postulated the existence of such natural blueprints, but have usually looked for them in the material substance and energy of the dense material world. The best candidates considered so far by conventional circles, are DNA – which constitutes only a reflex point, not an overall morphogenic field – and electromagnetic energy patterns. Though since biologists are not usually biophysicists, the evidence for this latter possibility is largely ignored.

However, it does seem likely that there is an electromagnetic information-encoding system. And DNA certainly has relationships to outer form, as well as to protein synthesis. But since neither molecules and electromagnetic energy are fundamental, but only effects or bubbles upon the vacuum energy ocean, the real place of existence for morphogenic patterns must lie within the vacuum and more subtle states, not in our world of physical effects.

This explains many of the phenomena highlighted by Sheldrake and others. Back in 1920, for instance, William McDougall ran a series of experiments at Harvard University, studying how long it took for rats to escape from a maze filled with water. To his surprise, he discovered that successive generations learnt the escape route more rapidly.

Was this an example of Lamarkian evolution, with parents passing on acquired characteristics to their offspring? Or was it simply that the rats left scent markers in the maze which were never sufficiently cleaned between experiments? The answer to both was, "No." For when other research teams in Scotand and Australia came to repeat McDougall's experiment using completely separate strains of rats, they found that their rats actually *began* their learning at the same level of expertise reached by McDougall's *last* generation. Somehow, the skill had been passed across material barriers, as if in some collective unconscious or as a field or vibration of energy common to all rats.

Sheldrake took the thinking further in his book, *A New Science of Life*, and in my own writings I have pointed our that this blueprinting system of energies arranged in a vertical spectrum, is the very mechanism of creation itself.

What is interesting is that nature, animate and inanimate, seems to operate – like our minds – according to acquired habits, as an aspect of more fundamental and intrinsic laws. And certain habits may be specific to individual species or even to the mineral kingdom.

So for particular forms, patterns or fields, it seems that there must be some common ground of morphic vibration, at – I would suggest – the vacuum state and more subtle levels. Individual forms in the physical world are thus derived from these more subtle energy fields and by a process of resonance or sympathy are automatically connected at an unconscious level to all other similar forms.

Thus nature remains an integrated whole, encompassing all adaptations in the rolling tide of change. This, no doubt, is what underlies the mood of an era on which all 'individual' minds are strung, like pearls on one chain. The moods of the 1920's, the '60's, the '70's, the '80's – the constant and characteristic patterning and repatterning of changing minds and circumstances – these we recognize so well, especially in retrospect. But we have more to say on this in a later chapter and especially in the next book in this series, *Natural Creation*. For ultimately all patterns are the result of activity within the Universal or greater Mind, the real architect of form and nature, a Cosmic, *Formative Mind* of which our individual minds are just one aspect. And this greater Mind is the one who weaves the web of pattern and form, time and space, over the face of the One Source of all being.

Looking, for example, at the mineral kingdom, Sheldrake notes how even certain organic compounds and other substances, never previously crystallized, when once crystallized, subsequently perform their magic more readily for other researchers worldwide, as if the pathway had suddenly been made easier for them. Even sealed containers of substances previously unknown in crystalline form, and where seed crystals could have never found their way uninvited, suddenly and otherwise inexplicably formed crystals. Laboratory workers have been so aware of this strange phenomenon that they have even postulated that miniature seed crystals must have travelled across the globe in the hair or clothing of visitors from other laboratories.

This flow, this mood, atmosphere and habit of the times is also expressed in synchronicity and coincidence. It is a part of the linkage of all minds at the formative level, the process by which – through the interlinking of our karmas, stored in our minds – the physical world is actually manifested. This mind-linkage is also, of course, how telepathy takes place. But mostly we are unaware of the process, because our mind is largely unconscious of its own inward activity, structure and influences.

Sheldrake was also intrigued by the habits of bluetits, who having discovered how to remove the metal foil caps from milk bottles in one part of the country – many years after the introduction of such caps – spontaneously discovered the technique in other areas, too. Bluetits are known from ringing studies to be rather parochial little birds, rarely travelling far during their short lives. So although the method naturally caught on in individual areas as one bird learnt the technique from another, there is clearly another process at work where *remote* learning took place.

Adding fuel to this perception is the observation that during the war years, bluetits were unable to continue their new found delight when the metal-capped bottles were replaced with cardboard. Yet, after the war, when the old style of caps returned, long after the most long-lived of bluetits could have survived, the old habit was *immediately* resumed.

It is also possible, of course, indeed probable, that many of the post-war bluetits were reincarnations of their pre-war ancestors, having taken many intermediate births, too, carrying their old impressions with them in seed form from birth to birth, just as we ourselves do. Though we cannot remember now from where we received our inclinations, personality and abilities.

But as a mechanism in nature, the linkage of all creatures at a more fundamental level than that of gross physical observation, would seem to be an intrinsic design factor, automatically creating coherence and integration. Holism is a part of the implicate order. Nature, as we have said many times, is not a motley conglomeration of horizontally causal associations. That is only the analysis of a reductionist mind, the most prevalent paradigm of twentieth century science, presently on the decline, though fighting a strong rearguard action.

So as a means of adaptation to a changing environment it would seem to be of tremendous benefit if skills and traits were automatically transmitted to distant members of the same species.

But really this is still only a reductionist analysis of the situation. Actually, there are no 'individual skills and traits' any more than petals can come into existence independently of a flower. There is only the whole pattern of manifestation which, in our minds, we may see as something divided. These divisions, however, lie in *our* minds, not in nature as a functioning whole.

There we have just one multilevel, multifaceted dance of creation and manifestation, interconnecting and interpentrating at all levels. With our physical eyes, we see just the surface, just the skin only. Hence our confusion and our ignorance. When we rise up within ourselves, then we see life in another way, where all is an expression of the Supreme One within all. Then there is no mystery – only awe, wonder, love and bliss.

INTERLUDE

Tales from Ancient Persia

Perhaps, as they say in India, it is time for a story. In the east there is a tradition of telling stories. Their literature is full with tales of every imaginable kind. Mystics of the east, too, since they always talk in the idiom and language of the people with whom they are dealing, have also used such stories and parables to put across their message.

During the Renaissance, usually said to have begun in the fourteenth century, there seems to have been a mood abroad, a change in thinking, a shift of emphasis. It was during this time that art and literature flourished intensely. Shakespeare was a part of the ongoing shift in the sixteenth and early seventeenth centuries. St. Theresa of Avila (1515–82), St John of the Cross (1542–91), Ramon Lull (?1235–1315), Meister Eckhart (?1260–?1327) and many others[1] all lived in Europe during this era. So too, did the spiritual community of the Albigensians, known locally as *les bon hommes*, the good men, that flourished in the south of France from the eleventh to the thirteenth centuries until they were destroyed by the soldiers of the Inquisition.

In India also, there was a similar era of great mystics who left behind them a considerable wealth of literature and spiritual understanding. It is known to Indian historians as the *Bhakti Movement*. Bhakti means devotion, for the mystics are always steeped in the love of God and talk of their inward experience of the highest reality in the most intensely loving terms. Sheikh Farid (1181–1365), Kabir (?1398–1518), Guru Nanak (1469–1539) and the lineage of nine mystics who followed him leading right up to 1708, Ravi Das (?1414–?1527), Mirabai (1498–1547), Tukaram (1598–1650) – all these and many more are a part of those times. These days, I think we would say that there

[1] See the *Mystic Experiences of Medieval Mystics* by Ponlain.

was a global paradigm shift, a shift in perception and consciousness, which took place during that era.

In the Middle East, the great mystics of Persia similarly left with us a legacy of great literature which still comprises the basic textbooks for a study of Persian. Hafiz (1320–1389) and Faridu'ddin Attar are still found upon the shelves of the university bookshops, here in Cambridge.

Amongst these Persian mystics was one who holds a place in the hearts of the middle east which is comparable to that of Shakespeare in the English-speaking world. His name was Jalalu'ddin Rumi or Maulana Rum, the Sage of Rum.

Rumi (1207–1277) was an academic, a scholar working in one of the Persian centres of learning. The somewhat apochryphal story goes that he was sitting one day upon the banks of a pool in the university gardens, reading through some precious manuscript, when a ragged dervish[1] appeared upon the scene.

"What are you reading?" he asked the young Rumi.

"It is a book of rare and valuable knowledge," Rumi replied. "I do not believe that you would understand such things."

Taking the book from the student's hand, the dervish carelessly tossed it into the pool. "You foolish man," exclaimed Rumi, "You have no understanding of the precious, irreplacable knowledge you have just destroyed. Why did you do such a thing?"

The dervish made no reply, but only knelt down and removing the book from the water restored it to Rumi's astonished hands in a perfect and dry condition. "This knowledge has little value," he said giving Rumi a most penetrating look, deep into his eyes. But before Rumi could respond, or so the story goes, the dervish was gone, leaving him questing for that higher knowledge which thought so little of a minor miracle.

Subsequently, he found the dervish once again and became his devoted initiate or disciple. Clearly, the bowl was already cleansed, for Rumi became a mystic in his own right and wrote many books, including a most wonderful series of six volumes, known as the *Mathnavi*, which he dedicated to his spiritual preceptor.

[1] A wandering holy man.

In fact, upon the very first page of this deeply spiritual work, he pays homage to his own master, the dervish Shamas-i-Tabriz, the Sun of Tabriz, and to all the mystics throughout history. He praises them as the:

> Godly, spiritual, heavenly, super-celestial, illuminated ones who possess mystical insight, the silent ones who behold, the absent ones who are present, the kings beneath threadbare garments, the nobles of the nations, the owners of excellences, the luminaries who display the Divine evidences. . . . The charge deposited by God amongst his creatures, His choice amongst His creation, the key of the treasuries of the empyrean, the trustee of the riches stored in the earth (the body), the Junayd (king of mystics) of the age, the entirely veracious son of an entirely veracious sire and grandsire.

Here he is referring to the natural law by which every true mystic has a master, in order to show to us egocentric humans, that we need a teacher, too, if we wish to experience the deepest mystic reality of our own life and consciousness. He wrote:

> His is a lineage upon which the sun hath cast its mantle and a renown of ancestry before which the stars have dimmed their beams. Their courtyard hath ever been Fortune's cynosure[1].

So speaks Maulana Rum, concerning his own spiritual teacher and so have all mystics spoken concerning the mystic adept who gave them light. Who would not feel so highly of one who had awoken him from the deep slumber of unconsciousness? Do we not feel grateful to those few, but special teachers who encouraged and nurtured our interests even in the things of this world?

Rumi's Mathnavi is written, in the tradition of the east, as a poem in rhyming couplets, comprised of stories and spiritual discourses interleaved so that at places he has stories, discourses and pithy observations on life all nested within each other, several deep! It is all beautifully organized, however, and frequent explanatory headings keep you in touch with where you are.

There is, as Rumi says, something in it for everyone. In that respect, it is like Shakespeare. If you just want a good,

[1]A person or object that attracts notice because of its brilliance or beauty.

even an occasionally ribald story, you can read it at that level. For the philosopher, it has much to stimulate and interest. For the observer of human life, it possesses much wisdom and an excellent appreciation of the psychology of human nature. For the poet and lover of literature, the phraseology and wording is exquisite. For conventional religious people, it contains much excellent advice on morality and ethics. For the mystically-minded it contains the whole spiritual story, though often hidden in metaphor and analogy.

In those days, it was not possible for mystics to be completely clear in their teachings, especially in what was made available to the general public. This was because they could easily have had their heads chopped off before they had hardly got started with their life's work. Christ was not the only mystic to have been badly mistreated. Mansur, Kabir, Paltu, Guru Amar Das and many others were killed or tortured under the instigation of the priests or intelligentsia of the day, who always see the universal teachings of mystics as a threat to their traditions, their power and their livelihood.

So Rumi taught through stories and allegories and I will relate here just two of the shortest stories from this poem that has almost as many verses as the *Iliad* and the *Odyssey* put together, and about twice as many as Dante's *Divina Commedia*. In fact, these 25,700 verses being considerably longer than the European *hexameter* and Spencer's *terza rima*, makes the *Mathnavi* even longer than the 33,500 comprising the *Faerie Queen*.

Rumi, you will remember, was a scholar and he tells the tale of the grammarian and the boatman, thus:

> *The story of what passed between the grammarian and the boatman.*
>
> A certain grammarian embarked in a boat. That self-conceited person turned to the boatman.
>
> The grammarian said, "Have you ever studied grammar?" "No", he replied. The other said, "Half your life is gone to naught."
>
> The boatman became heart-broken with grief, but at the time he refrained from answering.
>
> The wind cast the boat into a whirlpool: the boatman spoke loud (shouted) to the grammarian.

"Tell me, do you know how to swim?" "No," said he, "O fair-spoken good-looking man!"

"O grammarian," said he, "your whole life is naught, because the boat is sinking in these whirlpools."

The sage of Rum goes on to point out that *mahw* (self-effacement) is needed, not *nahw* (grammar). Of the various kinds of knowledge, he says, on "the day of death, the best equipment and provision for the road," is a knowledge of mystic reality. And referring to the pride of intellectual knowledge, he continues:

> Oh thou who hast called the people asses, at this time thou art left floundering, like an ass, upon this ice.
>
> If thou wert the most learned scholar of the time, behold the passing away of this world and this time.

Referring to our intellectual knowledge not only of this world, but also of mystical matters, he continues:

> We are carrying jugs full of water to the Tigris. If we do not know ourselves to be asses, asses we are.

Here he is referring back to another of his tales in which a poor Bedouin from the desert carefully carries what he considers to be of the greatest value – a jug of water – to the Caliph of Bagdahd, to present it to him as a gift. But the poor Bedouin did not realize that the capital was itself situated upon the river Tigris and the Caliph quite unneedful of water. So then, addressing those who only talk learnedly of mystic experience, but make no effort to actually achieve it, he says:

> After all, the Bedouin was excusable, for he was ignorant of the Tigris and of the (great) river.
>
> If he had been acquainted with the Tigris, as we are, he would not have carried that jug from place to place.
>
> Nay, had he been aware of the Tigris, he would have dashed that jug against a stone.

In the same way, all our intellectual knowledge has the same relative value as a jug of water in Baghdad, when compared to the knowledge gained by mystic experience. At this point, perhaps I should have stopped writing this book, but maybe such as this is useful to some people as a stepping stone towards a higher understanding.

There is one other tale which I would like to relate, from the great Maulana Rum's *Mathnavi* and which is quite appropriate to our theme. It goes like this:

How the mouse pulled the rope attached to the camel's nose-ring and became self-conceited.

A little mouse caught in his forelegs a camel's leading-rope and from emulation went off (with it).

By reason of the readiness with which the camel set out along with him, the mouse was duped into thinking himself a hero.

The ray of his thought struck the camel. He (the camel) said (aside), "I will show thee (presently)! Enjoy thyself!"

(All went well) till he (the mouse) came to the bank of a great river, at which any lion or wolf would have lost heart.

Then the mouse stopped and became paralysed. The camel said, "O my companion o'er hill and plain.

What is this standing still (for)? Why art thou dismayed? Step (forward) like a man! Go into the river!

Thou art my guide and leader; don't halt midway and be dumbfounded!" He (the mouse) said, "This is a huge and deep river: I am afraid of being drowned, O comrade."

Said the camel, "Let me see the limit (depth) of the water," and he quickly set foot in it.

"The water", he said, "is (only) up to the knee. O blind mouse, wherefore didst thou become dismayed and lose thy wits?"

He (the mouse) replied, "It is (as) an ant to you, but to me it is a dragon, for there are differences between one knee and another.

If it is (only) up to your knee, O excellent one, it is a hundred ells higher than the crown of my head."

He (the camel) said, "Another time, do not behave (so) boldly, lest thy body and soul be consumed by these sparks.

Contend with mice like thyself; a mouse has nothing to say to a camel."

He (the mouse) said, "I repent. For God's sake, get me across this deadly water!"

The camel took pity. "Hark," said he, "jump up and sit on my hump.

This passage has been vouchsafed to me: and I would take across hundreds of thousands like thee."

Rumi draws many spiritual meanings from this little tale. It is our habit, he says, to always want to be the leader in life, to feel that we know everything, to feel that we are the expert. Knowledge is a blind to us, because it makes us feel we know a lot, when actually we are really quite lost and ignorant.

We say, says Rumi:

> "Is there another leader superior to me, so that he should be worshipped by one like me?"

We do not like to accept that someone has a greater knowledge than us, especially a mystic kind of knowledge of which we may have no inkling or experience. We prefer to think they are deceitful or just writing symbolically of an intellectual philosophy. He is also equating the negative tendencies of our human mind to 'leadership', for we are led by our mind, willy-nilly, with – if we realized it – little or no real control. Our negative mind is, unknown to us, our leader. Do we know, for example, where our thoughts come from? Can we control their comings and goings? Yet, all day, we are occupied with them.

> Leadership (of your mind) is poison, except to the spirit (who should be the real leader) that from the beginning hath (in himself) abundance of the antidote.
>
> If the mountain is full of snakes, have no fear, for it is a mine of antidote within.
>
> When leadership has become a bosom-friend to your brain, any one who breaks (thwarts) you becomes (as) an ancient adversary.
>
> When anyone contradicts your disposition (habit of mind) many feelings of hatred arise in you.
>
> "He is tearing me (you say) from my (engrained) disposition, he is making me a pupil and follower (of himself)."
>
> Unless the evil disposition has become strongly implanted, how should the fire-temple (of passion) blaze up through being opposed?
>
> He may show some feigned courtesy to the opponent, he may make a place for himself in his heart.
>
> (But he really hates him), because the evil disposition has waxed strong; the ant of (worldly) lust has through habit become as a snake.
>
> Kill the snake of lust at the beginning: else, look you, your snake is become a dragon.
>
> But every one deems his own snake (his mind, his own human weakness) an ant: do you (then) seek the explanation of yourself (your real state) from him that is lord of the heart (the mystic).

> Until copper becomes gold, it does not know itself to be copper: until the heart becomes a king, it does not know itself to be an insolvent.
>
> Do service to the elixir, like copper: endure oppression (accept mystic instruction), O heart, from him that holds the heart in fee.
>
> Who is it that holds the heart in fee? Know well, it is the lords of the heart (the mystics) who, like day and night, are recoiling from the world.
>
> Do not find fault with the servant of God (the mystic): do not suspect the King of being a thief.

The king, in this instance, refers to the mystics, who because of our human nature we suspect of possessing motives similar to our own, we "suspect the King of being a thief." To use a modern expression, we do not realize just where the mystic is coming from. Real mystic knowledge is far superior to any kind of scientific or philosophical, intellectual 'knowledge'. It is immediate perception and experience. It is the egocentric nature of our human mind and intellect that keeps us away from an understanding of the mystic side of life.

This world is a supermarket of ideas, of people saying things. There is no end to books and philosophy. What we need is our own personal inward mystic transport, within. And then to increase even that into a yet greater awareness and experience, not to waste it, playing at being a 'guru', whilst still a victim of human ignorance and weakness.

But let us leave the last word to Rumi:

> The mind is suspect, not the sublime Reason (inward consciousness): the senses are suspect, not the subtle light.
>
> The mind is a sophist: beat it constantly (control it by meditation), for beating (meditation) does it good, not arguing with it.
>
> Take heed not to call me garrulous: I say only one in a hundred (words of what could be said), and that one is small like a hair.

—— PART II ——

The Unveiling of the Dance

Mind, Free Energy and the Creative Vacuum

There is an increasing body of opinion that recognizes the existence of tremendous amounts of energy in the vacuum, energy which offers us hope that one day we can capture this resource in our man-made machines and achieve what amounts to the dream of perpetual motion. This paper[1] addresses this question in the light of the supporting experimental evidence, to conclude that what is a dream today is, without a doubt, the certainty of tomorrow. Indeed, the breakthrough has already been made. It is just that we have failed to see, in its proper context, what is so clearly laid before us.

Dr Harold Aspden
University of Southampton, 1988

[1]*Ghost Mass and the Unseen Energy World as Revealed by the Anomalies of the Gyroscope*, Tothmattian Review, 1988.

Suppose that an aether strain corresponds to an electric charge, aether displacement to the electric current, aether vortices to the atoms; if we continue these suppositions, we arrive at what may be one of the grandest generalisations of modern science, namely that all the phenomena of the physical universe are only different manifestations of the various modes of motion of one all-pervading substance, the aether. The day seems not too far distant when the converging lines from many apparently remote regions of thought will meet on some common ground. Then the nature of the atom and the forces called into play in their chemical union, the interactions between these atoms and the non-differentiated aether as manifested in the phenomena of light and electricity, the structure of the molecule, the explanation of cohesion, elasticity and gravitation, all these will be marshalled into a single compact and consistent body of scientific knowledge.

A. A. Michelson, Lecture, 1899
Nobel Prize for physics, 1907

—— CHAPTER 6 ——

Science, Mind and Nature

Science and the Vacuum State

While a number of physicists, including Harold Aspden, Paul Dirac, Shiuji Inomata, Thomas Bearden and many others, have postulated the existence of the vacuum as a real energy field, the conventional view remains that it really is nothing – but with spacial dimensions. To contemplate that it could indeed be something carries too many implications, not the least of which is a return to the concept of an ether – a subject considered medieval, if not downright heretical to your average, materialistic scientist. Ether was never even mentioned in any of the science courses I took at school or university.

Be that as it may, modern physics is on the brink. A recent discovery, for example, that the speed of light is *variable* in a vacuum is taken as a possible verification that vacuum has a structure.

It has long been a sacred cow of science, more especially since Einstein, that the speed of light is a constant in a vacuum. After all, if vacuum really is nothing, then it will have no way of modifying the speed of light. If, however, vacuum has a substructure, with light (or electromagnetic radiation) being a patterning upon its surface, then its speed of passage is likely to be determined by the structure of the vacuum or space itself. Perhaps the vacuum matrix has something akin to density – the more dense, then the more slowly will light travel. Hey presto – the speed of light will be a variable in a vacuum.

Probably the nearest that quantum theorists have come to considering the vacuum as a real entity is in *quantum field* and *S-matrix* theories. There is no doubt that physicists do consider the vacuum to be of considerable importance, a seething mass of *virtual* particles, particles which arise and disappear at ultra-high speeds, and this fascinating topic will not be neglected.

Actually, physicists, mathematicians and most scientists understand that simplicity and elegance are of supreme importance in the formulation of natural laws. And whilst the laws of gravity, light, electromagnetism and so on, as we observe them outwardly, all seem to be individually capable of mathematical expression in simple terms, when you try and combine all of them into one set of equations upon the assumption that all you have are subatomic particles (whatever they are) and that vacuum is nothing, then you run into serious difficulty.

Such attempts at unification lead to horrendously complex mathematical calculations as well as a variety of fudges to get rid of infinite terms that keep on popping up out of the woodwork. And yet Harold Aspen published his book, *Physics Unified*, back in 1980 which takes the premise of a spacial matrix or lattice of energetic focuses or quanta (particles) and from this he derives all the known mathematical laws of physics, including Einstein's $e = mc^2$.

So why is his work and that of other similar-minded physicists mostly ignored by 'conventional' scientists? The answer lies in human inertia and academic institutionalism. Copernicus was considered a heretic when he suggested that the earth was not the centre of universe, but that it orbited the sun. It was the established belief that the earth was the centre of the entire universe. The whole philosophical framework of the intelligentsia of those times was built around the idea of a geocentric universe. So for some upstart to suggest a totally contrary point of view would have been a challenge to the identity and security of all those intelligent people. It is a rare person who can, halfway or more through his life, accept that some of his basic premises and beliefs are incorrect. Even though we were only *taught* them and had not worked them out for ourselves, they still become accepted as a part of ourself.

Similarly, during the nineteenth century, it was believed that diet could not affect health. In fact, many people, including established scientists and medical people, still believe it, despite all evidence to the contrary. The quality of hospital food confirms this. So when the Naval surgeon

James Lind demonstrated experimentally that the juice of lemons and oranges both prevented and cured scurvy, the Admiralty took fifty years (and hundreds of thousands more deaths) before they would believe it. Simply because they believed the formula of the times: "Diet does not influence health. So lemons and oranges *cannot* be a remedy for scurvy. So Lind *must* be wrong." They probably thought that he was a charlatan, seeking fame at any price, or out to make a quick guinea. Or that he was just a fanatic or maybe a complete nut. The one thing they did not think was: "Yes, that makes sense. Let's at least examine it as a working hypothesis."

What it means is that it can take a new generation to even begin to *teach* the possibility of a new idea. It can then take another generation to be presented with both possibilities (the old and the new) from which to decide, whilst in their youth, before ideas and mental patterns have become rigidly set.

I remember commenting to a colleague at Cambridge University when I worked there not so very long ago, "I wonder if there are any energy fields that have not yet been discovered?" My physicist friend smiled indulgently, "Oh no," he said, "I don't think so. I think we must have found them all by now." I wonder what he thinks his thoughts are. . . .

So physics is in the melting pot and needs to seriously consider the vacuum state as a real energy field. But the results of avant garde engineer-physicists are already said to be making inroads into this science, because an understanding of vacuum state manifestation leads one to design more efficient energy machines that do not require the use of nuclear fission or fusion.

The reasoning goes something like this. Electromagnetic and gravitational forces and fields are spun out of the surface of vacuum. It is within the vacuum state that they are allied, linked or unified. Thus gravity, mass and electromagnetic energy can all be traded against each other, or converted – the one into the other – through the medium of the vacuum state. The trick is in knowing how to safely make use of this connection.

Very simplistically, you can look at it like this, (see figure 6-1):

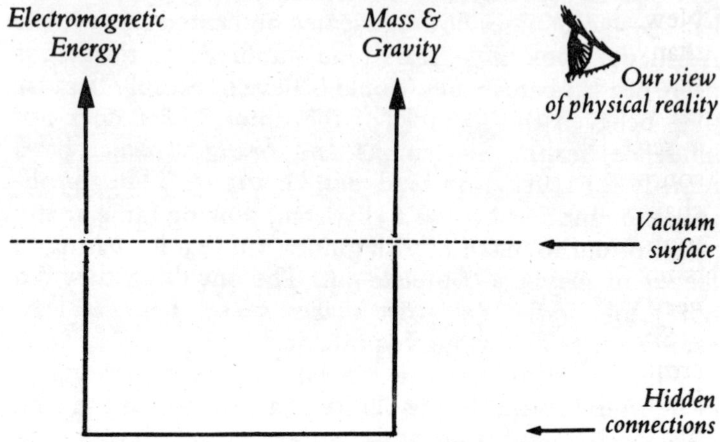

Figure 6-1. The hidden connections between gravity and electromagnetism.

We only perceive what is *above* the line and see them as separate entities, though intuitively realizing that they must be connected, hence the search for Grand Unified Theories. But if we could see beneath the surface, then we would understand the link.

So to engineer mass into electromagnetic energy (for example) we need to force the mass back into the vacuum state and then let it pop out as electromagnetic energy – vast quantities of it, according to Einstein's famous formula of $e = mc^2$, where 'e' is the energy, 'm' is the mass and 'c' is the velocity of light. This formula already links mass to electromagnetic energy, though its full significance is not fully appreciated.

Nuclear fission releases usable energy by 'bashing' the one into the other *above* the line, so to speak, and catching the energy that results. And it is a pretty dangerous way of going about things. And naturally, it creates some hefty disturbances *below* the line, too, since 'above' and 'below' are both part and parcel of the same thing.

However, the inventor Joseph Newman claims that he has produced just such an energy source, which is described in his book, *The Energy Machine of Joseph Newman.* But he cannot get a patent for it, because of reasons equivalent to, "Diet doesn't affect health" or "Everyone knows that the earth is the centre of the universe." Newman, however, has demonstrated his machine on many occasions, has signed affidavits from prominent scientists, and has installed such an energy source in a car which is reported to run very successfully using only a series of low voltage batteries as an outside power source. His motor car and energy generator is discussed in chapter nine. The beauty of the machine is that you get a tremendous amount of energy for your money! And that is not so good for the power companies. It is, however, very good for humanity.

Similarly, in the healing professions, Dr George Yao has created a series of microcrystal based devices, called Pulsors, which create harmony at the subatomic level, thereby affecting both the vacuum and subtle states, as well as the harmony of biochemical and bioelectrical activity within the body. These devices are frequently reported to induce a state of deep relaxation which the patient may not have experienced for a long time, if ever. This has also been my own personal experience of them.

In the world of computing, I read recently that a group has been formed at University College London to analyze brain function for the purposes of working out new models and paradigms for the creation of a new generation of computers modelled upon brain-mind functioning. This assumes that we understand brain-mind functioning, which we do not. However, the concept of molecular computers – turning molecules 'on' and 'off' between two states – is the most favoured, though my own suggestion would be to find ways of reading, mapping and influencing the vacuum state as a memory bank and processing source. Organized subatomic structure would be required to ensure a determinable matrix at the vacuum level and for this one could probably make use of ultra-pure crystals, whose power lies in their ordered atomic, and hence subatomic, structure. And, therefore, one presumes, in their vacuum substructure, too.

So just as I have described the brain as a vacuum state computer, so too could one electronically, through the use of crystals, research the possibility of an electronic vacuum state computer, taking the vacuum matrix of crystals as its data storage medium.

However, since the brain itself is already working at this level, it is probable that such a device would emit vacuum state waves which would disturb brain and body function. So all researchers should beware and be sure to find ways of adequately screening such devices. Some material along the lines of that used in George Yao's Pulsors might have the right properties for nullifying harmful vibrations, in the manner of a gyroscope.

The science of communication, too, will take on a new look with the realization that the vacuum matrix can be used for sending encoded messages at faster than the speed of light. It is likely that the use of wires and cables will be unnecessary, just as they already are now for radio and TV broadcasting.

In plant breeding, farming and agriculture, the possibilities are endless, since the creation of life-inducing, vacuum state waves and harmonics could enhance growth without the use of chemicals. For the destruction of pests one could devise specifically targeted vibrational emitters that left no residue and killed no other species. For each species has its own unique vibrational patterns which could be specifically disturbed or enhanced.

That plants respond to some people more than others is demonstrated without a doubt. The vibration is what we call green fingers, especially when it is associated with a practical knowledge of plant care. Plants respond to the vibration of music, too, and get on better with harmonious rather than discordant music. At the atomic and molecular level, music appears simply as a complex vibrational pattern, and naturally any movement at that level would affect the vacuum state, too. You cannot vibrate the bubbles without vibrating the ocean. And the formative energy field of all creatures lies within the vacuum and more subtle states. So naturally, any vibration at the gross physical level will be reflected in the more subtle states.

The possibilities are endless, but none are more rewarding than those opened up in the healing professions. For this understanding of the vacuum and subtle states gives us what we need for the further advancement of science – a basic conceptual framework or paradigm within which to understand human functioning.

The whole of biochemistry needs to be re-evaluated in

the light of molecular manifestation from the vacuum state. For the first time, the brain specialist can talk to the psychiatrist and psychologist with a comprehension of what they are dealing with and the roles that each can play.

The knowledge that specific 'diseases' have a vibrational counterpart which can therefore be combatted by vibrational means opens up the realm of new technology in the field of immunology and infectious diseases. Here, one can consult the practitioners of homoeopathy and radionics. In fact, many of the more modern thinkers in these professions are already experimenting with such technological devices that enhance their therapeutic success.

The understanding of placebo effects, of patient-therapist-therapy interaction, gives a far wider field in which to pursue healing and energy harmonization techniques.

The world of genetics must take a bow as it realizes that DNA is *not* the primary energetic encoder but is only a part of the total morphogenic process of creation from the subtle blueprint.

In fact, the entire vista of science takes on a new dimension once we understand that matter and life, energy and consciousness are created from within. Then we begin to see how man can work not in fear of natural forces, but in true harmony with nature.

The Linkage of Mind and Matter

The *Uncertainty Principle* of Heisenberg, who co-founded quantum mechanics in the 1920's, is fundamental to all quantum theory. It states that with all associated properties of subatomic particles, eg. position and motion (momentum actually), the measurement of the one automatically precludes us from ever *precisely* measuring the other. This is simply a practical problem. That is to say that the very act of measuring the position, for example, of an electron, prevents us from ever being sure about its momentum. And vice versa. But not only that, even the logical structure of the theory – the mathematical equations – are such that if one aspect is defined, the other becomes a matter of probability.

Instrumental measurement of anything requires *interaction* with that thing, thereby changing it. We can, therefore, only ever hope to measure a *relationship* or an *interaction*, because *we are, ourselves, involved*. There is no such thing as an *absolute* position or an *absolute* momentum of an electron. And if we attempt to define, absolutely, one aspect, the other aspects slip from our grasp.

Scientists and others have given this apparent conundrum many philosophical interpretations, but in simple terms, what it means is that the observer is integrally linked to the process of observation! Something with which we would all agree.

So what these statements, principles and so on are all, perhaps unknowingly, attempting to point out is that our mind is integrally linked to what we fondly thought was objective substance. And linked in an inherent or intrinsic fashion not "just because we are thinking about it." We are *participators* as the physicist John Wheeler, points out. There is no such thing as passive observation. The experiencer is dynamically linked to the experience.

It is an almost unconscious recognition of the reality that our outer life is created from within ourselves, through the medium of our mind. This is a form of expression with which many psychologists would agree. And it is quite in accord with eastern mysticism, too.

The interesting point is that this principle has been given a mathematical form and an experimentally verified basis.

Furthermore, there are a number of repeatable subatomic experiments, which could lead one to the conclusion that subatomic particles appear to possess the capacity to 'read the mind' of the experimenter! The measurement of electron spin, for example, is always found to be in the direction along which the experimenter has chosen to measure it. And this is true even if he makes two measurements, one directly after the other, before anything physical has changed (apparently) to alter the direction of spin. The electron always appears to be one jump ahead of him!

Similarly, there are experiments which show that light and indeed all subatomic particles possess *both* wave *and* particle-like properties. Attempting to understand these phenomena leads physicists to the bizarre conclusion that particles possess the potentiality of being everywhere all at once, or of the electron spinning in *all* directions, simultaneously.

These paradoxes may well contain aspects of the truth concerning physical reality, but one thing is certainly true, that all these paradoxes arise when we make the assumption that we, the observer, are *separate* from our observation. All our concepts of spin, wave or particle are indeed just that – concepts in our mind. In a very real sense, nature knows nothing of such things. It is what it is and our mental analysis is something different from the reality. By analysis, therefore, we are forever debarred from real comprehension of what is going on. The mechanism *underlying all this apparent confusion* lies in the fact that the vacuum state, upon which all subatomic particles appear as energy patterns, is linked to our subtle and mental energetic structure. This is the mechanism of manifestation. This is why the Indian mystics have said many times that the physical, astral and causal realms are all the creation of the *Universal Mind*.

Universal Mind is like a vast holographically-structured mega-computer where the primal power or undifferentiated energy of consciousness is wrapped around with pattern, vibration or form, giving rise to the laws of polarity and causality. It is the architect of cosmic justice, a mechanism which never fails since its power comes from the Supreme Consciousness or God. It is indeed, the 'Devil', Satan or the Negative Power. And within its dominion are said to lie the vast, heavenly, astral and causal regions, as well as the subastral, hellish zones.

According to the nature and contents of our individual *human minds* (a ray or spark of the Universal Mind), we are drawn automatically both during life and after death to those 'places' where we are most suited. We take birth again at the physical level or find a place, temporarily, in the more inward regions. And note that using religious terminology, God has Himself created the 'Devil'. The 'Devil' is the chief warden of the prison, but derives his power from the president. So there is a Divine purpose to our struggles with our inner nature, to the activities of the 'Devil'.

But the point is that it is the greater or cosmic *Mind*[1] which is the primary architect of cause and effect relationships, (such as science perceives), just as we feel that the highest form of human thought is *rational* – especially when enlivened by more inward intuition. So what we call nature is really only an aspect or expression of this deeper level of Mind operation.

So it is a credit to modern scientists that they have unravelled such an intrinsic aspect of Pandora's Box. But the full implications have yet to be grasped, because the philosophical aspects are so profound and point to a complete change in our conventional, western world-view.

Let me state it again, very simply. All our sensory perceptions of things in this world are subjective – within ourselves. They are nothing but energy patterns upon the vacuum surface linked inwards to the structure of our human mind. We are all co-creators and fellow shareholders in the universe. We have collectively created our circumstances through the medium of our own individual minds and under the dominion of the Universal Mind.

And the play is woven so cleverly that we do not realize that we are taking unreality for reality. We are lost in the world of our five senses and know of no other reality. We are led by the nose of our mind and senses and perceive only a slit-window view of the cosmic drama. We even resist all attempts at enlightenment. We have performed the ultimate conjuring trick – we have deluded ourselves. So much so that we have lost understanding of how the trick is performed. *This* is *Maya*, or illusion, the magician's dance.

So in reality, *there is no 'out there'*. The Indian mystic Kabir said, "The inward and the outward have become as one sky." My own spiritual teacher once commented, "Actually, what we see doesn't exist. What we don't see really does exist." Or as Juan Mascaro put it in his introduction to the Bhagavad Gita, "Just as the mind can see that all matter is energy, so the soul can see that all energy is Love."

[1] Although often difficult to differentiate between the two, I have used mind with a small 'm' to mean our individual human mind and Mind with a capital 'M' to refer to the greater, cosmic or Formative Mind.

Mystics say that what we think of as being 'out there' is Maya, an illusion. It is actually within us, projecting as our experience through the medium of our mind. We are all co-architects, co-creators of our joint illusion. Like the images formed frame by frame in celluloid upon a movie film and projected onto a screen, our life's destiny in this world is projected from within us. But we take the image on the screen as real and do not perceive the inward Source. The reality is within, not without. Its Source is also within us, not without. There *is* no without. "The inward and the outward have become as one sky." "What we see doesn't exist, what we don't see really does exist."

The 'outside' gross tattwas are thus reflected from the inside subtle tattwas and appear to be outside only due to the outward direction of our attention. We, as the perceiver, are our mind and we are perceiving, *within our mind*. There is no objective world, only the subjective. We speak of it as if it were 'out there', only for convenience. The seeds of our destiny karma are played upon the screen of our inward subtle tattvic screen and we perceive the play as the gross reality, though this does not mean that things only exist when we personally perceive them, for the fabric of illusion is more cleverly woven.

Another way of expressing an answer to this is to say that the vacuum or akashic state would remain as an unmanifested plenum of potentiality were it not for the minds and karmas of the souls inhabiting this world. We are all shareholders, co-creators of the world we inhabit. It is all of us living creatures that have together whipped up the akashic state into manifesting our karmas to us. Remove the souls and everything goes back to the akashic state. This is part of the mechanism of dissolution or *pralaya*. Our minds, linked by karmic bonds, have conjointly created all that we perceive or experience, for the karmas are actually stored as potential within our own mind structure.

Now how this mystic perception relates in detail to what physics should and will one day express, I feel unable to fully capture in words. Clearly, the answer lies in the nature of the vacuum state, in the energetic structure of the mind, in the relationship of the mind to manifested substance and in the essential gap between the concept and the thing itself. And I do go into this in greater detail in later chapters.

But consider, as a final comment in this section, a quotation from physicist and Nobel prize winner, Max Planck, at a lecture given in the historic Italian town of Florence:

> As a man who has devoted his whole life to the most clear-headed science, to the study of matter, I can tell you as the result of my research about the atoms, this much:
>
> *There is no matter as such!*
>
> All matter originates and exists only by virtue of a force which brings the particles of an atom to vibration and holds this most minute solar system of the atom together. . . . We must assume behind this force the existence of a conscious and intelligent Mind. This Mind is the matrix of all matter.

Mystics, throughout the ages, have always referred to this world as the domain of mind and matter. The Supreme Source, the Universal Consciousness, is One. As we have said, it is the greater Mind, of which our human mind is only one aspect, which creates the network of integrated patterns. But that integration, that apparent interwovenness, causality or sense of relationship, arises only because the underlying reality is, in itself, One. The relationships, the energy patterns which we perceive either outside or within our own minds – these are only 'surface phenomena', like ripples and bubbles on a still pool, (though it is a multilevel and multifaceted 'surface'). And they are conjured into existence by the activities of the greater Mind. We are looking, as it were, at a light through a patterned and multicoloured screen, though in this case, the screen is itself projected out of the light. The light creates its own network of obscurement, and this whole creation is supremely dynamic, vital and lively, with every part showing the signs of intelligent and constantly active order.

Subatomic Particles as Energy Chameleons, Part of a Holographically Structured Universe

Another approach towards comprehending the subatomic realm is to return to our understanding that subatomic particles do not actually possess spin, momentum or even position. These are *our* macroscopic analogies. They are actually slithy toves that gyre and gimble. In respect of a detailed analysis, what 'they' are and what 'they' do bears little relationship to things in our macroscopic world.

So when we attempt to actually measure their 'spin' or their 'speed' we impose our own point of view upon them. It would be like devising an experiment to determine whether white light were red. (We do actually know that white light *contains* all the colours of the spectrum, including red). But when we found the wavelength that corresponds to our experience of the colour red, we would not be justified in concluding that white light was *only* red. It might have other properties and constituents, too, as indeed it does.

Similarly, in our experiments, we measure only a small part of what subatomic particles actually are, even at the level of their outward, gross physical 'appearance', without even attempting considerations of their more inward structure. When we realize that these particles and forces do possess an inward, structured dimensionality, too, then we can understand that such experimentation is actually measuring only small aspects of a complex bubble, while altogether ignoring the creative ocean beneath or within.

Furthermore, while our theory may be able to comprehend in some small degree the amazing tapestry of energy relationships at the subatomic level, when it comes to experiment, we have no equipment which can even begin to probe such other-worldliness. In fact, our equipment and experiments are based almost entirely upon the models of *classical* physics, not even upon those of modern physics.

So when we look for particles, we find particles. When we look for waves, we find waves. If we could think of something else to look for, we would probably find that as well. For it is from the subatomic world that all macroscopic objects are comprised. One can imagine, therefore, that all the essential properties of the macroscopic world, and a lot else besides, must be present within the subatomic realm, perhaps within each and every subatomic particle.

As a result of this kind of thinking, some physicists

wonder whether the experimental set-up required to 'observe' an electron as a particle, let us say, actually *makes* the electron (the slithy tove), behave as a particle. J. J. Thompson, for example, shot a beam of electrons at a paddle wheel and the wheel turned. This is an experiment that many of us have repeated at school. So it is a fair assumption to say that an electron is a particle with mass, position and momentum.

But does the apparatus itself make the electron *behave* like a particle? Does it only *take account* of the particulate aspects of the electron, ignoring its wave-like and other characteristics? Or is the electron like some marvellous energetic chameleon, capable of *being* a particle with all its heart and soul, when certain physical parameters are applied to it and then, when asked to possess wave-like properties, immediately and obligingly reconfigures itself as a wave. There would be nothing overtly magical or mind-reading about this, it would simply be the effect of experimental parameters.

Interestingly, this chameleon-like nature of subatomic particles could also provide an alternative meaning to Everett's 'many-worlds' interpretation of quantum theory. For instead of many worlds, we would have 'many relationships' or 'many potentialities', but because of constraints upon the system deployed by our own unconscious minds, which also means our karmas or destiny, there is only one world – not many.

In essence, the electron, the photon or any subatomic particle is what it is. Not what we think it is! So is it, too, a microcosm, a part of an energy hologram which contains within it a world of potential that permits it to be anything that its fundamental configuration of mass, electric charge and so on, permits it to be? We have entered, here, a world of relationships where the part bears an imprint of the whole.

Just as the DNA within each cell carries within it an image of the whole, and yet the whole is not actually manifested therein, does every subatomic particle carry a potential for energetic relationship to the whole and to every other subatomic particle?

The British physicist, Richard Prosser, has actually worked out a valid mathematical model of subatomic particles based on the idea that each particle is actually a wave pattern filling all of space, spreading out throughout the universe. But these waves actually cancel each other out or sum to zero except at their tiny points of origin which we call a particle. In this sense, therefore, everything is automatically everywhere all at once, but manifests to us only at one particular point. For we have shown that summing effects to zero does not mean that they no longer exist – just that we do not immediately perceive the substructure.

"As above, so below." This mechanism of creation starts with the One Source and reflects itself within all the parts. Each part carries an imprint of the whole. Why should this mechanism not be present throughout *all* manifested substance? Surely one would actually expect that? Even in subatomic 'particles'.

The realm of the subatomic is strange and no physicist, conventional or otherwise, denies it. Erwin Schrodinger commented, "I don't like it, and I'm sorry I had anything to do with it." Neils Bohr said, "Anyone who is not shocked by quantum theory has not understood it."

Is the nature of just one electron, therefore, a complex world of shifting energy patterns and relationships both within itself and to all else in the universe? It would certainly seem so. Do you remember the well-known lines from William Blake?

> To see a world in a grain of sand
> And a heaven in a wild flower,
> Hold infinity in the palm of your hand,
> And eternity in an hour.

Will we also find them within each and every subatomic slithy tove?

No wonder quantum physicists and relativity theorists scratch their heads in wonder at what these little fellows get up to! It is not surprising that they invoke 'laws' of probability to try and explain in macroscopic terms, what on earth is going on.

But the secret of the subatomic world must lie in the mystic construction of the creation from within-out, a holographically woven tapestry of polarity, pattern and relationship, reflected in the nature of its inward structure and dimensionality.

Let us end this line of thought on a mildly philosophical note. Man often thinks he has free will, full control of his destiny. But how can he have complete free will when his body is made up of slithy toves, put together by a process of gyring and gimbling of which he has little comprehension? For if man does not have control of his slithy toves, then who does? They are clearly organized by some means or another!

Chameleons in Chemistry

The concept of an electron or any subatomic 'particle' being capable of reconfiguring itself according to circumstances is actually no more than is already known to take place at atomic and molecular levels. These energies rearrange themselves according to the patterns, relationships and circumstances in which they find themselves. Atoms and molecules transform themselves into a multitude of shapes with an amazing variety of properties at speeds even of billionths of a second. Actually, there is just one continual dance of energy. It is we, putting in our arbitrary starting and finishing posts, who then talk of a 'particular transformation' taking only a billionth of a second.

All the elements in the periodic table, from hydrogen to uranium, from oxygen to iron, are all said to be comprised of just electrons, protons and neutrons. The chemical properties of these configurations are based entirely upon how large is the aggregate of subatomic particles and how stable is that particular mixture. This is true of both atoms and molecules, however large or small.

There was a time when the atom was thought to be indivisible. Then came the experimental discovery of electrons, protons and neutrons. But to this date, we still have no really satisfactory theoretical model of how even the simplest atom of hydrogen holds together. We do not even have a complete model of an electron.

For many years, these subatomic particles were considered to be indivisible, but then came the theory of quarks which was required to explain experimental observations from particle accelerators where a multitude of smaller particles can be created from the disintegration of a larger one. Quarks are thought of as parts or aspects of subatomic particle structure, though no-one has yet demonstrated one in isolation.

More recent theorists realize that there can never be anything which can be labelled as the ultimate, indivisible blob of 'something'. That 'something' will always be an energy structure, with inward dimensionality and patterning. The best we can do now is to try to understand these relationships within the energy patterns. And this will occupy both the physics and the medicine of the twenty-first century.

The Laws of Nature

In all our physics classes we are taught about the *Laws of Nature*. Newton's Law of Gravity, Maxwell's Laws of Electromagnetism, Einstein's Theory of Relativity, and so on. But the question has to be asked, "What *are* these laws?" Applying the mystical approach, the answer can be found by looking from the top, down – from the within to the without.

The Universal Power, the Lord, the Supreme Being or Consciousness is *One*. In Him there is no differentiation. And His attribute is that of Love. Within the supreme reality, therefore, the only law is that of Love, because only Love exists.

When this Power creates, however, it is said that a differentiation – duality – is projected from within Himself, and the two sides of this duality begin the dance of manifestation. At first, it is highly refined, almost indiscernable, but by degrees it becomes more and more dense and complex, until it reaches the level we perceive and experience as our physical reality. Here the fundamental duality becomes so complexed that it is easy to fail to perceive it.

At a certain point along this line of descent, the duality becomes expressly crystallized in the formation of the Universal Mind. This is far higher or more deeply inward than the thought processes which comprise our human mind. And it is this Universal Mind which is the prime architect of duality or polarity. Furthermore, the inherent law of the regions within which mind holds sway is that of the interplay of opposites that comprise this polarity, of *yin* and *yang* in Chinese terminology or the *gunas* of Indian mysticism. This interplay is perceived by us as the causality which the Indian mystics call karma.

So within the Lord, the only real law is of Love, merging, oneness, but within the illusion of his projection or creation the law is of cause and effect, determinism, causality, relationship, connectedness. Causality represents the innate oneness and connection that is still apparent even when the One becomes the many. Causality is what happens, automatically, when we experience the One as the many. When we see connection and causality in the world, we are unknowingly perceiving the Oneness of the inward Source, but "through a glass, darkly." We have discussed this previously, but it is a beautiful and important insight of which to grasp hold, and bears repetition.

All our scientifically 'known' laws of nature are underlain by this one law. All equations have to add up correctly. The effect has to be equal to the cause. You cannot get something for nothing. The manner by which energy relates to energy does, however, vary depending upon the level from which you observe its activities. In the outward, gross physical world we see only local and obviously linear relationships. But once into the vacuum and more subtle states, then we perceive the far more integrated relationships which we may perceive outwardly as non-linear and non-local. These are the 'laws' underlying coincidences and synchronicity, for instance, as well as more specific, 'scientific' phenomena.

It is the same karmic pattern, too, which underlies the manner in which events that happen to an individual seem to 'fit' exactly with the psychology of that personality. A part of this mechanism seems to be obvious – we have familar patterns or habits of thought which automatically create analagous cirumstances around us. But there are those things which happen to us for which we can see no possible way that we were directly responsible. It is here that the hidden 'laws' of Mind and matter are functioning, a causal interplay within the energy fields of Mind and 'outer' substance.

So our laws of science are constantly being evolved or changed, for they are themselves *not intrinsic in nature,* but only a part of man's incomplete observation of and participation in the very simple law of causality, of duality, of differentiation, of interconnectedness, of integration.

Our mathematical formulations are thus abstractions in our own minds, partial observations or models of the patterns formed within the illusory worlds of duality. The only real law is that of Love and oneness, but when expressed within the regions of duality and division, this oneness becomes the primary law of these regions – causality and relationship.

So the real 'unified field' so sought after by physicists is actually that of Love, where there is only union or unity, no differentiation or duality and which is not 'out there' at all, but is the deep essence within us. And it is quite unapproachable by physics or even by the human mind, but only by consciousness or soul. What physicists actually mean by the unified field is that energy state in which all the basic forces with which they are scientifically familiar can be seen to be related or integrated – and this lies within the vacuum state. But this is not a condition of oneness, but only a point where it can be seen that all things are interconnected, as we know intuitively that they must be.

Recognition of this, however, does actually mean a return to the concept of an ether, an idea discarded around the turn of the century and a move generating great reluctance amongst conventional scientists, although it is said that even Einstein himself never really discarded the idea. The *new ether concept*, however, will be – from a technical and mathematical point of view – vastly more complex than its nineteenth and pre-nineteenth century counterparts because of all the new data we now possess regarding what is manifested out of the ether, the vacuum or akashic state. So there is plenty for physicists to get their mental and experimental teeth into and for engineers to work upon. And historically, of course, ideas do come in and out of fashion, so there would be no breach of precedent in returning via a new appreciation to an old idea. It could even be seen as having been a necessary part of the process in the evolution of man's understanding.

Scientific 'Explanations'

Emphasizing the kind of perception of the universe entertained by many scientists, are statements in all the textbooks and popularizations that, for instance, "Unpaired electrons *obey* the laws of Fermi-Dirac statistics," or "Apples *obey* the law of gravity." Actually, apples and electrons offer no such obeisance at all.

Similarly it is said that, "The behaviour of unpaired electrons is *explained* by the laws of Fermi-Dirac statistics", or that the "Falling of an apple is *explained* by the law of gravity." But the nature of electrons (paired or unpaired) or the way in which apples fall is not *explained* by any set of man's mathematical equations. We have made a close observation and expressed our findings or descriptions in a mathematical language, that is all.

Such 'laws' of nature are concepts or models in our minds, whether expressed in words or in mathematics. We even constantly modify these models or limit the circumstances under which they are valid or invalid, like Newton's classical 'law' of gravity.

Nature, in a very real sense, knows nothing of these models, present in the minds of men and women. Electrons do not *obey* a mathematical concept, nor do apples *obey* Newton's law of gravity. Part of the behaviour of electrons and apples is *described* by man, for his own satisfaction, by these mathematical constructs. Their behaviour is partially *modelled* – but it is most certainly not *explained*, nor is nature the *obedient* servant to a library full of mathematical equations. That is all man's idea about things, not that of nature, herself.

Man's theoretical science is actually only able to express or model the nature of *causal relationships*, not to understand the inward essence of things. Even statistical or probabilistic models only exist because there is an underlying causal relationship.

My favourite example is that of estimating the number of people in Cambridge on tuesday afternoons in November. Given the data from previous years, one can make a statistical assessment that may be quite accurate. But ask any one of those people how they came to be there and they will all have a totally deterministic reason.

Similarly, if we could bring an 'electron' within the focus of our inward consciousness, we would find that its existence had perfectly ordered and deterministic origins.

Science does not invite us to really understand nature as conscious participants and co-workers, although, like quantum theory, it may indicate, intellectually, that we are inextricably involved in the process. But we do not need science to inform us of that observation. It is staring us in the face, all the time!

This may all sound like an intellectual quibble, but actually it is not. For those scientists who really confuse their explanations or models with nature herself, genuinely feel that if they can find just one set of interlocking equations and concepts from which all phenomena can be safely *described*, then, they feel that they will have fully *explained* and understood the universe. And they promote this gospel to other people too, thus compounding the error.

But it is, actually, a self-deception. We still do not know what makes the sun come up in the morning or why we have two eyes, or what our life and consciousness is all about. In fact, an illiterate man or woman, living in the Himalayan foothills, whose face shines with the radiance of mystic transport and inward wisdom and whose soul rises to the inner regions, would be quite justified in describing such scientists as ignoramuses. I have met such people, too, and I would have happily exchanged all my own intellectual 'knowledge' of this world, for their far deeper wisdom and mystic *experience*.

So what we call the 'laws of nature' are incomplete observations. Our individual minds, being parts of the greater Mind, unconsciously appreciate the manner by which the creation is put together. The 'little', human mind thus observes aspects of or relationships within the greater Mind since the two are of the same essence. And it is these relationships which we call the 'laws' of nature.

We will never fully understand anything by analyzing its appearance from without. Such theories are only descriptions of observation and participation. *They work because they are designed to work* – they simply describe things as concisely and universally as possible. But the fundamental problem remains, "How does the universe come into being?" and, "How do *we* come into being?' Intellectually, the answer to that is: through the splitting of the One by the greater, Formative Mind. But the real answer comes from the direct inner experience of it, through deeper experience within one's own mind and consciousness.

It is also clear that if we do not know *how* what we call the laws of nature arise, we are in no position to declare that these 'laws' (our descriptions) can never be 'violated'. Doing so only indicates that we have lost sight of what such laws really are. To then stoutly defend them, unthinkingly, against all comers is thus more indicative of human psychology than of how nature works.

First we observe nature. Then we describe some of those workings mathematically. Then we insist that nature must *always* follow that description. Clearly we are putting the cart before the horse.

Looking at the problem from another point of view, if we are to think that mind and consciousness arise out of substance – nature – then we will always be left with the problem of where nature, and all its 'laws', came from. And there is never an end to that question. It is an infinite regress.

But if nature arises as a part of the proliferation of form, due to the activity of Mind, over the face of primal consciousness or being, then all such difficulties evapourate. For then we realize that everything – both outer substance and our own undeniable inner life, mind and consciousness – all originate from and remain an integral part of the one Ocean of Being. They have never been separate. 'We' and 'it' are part and parcel of the same thing.

Nature is thus seen to be a network of patterns, reflected and projected from within the same great Ocean of Being from which we also derive our own life or consciousness. The two are inextricably bound together. Physical science, therefore, is understood as the study of these patterns and relationships by our human mind – which itself is only another aspect of this hierarchical dance of energy patterns we call the creation.

Once this is understood, then never again will we expect physical science and human intellect to be able to grasp the ultimate secrets of creation. Science and intellect have their place. But to understand 'Being' one has to 'Be', to the fullest extent. And that means experience – mystic experience.

Natural Law

When, therefore, we speak of natural law, as opposed to man-made law, we mean it in the relative sense of living in harmony with the law of duality, of causality. It means moving towards the essence of oneness, of love, in all matters.

The prime architect of division is the Mind, and in our case, our human mind. It has the capacity when moving away from consciousness, to blind us and – when moving inward – of becoming a friend to the soul, to our consciousness, to our real essence of life. The 'enemy' to harmony both within ourself and in planetary affairs is therefore the mind of man itself and all our man-made laws are only designed to protect us from the activities that are projected from the uncontrolled minds of ourselves and others.

Spiritual progress and understanding are, therefore, synonymous with control of the mind. This is the primary aim of all meditation and yogic practice. And the more the mind is controlled and its attention focused within, then the more love is manifested within us and in all we do. Then we automatically become aware from the disquieting vibrations created within our own minds, when we have transgressed the laws of natural harmony and love – either in thought, word or deed. Then we automatically correct ourselves. This is living within the natural law. As one of the greatest Indian mystics of recent times, Maharaj Sawan Singh Ji, used to say, "Where there is love, there is no need for law.'

It's All in the Mind

Returning to the discussion of whether the physical world is outside or inside, one can approach the problem from yet another angle. One can ask oneself the question, "*Where* is time?" Is it outside in the physical world? If it is outside, then *where* is it? We cannot find a *piece* of time anywhere. Is it inside us, then? But what do we mean by *inside*? And what do we mean by *us*? What are *we*? And if we do not know what *we* are, then how can we be so sure about what is *outside* and what is *inside*?

What do we feel we know concerning time? I think that we can agree that time is an experience. A subjective experience. But time still passes when I am asleep or unconscious. It clearly does not *need* my own personal presence for it to 'flow' – whatever it is. But how do I know that time has passed when I wake up? Because I notice that certain things have changed – the position of the sun, the hands of the clock, the numbers on my digital clock, I am not tired any more – and so on. I relate to my experience of spatial events and feelings and call that change, *time*. In fact, I do more than *call* it time, I *experience* it as time, *in my own mind*. Okay, so time is in my own mind. Time is due to my feeling that I am separate from the physical world and is my mental measure of change in that world.

So far so good. What then is the 'physical world'. It looks as if it is 'out there'. But can I be sure of that? Well, we are already a little dubious about 'out there' and 'in here' because both relate to what *we* are, and we do not know the answer to that question. We might have a few *ideas* about what we are, but that is clearly different from what we *actually* are. This is the same as the difference between the word 'orange' and the experience of orange.

So what is the physical world, and where is it? 'Out there' or 'in here'? Let us take it from the ground up. The 'out there' has three spatial dimensions. That applies to all our five sensory perceptions whether we are seeing, hearing, smelling, tasting or touching. So space is a fundamental attribute of 'out there'. So what *is* space? The answer to that could tell us a lot, because everything that we perceive with our five senses is within space. It is modifications to space, energy patterns in space. But where do we perceive these changes that we call space? It is in our *minds*. In fact, all our perceptions are ultimately registered in our brains and experienced in our minds. They are 'in here'. But we also experience these changes as, 'time'. Now the edges between time and space seem to be getting blurred. . .

What about individual experiences of this world? The colour 'red', the taste of an orange, the sound of music for example? Where are they? 'Out there'? I think not. For these are all experiences and experience is always within our mind and our mind is within. It has an association with our brain. (In most people, anyway!) So the entire physical world appears to be in our own mind. So why are you and I both seeing the same outside world if it is all a personal subjective experience?

Well, how did we get to be 'here' in the first place? We do not know the answer to that one either. So maybe, if we could answer the question how we all came to be here together, each with our own subjective, mental experience of the world we could also answer the question of how we are all having *similar* experiences while being in this world. The two appear to be connected.

So we are all experiencing changes in the temporal and spatial conditions of the physical world, these experiences being within our own minds. And we are all linked together in some mysterious way, because we are all having similar experiences.

Now, we also analyze these experiences which appear to be 'out there' but are really, 'in here'. When we apply laws of logic and rationality we call it *science*. This analysis, this thinking is clearly in our mind. So science is all in the mind. The 'out there' is 'in here' and we then apply the 'in here' to further analyze the 'in here'.

So Newton's 'laws' of gravity and motion, Einstein's perceptions of the relative relationships between our temporal and spacial perceptions, the 'laws' of electromagnetism, the notions of electrons, photons, particle behaviour, atoms, molecules, chemistry, biochemistry and medicine – they are all within our own minds. Both the experience and the analysis. The whole shooting match takes place within us. And our 'science' is clearly a mental overlay to direct perception and experience. If we could therefore halt the processes of our thoughts we would most definitely perceive the world in quite a different way. *In other words, the nature of our mind and thinking processes determines the way we perceive and experience the world.*

This is also the aim, purpose and result of meditation, to control the mind, to change the nature of the mind, leading to a new and mystic perception of our inner life and physical experience. We think that the world is outside because of the direction of our *attention*. Attention is a fusion of mind and consciousness, of mind and life. The purpose of meditation is to untie this knot of mind and consciousness, of mind and soul. To still the mind, and thus let consciousness expand. Our soul is presently held uncomfortably in a small box by all our thoughts, ideas and emotions concerning what we think is outside. Our mind is held firmly in its outward direction by the *input* from our sensory perceptions and by our subsequent motor responses or *output*, the things we do and say. These actions originate in the mind and leave their mark there. Similarly with all sensory *im-pressions*. And our mental and emotional responses also leave their mark upon the mind within which they arise.

The mind is a subtle energy field that like the black-box in an aeroplane makes a record of everything that happens. But unlike the black box, it also *originates* everything that happens – all our experiences in the time and space of this physical world. At present, all that we experience of time and space is the physical world. Mystics, however, say that there are higher, more inward worlds where time and space still exist. These are the astral and causal worlds where *change is less intense*. This we experience as time being *expanded* and space becoming *more vast in extent*. We get a little idea of this in our day-to-day experience of time. 'A watched kettle never boils', for example. Subjectively, the passage of time is related to our state of mind.

So the mind is the originator and also the recorder of change. We call this second faculty, *memory*. The yogis called it *chit* and *manas* or *mind stuff*, the energy fields where impressions are first formed and then stored, and from which our destiny proceeds.

Destiny? Yes. Our mind (at its best) is *rational* and *intuitive*. *In-tuition* means being taught from within. So our mind is capable of receiving impressions from within. Mystics call this the higher mind – the astral and causal mind energy patterns, deeper within our being. The *rational* nature of our mind assumes order, cause and effect. But from where do we derive this feeling that the basic law of the universe is one of causality and relationship? It is from our mind. And what is our mind? Without mystic experience, we do not know. So once again, we do not know the intrinsic nature of our own science, of our own mind, of the physical universe in which we live. But we do, intuitively – and from experience – recognize an inherent operation of causal relationship. But it is clearly a law of the *mind*, since everything we experience is within our minds.

Mystics say that causality or karma is the only primarily existent law of nature. This I have mentioned earlier. Therefore, all the impressions which are formed upon our minds while we live in this world, react after the death of the physical body and recreate another drama or destiny in this world, which we once again go through.

In other words, we re-incarnate under the causal influence of our own minds. And since we are all connected through these impressions on our minds – we are all involved with each other – we take another birth in those surroundings and with those very people with whom we have been so fascinated and attached. We can even return as our own great grandson or daughter. We can move in very tight circles. And we then continue with these relationships and attachments, making new grooves, habits or impressions upon our minds, and back we come again after the physical bodies die. So at death, the body dies – the mind energy structure and the enlivening consciousness leave, and the physical atoms and molecules cease to function in an integrated fashion. The ghost has left the machine.

So, the mechanism of manifestation is from within our mind, under a cosmic law of cause and effect. But as I have said, it is an extended law. And there is far more to our mind than we can presently observe. The relationships within the energy patterns are clearly non-linear and holistic – the system acts as a whole, bringing us all into an integrated situation to work out our causally induced (karmic) relationships with each other. But it is most definitely causal. It is not based upon chance or probability.

I have a feeling that if the concept of 'probability' in quantum theory were replaced by 'potentiality' then the deterministic/statistical dilemma would be resolved. But this is for the physicists to work out.

It is the akash, the plenum of potentiality, the vacuum, the space, which is patterned by the non-linear, holistic, yet still causal patterns within our own minds, to form a physical world. That is why I have said that we are all co-creators, shareholders in this world. It is not really I who say this, it is true mystics throughout all the ages. They all say, "I have transcended time and space." Transcending is an inner, personal, mystic experience. It is not an intellectual insight concerning the illusory nature of time and space. That is just a stepping stone, a point on the journey. And a point at the very beginning, actually. It is a part of what makes an intellectual person *start* on the journey.

But since so few people even get to this starting point, many feel that they are near the end when intellectual and intuitive perceptions concerning the mystic reality begin to come to them. Actually, such realizations are simply the first awakenings from a deep slumber of physical entombment, the sleep of unconsciousness from millions of past lives.

Mind, Morality and Mystical Teachings

The nature of the mind, as an energy patterning system following an intrinsic law of holistic causality, lies at the back of all moral injunctions. Almost all world religions are founded upon the teachings of a mystic. Man, slowly and slowly, distorts these teachings through the interpretations of his own mind. Some suffer a worse fate than others. If a mystic wrote something, then we are only open to errors and intentional tampering during copying of the manuscript, and subsequently to the interpretations of translators, commentators, priests and so on.

But if, like Christ, his teachings were not written down until several decades after his death, then the message is readily misunderstood, misinterpreted, mistranslated and generally mangled. If the humans involved think that their interpretations are divinely guided, it only adds to the confusion. Mind is the instrument of illusion. Thinking itself to be divinely guided is just another of its tricks!

If, today, you attend a lecture and then tomorrow you try to write down what was said, it will only be the gist of what you think was said. If you then tell a friend and he tries to write it down, there may be only five or ten percent of the original content remaining. If this is then translated through different languages and gets modified in the process according to the interpretations of the translators and scribes, one can imagine how little will be left of the original lecture. And this has been the fate of Christ's teachings, of the Buddha and of many other mystics, too.

The sects and divisions within a religion arise due to differences in opinion as to what the mystic meant, but only after the mystic has departed. This happens even when the original writings of the mystic are preserved. So one can imagine what may have been the fate of teachings that were transmitted mouth to mouth for one or two generations before being written down.

Now people want to adapt religions to suit the times, but this is because the religion has become more of a social or moral philosophy. The essential and universal mystic message has long been forgotten. No saint or mystic came to found any religion or to make social changes. It is we who make organizations and religious philosophies out of the teachings after the mystic has departed. Then, because the meditational practice which was at the heart of the mystic's message has been lost and we have no inkling of the inward experience of which the mystic is really talking, we discuss and argue and turn what he taught into a formalized religion with set prayers and rituals. Then the divided human mind takes over, overlaying its tolerances and prejudices onto teachings it neither understands nor realizes are the description of an experience of Reality, and not open to modification.

Consequently, we have 'religious' wars and feuds between the various groups of humans involved. But what would the mystic think of all this? And what is God supposed to do with vying factions all praying to Him to help them exterminate the other group of humans and their beliefs? We may think that it is the religions which are fighting with each other, but actually it is the humans who are conducting the religions – they are doing the fighting.

God, that inward essence of life, is within all of us. There is only one God, but our mental conceptions of Him are as multifarious as our minds. We fight and argue over these *ideas* about Him. We have quite lost sight of what He really is. It is just our minds acting and has nothing at all to do with God!

So we have to develop a more universal outlook. This world is just a plane of consciousness, a level of perception, created by the mind and enlivened by the soul. We are all drifting around like dream characters, under the influence of the mind. Nothing happens without the involvement of our minds, however fleetingly or unconsciously.

True mystics are the ladders to the higher reality. They are the points where light shines in the darkness of illusion. They come, give their teachings, help the souls who are drawn to them to make their personal escape – and then they leave this world. Man, recognizing unconsciously the truth in their message, then clings to the remaining shell, the philosophy, and makes a religion or cult out of it. But by this time, another mystic has taken birth somewhere else and is performing his age-old function of guiding those souls who are ready, out of the sticky web of the physical plane. There is always a perfect mystic in this world, somewhere, for those who ready.

However, this is not a book on the fate of a mystic's teaching nor on the work they do on this plane. But the point is, that out of all this confusion, it is the moral precepts which survive more than all else. All religions agree on these basics of spirituality, however distorted the mystics' teachings may have become. No mystic founded any religion or any religious dogma and ritual. Man forms the religions after mystics have departed.

But the basis of the moral precepts is a very practical one, based upon the law of causality. In order to gain true *nirvana*, *Samadhi,* salvation, liberation of the soul – whatever name one gives it – it is necessary to control the mind, to escape from the law of cause and effect, to escape from the tight grip of our own mind. And this means being 'good', not 'bad'. In thought, word and action, because all of these leave an impression upon the mind energy and lead to our return to the physical domain. 'Good' is what helps us towards inward realization of the Source, 'bad' is what takes us away from that.

We need to inculcate that mental attitude which causes the least vibrational residue in our minds. That means living harmoniously, in all its possible meanings, and keeping a hold on our minds. This is truly the ultimate, personal physics, *meta-physics*. Scientifically, this is the ultimate experiment, too – to control our own mind through meditational technique.

For if everything is in our minds, then instead of studying the nature of the everything, does it not make more sense to study the nature of the mind itself? And then the soul or consciousness enlivening it, giving it motion and life? So meditation – with proper guidance, as with any experiment performed for the first time – is the ultimate science, the ultimate study. It is the study of the knower, not the known. And by coming to understand the knower, we automatically come to know that which can be known. Then we know the nature and limitations of science and use it in a very practical and harmonious way. We know what it can do and what it cannot do, and whether it is worthwhile doing those things, anyway.

Concepts, Ideas and Human Relationships

Our minds then, have ideas about 'reality', while 'reality' gets on with it and does its own thing. 'Reality' is different from the ideas we have about it in our minds! But yet there is a relationship between the two because our human mind is a part of the totality of Mind, that is – of nature, of what we think of as physical 'reality'. So our scientific ideas about nature are not totally awry – there is some correspondence. But our view is somewhat restricted. And because we do suffer in our human relationships with each other, it might be worth explaining how this same mind-mechanism operates in the realm of human emotion. This will be just a brief digression, though it is really a subject for considerably more thought.

Many relationships follow a pattern in which the two individuals, unable to really perceive or understand the content of the other's mind (this is our human situation), both have an image or concept in their own minds of how the other is and ought to be. But this image is based upon the mind patterns and self-orientated needs of the individuals, both emotional and physical, conditioned by the habits ingrained during childhood and from past lives. The result is that the partner does not fit this image, because it is not based upon how the other really is.

We can then go in one of two directions. Either we can modify our image as our perceptions of the other show us that he or she is not like our image. Or we can be continually frustrated when the person fails to fit our expectations. Usually we do some of both.

If we realize that our perceptions are imperfect and are related to our own mental/emotional background and personality patterns, then we have a chance to become more aware of the subconscious sea in which we live. Then we strive for a higher point of consciousness in our relationships. But if we insist, unconsciously, that our partner must enact our expectations, must fit our mental image, then we are doomed to failure and to misery.

We do, of course, present ourselves with good reasons why the other person should think and behave in a certain way. "It is their duty". "It is the way things are done in our society," and so on. But it is all a self-delusion. The only *real* law by which things are related is that of love – real, spiritual love that unifies, not our human passion that we call love but which contains a high degree of selfishness and self-indulgence. When expressed through the mind, the unity of love becomes the causality of relationships – human or otherwise.

So there are a multitude of possible outward social and environmental contexts which are all valid expressions of an inward harmony and love. By clinging subconsciously to our image and expectations of the way another person ought to be, we are setting ourselves up for disaster. Ultimately, we may become so frustrated that we develop a negative mental picture of our partner which is a severely distorted view of the reality. And it is *this image* with which we fight and quarrel and even go to court – not the person themselves, at all.

Under such circumstances, we are likely to force our partner into a similar way of thinking and emotionality, the result being a desperately unhappy relationship. In our present world situation, with exposure to so many belief systems, the human panorama of possible social circumstances results in many potential images of how a partner should be and behave; and with the feelings of insecurity engendered by all these possibilities, relationships increasingly break down. This is quite apparent in our western civilization and culture.

But again, this is a wide subject and there are an increasing number of modern schools of psychotherapy who work with a knowledge of the emotions as energy configurations, for the improvement of human relationships.

CHAPTER 7

How Fundamental are Scientific Fundamentals?

Scientific Endeavour

Contrary to some popular belief, science is not a solid body of incontrovertible fact, pushing forward the frontiers of knowledge until, by diligent application, the answers to everything will finally be found. It is actually more like a dinner party where someone has innocently asked: "What does everyone consider to be the meaning, purpose, explanation or goal of life?" And has then sat back to watch the fun. Everyone talks simultaneously, frequently with the one hardly listening to the other, each promoting his own particular point of view.

The resulting supermarket of ideas reflects the content of the individual minds present, flavoured strongly by cultural and social conditioning.

Life itself poses us this question and according to the atmosphere of the times we meander about trying to find answers. But there *is* a perennial philosophy, where inward mystic experience is described as providing the answers to all our perplexities. But when we have no intuitive recognition of the existence of such an experience, then unconsciously we are led into using our thought and sensory processes in order to make sense of our world. And we become unknowingly confused.

In present times, the prevailing idiom is that of so-called, rational science. The underlying philosophy is known as *reductionism* – where it is considered that the whole can be understood by an analysis of the parts. But even this body of reductionist knowledge has not been built up, step by step, by some organized planetary process, but has been more like the almost random clamouring of ideas around a dinner table.

Very few scientific minds are truly creative or ever care to question deeply the fundamental edifice upon which their day-to-day work is based. In fact, it is usually the young and fresh minds – uncluttered by years of uncreative, plodding endeavour and detailed investigation within an established framework and a preset paradigm – who make the most creative in-roads into the world of scientific knowledge and theory.

But even Einstein himself had serious doubts. In 1949, writing to his friend, Maurice Solovine, who had congratulated him on his seventieth birthday, he commented:

> Now you think that I am looking at my life's work with calm satisfaction. But, on closer look, it is quite different. There is not a single concept of which I am convinced that it will stand firm and I am not sure if I was on the right track after all[1].

In terms of basic concepts, science has lurched forward on the backs of a few creative individualists who came into prominence when the time was right for them. In many instances, their work was actually rejected at the time of its conception because of the pressure of prevailing opinion and thought, and only became acceptable to a later generation looking for a new direction.

All the same, the fundamental concepts of a science are rarely questioned, once established. It is difficult for any brave souls to fly in the face of peer pressure. It is more than their jobs are worth. It is sometimes said in America that there is only one thing more afraid of controversy than a government scientist, and that is two of them! And those, like myself, who come from outside the world of academia are largely ignored by the institutions of science. Those who are not ignored get ostracized and attacked like an invading beetle to a bee-hive. Their presence is emotionally uncomfortable to the majority who tow the party line.

But nature herself makes no such distinctions. All humans are the same in the eyes of both God and nature! Neither knowledge and experience, nor religion and access to God, can be claimed by one section of humanity as their particular preserve, through which all others must pass on

[1] *Out Of My Later Years*, Knopf, New York, 1948.

their way to the 'inner sanctum'. Everything lies within each and every man or woman. This is a part of the structure of the creation, and no amount of opinion, prejudice, bigotry or jealousy can change it. How can one own an idea, or knowledge, or even the sky or the land? Given the inherent subconscious weakness of the human mind, would God really place access to His secrets in the hands of just a limited section of the whole human community, as the priests and followers of almost every religion claim? Is even the limited knowledge of science to be found only amongst the halls of academia or in the research laboratories of large industrial concerns? Such thoughts lie in our own minds. They are not inherent in nature.

The initial response generated by Rupert Sheldrake's book, *A New Science of Life*, is a prime example of subconscious, habituated, scientific prejudice surfacing as 'rational peer review'. Britain's *Nature* magazine anonymously reviewed and castigated it as "A book for burning." "They are at it again in Little Essex Street," wrote a gleeful editor of rival magazine, *New Scientist*, eager to cast witty stones at a competitor. But are *New Scientist* any the more open to new ideas? Unfortunately, they are not! After all, they have a commercial magazine to run, catering for the conventional majority. So the system becomes a closed, locked-in, loop.

And this is human nature in all its manifestations. Our minds are held tightly, operating only within the small sphere permitted by our karmas, rejecting all attempts at enlightenment.

Just like when you attempt to suddenly awaken a slumbering person, his first response may be one of anger at being awoken, so too do we tend to reject unthinkingly all ideas which indicate a path of thought down which we have never previously trod. And we present what appear to be good and rational reasons for the rejection, too – but the unconscious, emotional motivations are nonetheless active.

So the path trodden by all of modern science can be seen in this light. The advances in physics and more especially the mathematical and theoretical modelling of events and phenomena are no exception.

The basic concepts have in many cases been questioned and modified only rarely, if at all, even though it is accepted that the models are inadequate and incomplete. That is why research continues. Yet a towering edifice is built upon them, which is now threatening the continuation of our present human civilization. It has already led to the destruction of innumerable other living organisms, including entire species. And if a human activity leads to so much destruction and disharmony, then we may safely presume that fundamentally, we are on the wrong track.

Physics has progressed historically, not rationally, steered on its way by the pioneering of a few rugged individualists. These few have now become the heroes, the religion and the dogma. The institutionalized impetus of the system, backed up by the marketeering motives of industrial concerns and the power-motivated desires of politicians, makes an imposing, smooth-sided edifice which the individual can find difficult, if not impossible, to scale.

The adventurers, however, have always been present and will always be amongst us and later I will be discussing the work of just a few of these.

The State of Science

So science has become like a house which has had so many pieces added in a piecemeal fashion that the resulting edifice has no real coherence and no direction. Government funded research provides hundreds of thousands of bread and butter 'scientists' with a job. But the research undertaken is frequently more like an army of uncoordinated builders all gleefully adding on rooms, roofs, even foundations, to a monstrous structure. With no-one ever really questioning the fundamental rationale for its existence. Most scientists follow recipes based upon principles laid down in the standard scientific cookbooks.

Certainly, there is no overall comprehension of what science is, or what physical substance, energy, life and consciousness actually *are*. The essential quest has been unknowingly abandonded as the humans involved have become further and further enmeshed in the frantic activity. But this is the situation in all of life, as far back as history goes.

I do not suggest that science ever possessed such a direction, but in the early days, those who followed a scientific bent were individuals, fascinated by some aspect of physical manifestation. They were called natural philosophers. They were intrigued and energized by the remarkable nature of things and wanted to find some answers. Even Newton never thought that he had discovered the essential *nature* of gravity. But now, if I may be forgiven for saying so, one rarely finds a scientist who is really aware that he is alive. The endless university round of lectures, seminars, supervisions and tutorials, plus a wife, kids, home and mortgage leave little space for the flame of real enquiry, for a spark of real life and creative, detached thought, perception and insight.

And the big prizes and motivations have become Nobel prizes and professional acolade. So the concommitant increase in ego and pride actually puts a damper on further creative thought, because it draws the mind's energy and attention away from inner concentration and out into the mundane world. So the source of inspiration is quite rapidly lost, even if temporarily found. This is why so many 'advances' are made by young people, with fresh minds, idealistic perhaps, and uncluttered by things that their elders think they know and adhere to with a strength and faith that would do credit to any observer of religious dogma.

Science, Emotion and Human Weakness

It is an unfortunate fact that humans like to be right; they like to be first; they like to have done something new; they like praise and glory. They do not like to acknowledge that they are only a part of a chain. This is our human nature and it is as much a feature of science as it is of family and tribal life[1]. The human emotions are identical.

[1] I remember watching a documentary film concerning the life of a forest dwelling community in West Africa. Sitting in his cleverly constructed cottage made out of natural and readily available materials, a man was preparing a nerve poison, requiring a number of different and essentially chemical processes. Watching him apply this final mixture to the tip of an arrow was his anxious wife. The film was subtitled. "Do be careful, dear," she said, "It's very poisonous". "It's all right – I know what I am doing," responded her husband. Human feelings are the same everywhere!

One would have thought that we would be more aware than we are of our state of ignorance and would be so happy to see our fellow humans pushing back the frontiers of our group ignorance. But not a bit of it. And this egocentric and competitive behaviour pattern, this mental-emotional energy configuration, actually helps to keep us ignorant! It is the sheer depth of our subconscious entanglement in these human emotions that keeps us in ignorance of the higher mystic reality. As humans, it is axiomatic to say that we understand things in our minds, so the degree and intensity of human emotion, which is largely subconscious, unconsiously influences all perceptions and understanding – whether scientific, social, political or spiritual. This subconscious constraint, in itself, is enough to deprive us of any real free will, to totally collapse any probability wave function.

Scientists behave in many respects like religious priests, when confronted by new ideas, even from one of their own colleagues. Especially if it is a lesser known colleague! Disputes over who discovered what first, or who thought up a certain idea first, are frequent and can be most acrimonious. And these emotional clouds over the mind actually prevent us from returning to the sea whence all these ideas and intuitions come.

We do not own anything, least of all an idea or a perception of nature's mechanisms. Rather, we should be abashed at our utter ignorance of nature's processes and be humbled thereby. In a good family, all work together for the common good. It is irrelevant who discovered what. It was the natural outcome of the way things were going, anyway. Like the mouse who thought he lead the camel but whose part was only circumstantial, we can hardly take credit for being on the crest of the wave when it broke!

But I have experienced colleagues who have purposely prevented particular scientific papers or books from reaching others, purely out of jealously that their position as an 'authority' on the subject might be undermined. Or their criticism of a 'new' idea was unconsciously motivated by jealousy rather than purely rational science or an honest disagreement. And there are also those who give unstintingly and selflessly. The latter, of course, are the happier and more peaceful people and frequently have a deeper intuition of nature's processes.

Then there are those who pretend to understand more than they do, refusing to divulge their 'secrets' because the information is 'proprietory' or – an even better one (!) – because "you wouldn't understand."

Expansion of consciousness by meditation actually entails the control of all these hidden, yet very simple, human, emotional weaknesses which presently control us. Then we develop a greater capacity for tolerance, open-mindedness, universality, clarity and lucidity – for wholeness. And with greater wholeness and personal mental-emotional integration within us, we automatically perceive a greater wholeness and integration in the 'outside' world.

So science is not truly rational – it is the outcome of human mental-emotional activity. The democratic process of discussion and experimentation helps to some degree in removing its rough and inconsequent edges. But the scientific 'conclusions' will always lie only within the constraints imposed by the general level of consciousness of the majority concerned. If the level of consciousness shifts, as we are presently experiencing, then our 'science' suddenly shifts, too, and hurries along to catch up with the higher general perception we then have of our physical domain.

Science, Holism and the Shift in Consciousness

The more one reads descriptions of the universe by scientists, philosophers and mystics, the more one realizes that the theory of the universe presented by each individual exactly mirrors – not the universe – but the content and structure of the individual's mind. Put in another way, given the energetic nature of the inner human constitution, it happens *automatically* that the mind of each one of us expresses itself in the way it does. That is a 'law' of nature, part of the karmas by which we find ourselves where we are – both physically as well as emotionally and mentally.

As we individually evolve in consciousness, our point of view changes automatically. To begin with, we may even dine out on the 'new' ideas we are 'having', by writing books and papers, giving lectures at conferences and so on. Later on, we realize that ideas are no more 'mine' than the sparkling of summer sunshine in the early morning dew. At the present time, there is most definitely an upward and global shift in consciousness taking place within many individuals, if not in large sections of the population, and a shift in perception is exciting to the individual. It results in an increasingly whole and universal inward condition, but which still has a long way to go. The result is that the theories of the universe which occur to such humans, reflect this wholeness.

Hence, the once cultish concept of holism is increasingly finding its way into conventional institutional thought. Holism, as a perception of the structure of the universe, is as old as man, though the word may be a comparatively new one. Mystics have expressed the fundamental oneness and interconnectedness of everything for as long as we can trace the history of man's perceptions.

Now, even our reductionist, analytical scientific process is finding itself unable to cope with the wealth of detail that it finds. For scientists are increasingly realizing that knowledge of local causality and connection does not tell you how the whole operates. And this is as much applicable to subatomic particles, to atoms and molecules, to a single cell, to the human body or to human psychology as it is to the entire universe, known and unknown. The idea is encapsulated in the very word we use for everything we know of – the *uni*-verse, one world, one 'turning', one complete, self-consistent system. It would be pleasant if our Uni-versities were also constructed along such lines!

Now, we even have such people as Paul Davies, professor of theoretical physics at the University of Newcastle upon Tyne, commenting with considerable insight upon his own discipline of physics, for long held to be the most fundamental of all sciences. Davies realizes that such 'fundamentalism' is relative only to reductionist thought processes, physics being the ultimate analysis of the 'parts' of nature.

But the beautiful thing is that having arrived at this 'fundamental' level, we find that it leads us back to a web of relationship in the energy patterns where everything is interconnected in one whole. So even reductionist logic has led back to holism. But the extent of that holism, to include our own mind and consciousness is still not fully grasped, even by many of the physicists who embrace the holistic concept. The habit of classical, reductionist thought goes very deep and the inward intuition, or even vision, of holism, of one universe, both inward and outer, is not something that can be taught.

Analytical reductionism, the splitting of the world into fragments by our divisive minds, is a level or state of consciousness. It matters little whether this is expressed as social, emotional, personal, political or scientific. The divided mind will perceive a divided universe. The integrated, whole mind will see one whole universe. So as we inwardly grow from the divided perception to the whole, our manner of expression automatically changes.

We may not be aware, at first, that this is what is actually happening. When we begin to wake up, we may pass some considerable time in a state of slumber, of semi-consciousness. For humans, the process is continuous. We are locked into a system where we are either slowly awakening or returning to the sleep of a deeper unconsciousness. We are never static, we go up or down on a daily basis. So, slowly, we come to understand that intellectual analysis tells us little of the intrinsic nature of the way we are and the way we perceive the universe. It is at this point in their thinking that people like Paul Davies then suggest: "I do not see any reason to dignify the former (particle physics) but not the latter (the holistic organization of networks or processes) with the label fundamental."

In other words, the mechanisms of holistic integration are now seen as more fundamental in nature than sub-atomic particles, ie. the whole is more fundamental than an analysis of its tiniest 'parts'. Hurray, one might exclaim! But hold on, for the process of change happens slowly and there are degrees to which the fundamental holism of nature is understood – conditional upon the mind set of the individual expressing or using it. So the buzzword of modern scientists is becoming that of 'self-organization in chaotic systems'. Ilya Prigogine received a Nobel prize for his work along these lines only a few years ago and his ideas are now beginning to penetrate beyond the bounds of the thermodynamic systems in which he first expressed them.

Matter and energy, scientists have noted, appear to possess the ability to 'self-organize'. But the question is not usually asked as to where that ability arises. It is intrinisic, they say. But this is like saying that a fundamental particle can exist as a little solid ball of something, but that we do not need to know the nature of that something. Clearly, neither such statements are correct.

Scientists are now torn between the classical view that nature increases in disorder or entropy, or that it is continually self-organizing into greater and greater complexity. This has now become the neat answer to the mechanistic, neo-Darwinist theories concerning the origin of life from inert matter. Evolution, they say, is just an example of the ability of matter or energy to self-organize. But from the truly holistic or mystic point of view, the whole universe is neither tending towards chaos, nor is it self-organizing. It is always – within its total self – completely in equilibrium.

This is automatically a function of the One expressing itself as the many. The oneness, the ultimate equilibrium, will always be present. This is how things are held together. But one's holism has to be mystical to comprehend this, for the Oneness is within. You cannot find it in anything that is manifested purely to our senses. Such understanding comes only from an inward point of consciousness.

So we are again brought back to the balance of yin and yang in all manifested things. Or, more fully, the expression of the three gunas – positive, zero and negative. For the zero is the point of inward creation from which the plus and the minus, the pairs of opposites are derived.

Knowing, then, that this is the nature of human understanding and that it is meant to be in just this very fashion, too, mystics will rarely, if ever, venture into controversy. For controversy is the expression of a confused mind divided against itself, and hence against others, too. One cannot intellectually convince others of something which arises, like the cream on milk, purely as a result of an expansion of consciousness. The ideas, the science, the expression – all these are secondary reflections of the degree of consciousness of the individual.

For the outward expression to change, the inward consciousness needs to change first. So to try and change the expression when one has no means of changing the level of inner consciousness, is doomed to failure. It is like putting on clean clothes, without ever having a bath. Expressed socially, for example, this is why simply imprisoning wrong-doers fails to change their activities. What is required is an inward change of perception and this can never be forced upon anyone, however intellectually intelligent a person may be.

So mystics generally keep quiet about controversial issues, especially where their point of view may lead to argument. From personal experience, however, I can add that in private, their comments can be hilariously revealing as to the true ramifications of human nature, though even then one is left with a warm and loving feeling concerning the nature of our human foibles. But one is left in no doubt as to where we stand.

In many respects, mystics see our human theorizing about the way things are, as so much childish chatter. To instruct the child to cease behaving childishly is irrelevant and will only stunt the child's natural growth. As with good parents, the childishness is a matter for affection, not judgement. They know that the child will grow beyond such prattle. They have seen it happen before and understand the process.

Scientific Concepts

As we have said, much of science is built on concepts, the meaning of which – in terms of real human experience – is unclear or altogether lacking. The foundation of modern mathematics was Euclidean geometry. The geometer dealt with such abstract notions as 'points', 'lines', 'planes' etc – all *in the absence of mass.* Clearly a theoretical science. With the introduction of Descartes' fundamental work on algebra in the seventeeth century, followed by the independent invention of calculus by both Leibniz and Newton, physics and mathematics received a tremendous impetus, as the power of their methodology was increased.

The application of this conceptual approach to the mechanics of Newton then set physics upon the path that we know so well today. But was it the right track for the understanding of primary realities? Can one apply the theoretical concepts of geometry (as it is commonly understood) to gravity or mass, for example, and derive a basic understanding of what gravity or mass actually *are*? The answer is, "No". We still, by this method, have no idea what *anything* actually *is*!

Newton did not really 'discover' gravity. He never even claimed to understand its nature. He simply found a mathematical formula to describe a part of its activity. Similarly, with his work on mass, mechanics and optics. The fundamental question of what these experiences of our physical world actually *are* remains unanswered by physics, because the *experiencer* is ignored as a part of the process of experience. The *observer* is omitted in the study of observation. There is a glimmering of light in some interpretations of quantum theory, but the mind, awareness and consciousness of the observer are not an integral part of these theories as they are conventionally expressed.

And so the story of scientific 'discovery' continues. Electricity and magnetism were brought into the field of mathematical theorization. Maxwell's work, showing the interrelationship of electricity and magnetism, introduced the concept of *force fields*. But at the present time, this concept of a force field has become something of an embarrassment because particle physicists can find no such thing as a *force field*. They can only find particle-like and wave-like entities.

So gravity becomes reduced (in the theory) to an interaction of *gravitons* (though no-one has ever seen one) and electromagnetism becomes an expression of *photons* and *electrical charge*.

Electrical charge is yet another concept which has a meaning as a mathematical and logical expression only and is tremendously useful in determining the quantitative nature of *effects* in electronics and electrical engineering, but it cannot be said to be a fundamental explanation of electrical phenomena. Nobody knows what charge actually *is*. Even when described by quantum theory as a 'flux of virtual particles', the essential lack of understanding still remains. What, one may ask, do virtual particles consist of? A question we will defer to a later chapter!

Einstein worked at combining the concepts of space, time and gravity, with some considerable success, but his theory cannot be easily combined with the statistical mathematical formulations concerning the world of subatomic particles. His theory is used extensively to help describe what goes on at the high velocities at which subatomic particles move. Ironically, it was even Einstein himself who did a large part of this basic work concerning the use of statistics to help describe particle behaviour. But he never envisaged that a statistical and probabilistic model would develop such credence as a description of physical reality. He always felt that somewhere underlying it all there must be a deterministic, ordered, causal pattern.

So it has all become very messy. It is a mansion that has been built piecemeal and does not fit together very well. And there are so many anomalies – experiences and experiments which are inexplicable according to current theoretical models – both within the realm of scientific discovery, as well as outside.

What is lacking is a fundamental viewpoint based upon the inner, mystic *experience* of the individual. Our grossly physical science has no place for the very thing which we all treasure more than any knowledge – our innner life and consciousness itself, even its continued physical existence in our present body.

This is very clear. For if the University Library or any of the faculty libraries here in Cambridge were to catch fire, the immediate emphasis would be, quite rightly, upon saving life – not knowledge. The academics would come running out leaving their accumulated scientific 'knowledge' behind them! But concerning that very inner spark of consciousness, the physical and biological sciences have got absolutely nothing to say.

So we are fooling ourselves if we think that scientific knowledge is of more importance and relevance to us than our own inner life. Science is a body of concepts that relate to each other only uneasily. It does its best to provide a logical framework within which experiences can be modelled and general principles established, but it falls far short of the ideal. Medical science has no real model at all of the human body, or even of just one cell. Reductionist analysis of the parts according to certain preconceptions does not constitute a model. And the reason is because life and consciousness are ignored and the inherent limitations of the intellect are not appreciated.

But most importantly – as regards the remainder of this book – these concepts can be changed and can be improved upon. Just as it seems a truer reflection of reality to say that the earth is round (not flat) and moves around the sun (is not stationary), so it is more correct to say that all manifested objects perceived with our senses or with instrumental extensions of them are actually patterns upon the vacuum surface which is inwardly linked in to our mind structure. What we want to know is how that primary patterning is ordered.

An understanding of this explains many of the experimentally observed anomalies of science and has also resulted in technology that actually works and is being developed at this very time, or in the recent past, most frequently by private individuals. Unfortunately, the history of the manner in which these individuals have been ignored or even persecuted by institutionalized science and industry is quite salutary.

Tom Bearden, propounder of the Scalar Wave Electromagnetic Theory and a creative scientist possessing an understanding of the relevance of mind and consciousness to scientific theory, is fond of pointing out that even the basic concepts of physics are poorly defined. Most scientists assume that concepts such as 'mass', 'time', 'field', 'force', 'charge' and so on, are clearly defined. The edifice of their scientific education or conditioning is built upon these concepts. But as we have pointed out, the meaning of these concepts is due more to the historical development of science than to any absolute or coherent definitions.

Burniston-Brown, writing in the *American Journal of Physics* (Vol. 28, p.475, 1960) on *Gravitational and Inertial Mass* comments, "One of the most astonishing features of the history of physics is the confusion which surrounds the definition of the key term in dynamics – mass." Without exception, this applies to all fundamental scientific concepts. Not one of these ubiquitous and familiar, fundamental terms is unambiguously understood.

This, of course, is a reflection of man's basic confusion concerning his existence, overlain by the fact that the minds of men are in constant flux. We are back with the dinner party syndrome. And as we have pointed out, the concept or thought concerning a thing is quite different from the thing itself. The 'thingness' of things can never be comprehended by intellectual concepts. Rather, such conceptualization becomes a barrier to the higher experience which perceives the 'thingness' directly.

Actually, many scientific concepts are so hard to grasp, intellectually, that when a science student finally gets the idea and its meaning into his mind, he (probably unconsciously) heaves a sigh of relief and never questions the verity or absoluteness of the concept. It becomes a matter of intellectual pride – knowledge often breeds a sense of superiority – that he can hold such thoughts in mind and work intelligently with what he thinks are their meaning.

To sit down and quietly question all that one has been taught can lead to a discovery of one's essential ignorance and loneliness – a good starting point for the mystic ascent and a good approach to science and life generally, too. But it is not an easy thing to do.

For the purposes of further scientific advancement, however, it is necessary to question all the basic concepts. For if we have reached a point where we can blow ourselves to pieces and destroy the ecological balance of the planet, where huge numbers of other species are becoming extinct on a daily basis, then surely this indicates that our fundamental understanding of life is awry? We are clearly missing out on something, somewhere. And that something, of course, is the spiritual dimension of inward life and consciousness.

The fundamental duality intrinsic in all the mind regions represents the basic dilemma of all human science and activity. The problem of 'I' and 'it' will always remain, however deeply one analyzes the 'it'. As long as 'it' is separate from 'I', whatever 'it' happens to be, one can never know 'it's' real nature. As long as the observer and the observed are experienced as being separate – even if we understand intuitively that they are one – we can always ask questions of the 'it'. "What is 'it'?" And the question can never be fully answered. In fact, answers only lead to more questions. "What are the 'its' that 'it' is made of?" and so on.

But when the 'I' merges with the 'it', in an expanded consciousness, then the problem concerning the real nature of 'it' is not resolved, but is *dissolved*. It ceases to have any meaning, in a higher sense. We can still ask questions of 'it' while functioning at the physical level, but then we know the relative nature of both the questions and answers. We do not expect to receive fundamental answers in this way.

Nikola Tesla and the Early Days in Electricity[1]

Let us now turn to specific, *experimental* scientific endeavour of the last hundred years. Endeavour that has resulted from a reappraisal of basic scientific concepts, plus a willingness to tackle, rather than sweep beneath the carpet, observed anomalies that do not fit within prevalent theories and conceptual structures. We must start this story with Nikola Tesla.

I have already written of Tesla's work in *Subtle Energy*, but his influence is so far reaching that no tale concerning the emergence of modern technology is complete without mentioning him. The undisputed father of alternating current technology, the electric power which drives the motors, heating and lighting of our modern homes and industries, Tesla has been largely forgotten or, some say, purposely suppressed. Yet many of the pioneers of electrical invention throughout this century and to the present day acknowledge his work as a tremendous inspiration in their life.

Tesla was a loner, who established no permanent corporate or research ties and this perhaps led to his ultimate isolation. But throughout all of his work, one perceives the undercurrent of a man who had discovered or understood more than was good for him. Or so it was thought by his contemporaries. They were probably alarmed by his visionary ideas, many of which have since come to

[1] My main biographical source on Tesla has been Margaret Cheney's, *Tesla: Man Out Of Time*.

pass, and they no doubt felt confused – unable to know whether to believe in the man or not.

Born in Yugoslavia in 1856, he moved to Paris when he was twenty-six. Back in Bucharest, he had worked for a while with the early telegraph systems and in Paris he worked for Edison's electric company where he rapidly became the chief trouble shooter for Edison's French and German power plants.

In 1884, when he was twenty-eight, Tesla moved to New York, remaining in the employment of Edison's company. Edison's electrical systems – his motors and lighting etc. – worked on direct current (DC), and although Tesla helped Edison in many significant ways, he had, when in Paris, already formulated in his mind a complete polyphase, electrical system based on alternating current (AC). After falling out with Edison over proposed rewards that were never forthcoming for redesigning Edison's primitive DC dynamos, Tesla finally founded his own company in April 1887 and set to work building his AC system of transformers, motors, dynamos and the all-important control systems. During the next four or five years he applied for and was granted a total of forty patents.

But Tesla was not the only one working on alternating current systems. Enterpreneur and himself an inventor (of the railroad air brake), George Westinghouse had acquired the patents to the AC distribution system of Gaulard and Gibbs. Setting his own chief engineer, William Stanley, to work on a transformer system, it was successfully tested in 1886 and by the end of that year, Westinghouse was operating the first commercial AC system in America. By the end of 1887, he had more than thirty such plants installed.

Westinghouse, however, still lacked a satisfactory alternating current motor and when in 1891, he connected with Tesla and visited him in his laboratory, one can imagine his excitement at what he saw.

Westinghouse bought Tesla's patents for about $60,000 which included $5000 in cash and the rest in Westinghouse shares. Tesla was also to receive a $2.50 royalty per horsepower of electricity sold. Within four years, these royalties were to be worth a staggering sum, a sum to which Tesla relinquished his rights in order to help his friend avoid commercial disaster.

Tesla now began working for Westinghouse as a consultant earning $2000 per month – a princely salary for those days. Westinghouse was clearly taking no chances that the incredibly creative and inventive mind of Tesla would be offered a job elsewhere! The existing system used by Westinghouse at that time utilized current oscillating at 133 cycles per second. Tesla's system operated on 60 cycles and after getting off on the wrong foot with Westinghouse's engineers, several months passed in an attempt to adapt Tesla's system to run at 133 cycles. Ultimately, Tesla's system was adopted just as it had been designed and the AC frequency of 60 cycles has been the American standard to the present day.

Edison's response was to bring his huge propaganda machine into operation, declaring – as he had done with his rivals in the gas industry – that AC was dangerous. He used leaflets, the newspapers and word of mouth. It was not only Edison's financial investment in DC that was at stake, it was the challenge to an egocentric genius that he was wrong. For Edison had proclaimed it as his scientific 'opinion' that an AC system would never work. Perhaps his motivations in this proclamation, too, were also commercial and he was only throwing up a pseudo-scientific smoke screen to keep out such competition to his lucrative electrical power business. Such motivations would need to have had little degree of consciousness in them. Edison would have probably believed his thought processes to be quite scientific. This is too often the nature of scientific criticism. The thin veneer of rationality overlies a seething mass of quite ordinary, subconscious, human emotion.

It is even related that people living in West Orange, New Jersey, in the vicinity of Edison's huge laboratory complex found that their dogs and cats were disappearing. Subsequently, they discovered that Edison was paying local boys twenty-five cents a head for these pets, which he then electrocuted with alternating current. He also arranged shows in which a phoney 'professor' electrocuted calves and large dogs on stage. This was all intended to scare people away from the use of AC power installations. The sale of energy was in the process of becoming the big business we know today, and greed is a powerful motivator.

Simultaneously, Edison issued scare leaflets with the word 'WARNING' printed in red letters at the top. The gist of his 'warning' was that if people were not careful they could find themselves being terminally 'Westinghoused'. This was a word he attempted to bring into the language with highly negative connotations. He also forecast that within six months of Westinghouse installing a system of any real capacity, someone would be killed by the AC current.

Edison ranted on virulently, and reluctantly Westinghouse had to respond with a truer version of the situation, quoting real facts and figures to allay public anxiety. The country, too, was expansion-minded after a period of depression and Westinghouse's AC system ultimately gained precedence, even despite the efforts of the power hungry, J. P. Morgan, and combined industrial conglomerates, to put him out of business. J. P. Morgan had by this time gained control of Edison's company, merging it with a previous acquisition in the electrical field, the Thomas-Houston Company, to form the General Electric Company we know today. It was at this juncture that Tesla so generously relinquished the rights to his patent royalties. Without this gesture, Westinghouse would have been forced into liquidation or have been taken over by Morgan. In the event, Westinghouse merged with several other smaller electrical power companies and America was saved from a complete Morgan monopoly.

The accrued royalties were by this time rumoured to be worth about $12 million and their continuance would have made Tesla one of the richest men in the world. But, as ever, he was deeply engrossed in his research and realizing the plight of a friend who had believed in him, he readily let Westinghouse off the hook. The Westinghouse company's annual report of 1897 shows that Tesla was only paid $216,000 in final settlement of all claims. For the next decade, he had sufficient funds, but increasingly his financial sources dried up and one of the world's greatest inventors found himself treading a lonely path on limited resources. His inventions were too far-reaching and too 'dangerous' a challenge to already existing technology and the businesses entrenched around it, to be acceptable to minds engrossed with egocentric glory, personal power and high financial rewards.

During the dirty battle for control of the electrical energy industry, Charles Coffin, president of the new General Electric Company, who thought that they were about to take over Westinghouse's company, had boasted recklessly to Westinghouse that they were "cutting prices fearfully", so as to "knock out" other electrical firms. He advised Westinghouse to do the same. The important thing, he urged, was to install *any* electrical power system that they could sell, because the cost of changing over later would be prohibitive. The customers would therefore be locked in to buying electrical power and associated electrical devices from them alone.

Coffin also earnestly advised Westinghouse to raise the price of his street lamps from $6 to $8 each, so that a payment of $2 'boodle' could be paid to the local aldermen and politicians without loss of profit. But Westinghouse wisely declined.

This kind of commercial reasoning and greed is common even in the present day, but if viewed with a detached mind one can see that to manipulate and pressurize one's fellow humans in such a manner is a pretty shoddy way to treat members of one's own human family. This attitude is unfortunately prevalent in the present cycle of man's affairs upon the planet.

Westinghouse, however, believed that a superior system would oust an already installed inferior one. It was certainly true, and his competitors knew it, that he had the better system. All the same, the commercial desire to sell the energy of the universe to one's fellow humans and to manipulate them thereby began in earnest at this time and continues to the present day. All attempts to make cheap energy available have been firmly quashed, though now, I believe, due to environmental conditions, the tide is turning.

One of my purposes in relating this story is to point out the intensity of the fight for control of the energy industry during its inception at the end of the last century. The underlying motivation was greed and ego – it was never that of human betterment. It has been a continuation of this industrial attitude which has led our planet to its present point of ecological crisis. It also provides the rationale for why cheaper and cleaner alternatives have been ignored or suppressed.

Well, the story continues and makes a fascinating read, but Tesla went on to experiment with a number of other inventions with which we are now quite familiar. Back in 1893, he had given the first public demonstration of radio-wave transmission, describing his experiment in full detail. But before he could take his work to the point of transmitting voice signals, he had to temporarily shelve his research in order to help Westinghouse prepare for the Chicago World's fair of 1893, where Westinghouse had landed the contract for the installation of all the electrical power and lighting equipment.

Then in 1895, a young Italian, Marchese Guglielmo Marconi, arrived in London with a wireless set similar to that demonstrated a year earlier by the British inventor, Sir Oliver Lodge. It did, however, have features common to Tesla's earlier equipment, though whether Marconi knew of Tesla's much publicized work or whether it was one of those coincidences of science is not known. Marconi certainly denied that he had ever heard of Tesla's system and there are many instances of simultaneous, but independent, invention in the annals of science. They call it synchronicity. When a wave breaks, it does so in many *apparently* independent places. If one cannot see the connecting wave, events may appear as coincidental.

Tesla was on the crest of the wave in many other of his inventions. It was he who first speculated upon the possibility of radar, in an article for *Century Magazine* in June 1910. Then in August 1917, only shortly after German U-boats had been sinking almost a million tons of Allied shipping a month and the first airborne bomb attacks had been carried out on Paris and London, he presented the main features of modern military radar in an article published by *The Electrical Experimenter*. Radar, however, was not actually developed until almost twenty years later, shortly before the second world war.

Tesla also designed and built the first fluorescent tube and the bladeless turbine. And he also presented the first cogently argued case for robots, for computer technology and for solid and liquid fuelled rockets.

All of this intensely practical research by Tesla and many others into the use of electromagnetic energy drove the scientific thought of the day into considerations on the *nature* of electromagnetism. All the basic work on X-rays, the discovery of the electron, the splitting of the atom and so on were a part of this era. It was also during this period of intensely focused thought that Einstein put forward his theory of relativity and that the basic principles of quantum theory were first formulated.

Even so, the leading scientists of those days could not foresee the future of their discoveries. Lord Rutherford, who discovered the atomic nucleus in 1909, was still heard to say in 1933, "The energy produced by the breaking down of the atom is a poor kind of thing. Anyone who expects a source of power from transformation of these atoms is talking moonshine." Similarly, Dr Millikan had commented in 1928, "There is no likelihood that man can ever tap the power of the atom. The glib supposition of utilizing atomic energy when our coal has run out is a completely unscientific Utopian dream." Some Utopia!

Tesla, however, maintained his belief in the ether as the source of all substance. This, he thought, was the fundamental, unifying theory of physical things. And because of this understanding he was able to conceive of waves in this ether that would transmit energy at a distance, without the use of wires. He built two of the most extraordinary electrical experimental stations ever constructed, the first in Colorado Springs and later his famous Wardenclyffe Tower on Long Island, New York. Here Tesla hurled lightning bolts of millions of volts, experimenting with a world radio broadcasting station and – unknown to some of his backers – with his ideas concerning the wireless transmission of energy. These backers included J. P. Morgan, ever hopeful of extensions to his empire.

His plans included putting the earth into some kind of "resonance circuit". From this point on, Tesla's direction was different from that of his more down to earth contemporaries and he suffered increasing scientific isolation. He was quite unable to accept Einstein's theory of relativity and curved space. He remained adamant that there was "no energy in matter other than that received from the environment". In this respect, he was wrong, but his comittment to the existence of an ether led him into directions which only in recent years have once again become possibilities. He postulated the probability of fractional charge on subatomic particles, for example, a matter upon which physicists are still divided.

He also claimed to have invented devices for hurling extremely concentrated beams into outer space, a subject reminiscent of modern day particle beam (Star Wars) weapons. Similarly, he claimed to know how to send signals to other planets, today a matter of routine for NASA's interplanetary Explorer modules.

None of these more esoteric devices was ever demonstrated or patented, so we will never know. Perhaps, in his intuitive mind, he could perceive how these things could be, but the direction that atomic theory had taken was alien to his thinking and he found himself out on a limb. His visionary concepts, however, have been a continuous source of inspiration to those who know of his work and part of his interest lies in the practical demonstration that by pursuing a different conceptual approach, he was able to envisage and build things beyond the scientific imagination of others.

Free Energy

Changing tack and moving into the present day, there are really two ways in which vacuum state technology is emerging:

1. The direct transformation of zero point vacuum energy into useful energy in the form of electricity or electromagnetism. This is then used for transport, heating, lighting, driving electric motors and so on.
2. The linkage of gravity to electricity, producing an electro-gravitic device in which gravity is controlled by means of electrical charge. This creates an anti-gravity thrust, providing a means of transport both within the atmosphere and in outer space, if the

device is also anti-inertial[1]. The medium within which such a craft is moving is, thus, largely immaterial.

Both these systems of directly utilizing vacuum energy have, apparently, been developed, though devices are not yet commercially available. In addition, both systems are intrinsically highly efficient and one of the major problems appears to be the control of this efficiency. If more energy is taken out of the vacuum state than can be used, then the total efficiency of the device is greater than 100 percent (in conventional terms) and the excess energy causes major practical difficulties of storage or dissipation.

Such *super-efficiency* also causes problems of another kind amongst industry. For the entire oil, electricity and gas industries, with all the gadgets we use which run on them – motor cars, aeroplanes, heating, lighting, electrical devices, etc. – all become either directly superceded or their power source can theoretically be replaced by a simple device, installed in each home, or in the device itself, to supply all existing devices with power. Hey presto – no more electricity or fuel bills, just a purchase of the vacuum energy converter.

One can imagine the impact of such a prospect upon these major international industries. Much of their activity would become obsolete and their man-power redundant. The resulting economic, political and employment problems would (and will) be immense. However, the energy is clean, one supposes, though the problems of scalar (vacuum) waves produced as 'by-products' must be considered. But the massive environmental problems presently facing our planet would therefore be greatly allieviated.

Nature keeps its own balance, they say, and if man is meant to move into a technology where such devices are available, then the social structure will automatically be

[1]*Inertia* is the tendency of something to stay put, even in the absence of a gravitational field. Even in space, for example, astronauts need to push something in order to make it move! A purely anti-gravitational device would be of little use in providing thrust once one has escaped the gravitational attraction of a massive object, and is in a weight-less, though not inertia-less, condition.

readjusted in one way or another. Maybe this will entail considerable planetary unrest, with the 'old order' being moved aside, much as happened during the period of the last two world wars. In combination with this, an upward or inward shift in consciousness, such as we already see taking place, prepares us human beings for a change in values and emphasis.

The current world obsession with money, power, work, survival and busy-ness will be seen more as the illusion which it really is. And perhaps man will develop a more fundamental and universal understanding of essential spiritual and human values, and strive to express them in his life. Then the motivations which drive us to pollute our planet, exploit our fellow creatures, human and otherwise, and ravage what could otherwise be a beautiful environment for us to live in, will be brought under greater control and the world will become a better place. Let us hope that this is not just a utopian dream.

The sheer insanity which prevails in (almost) all the major cities of the world – the traffic jams, the pollution, the wastage of resources, the social unrest – cannot be expected to continue. It has to change. Something has to give. Do we really think that London or Los Angeles or Tokyo will be just the same in fifty or a hundred years time? History tells us that everything changes, and these days, very rapidly. Do we really expect that in fifty years, vast numbers of humans will still spend hours each day stuck in traffic jams? That the stress of our modern lifestyle will still be acceptable as a way to live our lives? I do not think so.

People reacted against the Victorian workhouses and made the necessary social changes. The advent of electrical power made people fearful for their jobs, but it did not prevent electricity from spreading its web into every corner of our lives. Do we think that electrical power is the last great invention? Again, history does not suggest it.

The changes in both social and technological emphasis will come. The stage is already set. But we can ease its coming or resist it. We can suffer or enjoy. But come, it will, and I believe, pretty rapidly, too.

Electro-gravity and the Gravitational 'Constant'

I am much indebted, in what follows, to the investigations of Rolf Schaffranke, as detailed in his fascinating and cogent little book, *Ether Technology*, as well as in some other of his writings. Now mostly retired, Schaffranke was one of the youngest co-workers with the famous rocket expert, Wernher von Braun, at NASA in Huntsville, Alabama and was later employed by Boeing. He has done much invaluable sleuthing and presentation of the state of the art in gravity control devices and theory. If you are interested in repeating some of this work and taking it further, his book is an excellent starting point.

In the macroscopic world of scientific engineering, the concept of perpetual motion is considered to be impossible, because energy is always required to maintain any system in motion. This is not disputed. However, in the subatomic realm of particle physics, it is accepted indisputably that particles do spin and orbit, *perpetually*. As we have pointed out, spin and orbit are really misnomers, since the motion bears little resemblance to analogies from our macroscopic world. But motion is a part of subatomic manifestation and without it, particles would not exist. And this motion, they say, has existed for billions of years and will continue to exist for billions more.

So the concept of perpetual motion at the subatomic level is already an accepted reality, though no one understands (in scientific terms) from whence arises the energy that comprises their being.

These topics, of course, are a matter of discussion, even in conventional scientific circles, though we may not be too far wrong to assume that much of the experimental aspect of this work is classified material, undertaken by those with a military motive.

In June 1972, however, an open technical report, number AFRPL-TR-31, was prepared by a group of twenty eight scientists from the U.S. Air Force Command, Edwards, California. Entitled, *PROJECT OUTGROWTH, Advanced Propulsion Concepts*, the report attempts to predict possible developments in the field of propulsion in the near future. It was designed, it says, "To encourage and motivate talented and interested scientists and engineers once again to strive for 'advanced propulsion concepts'." Amongst those listed under the category heading of *field propulsion* were:

Electrostatic Effects
Alfven Wave Propulsion[1]
Electromagnetic Spacecraft Propulsion
Superconducting Particle Accelerator
Antigravity Propulsion

Field propulsion includes methods that incorporate a use of electric, magnetic and gravitational forces, and presume an advanced knowledge and understanding of these fundamental forces. Something we do not as yet possess.

This report continues:

> Before attempting to control gravity, it will be necessary to know exactly what causes gravity. Many reputable scientists, including Michael Faraday, Max Born, and Albert Einstein, have attempted to explain this phenomenon by relating electromagnetic and gravitational forces. Other scientists are convinced that an *entirely new discovery in fundamental physics* is necessary for a full understanding of gravity. Physicists generally assume a relationship between electromagnetism and gravity because both obey the inverse-square law which says that the force of both fields decreases with the distance in the same mathematical relationship.
>
> There are some intriguing differences between the two forces, however, since electromagnetism consists of two identifiable components – an electrical field and a magnetic field – while gravity appears to have only one component. In addition, electrical charges can repel and attract, while gravity always attracts.

Actually, recent experimental research[2] concerning the measurement of gravity in deep mines suggests that gravity may be comprised of two forces – one attractant and the other repellent. It is the *sum* of these two that we have been describing as gravitational attraction all these years. This brings it into line with electromagnetism and

[1] *Alfven waves* are formed in ionized gases at high temperatures in the presence of a magnetic field. Electricity can be produced by collecting the free electrons which result.

[2] Frank Stacey et al., University of Queensland, Australia, Physical Review D, vol 36, p2374.

the other forces of nature which exhibit the fundamental duality or polarity of all created energy patterns. This is the yin and yang of the universe.

It also underlines what was said earlier, that forces are effects, not primary realities. Science observes the summation of these effects, but makes an error if it considers them to be primarily existent. Since we are suggesting that all physical phenomena are actually such effects, what we would like to understand is the nature and arrangement of the substructure underlying them.

Again, concerning gravity, Borel, the French mathematical physicist wrote:

> There was, however, something rather strange in this phenomenon of gravitation, something that distinguished it from other physical phenomena. This was its utter immutability and its absolute independence of all external actions. Light is arrested by opaque bodies, deviated by prisms and lenses: electrical and magnetic actions are modifield by the neighbourhood of certain bodies; gravitation alone remains the same. . .

So the nature of gravity is not at all understood, even in a scientific way. We have certain theories, but they do not all fit together. There is no one mathematical expression of all energetic interaction that permits an understanding of all material forces. It is not surprising, therefore, given that we have only flawed theoretical concepts, that empirical experimentation has continuously thrown up anomalies that do not fit within our existing models of physics.

There is incontrovertible evidence, for example, from a number of sources, that neither the gravitational 'constant' nor the speed of light in a vacuum are constant after all. Since Einstein's theory of relativity is founded upon these two assumptions, if either one of them is shown to be incorrect, then Einstein's theory is seen to be more relative than he thought! In short, it would be wrong, *as a fundamental model*. Though, like Newton's observations, it would still have its relevance and use.

Conventional scientists do not dispute this, for otherwise they would not be engaged in the search for more fundamental models than relativity and quantum theory. Einstein, however, occupies the place of a hero in the scientific world (and even outside it) and it is difficult for physicists, both psychologically and in actuality, to challenge his work.

You will perhaps be interested to hear of his research concerning the gravitational constant and I will mention some of it here. In the June 11, 1964 issue of *Nature* magazine, a former student of Einstein, Dr Erwin Saxl published the results of some most convincing experiments. He made the following comment:

> When working as a post-doctoral student with Einstein, we discussed the possibility that there were *interrelations between electricity, inertial mass, and gravitation*. These experimental results make me wonder whether they may properly be so interpreted

Dr Saxl's experiments had been conducted in his own private laboratory over a period of the previous ten years, using extremely sensitive and highly sophisticated electronic equipment, much of which he built himself out of his own resources. It cost him around $40,000. He also expressed his thanks to Professor Hans Thirring for presenting the original disclosure of his results before the Austrian Academy of Science. Since it comes from outside the realm of institutionalized science, however, his work has simply been ignored by the majority. There is, after all, no scientific fame or fortune in someone else's work.

The *Boston Sunday Globe* reported his findings on June 14, 1964 under the banner:

> *Gravity Not Constant, Einstein Pupil Makes Discovery*.

The article went on:

> A one-time pupil of Albert Einstein has obtained experimental evidence that upsets one of the most firmly established concepts of modern physics. . . . He has found that the so-called 'gravitational constant' – a number heretofore believed to be unchanging – *appears to vary under dynamic conditions*.
>
> At the same time he has found evidence that gravity and electricity, until now believed completely unrelated, *do in fact interact*. If his experiments are confirmed, it will mean rewriting the books from start to finish. In sum, it will be one of the most important scientific discoveries in history, on a par with Newton's laws of gravity and Einstein's theories of relativity, adding a completely new dimension to both their concepts of the universe. This is the first time that gravitation and

electricity have been connected experimentally, and if the evidence could be confirmed its scientific import would be staggering.

Such thoughts, however, are not unique. Michael Faraday, the great experimenter who demonstrated the link between electric and magnetic fields around 1830, discovering electromagnetic induction which led to the invention of the first electric motor, stated in a lecture given to the Royal Academy on November 28, 1850, "Here end my trials for the present. The results are negative. They do not shake my strong feeling of the existence of a relation between gravity and electricity, though they give no proof that such a relation exists."

We must remember that although this statement was made over 135 years ago, it is the work of Faraday and soon after, that of Maxwell in 1865, which has provided the fundamental basis for much of our twentieth century electromagnetic technology. So historically, we are just about ready for a new technological and theoretical paradigm shift.

Many other scientists, too, have puzzled over the fact that if the gravitational laws of attraction as presently understood are true, then it is difficult to comprehend why the enormous masses of the galaxies do not cause a collapse of the universe. Or why, within an atomic nucleus, the particles do not collapse.

By understanding that there is a dynamic interaction between electricity and gravity, the situation can be viewed in quite a different light. This, after all, is what all the theoretical physicists are looking for in Unified Field Theories.

What was unique in Dr Saxl's work was that he measured the gravitational 'constant' in a *moving* system. Using a rotating ceramic pendulum with a beam of light as a reference point he was able to measure its speed of swing (*angular speed*) with an accuracy of *one part in 10 million.*

According to standard theory the fact that the pendulum was rotating should make no difference to the value of the gravitational force influencing its swing. In fact, Saxl discovered that it did.

Furthermore, when he applied an electrical charge to the pendulum, in his own words, "All hell broke loose."

Specifically, he discovered that *when the pendulum carried a negative charge it took a shorter time to swing across the same arc than when it was positively charged.*

Extensive additional experimentation and checking revealed to him that there is a direct linkage between gravity and electricity. We can assume, I believe, that Saxl would have taken into account the magnetic and electrostatic fields surrounding the earth, as well as atmospheric ionic factors which may have influenced his results. This would be standard laboratory technique.

"In space we know there are billions of electron volts, and we're dealing with masses of fantastic magnitude," observes Dr Saxl. "If my little pendulum, moving over such tiny distances and with such modest voltage shows a distinct electro-gravitic effect, what forces may be operating in intergalactic space where the parameters are multiplied infinitely in both electric charge and mass?"

Similarly, if electro-gravitational forces are playing a part in atomic structure, then the apparently enormous concentrated mass present in a nucleus may indeed be much less than presently calculated and may satisfactorily explain why atoms do not collapse.

Moreover, the existence of electro-gravitational forces permeating the universe would also be likely to influence the speed of light. The primary evidence for an expanding universe is the 'red-shift' – an apparent shift in wavelength due to the speed of the object (eg. a star) relative to the observer[1]. But Saxl points out that this red-shift *could* also be due to interaction between the gravitational and electric fields. The universe might not, therefore, be expanding, after all. And such a possibility would also put paid to the idea of a primaeval Big Bang in which everything appeared out of nothing and began expanding just as fast as it could.

So you can see why, with all the vested interest in the more conventional ways of thinking, the demonstration of the very thing scientists are looking for is conveniently ignored.

[1] This is similar to the reason why an ambulance siren changes pitch (or frequency/wavelength) as it passes you in the street. The emitted waves are 'stretched' as it moves away and 'compressed' as it moves towards you.

Dr Saxl's work continued, however, and the data was fed automatically into a powerful computing system. With the long experiments which this has made possible, Dr Saxl has uncovered periodic variations in the gravitational constant which are related to the positions of the sun and moon. And as we shall see in the ensuing chapters, this is not the first time that such changes have been noted.

The Speed of Light

Having discovered that gravity is not a constant, but does, like everything else, interact with other energies, what about one of the other basic dogmas of modern science, that the speed of light (electromagnetic energy) is a constant in a vacuum? Einstein's Special Theory of Relativity makes the basic asumption that it is unvarying. The same theory postulates that the speed of light is as fast as you can go, that it is the ultimate speed limit. At that speed, mass becomes infinite.

Well, mathematicians always begin to suspect their calculations when infinities start popping up out of the woodwork. It is an indication that there is something wrong with their model. That it could be better. But is there any experimental proof of variations in the speed of light in a vacuum? Yes, there is.

And more than just that, for as the successors to Michelson's experimentation discovered in 1932, using a mile long length of tube in Pasadena, California, there are variations of twelve miles per second and more. These *vary with the season* and also within a shorter cycle of about two weeks. In the end, the scientists took an average of all the readings, which was announced in 1934 to be 186,271 miles per second.

More recent research by physicists at the University of Alabama, using atomic clocks, spinning discs and gamma rays, have also shown that this constant does vary with a periodicity dependent upon the angular velocity of the disc. But they have had considerable difficulty getting their work published, because, "Everybody knows that the velocity of light in a vacuum is a constant." These experimental results, however, are quantifiably explicable by their model of the physical vacuum as a web of energy focuses, ultra-minute 'particles', or spatial quanta.

While light seems to show little inclination to fully 'obey' our 'laws' concerning its activities, scientists studying other systems have found that electrical signals do sometimes appear to travel faster than light. Alexis Guy Obolensky has been performing such experiments since 1977, reporting on a detailed series conducted in August 1988 at the Technithion-Bromion Laboratories in Sloatsburg, New York[1]. The results were subjected to rigorous numerical analysis.

In his apparatus, two electrical signals were received simultaneously and almost instantaneously after travelling from the same source – at over 100 times the speed of light – down two separate and unequal paths, (up to 105 feet long). The signals were monitored on an ultra-high speed oscilloscope.

There was also a further low energy signal that seemed to be travelling at twice the speed of light. Furthermore, other speed-of-light signals were detected which varied with the compass orientation, the time of day and the polarity of the current. These were like the electromagnetic signals flowing in an aerial, but the periodicity cannot be readily explained.

Obolensky offers no explanation for these results, but only points out that they are not describable by Maxwell's laws of electromagnetism. Other scientists are predictably sceptical, of course, (some 'laws of nature' are totally predictable!) and further experimentation is required to elucidate exactly what is going on.

Finally, we must mention Alain Aspect's famous and accredited quantum physics experiment with photons (1982), which indicates conclusively that interactions can occur at speeds far in excess of the speed of light, thus breaching the requirements of Einstein's field theory.

So, all in all, gravity and the speed of light are known to be incompletely described by any of our existing 'laws'. They also vary cyclically and seasonally. It's all very interesting. . .

[1] *Electronics and Wireless World,* December 1988.

Some Good Advice from a Savage

A prerequisite for solving our self-created environmental planetary mess is a world view that must bear some relationship to the highest spiritual reality. Without this, there is no basis upon which to determine our actions, no intuitive comprehension of natural law, no rationale for unselfish behaviour.

The following letter, written in 1855, was sent to President Franklin Pierce of the United States by Chief Sealth (now Seattle) of the Duwamish Tribe of the State of Washington, in response to a demand to sell his people's land. It has been preserved in Washington and is one of the most poignant statements I have ever read concerning man's place on this planet.

I place it here because a book such as this is written at this time in man's history to help him understand his place and role in nature, within the terminology and idiom of our present culture. Within his context, Chief Sealth clearly understood this place.

> The Great Chief in Washington sends word that he wishes to buy our land. The Great Chief also sends words of friendship and goodwill. This is kind of him, since we know he has little need of our friendship in return. But we will consider your offer, for we know that if we do not do so the white man may come with guns and take over our land. What Chief Seattle says, the Great Chief in Washington can count on as truly as our white brothers can count on the return of the seasons. My words are like the stars – they do not set.
>
> How can you buy or sell the sky – the warmth of the land? The idea is strange to us. Yet we do not own the freshness of the air or the sparkle of the water. How can you buy them from us? We will decide in our time. Every part of this earth is sacred to my people. Every shining pine needle, every sandy shore, every mist in the dark woods, every clearing and humming insect is holy in the memory and experience of my people.

We know that the white man does not understand our ways. One portion of land is the same to him as the next, for he is a stranger who comes in the night and takes from the land whatever he needs. The earth is not his brother, but his enemy, and when he has conquered it, he moves on. He leaves his fathers' graves behind and he does not care. He kidnaps the earth from his children. He does not care. His fathers' graves and his children's birthright are forgotten. His appetite will devour the earth and leave behind only a desert. The sight of your cities pains the eyes of the red man. But perhaps it is because the red man is a savage and does not understand. . . .

There is no quiet place in the white man's cities. No place to hear the leaves of spring or the rustle of insects' wings. But because perhaps I am a savage and do not understand – the clatter only seems to insult the ears. And what is there to life if a man cannot hear the lovely cry of the whippoorwill or the argument of the frogs around a pond at night? The Indian prefers the soft sound of the wind darting over the face of the pond, and the wind itself cleansed by a mid-day rain or scented with pinion pine. The air is precious to the redman. For all things share the same breath – the beasts, the trees, the man. The white man does not seem to notice the air he breathes. Like a man dying for many days, he is numb to the smell of his own stench.

If I decide to accept, I will make one condition. The white man must treat the beasts of this land as his brothers. I am a savage and do not understand any other way. I have seen a thousand rotting buffaloes on the prairies, left by the white man who shot them from a passing train.

I am a savage and do not understand how the smoking iron horse can be more important than the buffalo that we kill only to live. What is man without the beasts? If all the beasts were gone, men would die from great loneliness of spirit, for whatever happens to the beast also happens to man. All things are connected. Whatever befalls the earth befalls the sons of the earth.

Our children have seen their fathers humbled in defeat. Our warriors have felt shame. And after defeat they turn their days in idleness and contaminate their bodies with sweet food and strong drink. It matters little where we pass the rest of our days – they are not many. A few more hours, a few more winters, and none of the children of the great tribes that once lived on this earth, or that roamed in small bands in the woods, will be left to mourn the graves of a people once as powerful and hopeful as yours.

One thing we know that the white man may one day

discover. Our God is the same God. You may think now that you own him as you wish to own our land. But you cannot. He is the God of man. And his compassion is equal for the redman and the white. This earth is precious to him, and to harm the earth is to heap contempt on its creator.

The Whites too shall pass – perhaps sooner than other tribes. Continue to contaminate your bed and you will one night suffocate in your own waste.

When the buffalo are all slaughtered, the wild horses all tamed, the secret corners of the forest heavy with the scent of many men, and the view of the ripe hills blotted by talking wires, where is the thicket? Gone. Where is the eagle? Gone. And what is it to say goodbye to the swift and the hunt, the end of living and the beginning of survival?

We might understand if we knew what it was that the white man dreams, what hopes he describes to his children on long winter nights, what visions he burns into their minds, so that they will wish for tomorrow. But we are savages. The white man's dreams are hidden from us. And because they are hidden, we will go our own way. If we agree, it will be to secure your reservation you have promised. There, perhaps, we may live out our brief days as we wish. When the last redman has vanished from the earth, and the memory is only the shadow of a cloud moving across the prairie, these shores and forests will still hold the spirits of my people, for they love the earth as the newborn loves its mother's heartbeat.

If we sell you our land, love it as we've loved it. Care for it as we've cared for it. Hold in your mind the memory of the land, as it is when you take it. And with all your strength, with all your might and with all your heart – preserve it for your children, and love it as God loves us all. One thing we know – our God is the same God. This earth is precious to him. Even the white man cannot be exempt from the common destiny.

— CHAPTER 8 —

Free Energy and the Real Space Age

Thomas Townsend Brown and the Gravitor[1]

While it is understood that the static forces of electrical charge and magnetism interact as electromagnetism, we have not, as yet, in conventional circles, identified the corresponding link between gravity and electricity, nor indeed between gravitation and magnetism.

These forces can be portrayed as a triangle, viz:

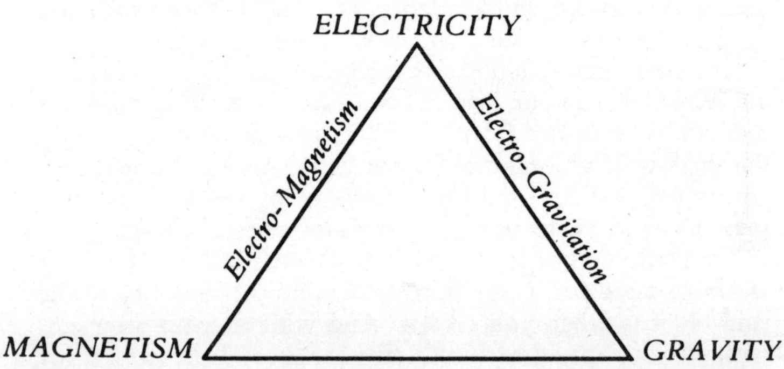

While the majority of our modern technology has resulted from exploitation of the electromagnetic side of this triangle, the electro-gravitic side has been sorely neglected.

Referring once again to Schaffranke's excellent little book, he tells the fascinating tale concerning the work of one Thomas Townsend Brown.

Townsend Brown's work came as a result of certain suggestions put to him in 1923 by Professor Biefield of Denison University and the experiments which followed led to the discovery of a linkage between electrical charge and gravity, the *Biefield-Brown* effect.

[1]My main source of information concerning Thomas Townsend Brown's research has been Rolf Schaffranke's *Ether Technology*.

Townsend Brown's first experiments were performed with suspended charged capacitors, with the amazing observation that when the capacitor was charged *it exhibited a forward thrust towards the positive pole*. Reversing the polarity resulted in a reversal of the direction of thrust. Thus:

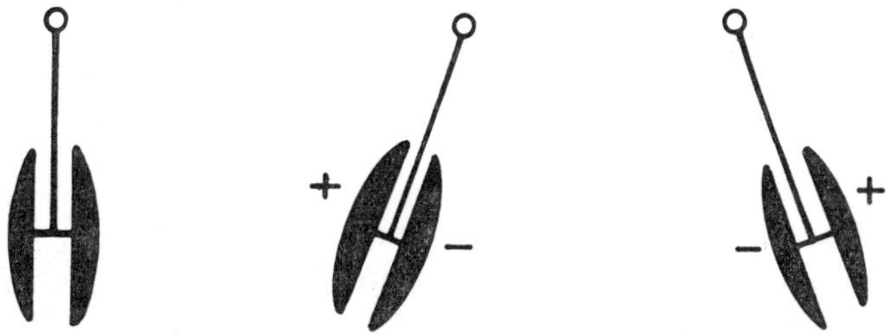

Uncharged *Charged* *Charged*

Similarly, when the capacitor was mounted vertically upon a beam balance, an 'anti-gravity' effect was observed, thus:

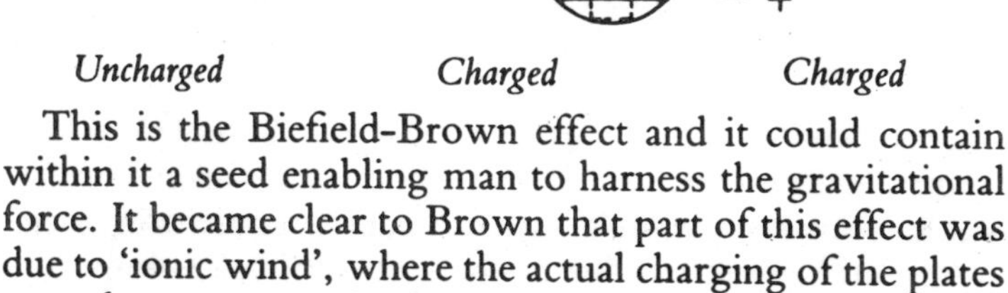

Uncharged *Charged* *Charged*

This is the Biefield-Brown effect and it could contain within it a seed enabling man to harness the gravitational force. It became clear to Brown that part of this effect was due to 'ionic wind', where the actual charging of the plates caused movements in the air, resulting in their displacement. Consequently, he performed the experiments in a high vacuum and observed that a significant percentage of the effect remained. This effect is proven and is repeatable. It is one of the scientific anomalies that are inexplicable by conventional scientific wisdom, although the theoretical work of Dr Inomata, discussed in the next chapter, not only predicts this very effect, but also quantifies just exactly how much it might be. He has also successfully performed the experiment in his own laboratory.

Working on ways of using this effect to power a vehicle,

Brown's research led him to the development of a shape that was the most efficient in the production of electro-gravitational lift. It looked something like this:

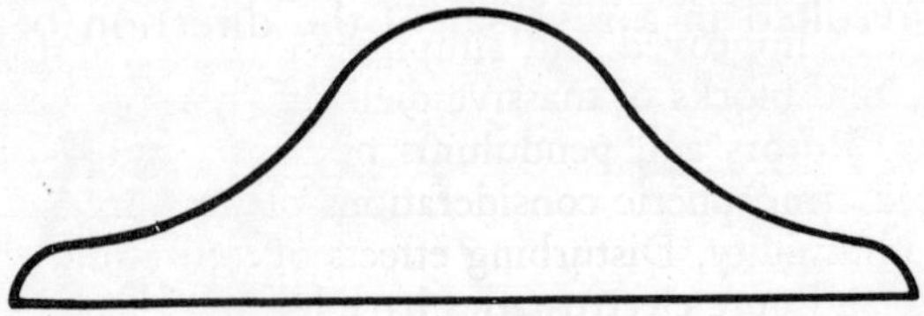

The shape is that of a disc or saucer. And note, mind you, that this was in 1926, before the words 'UFO' and 'FLYING SAUCER' had even been coined. And before anyone had ever reported the electrostatic glow that is often reported as surrounding flying saucers.

By arranging the disc or saucer in segments that could be selectively and deterministically charged, Brown reasoned that it would thereby be possible to control the movement of such a vehicle.

Brown, in fact, developed and successfully patented a method of electrostatic propulsion (Pat. No. 2,949,550) which he demonstrated upon a scale model travelling around a stationary pole. When this model was run in a vacuum, there seemed to be no limits to the speeds possible and it needed to be shut off before developing enough energy to disintegrate.

One of the most interesting factors concerning the reports of flying saucers is that one would think that the whole craft, both vehicle and occupants, would be subject to unbearable stresses due to the sudden accelerations and changes in direction. But Brown pointed out that both craft and occupants would respond identically to the distortion in the local gravitational field, so no such stresses would be felt.

By analogy, this would be similar to what happens when an elevator moves *down*. Since both the elevator and the passengers share the same gravitational tendencies there is no differential in movement between the two. And if the acceleration is smooth enough, there is barely any perceptible movement.

Brown's work was ultimately written up, his first paper

being published in 1929 in *Science and Invention*, under the heading, *How I Control Gravitation.*

He wrote:

> Since the first tests, the apparatus and methods used have been greatly improved and simplified. Molecular gravitors made of solid blocks of massive dielectric have given greater efficiency. Rotors and pendulums operating under oil have minimized atmospheric considerations of pressure, temperature, and humidity. Disturbing effects of ionization, electron emission, and pure electrostatics have likewise been carefully analyzed and eliminated. After years of refinement in methods, we succeeded in observing the gravitational variations produced by the moon and the sun, and the much smaller variations produced by the different planets. It is a curious fact that the effects are most pronounced when the affecting body is in the alignment of the differently charged elements, and least pronounced when it is at right angles!
>
> Much of the credit for this research is due Dr Paul Alfred Biefeld, Director of Swasey Observatory. The writer (Brown) is deeply indebted to him for his assistance and for many valuable and timely suggestions.

Concluding his paper, he wrote:

> The Gravitor, in all reality, is a very efficient motor. Unlike other forms of motor, it does not in any way involve the principles of electromagnetism, but instead it utilizes the principles of *electro-gravitation*. A simple gravitor has no moving parts, but is apparently capable of *moving itself from within itself.* It is highly efficient for the reason that it uses no gears, shafts, propellors, or wheels in creating its motive power. It has no internal mechanical resistance and no observable rise in temperature. Contrary to the common belief that gravitational motors must necessarily be vertical acting, the gravitor, it is found, acts equally well in every conceivable direction.
>
> While the gravitor is at present primarily a scientific instrument – perhaps even an astronomical instrument – it also is rapidly advancing to a position of commercial value. . . Multi-purpose gravitors weighing hundreds of tons may propel the ocean liners of the future. Smaller and more concentrated units may propel automobiles and even airplanes. Perhaps even the fantastic 'space cars' and the promised visit to Mars may be the final outcome. Who can tell?

Brown commenced this work before World War II. During his war years, he rose rapidly to the rank of

Lieutenant Commander and Commanding Officer of the U.S. Navy Radar School in Norfolk, Virginia. But, overworking himself, he finally collapsed and after recovery and retirement from the Navy, he took a position with Lockheed-Vega.

After the war, his experimental work was repeated by a group of naval students at Pearl Harbour and demonstrated in the presence of U.S. Admiral Radford, who congratulated Brown on his discovery. The Navy, however, refused funding for further research because of the negative opinions of other scientists.

So Brown's work was largely ignored. His friends arranged demonstrations for the business world and government officials, but although considered of interest, they were thought to be of little value. Nobel prizewinner, Dr Millikan, in declining to attend one such demonstration is said to have commented, "Such a thing is impossible and out of the question."

In England and France, his work was described in air and space magazines but the expected recognition never materialized. A small corporation was formed to carry on further research in the absence of government finance and over seventy-five patent applications were filed in twelve major countries. The system was developed to the point where one particular device was capable of lifting itself when voltage was applied.

In 1956, however, Brown made the mistake of showing an interest in UFO's, even founding a Washington-based organization, NICAP. At this, the conventional scientific community buried their heads and the facility to publish in American scientific journals was withdrawn.

Probably the last scientific article to appear, in the spring of 1956, concerning Brown's discovery was printed in the internationally read Swiss magazine, *Interavia.* It was headed, *Toward Flight Without Stress or Strain . . . . Or Weight.* Written by a reputable journalist who had been vetted by the magazine, the article stated:

> Electro-gravitics research, seeking the source of gravity and its control, has reached a stage where profound implications for the entire human race begin to emerge. Perhaps the most startling and immediate implication of all involved aircraft, guided missiles, atmospheric and free space flight of all

kinds. . . . And towards the long-term progress of mankind and man's civilization, a whole new concept of electro-physics is being levered out into the light of human knowledge.

Regarding the technical details of Townsend Brown's work, the article continues:

> A localized gravitic field used as a pondero-motive force has been created in the laboratory. Disc airfoils two feet in diameter and incorporating a variation of the simple two-plate condenser, charged to fifty kilovolts and a total continuous energy input of fifty watts have achieved a speed of seventeen feet per second in a circular course twenty feet in diameter. . . . More recently, these discs have been increased in diameter to three feet and run in a fifty-foot diameter air course under a charge of 150 kilovolts (KV), with results so impressive as to be highly classified. Variations of this work done under a vacuum have produced much greater efficiencies that can only be described as startling. Work is now under way developing a flame-jet generator to supply power of up to fifteen million volts.
>
> The most successful line of the electro-gravitics research so far reported is that carried on by Townsend T. Brown, an American who has been researching gravity for over thirty years. He is now conducting research projects in the U.S. and on the continent. He postulates that there is, between electricity and gravity, a relationship parallel and/or similar to that which exists between electricity and magnetism. And as the *coil* is the usable link in the case of electromagnetics, so is the condenser that link in the case of electro-gravitics.
>
> Years of successful empirical work have lent a great deal of credance to this hypothesis. The detailed implications of man's conquest of gravity are innumerable. In road cars, trains and boats, the headaches of transmission of power from the engine to the wheels or propellers would simply cease to exist. Construction of bridges and big buildings would be greatly simplified by temporarily induced weightlessness, etc.

Finally, intrigued by the possible UFO connection, the author speculates:

> Of course, there is always a possibility that the unexplained 3% of UFO's – 'Unidentified Flying Objects' as the U.S. Air Force calls flying saucers – are in fact vehicles so propelled, developed already and undergoing proving tests. . . . But by whom? The U.S., Britain or Russia? However, if this is so, it is the best-kept secret since the Manhattan Project, for this

reporter has spent over two years trying to chase down work on gravitics, and has drawn from Government scientists and military experts the world over only the most blank of stares. This is always the way of exploration into the unknown.

Later that year, Lucien A. A. Gerardin, head of the Nuclear Physics Section, at Compagnie Francaise Thomson-Houston, published a follow up article giving his thoughts on the theoretical basis of Brown's work, though this is somewhat too technical for these pages.

Similarly, following Brown's earlier visit to Europe, the *Journal of the British Interplanetary Society* printed a detailed appraisal of electro-gravitics by A. V. Cleaver, Assistant Chief Engineer of the Aero-Engine Division of Rolls Royce.

Both these articles are worth reading if you want to take this subject further (see bibliography).

Finally, Schaffranke managed, in 1973, to track down the whereabouts of Townsend Brown, discovering him in retirement at the age of sixty-eight, living in the Bahamas.

In reply to a letter from Schaffranke, he wrote:

> The experiments in vacuum were conducted at Soc. Nat. Construc., Aeronaut, in Paris in 1955–56, in the Bahnson Laboratories, Winston-Salem, North Carolina in 1957–58 and at the General Electric Space Center at King of Prussia, Penna, in 1959. Laboratory notes were made, but these notes *were never published* and are not available to me.
>
> The results were varied, depending upon the purpose of the experiment. We were aware that the thrust of the electrode structures were caused largely by ambient ion momentum transfer when the experiments were conducted in air. Many of the tests, therefore, were directed to the exploration of this component of the total thrust.
>
> In the case of the G.E. test, caesium ions were seeded into the environment and the additional thrust due to the seeding was observed. In the Paris test miniature saucer type airfoils were operated in a vacuum exceeding 10mm Hg.
>
> Bursts of thrust (towards the positive) were observed every time there was a vacuum spark within the large bell jar. These vacuum sparks represented momentary ionization, principally of the metal ions in the electrode material. The DC potential used ranged from 70 KV to 220 KV
>
> Condensers of various types, air dielectric and barium titanate were assembled on a rotary support to eliminate the

electrostatic effect of chamber walls and observations were made of the rate of rotation.

Intense acceleration was always observed during the vacuum spark, (which incidentally, illuminated the entire interior of the vacuum chamber.) Barium titanate dielectric always exceeded air dielectric in total thrust. The results which were most significant from the standpoint of the Biefeld-Brown effect was that thrust continued, *even when there was no vacuum spark*, causing the rotor to accelerate in the negative to positive direction to the point where voltage had to be reduced or the experiment discontinued, because of the danger that the rotor would fly apart.

In short, it appears there is strong evidence that the Biefeld-Brown effect does exist in the negative to positive direction in a vacuum of at least 10 Torr. *The residual thrust is several orders of magnitude larger than the remaining ambient ionization can account for.*

. . . The condenser 'Gravitor' as described in my British patent, only showed a loss of weight when vertically oriented, so that the negative-to-positive thrust was upward. In other words, the thrust tended to 'lift' the gravitor. Maximum thrust observed in 1928 for one gravitor weighing approximately 10 kilograms was 100 kilodynes at 150 KV DC. These gravitors were very heavy, many of them made with a molded dielectric of lead monoxide and beeswax, and encased in bakelite. None of these units ever 'floated' in air.

There were two methods of testing, either as a pendulum, in which the angle of rise against gravity was measured and charted against the applied voltage, or, as a rotor 4ft in diameter, on which four 'gravitors' were mounted on the periphery. This 4ft wheel was tested in air and also under transformer oil. The total thrust or torque remained virtually the same in both instances, seeming to prove that aero-ionization was not wholly responsible for the thrust observed.

Voltage used on experiments under oil could be increased to about 300 KV DC and the thrust appeared to be approximately linear with voltage.

In subsequent years, from 1930 to 1955, critical experiments were performed at the Naval research Laboratory, Washington D.C.; the Randall-Morgan Laboratory of Physics, University of Penna, Philadelphia; at a field station at Zanesville, Ohio and two field stations in Southern California, of the torque of multi-segmented rotors containing hi-K dielectrics. The torque was measured continuously day and night for many years. Large magnitude variations were consistently observed under carefully controlled conditions of constant voltage, temperature, under oil, in magnetic and electrostatic shields, not only underground but at various elevations.

These variations recorded automatically on tape, were statistically processed and several significant facts were revealed. *There were pronounced correlations with mean solar time, sidereal time and lunar hour angle. This seemed to prove beyond a doubt that the thrust of 'gravitors' varied with time in a way that related to solar and lunar tides and a sidereal correlation of unknown origin.* These automatic records, acquired in so many different locations over such a long period of time, appear to indicate that *the electro-gravitic coupling is subject to an extra-terrestrial factor, possibly related to the universal gravitational potential or some other (as yet) unidentified cosmic variable.*

In a second letter to Rolf Schaffranke, replying to further questions, dated April 5, 1973 he wrote:

The apparatus which lifted itself and floated in the air, which was described by Mr Kitselman, was not a massive dielectric as described in the English patent.

Mr Kitselman witnessed an experiment utilizing a 15 inch circular, dome-shaped aluminium electrode, wired and energized as in the attached sketch, (see figures 8-1). When the high voltage was applied, this device, although tethered by wires from the high voltage equipment, did rise in the air, lifting not only its own weight but also a small balance weight which was attached to it on the underside. *It is true that this apparatus would exert a force of upward of 110% of its weight.*

The above experiment was an improvement on the experiment performed in Paris in 1955 and 1956 on disc airfoils. The Paris experiments were the same as those shown to Admiral Radford in Pearl Harbour in 1950.

These experiments were explained by the scientific community as due entirely to 'ion-momentum transfer,' or 'electric wind.' It was predicted categorically by many 'would-be' authorities that such an apparatus would not operate in vacuum. *The Navy rejected the research proposal (for further research) for this reason.* The experiments performed in Paris several years later, proved that ion wind was not entirely responsible for the observed motion and *proved quite conclusively that the apparatus would indeed operate in high vacuum.*

Later these effects were confirmed in a laboratory at Winston-Salem, N.C., especially constructed for this purpose. Again, continuous force was observed when the ionization in the medium surrounding the apparatus was virtually nil.

In reviewing my letter of April 5th I notice, in the drawings which I attached, that I specified the power supply to be

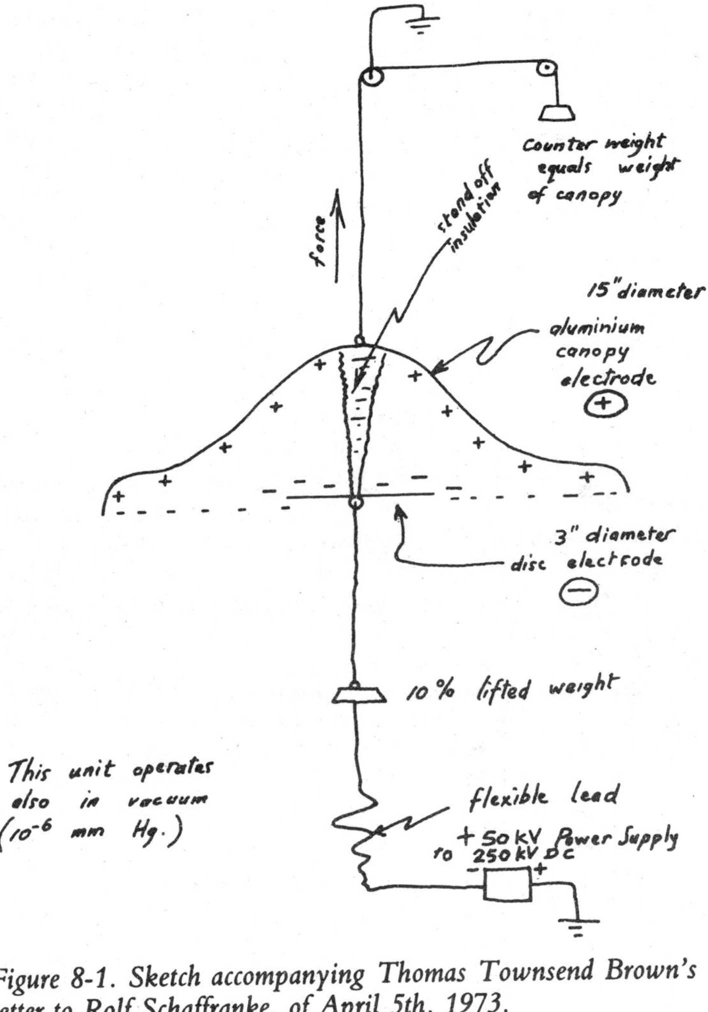

Figure 8-1. Sketch accompanying Thomas Townsend Brown's letter to Rolf Schaffranke, of April 5th, 1973.

50 KV. Actually, I should have indicated that it was 50 to 250 KV DC for the reason that the experiments were conducted throughout the entire range, (see figure 8-1). The higher the voltage, the greater was the force observed. It appeared that, in these rough tests, that the increase in force was approximately linear with voltage. In vacuum the same test was carried on with a canopy electrode approximately 6 inches in diameter, with substantial force being displayed at 150 KV DC. I have a short strip of movie film showing this motion within the vacuum chamber as the potential is applied.

There seems to be no doubt from the foregoing that Townsend-Brown did indeed discover an electro-gravitational linkage, though considerably more research would have been required to develop the effect into a usable, practical device. But this is the manner of all new research.

Man and His Artefacts

Let us for a moment make a short digression into the nature of man's artefacts.

Man has only five modes of sensory perception and five modes of action response. These modes of action and perception each have a mental analogue (or *indriya*, in yogic terminology) to energize and interact with the outward organs[1]. And since we have no other such mental aspects or functions, we are actually unable to conceive of any other possible instrumentation. Our instrumentation and devices, therefore, can be seen as having only ten possible major modes – five receptive or yin and five active or yang. Study the table in figure 8-2 for a while and you will see what is meant.

Sense Perception	*Examples of Instrumentation & Devices*	*Action Response & Devices*	*Examples of Instrumentation*
Eyes/Sight/Form & Colour	Cameras Lenses Television Instrument Panels	Ability & desire to move about using the legs especially	All kinds of vehicle transport
Ears/Hearing/ Sound	Microphones	Throat and Mouth/Speech	Loudspeakers Tape Recorders Audio Equipment Musical Instruments
Skin/Touch/ Feeling	Various tactile sensors	Hands/ Fingers/ Manipulation	Robotry Steering Controls
Tongue/Taste/ Flavour	Chemical testing of liquids & solids	Sexual activity	Sexual stimulation devices
Nose/Smell/Scent	Chemical testing of gases	Elimination	Enema & colonic equipment

Figure 8-2. Table showing the relationship between the five sensory perceptive mechanisms, the five motor responses and man's artefacts.

[1] This is fully discussed in my book, *The Web of Life*.

In fact, of these five yin and yang modes, it is clear that the majority of our day-to-day artefacts are largely concerned with replicating the functions of just the first three. On the sensory (yin) side, these are our seeing (eyes), hearing (ears) and feeling (skin). The corresponding motor responses (yang) are: moving about and going places (mostly using our legs), making communicative noises (mouth-throat), and physically manipulating our environment (mostly using our hands and arms).

Many human activities and artefacts clearly involve a mixture of these yin and yang modes, but I think you will find that there is no physical activity or sensation which does not fit into these five simple categories.

Eating, for instance, is a complex involving practically all of the above, while a book exists because of our faculty of sight as well as our mental capacity for language. It also requires the hands for manipulation in order to turn the pages. It may also involve the ears, throat and mouth, in reading aloud and in hearing.

Man's activities may appear to be complex, but actually he is only involved with extending capabilities with which nature has already endowed him. This is an expression of our tattvic constitution as discussed in chapter four and considerably expanded upon in *The Web of Life*. Basically, each sense organ and motor action arises as an interaction between the mind and the five tattwas in their subtle form, and in both their yin and yang aspects.

So our instruments and devices are always simplifications of individual skills or functions which we ourselves already possess, in some degree. Only a *living* human being can perform them all. Only man, or a *living* creature, has an inward consciousness. Only in consciousness can we be simultaneously aware of so many factors in our environment. Consciousness is the inward point of wholeness and integration, linking all our sensory and motor functions into one continuous experience. Our mind presents us with a divided universe, a place of pieces and parts. Consciousness tells us, through intuition within our mind, that the parts are integrated and connected into one whole. That they are all creations of the one whole. Consciousness is the inward essence of our life and being. It is what we really are. And our individual consciousness, however submerged into mind and matter it may have become, is a drop of the Universal Consciousness, the Supreme Being or God.

This inward spark of life is clearly missing in all our instrumentation. Hence its limitations. Even the most sophisticated of robots or devices behaves like an idiot and can only perform a limited range of functions as programmed and predetermined by human beings. The only adaptability to circumstance possessed by a computer-controlled device is that which has been foreseen by its human creators and preprogrammed into its construction. The gap between consciousness and inert devices is immense.

Consciousness, or the life force, is the only power that can control the tremendously complex biological, biochemical and physiological functioning of living bodies. It patterns, organizes and administers it. We are unaware or unconscious of the process because of the scattered activity of our mind. It is well-known, however, that by application of our concentrated attention, we can control bodily functions normally out of the range of consciousness. Biofeedback[1] experimentation has shown this quite conclusively, and interestingly enough, it is those who meditate – who are already conversant with inner methods of controlling and concentrating their minds – who prove to be the most successful subjects.

But when the soul or consciousness departs, no amount of cleverness on the part of the assembled humans is able to make that now dead body perform any of the functions that it possessed perhaps just a few seconds previously.

We may have been provided, as it were, with an almost perfect (not quite perfect, since the person or creature is

[1] Biofeedback is a goal-oriented technique where a subject attempts to mentally control his blood pressure or heart rate, for example – functions normally considered beyond the range of voluntary control. He receives reinforcement as to how well he is doing, usually through visual or auditory signals – flashing lights, gauges, changing musical tones and so on. It forcibly demonstrates the linkage of mind energy to biochemistry and physiology, though, in fact, so does bending a finger or performing any normal voluntary act. The same linkage underlies the placebo effect and all psychosomatic phenomena. Actually, the whole of physical life, on a continuous basis is determined by the existence of this mechanism.

dead!) body, once capable of expressing life, but yet we cannot make it perform *any* cogent function. Yet still we may not realize the totally different nature of the life force within from the gross physical body which is all that remains after death. But this inward life is our day-by-day *experience*. Nowhere is it possible physically to discover or actually perceive *any* of that *experience*. No one else can find, nor can we adequately express, just what it is to experience even the colour red. We may have agreed on a sound or word to express and communicate that experience. But the experience stays within and we have no way of knowing if what you experience as the colour red is the same as I experience, or if such a comparison even has any meaning.

All our sensory perceptions are within us, experienced in our mind, and all the dissection in the world will fail to find *any* of those daily (or nightly) experiences. All *experience of life* is within and beyond the ability of instrumentation to either mimic or monitor.

So it is within this context that we should understand the limitations of our devices and artefacts. They should be made for our human betterment, for our convenience and ease, to make life in this world more bearable.

The motivation of money, to exploit and tempt our fellow humans, to play on human weakness for our own personal motives of power or profit – these are unworthy and incorrect ways for humans to behave towards each other. This does not mean the introduction of state control – which is just another form of short-sighted manipulation for personal self-centered motivations. It means a universal understanding of relative values.

But this can only come when we humans realize our own innate spirituality within – when we begin to follow the natural law which includes kindness, tolerance, and an expanding consciousness, awareness of subtle vibration and atmosphere, contentment, control of all passions, humility, honesty and all the other virtues that make us happy and contented within. Ultimately, these are all expressions of great inward love – love as the fundamental quality of consciousness and life, not as an emotional sentiment, though the latter is a reflection of the former.

But this world has never been such a heaven and perhaps

it never will within the foreseeable future. But that does not excuse us from making no effort to improve our own inward condition. It is from changing ourselves that changes in social interactions and structures actually take place. We do not change the world for the better by setting out to do so, but by focusing our primary attention upon our own self-improvement – meditation, expansion of consciousness. Then we do what comes naturally from within and the world we relate to automatically changes. In this way we also avoid the increase of ego that automatically blocks further spiritual progress when we think that we are being of great personal value in this world. This is the ego of the 'professional' philanthropist, though no doubt the world needs such people.

Then, at least, we will take stock of our, so far, disastrous adventure into technology, which would appear to be in imminent danger of destroying much of the life on this planet. We have already eliminated large number of species without much thought or concern. This human ego and greed must be controlled. We must each honestly examine our true sense of values and then have the courage to act accordingly, within the context of our own sphere of life. And you will be amazed how much support you receive both from within and from your fellow humans when one makes such a determined effort.

John Searl's British Ether-Vortex Turbine[1]

The story of John R. R. Searl's work begins in the early 1950's. Back in 1949, at the age of seventeen, Searl was employed in Birmingham by the Midlands Electricity Board, working as an electrical engineer. He had no formal education in the subject other than the training provided by his employers, but was greatly intrigued by electricity, being largely self-taught. This can have its advantages, for one is not so readily indoctrinated with the preset ideas of the day. In fact, the great Michael Faraday was another with no formal scientific education and even

[1] This description is largely derived from a scientific report by Searl's associate P. L. Barrett B.Sc., published in Rolf Schaffranke's book, *Ether Technology*.

Einstein was working, not as a physicist, but in the patent office, when he published his first paper on relativity.

Actually, all courses of human 'knowledge' and science should be preceded by a disclaimer, pointing out that we humans do not really know very much, but this is the way it appears to us at the present time. And any improvements would be most welcome!

Anyway, experimenting with electrical motors and generators, Searl noticed that a small electromotive force (EMF) was generated in spinning metal parts. The negative charge was at the periphery, with the central axis becoming positively charged. He concluded that free electrons, (which possess a negative charge) were being spun, by centrifugal force, to the outside of the rotating slip rings which he was using, (see figure 8-3).

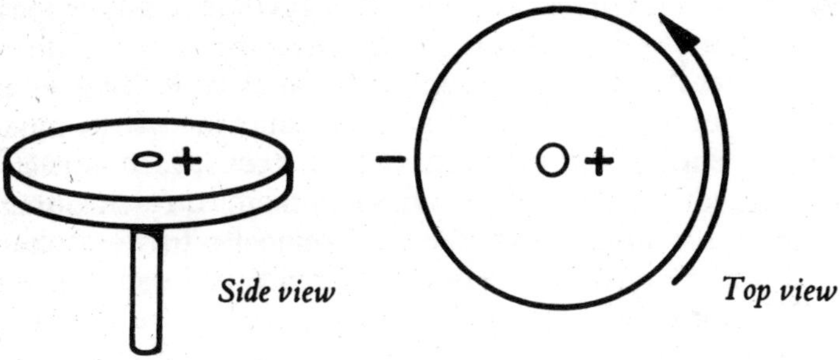

Figure 8-3. An EMF is produced by rotating a metal ring.

Deciding that the best material to use would be a good electrical conductor containing a large number of free electrons, he designed a generator based upon the principle, constructing a three foot disc which was provided with initial impetus by a central motor of conventional design. In addition, the rotating disc was segmented, with electromagnets installed around the periphery through which these rotating segments passed. These electromagnets were actually powered by the EMF created by the rotating disc and were intended to boost the EMF still further.

The initial and continuing driving impetus, however, came from the central initiating motor. So far, so good – this is quite conventional thinking and a rather neat idea for the production of electrical power from free electrons[1].

This work is of historic interest only, however, indicating the way Searl was thinking, for his breakthrough, if such it was, appears to have come from his work with magnets in a similar rotating device.

Searl discovered an unusual magnetic phenomenon, but one which is still within the bounds of standard magnetic theory, (though the theory does not tell us how magnetism *arises*, just how it *behaves* most of the time).

He prepared two bar magnets in which the polarity was from top to bottom, rather than from end to end, (see figure 8-4). These are placed one on top of the other. Then, two short and stubby cylindrical magnets are placed alongside the two bars, as shown. Since north attracts south and vice versa, these two magnets stick to the sides of the bars by normal magnetic attraction.

Magnet A is then given a push, as shown. Rolling along the side of the bars it reaches and rounds the sharp, right-angled corners at the end. As it does so, magnet B spontaneously begins to move away from it. As magnet A continues rolling down the side opposite to its starting position, magnet B also moves around the other end.

The two magnets now oscillate rapidly at about 10 oscillations per second, up and down the two sides, until finally after two or three minutes they come to rest in central positions opposite to their original starting points. The initial impetus and energy for movement is supplied by hand and the magnetic attraction and repulsion modifies the course of this original input.

Now although this effect can be demonstrated using normal ferrite, permanent magnets, Searl actually used magnets of an unusual composition and they were also treated in a special way during manufacture.

To understand what might be going on we need to understand a little concerning the nature of magnetism. The magnetic effect can be traced to the spin of unpaired electrically charged electrons in the atoms of magnetic

[1]Searl's explanation of centrifugal force and free electrons may not, in fact, be correct. The phenomenon is real, but could also be due to an induced electric current arising as the conductor is rotated in the earth's magnetic field. This is described by standard electromagnetic theory.

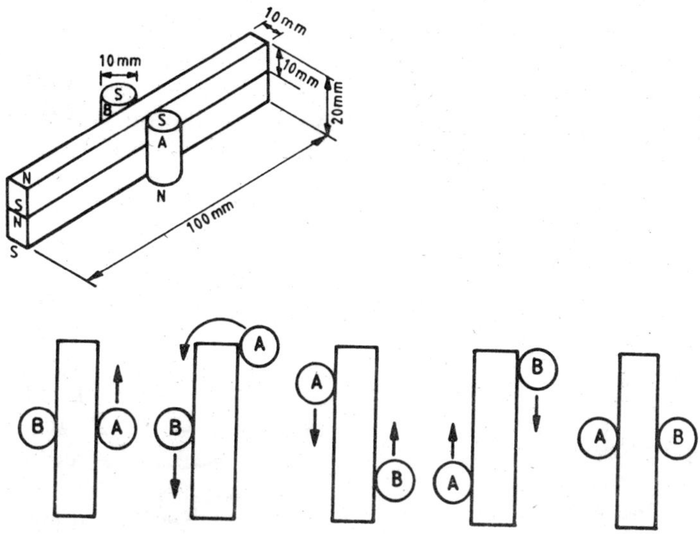

Figure 8-4. John Searl's magnet experiment. Two cylindrical magnets roll around two bar-shaped magnets which are placed on top of each other. They need to be started in motion by hand.

materials. Magnetization is the process of aligning these atoms, creating the macroscopically observable effect we call magnetism. But the particular treatment given by Searl to these magnets is assumed to give some further alignment or ordering, perhaps to other aspects of the spinning motion of the electrons.

Normal magnets, for example, absorb microwave radiation,. and it is assumed that the energy so absorbed is either translated into angular, kinetic motion within the electrons or results in their adopting new energy states. The exact nature of the treatment unfortunately remains confidential, but it is most probably something along these lines.

Using these specially treated magnets, Searl then modified his original experiment. He had quickly realized that forming the bars into an anulus (a ring) would considerably reduce the friction which caused the rollers in his first experiment to come to a rapid halt, because much energy was expended in friction and in going around the right-angled corners, (see figure 8-5a).

In this he was successful beyond his wildest imaginings, for he discovered, so he says, that when the number of rolling magnets goes beyond a certain minimum number, they continue to rotate *indefinitely*, (see figure 8-5b).

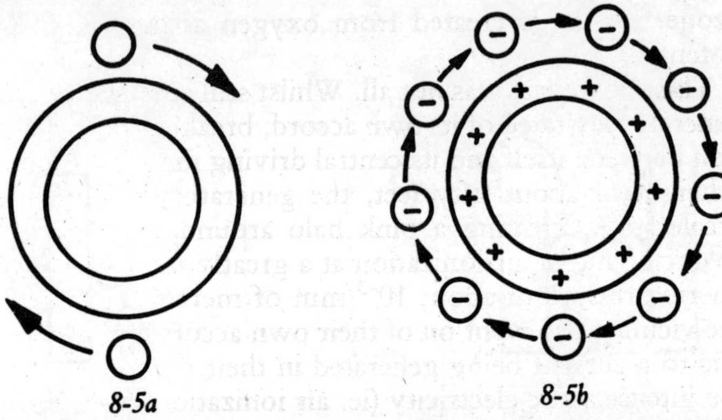

8-5a 8-5b

Figure 8-5. Searl's arrangement for continuous rotation of cylindrical magnets around a magnetic anulus. A high electrostatic charge is said to develop between the rollers and the ring. The design of the roller track allows them to be kept separate from the anulus by centrifugal force, preventing a discharge of the electrostatic potential. At the high potentials developed, however, one would expect a flashover, like lightning, equalizing the charges. This is yet another anomalous aspect.

And more than that – an electrostatic potential also develops between the rollers and the anulus.

Neither the continuous rotation, nor the electrostatic voltage can be described using standard magnetic theory. But there was yet a third, even more intriguing, anomalous effect. Beyond a certain threshold of rotational speed and electrostatic differential, Searl claims that *the whole device decreases in its effective weight*. That is, it interacts with the gravitational field.

Searl therefore built a circular device in which the initial rotational movement was provided by a central motor. In addition, he used three concentric sets of magnetic rings and rollers, like three ball-races, one inside the other.

By 1952, the first machine had been built, with Searl and

a friend testing the generator in the open. They were not, however, prepared for what happened next. The rotating disc was set in motion and the expected electrostatic difference was generated, but at an unexpectedly high potential in the region of 10^5 volts. Nearby objects exhibited the effects of static electricity, while the accelerating rotor crackled and emitted a characteristic smell of ozone. Ozone is created from oxygen at high electrical potentials.

This, however, was not all. Whilst still accelerating, the generator levitated of its own accord, breaking the connection between itself and its central driving motor. Rising to a height of about fifty feet, the generator continued its acceleration, creating a pink halo around itself. This is characteristic of air ionization at a greatly reduced atmospheric pressure of about 10^{-3} mm of mercury. Radios in the vicinity also went on of their own accord, presumably due to a current being generated in their circuits through the intense static electricity (ie. air ionization, a multitude of electrically charged air molecules) or because of electrical currents induced by the intense EMF.

Finally, the entire generator accelerated at such a speed and generated so much lift that it disappeared from view at a fantastic velocity and is thought to have disappeared into outer space!

Since then, Searl and others have made more than ten such craft, all of which have been similarly lost. Larger craft, of twelve foot diameter, have also been constructed and two of thirty foot diameter. Considering the sheer weight of the magnets, these craft must have been pretty heavy and Searl states that the more the mass, the greater the levitational effect. Mass is somehow being persuaded to exhibit anti-mass effects – and the more you have, the more the effect!

One immediately asks why Searl's work is not known on a world-wide basis. The answer is that he *is* known about in government circles as well as to some scientists. His levitating device, however, contravenes the descriptions of nature's processes given by conventional physics, so university and government scientists are naturally reluctant to put their jobs and reputations on the line by showing an interest in what is essentially a flying saucer!

There may well have been other suppressing pressures brought to bear, too, about which we can only surmise, but clearly the craft has both military applications as well as a strong potential to upset the huge international energy and transport industries. Reason enough, perhaps, for powerful people to wish to suppress such information and technology, though actually the greatest 'suppressant' of all is sheer mental inertia or habit. Everyone is so busy with the activities of their own life that even potentially world-shaking discoveries are almost unconsciously ignored. They may be heard about, even receive temporary public acclaim, but are soon forgotten unless they happen to impinge in some material way upon the course of an individual's life.

Perhaps I should tell you here of a true story related to a highly reliable and honest friend of mine. A friend of his, a homoeopathic doctor, while upon a trip to South America – a subcontinent with an especially rich herbal flora – returned with a herb which when taken prevented a woman from becoming pregnant for a period of about one year. A useful herb, you will agree. What its biochemical constitution is I do not know, but it is well known that a number of herbs contain steroids very similar in structure to female oestrogen (sex) hormones. Presumably this herb possesses properties along these lines.

Having established a source of the herb, he was engaged upon the necessary research and trials to place it on the market when, one day, a gentleman in a grey suit walked into his consulting room. "I represent XXXX[1]", said the gentleman. "We have heard that you are intending to market a powerful contraceptive herb. We will give you $10,000 not to do so. If you do go ahead, you will be killed." The good homoeopath accepted neither the pay-off nor the offer of murder – he withdrew his plans in preference of a quiet life. Discretion is the better part of valour, and the story demonstrates the lengths to which vested interests will go to protect their activities from financial erosion.

[1]Unfortunately, to quote the name of this large international business organization with interests in the contraceptive industry might lay me open to charges of libel, since (although true), the evidence is 'only anecdotal'.

Returning from this cautionary tale to that of John Searl, his device demonstrates the following characteristics:

1. Anti-gravity or levitation.
2. Extremely high electrostatic gradients.
3. An odd magnetic effect, in addition to the electrostatic effect, which induces electrical currents in closed loop conductors, even when there is no relative movement. This implies a production of energy from an 'unknown' and apparently unlimited source. This source, one imagines, is the energy inherent in the vacuum state.
4. Once past a certain threshold, the power output exceeds the power input. The machine therefore exhibits *perpetual motion*. The energy is again derived, presumably, from the vacuum ocean, so the laws of energy conservation, or of getting something for nothing, are not violated. Their extent, however, does need to be re-understood and enlarged. The estimated power output is in the region of 10^{13} to 10^{15} watts. That is about a million, million times as much power as is used by a 100 watt electric light bulb.
5. Again, above this threshold, the generator appears to possess no *inertia*. This brings us back to our various comments concerning the nature of *mass*, another of those fundamental and curious properties of matter. Note that *mass*, the resistance of a body to being placed in motion, or its inertia, is *different* from its *weight*. Weight is the attraction of one body to another due to *gravity*. That is what keeps us from zooming off into outer space when we jump up in the air. Generally speaking, weight and mass are considered to possess equal values. But in space, for example, it is clear that they are different. For while astronauts and their equipment are *weightless* (no appreciable gravitational attraction), they are not *massless*. It still requires an effort to push something and to get it moving. This is its inertia. Conversely, since gravity is an attraction between masses, if an object is *massless*, it will experience no gravitational attraction. That is, it will also be weightless.

So for Searl's device to somehow nullify inertia, or mass, relative to the surrounding space, is of fascinating importance. For the effort then required to accelerate the craft would be almost zero – the only drag would be that of friction against air, or the medium in which or upon which, it was moving. In space, or in a vacuum, when no such drag or friction would be applied, infinite accelerations would be possible.

Can we accept this facet of Searl's machine? Well, do we really know what mass and gravity actually are? We do not. As we have pointed out, having a mathematical formula or equation to describe something or its relationships does not constitute a knowledge of what that thing is, *of itself*.

6. By controlling the distribution of electrical potential upon the surface of the craft, the whole device can be steered. The generator itself automatically orientates itself at right angles to the planetary gravitational field. It thus has an inherent tendency to shoot off into space. When forced to fly in a horizontal direction by control of the electrostatic potential, the craft adopts an attitude suggesting a balance between its own self-generated field and that of the earth's gravitational field. It is suggested, therefore, that the craft may thus create its own gravitational and/or inertial field.
7. The air around the device becomes heavily ionized, due to the electrostatic charge. There is nothing unusual about this. In fact, the charge is so intense that the air is repelled, (like charges repell each other as do like magnetic poles), causing a near-vacuum around the generator. This is an added bonus since it reduces atmospheric friction and subsequent problems with overheating.
8. Searl also noticed that after working near his craft or generators, that dielectric materials such as his own body tissues, developed a *permanent electrical polarity*. This is analagous to the permanent north and south poles of a magnet. Recently, some research has been conducted into the use of permanently charged dielectric materials. The phenomenon is reasonably

well understood, in a conventional way, but it means that Searl's device is able to permanently affect the condition and movement of subatomic particles in nearby materials.

9. When the craft is stationary, upon the ground, and is suddenly switched on, it takes with it a neat round hole of earth, as it rises up, leaving a familiar sign of its presence. Similarly, Barrett reports that if the craft hovers too long above the ground, the soil gets burnt due to the inducement of electric currents in it, creating heat out of electrical resistance, (another interesting phenomenon when viewed from the point of view of vacuum manifestation). The nervous system of living creatures is also disturbed as one can readily imagine.

Searl, of course, became quite obsessed with his research, leading eventually to the breakdown of his marriage in 1982–83. He is a person of tremendous enthusiasm and although almost all of those who have spoken to him are convinced of his sincerity, he does not possess a detailed theoretical knowledge of how his devices worked. One could equally say the same of all electrical devices even today. In the absence of any complete idea of what an electron is, or how nature herself comes into being, we are using the forces of nature blindly.

So Searl, like many inventors before him, was essentially working from an intuitively inspired empiricism. The theorists normally come in afterwards to model the phenomena and provide the ground for further experimentation. The destruction of his notes, therefore, was disastrous for he cannot reproduce his work from first principles.

Searl's descriptions are largely general and non-technical, leading some people to question his honesty. Others who have visited him, however, have noted his sincerity, generosity of spirit and sense of responsibility both for those working for him as well as for all the peoples of our planet.

Intuition, Higher Mind and the Source of Insight

Searl has commented frequently that much of the intuition of how to proceed, came to him in dreams. It is an experience common to many of us that our unconscious mind is clearly active on a problem even when we are unaware of it. Frequently, one may awake in the morning with a clear understanding of a solution to some difficulty which was bothering us the previous day. "I'll sleep on it," is a common expression embodying this experience.

Similarly, it is often when the mind is relaxed and has temporarily left off the intricate and detailed, logical and intellectual pursuit of a solution that the answer comes to us. "Eureka", we cry (perhaps), as we lie in semi-somnulescent torpor in a hot and steamy bath.

As we have said, this world is actually patterned and formed by the Formative Mind. Mind, too, has many levels between our human mind and the Universal Mind. So the mind within us knows all the answers, though not in intellectual form. This is really part of our uncharted superconsciousness, rather than subconscious. And this *higher mind* structure constitutes our intuition.

Out of an egocentric, intellectual, and unconsciously emotional, mental pressure, we cut ourselves off from the source of enlightenment upon many issues in our daily lives, as well as the answers to many scientific and philosophical conundrums.

So, as a technique, we can learn to actually make conscious requests of our inner or higher mind to show us the clear path to follow, even on matters in the forefront of human scientific endeavour. This is where scientific insights come from, anyway, and it is to this ocean we must return for further realization. We can, therefore, simply ask our higher mind for the answers and then wait for the response to come through, which it does, often when we least expect it. We do, of course, need to maintain the discrimination and understanding that our mind can also mislead us. We do not know where any of our thoughts come from, and simply taking any old rubbish that comes into our head as the truth, (even 'divinely' inspired, 'channelled' or 'from the other side'!), is a sure recipe for disaster. People call it 'kidology', or simply fooling yourself and others! I do not say that no-one is ever guided by conscious powers from within. Quite the reverse. But that does not mean that we should abrogate all responsibility and common sense to the whims of our own imaginings.

We have to develop our discrimination.

Humility, absence of ego, is the key – sitting down before nature's secrets as a little child and humbly requesting enlightenment. If I have, in the back or forefront of my mind an egocentric desire that I should work it out for myself, for display to all mankind (and maybe even win a Nobel prize), then I close the doors to the real source of inspiration. Then the patterns of the higher mind cannot infiltrate the tightly wound up human mind.

So if Searl obtained his understanding in dreams, there is nothing unusual in that. Our inner human mind contains vast realms which we cannot understand intellectually. Dreams are just one way in which our higher mind can gain access to our tightly locked-in, human state of ignorance, leaving fleeting bursts of realization, flashes of insight which could, if we only knew how, be our daily and continuous experience.

In Search of the Electro-Gravitic Threshold

The reader will no doubt have noticed that both Searl's and Townsend-Brown's work involved extremely high electrostatic potentials. But while Brown's gravitors demonstrated an effect that was never turned into a usable craft, Searl's discovery of a relationship between his special magnets and the development of high electrostatic potential, gave his generator the ability to reach the threshold beyond which enough energy was extracted or converted out of the vacuum state to make it more than self-propelling and self-sustaining. But the practical problem is again one of control and refinement.

Note, too, how Searl's anti-gravitational effect is also produced by a differential in electrostatic charge. So there is a probability that, like Townsend-Brown's work, part of the effect is due to electrostatic thrust and air ionization. But this is clearly not all. This high electrostatic potential seems to be a characteristic requirement of these electro-gravitational devices. And it is understandable, for it is a separation of polarity which produces energy potential or strain within any energy system.

So the strain builds up, until at certain thresholds, it gives way to a change in state or energetic activity, just as substances *suddenly* become solid, liquid or gaseous as their temperature gradually rises or falls and the atoms or molecules rapidly assume a different arrangment to each other. They do not change slowly into a range of semi-gaseous or semi-liquid or semi-solid states, but when the strain (in this case temperature, that is atomic and molecular vibration) reaches a certain threshold (determined by other factors such as the mechanical pressure on the substance), the change of state or inward energetic condition is suddenly flipped into another state.

Generally speaking, when one or more factors or constraints are applied or added to any energy system, it is characteristic of nature's processes to attempt to include the new factors within the existing equilibrium. When, however, the new factors or input energy push the system beyond the point at which the old kind of equilibrium can be maintained, then – rather than becoming chaotic – nature reconfigures or reorganizes herself into a different state of equilibrium. Nature has an in-built preference for order and equilibrium, everything is arranged that way.

In recent years, this principle has been observed and analyzed by Ilya Prigogine in his work on the thermodynamics of chaotic or non-equilibrium systems, and for which he received a Nobel prize in 1977.

There is, however, an underlying, more inward pattern and what we observe as this tendency in nature towards equilibrium is underlain by the extended causality of the One within the many. It is part of the way in which the polarity of opposites or the world of duality is manifested.

This is true of *any* system in nature, since everything is energy. And it as much includes sociological circumstances, psychological states, the balance of our planetary ecosystem and the interplay of mind and spirit in human affairs, as it does the interrelationship of atoms, molecules and thermal agitation in the solid, liquid and gaseous states.

Similarly, it seems probable that the inherent relationship of electrical charge, gravity and magnetism, normally hidden within the vacuum matrix comes into play as an outwardly observable phenomenon when certain criteria of charge and motion are reached. At or above a particular threshold the system flips into a new equilibrium in which the relationship of gravity and electromagnetism is outwardly manifested when previously it was hidden.

Note also that although Searl's original experimentation required rotation or motion to generate this important differential in electrical charge, the circular motion of the magnetic rollers seems to play an essential part in creating the effects. Searl therefore stumbled upon his effect almost unwittingly.

In fact, is some respects, Searl's craft bears resemblances to the electrical configuration of an atom. Others have noted the same feature and the theme is taken up by modern work on levitating gyroscopes, discussed in chapter ten. Are we witnessing an accumulative, macroscopic effect of subatomic ordering? Just like the magnetic field surrounding individual electrons sum together in the magnetic field of a magnet?

You will also recall that this motion was an inherent aspect of the gravitational effects discovered by Dr Erwin Saxl in his original experiments with a moving pendulum, even in the absence of charge. When he applied an electrostatic charge, the effects were even more pronounced.

John Searl's generator, therefore, includes the gravitational effects demonstrated by Townsend Brown due to variation in electrostatic charge, the change in gravitation due to movement as described by Dr Erwin Saxl. It also demonstrates the threshold, or change of state, which Townsend Brown also experienced. Perhaps we can believe Searl when he maintains that all the craft he has ever built have disappeared into outer space!

The report by P. L. Barrett, as printed in Rolf Schaffranke's book, also discusses some of the theory by which they attempted to explain Searl's effect. He also refers amusingly to games Searl played with unsuspecting motorists, as well as with electrical power lines. It seems that Barrett was a civil servant and a member of Searl's team. Searl, however, did not completely trust him, feeling that he was intending to steal his secrets and, indeed, Barrett did later move to the U.S.A., where he filed at least one patent based upon Searl's work. Nothing practical, however, appears to have come of it.

Furthermore, Barrett suggests that Searl's craft does not pass *through* space, but "carries its own space with it." It travels *past* space, he says. Clearly we need to experiment more with such devices, developing concepts and mathematical models which help us to understand the energetic structure of vacuum.

Barrett's theory is of ether flux and he too suggests that a threshold is reached within the fabric of space or vacuum when it is strained or stressed with high electrostatic or magnetic potentials, such that the generator develops its own gravitational and inertial field effects. Also, when stressed in such a way, the vacuum matrix relieves its stress by releasing its energy as further electric charge. In Searl's generator, this energy is fed back into itself, increasing the stress until the critical threshold is reached where gravitational and inertial field effects take place.

This is analagous to the critical threshold required for an atomic chain reaction to occur, leading to an atomic explosion, with a huge release of energy. Remember that even in the 1930's, Rutherford and other distinguished scientists wrote that it was impossible to extract energy from the atomic nucleus because you needed to put more energy in (to create the fission) than you could ever get out. This was even in the presence of Einstein's famous formula of $e = mc^2$, the energy(e) in mass(m) equals that mass multiplied by the square of the speed of light(c).

In fact, a short time before the first atomic bomb was exploded over Hiroshima, Admiral William D. Lacey, Chief of Staff to the American President expressed his opinion, that it, "Is the biggest fool thing we have ever done. The bomb will never go off, and I speak as an expert in explosives." (*Truman Memoirs*)

We all have a natural and healthy question mark in our minds over new ideas and concepts. It is healthy for as long as it is a part of honest enquiry rather than prejudice, reflecting an unconscious desire to cling to habituated thought patterns. But the time does come when those same ideas are commonplace and are even taught to school children – until once more replaced by other 'new' ideas.

One final detail needs to be covered. Where is Searl today and what has become of his research? Well, he is still alive and very much kicking! Searl continued his private research from his home in Mortimer, Berkshire. During the early 1970's, he is reported to have been flying his levity discs and the *Sunday Mirror* of November 28th 1971 even printed a photograph (see figure 8-6) and a short story. I have several negatives of Searl's disc in flight, but cannot, unfortunately, be certain of their authenticity or otherwise.

Figure 8-6. Searl and his flying saucer. This photograph is very similar to the one published in the Sunday Mirror *of November 28th 1971. Authenticity unknown.*

There is no doubt, from photographs taken at his home workshop, that at least some of the flying discs were of considerable size and it is not altogether surprising that in

1982 some trouble with the Electricity Board culminated in the break up of his marriage and family. That must have been the final straw – such obsessive inventors cannot be the easiest of people to live with.

Searl had to move from his home in Mortimer and until very recently, he has had no real facilities with which to continue his research. Moreover, he was not a professionally trained scientist and never kept adequate notes of his work, so it is difficult for others to repeat what he has done. He himself worked empirically and intuitively, never really understanding how his devices worked. This is no deep criticism, for all of our modern electrical and electronics technology has beed created without a clear understanding of the real nature of an electron. Or – in more general terms – we can play about with the energy patterns of the universe without ever coming to understand how they are maintained in existence or how they ever got there in the first place.

But in the emotional mayhem of his family problems, many of his notes and much of his equipment got thrown out or burnt. So little is left of his experiments but what lies in his memory – *and* – twenty to twenty-five of his special magnets which he guards with the greatest care!

All the same, the latest news is very encouraging. Searl's work is being actively researched by the Californian company, Hydro-Stack, whose president Devon Tassen, committed $250,000 in 1988 to the production of a prototype domestic power unit, based on Searl's work. They have installed a magnet press, plus the electronics required for the special manufacturing treatment and the first magnets have already been successfully produced.

Meanwhile, research has been initiated at one of our British universities, though due to ongoing discussions of funding with international industrial concerns, they are unable to reveal details of the present state of progress. Searl himself, now in his late 50's, is living in London, has formed his own company, DISC, and was interviewed on BBC Daytime Live TV on October 28th, 1988. The story has not yet ended.

—— CHAPTER 9 ——

An Abundance of Free Energy

More Free Energy Devices

We have discussed, at some length, the work of Tesla, Thomas Townsend Brown and John Searl, but they are not the only ones who appear to have got particular devices actually working. In fact, doing a rapid count of all the work I know of, over twenty different free energy devices must have been built over the past few decades, demonstrating the phenomenon of vacuum energy translation. And many are working at this very time, though in varying stages of development.

In fact, the third international New Energy Technology symposium and exhibition was held from June 25th – June 28th, 1988 where many of these devices were demonstrated or discussed. This exciting meeting and focal point was held in Ottawa, Canada, organized by the Planetary Association For Clean Energy. So we will now venture in to the world of some of these other inventors and see what further common factors emerge.

Dr T. Henry Moray and His Radiant Energy Device

Dr Henry Moray was an American electrical engineer and inventor who worked from 1909 to 1943 on the development of what became known to him as 'Radiant Energy.' The heart of his device utilized a component (known as a Moray valve) consisting of a semiconducting heterojunction (a complex interface) using ultra-pure germanium. This was long before the days of the transistor, where the semiconducting properties of germanium have been extensively exploited. During the 1930's, Dr Moray applied for several patents. These, however, were rejected on the grounds that a cold semiconductor cathode could not emit sufficient electrons. The development of the transistor some two decades later demonstrated that Moray's central component could actually operate just as he had described it.

During this time Moray demonstrated his device to numerous interested people and a company was actually formed for its commercial development. Considerable interest was aroused, which ultimately led to his harrassment and to repeated threats. In fact, Dr Moray was actually shot in his laboratory in 1940 and remained the subject of frequent threats until he retired from active research in 1943.

Further attempts to secure government funding during the 1950's and 1960's failed, largely due to Dr Moray's insistence upon secrecy. The government were naturally unwilling to put up funds without adequate explanations of how they were to be used and without receiving a share in the results.

Dr Moray utilized a multi-stage system in which the first stage required a primary power input to excite initial current oscillations in the first stage of the circuit. This oscillation was then tuned to the frequency of the 'energies of the universe'. The resulting resonance resulted in an increase of amplitude and hence power. The peaks of these amplified oscillations were allowed to 'spill over' into the second stage, where the same process was repeated. Continuous stages were added until usable power was generated of suitable frequency, voltage and current.

By this time, the device had become self-sustaining as long as it remained correctly synchronized and in resonance with the natural frequencies of Moray's *Sea of Energy* or radiant energy field, and as long as the external power produced was correctly handled.

Moray conducted numerous public demonstrations but no one was ever able to detect any evidence of fraud. His device, as demonstrated, was silent and possessed no moving parts. A potential difference of 225,000 volts could be generated between the primary terminals and a characteristic smell of ozone accompanied its operation, indicating voltages in excess of 10,000 volts. Once running, it required no further power input and ran with no apparent heating up, producing between 10,000 and 50,000 watts from a unit weighing no more than sixty pounds.

Moray's *Sea of Radiant Energy* is, no doubt, our vacuum sea of zero point energy and it is interesting that he felt that the physical universe possessed constant rhythms of oscillation within this sea, which could be utilized for the amplification of electrical potential, when tuned correctly. This, of course, cannot be the whole story for the transformation of that energy into usable electrical polarity must surely require something more than just fine tuning. Perhaps, the Moray valve or one-way gating device to trap vacuum energy as electrical potential was also required. Actually, it has never been made sufficiently clear whether Moray's valve was 'simply' a regular amplifying transistor, but two decades ahead of its time, or whether it was something even more sophisticated – gating vacuum energy into usable electrical power.

As we have seen, Tesla also worked with high voltages and planned to put the whole earth into resonance, so that anyone, anywhere, could tap into the electrical vibration for their free power source. No wonder J. P. Morgan, one of the greatest, power-hungry, money-motivated, mega-industrialists at the turn of the century, with deep financial interests in the energy industry, finally withdrew his backing from Tesla's Wardenclyffe Tower project. Maybe he also thought that Tesla had really gone over the top this time. Either way, Morgan had nothing to gain by his continued support of Tesla and being a man more interested in profit and personal fortune, no altruistic thoughts or even sheer scientific curiosity would have driven him to the continued support of what would have appeared to him as a risk enterprise.

And perhaps it was a good thing too. I shudder to think of the health implications of such total electrification of the earth, if Tesla's scheme had worked. I am already concerned with the zapping of all our planetary atmosphere with radio, TV and microwave radar signals, what to say of global, vacuum state resonance!

Anyhow, Moray died, taking his secrets with him, and though his son continues to encourage scientists to follow up his work, no one to this day has been able to rebuild the machine. The main problem seems to be reconstruction of the Moray valve.

Perhaps, like John Keely, described in my book *Subtle Energy*, Moray's own distinctive subtle energy patterns were an essential factor in the equation and were somehow input to his own device, through the strength of his own mental intent and purpose.

Howard Johnson's Permanent Magnet Motor

In the Spring 1980 edition of *Science and Mechanics*, a report was made of a new kind of motor, patented in 1979, by Howard R. Johnson of the U.S.A. At that time, "A 5000 watt permanent magnet powered generator is already on the way and Johnson has firm licensing commitments with at least four companies." Howard Johnson's motor does exist, does work and is the subject of considerable scientific controversy.

Conventional electric motors, whether AC or DC operate through employing electromagnets to act upon one another to create usable power. Similarly, permanent magnets can be used to convert their magnetism into mechanical motive force in suitable materials (iron, for example), thereby performing physical work. Conventional scientific wisdom states, however, that no usable work can be derived from the sole use of permanent magnets. The possibility of such a motor has, however, been considered for a long time and its beauty is that it is powered, not by connection to an electrical supply, but purely by the energy of magnetism. Johnson's is the first device which appears to work, though some scientific theoreticians are sceptical of it since it seems to violate the laws of conservation of energy, as they are presently understood.

This, however, is no problem to those who understand the vacuum state energy field. Magnetism is actually known to be associated with the unpaired electron spin characteristic of magnetic materials and one possibility is that the energy is extracted from this kinetic spin energy within the electron. When Johnson was asked whether such spin was being diminished during the operation of his motor, he replied "I didn't start the electron spins and don't know any way to stop them – do you?" 'Perpetual motion' seems already to be an intrinsic aspect of nature.

Hans Coler's Permanent Magnet Energy Generator

Permanent magnet energy machines are by no means new. As long ago as 1925, the German researcher, Hans Coler, built a device which generated a 10 watt output. Professor Kloss of Berlin University asked the German government to give it a thorough investigation, but both the investigation and a patent were refused on the grounds that it was a "perpetual motion machine" and therefore "impossible."

In 1933, however, Coler built a 70 watt version and found some good commercial backing. By 1937, he was running a model with 6000 watt output, continuing his research throughout the war years under the auspices of the German Admiralty.

In 1945, Coler's apparatus was destroyed by a bomb attack on the city of Kolborg. The Allies, however, were not without knowledge of his work, probably because of his connections with the German Admiralty. So after the war, Coler was duly visited and interrogated by British Intelligence. He even obligingly built a small working model for them, consisting only of permanent magnets, copper coils and electrical condensers.

The resulting British Intelligence report, from which this information is summarized, was written in 1946 and declassifed in 1962. Valuable and interesting technical details were also supplied with this report, but the nature of Coler's theoretical explanations are not clearly stated. In fact, the author admits tht he could not follow them. Mention is made, however, of "space electrons," so perhaps Coler was yet another who saw things in terms of a spacial matrix of energy.

Dr Shiuji Inomata and Japanese New Science

> The twenty-first century is expected to be an era of new science, during which the development of the precognitive and telepathic powers of mankind through the energy of consciousness and shadow may well become possible.

So writes Dr Shiuji Inomata in his article on *Psychotronics*, printed in the New Science section of the prestigious 1988 Japanese *Yearbook of High Technology and Science*. Dr Inomata was also good enough to write one of the two forewords to this book. The Japanese clearly take New Science seriously.

The *Yearbook* is divided up as follows:

1. Fine Chemicals
2. New Ceramics
3. Superconductivity
4. New Generation Computers
5. Artificial Intelligence
6. **New Science**
7. Medicine
8. Biological Engineering
9. Computer Chemistry
10. Bio-Science

Section 6 on **New Science** further contains:

6.1 Consciousness and Matter (S. Sasaki)
6.2 Biofeedback Method (K. Shiga)
6.3 Electromagnetic Field Combustion (E. Fujita)
6.4 Qigong (S. Nakazaki)
6.5 Generation of Electric Power by Magnetic Motor (K. Minato)
6.6 Remote Viewing (T. Aoki)
6.7 Earthquake Prediction by Measurement of Electric Potential in Plants
6.8 Asakawa Effect and its Application (K. Suzuki)
6.9 Psychotronics (S. Inomata)

In 1987, Dr Inomata published his book, *Paradigm of New Science – Principia for the Twenty-First Century*, which is presently being translated into English. The book has been so popular that it sold out of its first two editions within just a few months. This demonstrates the readiness of the Japanese to accept and understand concepts concerning the vacuum state. Ciba-Geigy, who have international research laboratories in Tokyo, take Dr Inomata very seriously and in the spring of 1988 financed a trip for him to talk to a group of people at their international headquarters in Switzerland. From there he made a short trip to London where I had the good fortune to meet him and his wife along with a small number of scientists who had collected together for the purpose. Gunnar Sandberg from the University of Sussex was there, as was Arthur Ellison, professor of electrical engineering at London's City University and president of the British Psychic Research Association. We had a fascinating day.

Dr Inomata has worked in many research areas, including acoustics, speech research, bionics, robotics and psychotronics, and since 1972 has been engaged in reorganizing contemporary mass-energy physics to include what he calls 'consciousness' parameters. He is presently the senior scientist at MITI's Electrotechnical Laboratory, and president of the Japan Psychotronics Institute (JPI). So Dr Inomata is highly qualified, is presently active in research, posesses a keen and lively intelligence, and is, in addition, a kind man, of humble mien.

His model is one of the vacuum state as a real energy field, which he also calls *shadow energy*, *virtual energy* or *pan-psychist consciousness*. He also envisages it to be the same as the Chinese *Ch'i*, or the *void* of Buddhism. My own understanding is that this vacuum energy field, though impressed and patterned by the mind into becoming what we perceive, is not conciouness itself, but only a gateway in the grand, inner hierarchy of the creation.

But as regards the mathematics and physical implications of Dr Inomata's theory, this difference has little relevance.

Dr Inomata has set about reworking the equations of electromagnetism and gravity to include the vacuum energy, which he designates as Q – the substrate from which all other physically manifested energies are derived. This includes Einstein's famous $e = mc^2$. Dr Inomata's basic relationships can be seen in figure 9-1.

On the basis of this triangle of relationships, Dr Inomata goes on to mathematically integrate its various implications into the world of electromagnetic and gravitational theory, and thermodynamics. He is quick to point out, too, that his model provides the energy transmutations required to scientifically understand some paranormal events, especially psychokinesis, and the manifestation and de-manifestation of tangible objects. This includes the metal-bending antics of Uri Geller and the host of children who have also turned out to possess paranormal abilities.

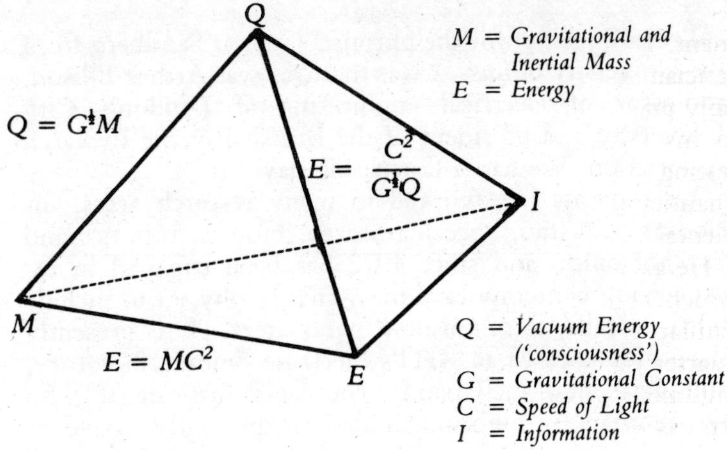

Figure 9-1. Dr Inomata's Mass-Energy-Consciousness Triangle, with his conversion formulae. Note how information (I) is a derivative, connected to all three of these.

In a report printed in Britain's *Nature* magazine, for example, it was stated that under the influence of Uri Geller's mind energy, part of a semi-conductive material inside a sealed capsule had disappeared.

Dr Inomata's vacuum state theory permits us to quantify exactly how much increased vacuum energy this disappearance would have occasioned, for the energy of mass and substance was not destroyed, only transmuted into the shadow, virtual or vacuum state.

Similarly, it was reported during that same period that the mass of a spoon, bent by a boy with paranormal powers, had decreased by three milligrams. Again, mass had been withdrawn back into the energy of the vacuum. With the new vacuum state theory there is absolutely no problem in understanding this.

In one of his papers concerning the polarities within the vacuum state, Dr Inomata concludes:

> It goes without saying that the image of a vacuum as a sea of positive and negative energies also conforms to that of eastern philosophy which says that vacuum is a sea of Ch'i, governed by the negative and positive principles of yin and yang.

One of the beauties of Dr Inomata's presentation is that it works through from the theory to practice and experiment. Dr Inomata is both experimenter as well as theoretician. The mathematics of his theory, for example, not only predict the Biefield-Brown effect (which he discusses in his book), but also quantifies it. Full experimental testing of this effect, therefore, is capable of proving the quantitative aspects of Dr Inomata's work. This experimental research remains to be done.

He also discusses Joseph Newman's work, (see below) which he takes seriously, and even demonstrates a coil, similar in concept to Joseph Newman's, which contains a quarter of a million turns of fine copper wire only .06 millimetre thick. When energized with 300 volts, this coil attracts non-magnetic objects such as pieces of wood (Dr Inomata has used toothpicks in initial trials), and he suggests that the coil is creating a gravitational field out of the vacuum energy. This is also predicted by the mathematics of his theory, though he is the first to admit that it is very difficult to experimentally distinguish between electrostatic and gravitational field effects. But the formation of a gravitational field due to electromagnetic activity is not, of course, 'permitted' by the mathematics of conventional physics. Again, the experimental testing remains to be performed.

Dr Inomata is also deeply interested in permanent magnet motors, since they can only be fully understood by vacuum state theory. He is familiar with the work of Howard Johnson, Joseph Newman, John Searl and all the others. But perhaps the most successful of these and the strongest proof of vacuum state theory, comes from Japan itself. It is the permanent magnet motor of Kohei Minato.

Kohei Minato sees magnetism as one of the great forces holding the universe together. He is also a musician and writing poetically in the 1988 *Japanese Yearbook of High Technology and Science*, he says, in translation:

> The entire universe is imbued with magnetism, from the vastly distant nebulae down to the most minute elementary particles. The earth on which mankind exists is also a gigantic magnet. Magnetic fields are present in the interstellar space of the galactic system as well as in the more remote regions of the universe. The nebulae, which are composed of various kinds of cosmic dust or gaseous atoms, and are destined to evolve into stars, also possess magnetic fields.

These nebulae of gas or dust are constantly subjected to the action of gravitational forces, which act to retract each nebula into its centre. However, the magnetic lines of force are also drawn in, along with this matter. Except for the fact that the state of the system is maintained by this magnetic field, which revolves along with the system as a whole, the immense gravitational forces, acting over long periods of time, would crush the galactic system, concentrating the mass of the system at its centre. The ensuing gravitational collapse would be followed by a violent explosion.

Thus, the magnetic field constitutes a robust framework which protects the galactic system from the destructive action of gravitation[1] Furthermore, if the earth did not possess a magnetic field, then it would long since have been devastated by cosmic rays and reduced to a desolate state, uninhabitable by living organisms.

Thus, magnetism is a vast celestial entity which maintains order in the physical universe.

Perceiving magnetism as one of the primary cosmic forces, Minato designed his 'magnetodynamic rotational device' as a copy of our solar system. Again quoting from his article:

> The part corresponding to the sun is a shaft fixed by bearings, and in the position corresponding to the planets is a group of permanent magnets which are arranged at constant intervals on a circular orbit. The basic idea of the present system consists of two identical coordinate systems of this kind, each with the same function and arrangement, which mutually interact and revolve together.

The world of 'New Science' is a wave which is breaking almost simultaneously in many parts of the world at this present time, and will no doubt gather momentum as we proceed towards the end of this millenium (according to our Christian calendar). But whether within or without the academic and industrial institutions, the New Science is presently represented by individual workers and small associations, as well as by this wave of perception that science is only an expression of man's inner condition. And that the keynote of our activities should be the innate

[1] From the point of view of modern astrophysics, the situation is actually considerably more complex than this!

spiritual nature of man. All else should be understood within this context.

As a new paradigm, this understanding is spreading fast, but it still takes time, and much of the onus of networking and spreading the news is performed on an individual basis by dedicated people, dotted all around the world. One of these is Mitsuo Nakada, to whom we are indebted for translating these sections of the 1988 *Yearbook*.

In a letter dated March 1st, 1988, he wrote to me concerning Kohei Minato's device:

> It was some years ago that Mr K. Minato invented the magnetic motor, which was demonstrated on television and featured in magazines and newspapers.
>
> When I heard the news, I visited Mr Minato's office to ask questions about the magnetic motor. He willingly showed it to me and I actually watched the motor rotating. I was then convinced that the principle of energy conservation, as presently understood, is wrong and that Dr Inomata's theory is correct.
>
> I heard that tens of thousands of people who had watched the magnetic motor rotating had been very surprised and that some of them had not been able to believe what they had been watching.
>
> Then I tried to persuade our members of the Technology Development Division at the Japanese Ministry of Transport to begin work on the magnetic motor, but they could not believe what I said. So after that I have been researching personally, since I had thought that the magnetic motor would drastically change everything.
>
> The detailed information concerning the magnetic motor is confidential and Mr Minato does not reveal it. He told me that some aspects of the design are critical for the motor to operate – the angles and spacings of the magnets, for example.
>
> I know of both Howard Johnson's permanent magnet motor and Joseph Newman's energy machine. The Japan Psychotronics Institute (JPI) has an American member and he wrote to Mr Johnson requesting details as to the present situation of his magnetic motor. Mr Johnson replied that the magnetic motor was not yet in practical use, and he was continuing his research on the magnetic motor in Virginia.
>
> The problem with Johnson's motor is that it cannot produce sufficient torque (rotational force) to rotate a dynamo. It has been suggested that this is because Johnson's motor rotates by using the minute difference between repulsive and attrac-

> tive magnetic force, while Mr Minato's magnetic motor rotates using only the repulsive force, which can therefore provide sufficient torque.
>
> This American member also confirmed that Newman's energy machine does actually work. And a Japanese member of JPI who has looked into Newman's energy machine in the U.S.A., also gave a lecture on it at one of JPI's regular meetings last January.

In his letter to me, Mitsuo Nakada went on to describe yet another Japanese magnetic motor, discussed and described in Dr Inomata's book. He also comments that many Japanese manufacturing companies have asked Mr Minato to work with them, though all but one have been rejected. Ciba-Geigy have also wanted to work with him, but whether their request was successful or not, Mr Nakada did not know.

Finally, he makes a general comment that the present world economic crisis, especially that of the U.S.A., with its vast international ramifications, is likely, ultimately, to bring about great social chaos and depression. From upheavals such as this, it is then possible for a new social order to emerge in which New Science is acceptable.

> Even now, the Chernobyl nuclear accident and the decrease in the ozone layer, are making many people look for new energy sources, outside of nuclear energy, oil and coal. I think that this will make magnetic motors and devices like Newman's energy machine, far more widely used.
>
> Recently, people have become interested in supernatural phenomena. Even governments have an interest in this field. Our Ministry of Post and Telegram, for example, is studying telepathic communications for use in possible future mass communication. The Ministry of International Trade and Industry has an interest in the magnetic motor, too, while the Ministry of Agriculture and Forestry had budgeted to help development of the magnetic motors to be used in the field of agriculture, though this plan seems to have been unsuccessful.

From the foregoing, it is very clear that despite the predictable inertia in some quarters, due to ingrained and habituated scientific thought patterns, at least some of the Japanese are taking New Science generally, and the production of free energy in particular, very seriously. Let us hope that their lead is followed by western countries in the very near future. Under present world conditions, it is essential.

A Few More Free Energy Devices

In West Germany, a *gravity field* converter has been built and fitted to an electrically powered motor scooter. The converter continuously charges the battery from which the scooter is run, the operation being noiseless, fuelless and pollution-free. The scooter had run approximately 20,000 kilometres by 1982, on a power output of 2000 watts. It was said at that time that a factory was in the process of being set up in the town of Oldenburg for the production of a domestic heating unit, running upon the same generator, and motor car designs are supposed to be in the research stage. Details of the design are unfortunately proprietory and are not available, but German doctor and scientist Dr Hans Nieper, founder of the German Association for Gravity Field Energy recently told me that development had been halted because there is a problem of how to deal with the excess output power. This excess could not be stored or dissipated successfully, with the result that the translator heated up too much.

Research and development takes much time, money and resources and when faced with a technical difficulty that cannot be overcome in any obvious way, a project may very easily be put on the back-burner. Generally speaking, the gravity-field or *tachyon field* spoken of is the same as the vacuum state, though I have a feeling that the concept refers to just one aspect of the vacuum state structure. None of the specific details are available from the Germans, so it is difficult to say exactly.

All the same, research in West Germany has not been completely quiescent. On September 12th 1988, Ulrich H. Schumacher of 35 Bielitzer Strasse, 4800 Bielefeld 18, announced the availability for sale of a range of domestic and industrial free energy generators based upon permanent magnet technology. Five models, generating electrical power from between 6 to 76 kilowatts are available. Manufacture takes about three months from the date of placing the order. Is this the long-awaited breakthrough? As this book goes to press, we await further information, (see *Further Information* at the end of this book).

In France, Raymond Kromrey has developed a gravity field generator which seems somewhat similar to Howard

Johnson's permanent magnet generator. Kromrey, like all the others, talks in terms of electro-gravitation and stresses the need for a re-evaluation of all current dogmas in physics. The output once again greatly exceeds the apparent input, one prototype supplying approximately 700 watts at motor speeds of between 600 to 1200 revs per minute. A number of patent applications have been granted, apparently against heavy opposition from French industrial concerns. France, you may know, is the European country most heavily committed to nuclear power, with their stated aim of becoming a major exporter of electricity to neighbouring countries. They have about forty operational nuclear power stations out of a Western European total of a little over 140, with a further twenty under construction.

John Bedini, in the U.S.A., has built a Kromrey converter from the patent information, noting in his 1984 report (*Experiments With a Kromrey and a Brandt-Tesla Converter*) that the patent details had been altered, resulting in a non-functioning device.

Bedini discovered the required modifications and, testing his gravity-field converter, was able to demonstrate a greater than 100% efficiency. He has also released sufficient details for others to repeat his work and this work has already been performed by Jim Watson, reportedly scaling it up into a much larger version.

Meanwhile, in India, Paramhansa Tewari, author of *Beyond Matter* and head of quality assurance at the Nuclear Power Corporation in Bombay, has for some years been working on a 'Space Power Generator', designed to extract energy directly from the vacuum state. Several models are in operation, but he has yet to achieve the magical 'over-unity' output which would conclusively prove that its source of energy was the vacuum. But he is ever hopeful!

It is possible that some of the experimenters under discussion have not achieved everything they may think they have. But this does not invalidate the fundamental basis of understanding underlying their attempts. After all, the atom was not split in a day. To 'extract' usable energy from the vacuum state is an even more difficult task. But first comes the idea, and then the experimental proof. In this instance, most of the experimenters lack the research facilities of the larger institutions, so they are to be congratulated for having gone so far with such limited resources.

It is true that the world of free energy research (like most science) is full of false starts and over-enthusiastic claims, but at least they have dared! It is so easy to criticize, to mock and to play the cynic – to react subconsciously without truly considered and conscious appraisal. But to follow a path knowing that there will be many who will sit at the wayside and scoff requires inner courage and conviction. Qualities, surely, to be encouraged? For the benefit of all humanity.

The Swiss M-L Converter

Situated near Bern in the little town of Linden, in Switzerland, there is a spiritual community, Methernitha, where one of the most successful free energy converters is in use, I believe, at the time of writing.

The commune who support themselves by market gardening and a variety of manufacturing activities has been visited by members of the German Association of Gravity Field Energy (GAGFE) on at least five separate occasions and the following is derived from the reports of these engineers. In particular, the Swiss electronics engineer, P. H. Matthey, visited the centre on October 20th, 1984 along with several other Swiss engineers. Dr Hans Neiper, president of GAGFE, visited the centre on October 28th, 1984.

The converter which was demonstrated, and possibly one or two others, have been in operation since 1982. It was seen to be providing some of the electrical power to heat a greenhouse of 5500 square feet, at an altitude of 2600 feet, and in the winter, too. Its power output is in the order of 3–4 kilowatts at 230 volts DC.

Perhaps I should point out right away that the community do not wish to present the details of their technology to the world at large. They fear, perhaps rightly, that to present mankind with such an unlimited source of energy would do little more than fuel his rapacious appetite for destruction and disharmony. They may indeed be right, but it seems that this secret has already been unlocked by so many other workers, that the cat is already well and truly out of the bag. That the time has come for mankind to struggle with the implications of possessing so much power. Indeed, he is already struggling with the social, humanitarian and ethical implications of electricity, nuclear and all other sources of power.

The M-L converter consists of two phases. Firstly, there is a modernized, self-propulsion version of the old-fashioned Wimshurst electrostatic generator. Basically, two discs made of electrostatically active acrylic are contrarotated with only a tiny space between them. The consequent electrostatic potential generated is stored as its positive and negative constituents in two large electrical capacitors. In this case the craftsman used Leyden jars.

The high electrostatic potential is then used in the second, solid-state phase of the system, which adjusts the voltage and frequency of the output, for use with standard electrical equipment. But this Wimshurst-style generator utilizes permanent magnets wound with coils, which when tuned to their 'natural resonant frequency' provide substantially increased power output. This is a further aspect of the solid-state phase of the converter and is a part of the mechanism by which energy is derived out of the vacuum state. But the full process utilized is not completely understood either by those who have visited or who have made later assessments.

Don Kelly[1], in his analysis, points out that the choice of the Wimshurst electrostatic generator is by no means arbitrary, but must have been chosen because it is the only type of generator which provides a polarity separation between the negative and positive charges. As we have seen, high electrostatic potential difference seems to be required to reach the threshold conditions at which vacuum energy conversion takes place. In fact, the Whimshurst generator strips the electrons off air molecules. The resulting positive air ions are collected into one Leyden jar, while the negative electrons are trapped in the other.

[1] *The Manual of Free Energy Devices*, and other reports, containing an in-depth technical appraisal of almost all the free energy machines that have ever been built.

It is clear that visits to Methernitha were rather special occasions for the visiting engineers. Quoting from 'L.L.', in a report printed in Dr Nieper's, *Revolution in Technology, Medicine and Society*, one reads the following:

> I promised certain people who are interested in tachyon converters and who would have enjoyed coming with us, that I would write a report. Unfortunately, one can capture the mood only imperfectly on a typewriter, unless one belongs to the small guild of poets.
>
> The so-called 'Electrostatic Generator' was functionally constructed, completely symmetrical, about 110 cms wide, 45 cms deep and 60 cms high, and weighed 20 kg (without the cover, which was made from clear acrylic plastic). Its body was made from acrylic plastic, a light metal lattice, insulated copper wires, a mysterious crystal-diode rectifier and gold-plated electrical connections. Everything was hand-made with the finest craftsmanship, and with an elegant beauty which caused great fascination in each of us.
>
> The operating principle has been known for a long time. The air molecules between two acrylic plastic discs (about 45 cms in diameter), which counterrotate closely together, side by side, become activated through electrification by friction. This causes the discs to be continually charged, until a flashover equalizes them. To limit the electrical voltage to a desired amount, the positively charged particles (atmospheric ions) on one of the counterrotating discs and the negatively charged particles (electrons) on the other disc, are each extracted by means of separately adjustable lattice-electrodes and are fed into a Leyden bottle, which collects the energy.
>
> On the outer rim of the rotating discs the electrons are extracted with another lattice-electrode, and according to our understanding, are used for the control of the converter. The speed of the discs, on which a fan-like structure of 50 lattice-electrodes is etched out, is 60 rpm. This speed is synchronized by magnetic impulses. The secret lies in how these two discs become charged, using strong horseshoe magnets, which are parts of electrical resonance circuits.
>
> It is understood that the technical information made available must remain insufficient to serve as the basis for the construction of such a converter. This is because it is considered that unlimited energy should be restricted to a society which practices love and peace for its fellow man, and does not engage in exploitation and war.
>
> The demonstration of the following experiments was very impressive. One of the experts, using the tip of his fingers,

started the two discs rotating in different directions, until the converter was charged up to such a degree that it synchronized itself and continued to rotate smoothly and noiselessly, without any source of power. A centrally mounted disk of about 10 cms in diameter was glimmering in all the colors of the rainbow.

After only a few seconds, the Leyden bottles were ready for operation, so that 300 volts DC with a current of 10 amperes could be extracted at the terminals – and this could be done continuously, for hours, or for years, without any wear!

To demonstrate the power available, we connected alternately, via a cable, either a high-power incandescent lamp or a heating element, each of which was rated for 380 volt service. The brilliant light from the lamp was blinding and illuminated the complete hall, all the way to the farthest corner. The heating element became so hot after a few seconds that it could not be touched. This experience was for all of us certainly a look into the future – into a new era.

It became evident for everybody who saw this converter functioning, that the teachings of orthodox science must undergo a complete revision in order to be taken seriously. Today there are already dozens of known violations of the orthodox energy laws.

This converter produces, every day of the week, via an inverter and an accumulator, current for the electrical network of the company, into which additional current from two to three wind converters (self-made, of course) is also channeled. The pilot model of this converter was built a long time ago when the inventor had at his disposal only waste materials such as chocolate wrappers, plastic containers, nails, copper wire, and leftovers from the workshop. It delivered sufficient electric power for one light bulb.

This then is the Swiss M-L converter – clearly poetry in motion – with its combined features of energy extraction from the vacuum state and high quality, handcraftsmanship.

The Energy Machine of Joseph Newman

ENERGY MACHINE WOWS CROWD AT SUPERDOME – *Metro News*, Michael Perlstein, Saturday April 12th 1986.

NEWMAN OPERATES ENERGY CAR – *Mobile Press Register*, June Heydt, February 5th 1987.

LUCEDALE INVENTOR HITS THE ROAD. SUCCESS! NEWMAN'S 'GYRO-POWER' CAR WORKS – *The Clarion Ledger*, Valeri Oliver, February 5th,1987.

IT DOES, DOES RUN, RUN, RUN – *George County Times*, editorial opinion, February 12th,1987.

Figure 9-2. Joseph Newman's Energy Car. Photograph by courtesy of the Mobile Press Register, *dated February 4th 1987.*

"Yes, it does run. Joe Newman's invention of a battery powered automobile, does defy the (accepted) laws of physics." So starts the editorial column in the George County Times. It goes on to point out that for over eight years, the people at the U.S. patent office have steadfastly refused to give Joseph Newman a patent for his generator, on the grounds that "it couldn't work."

More than any other inventor, Joseph Newman has gone all out to present his device to the media and to the public at large. And his book, *The Energy Machine of Joseph Newman*, gives details of the theory and construction of his device, though it is not very clearly presented. This is a welcome and altruistic attitude, for a device that only one person knows how to build is really rather useless! However good it may seem to the inventor, if it dies with him, it not much more than a curiosity whose authenticity will be questioned ever after even by those who understand that such things could exist.

Somehow, one always suspects motives that result in secrecy. Either they hide dreams of a profit and power-reaping empire or they may even be a cover for the works of a charlatan, or they may simply hide the fact that the inventor does not fully understand how his invention really works. There is no discredit in that, since – as I have pointed out previously – we have all been using electricity quite happily for nearly a century without any really clear idea of just what an electron is.

If a person is not clear, we can never know for sure where they are coming from. Sometimes, it may obscure only a complex and emotional personality, where the ownership of a secret gives its keeper great personal and egocentric satisfaction. But such obsessions are also hard to relinquish. They may even be encouraged as a part of the social climate and idiom. It is said, for instance, that a great wealth of knowledge in the field of acupuncture has died out with the demise of certain Chinese families. They took their health secrets to the grave with them, rather than pass them on or write them down.

In a terse 44 words, Newman's first application to the Patents and Trademarks Office (PTO) rejected because the machine "smacks of perpetual motion."

Actually, without going into all the details which are readily available from Newman, the most unusual and seemingly unconstitutional actions of Judge Jackson who presided over Newman's appeal against the PTO appear to have entangled him in a highly expensive legal morass.

In 1984, Jackson – who understandably found the science beyond his threshold – rejected, without reason, the findings of his own appointed court expert and special master, William E. Schayler. Schayler had been appointed to make a detailed scientific appraisal of Newman's work, reporting that:

> The evidence before the PTO and this court is overwhelming that Newman has built and tested a prototype of his own invention, in which the output energy exceeds the external input energy; there is no contradictory factual evidence.

Similarly, Schayler stated that the PTO,

> *intentionally* did not consider the formalities of Newman's application or the patentability of Newman's claims under 35 USC sec 102/103.

Judge Jackson was clearly prejudiced, his mind patterns being quite unable to accept something contrary to his own beliefs. Perhaps, too, some unknown pressures were also brought to bear upon him, though many of those finding themselves in a struggle against 'the system' have been prey to paranoid feelings of victimization and suppression, when really there had been no 'plot' to suppress their work, but only the subconscious inertia of 'established opinion'.

Newman also claims that PTO commissioner Gerald Mossinghoff had previously arranged to have $100,000 of Energy Act funds (intended for the development of new energy systems) to be utilized in discrediting him. Messinghoff ran little risk of being taken to account by the National Bureau of Standards (NBS) since NBS 'expert' Jacob Rabinow had made a sworn, legal declaration that Newman's device did not operate. And this was without his ever testing it.

Later, Jackson was sternly rebuked by a higher appeal court for ordering "highly irregular" testing procedures for the National Bureau of Standards (NBS) to follow, which denied Newman the "fundamental fairness" guaranteed to him by law. These procedures included an order to Newman that he should surrender his machine to the NBS for them to dismantle or destroy, if they saw fit, no doubt to check for a hidden source of power. Neither were the NBS instructed to prepare a testing programme in advance, for Newman to check, and they were also given an open-ended period for testing. Newman was also denied the right to have present an expert of his own choice; and finally, the results were to be kept sealed "until we determine that it ought to be exhibited to the public."

Perhaps it should be said that the purpose behind acquiring a patent is not only to protect Newman's personal rights, for his book already explains how to replicate his work. The point is that a device protected by patent is far more likely to be developed under licence by a large industrial concern if they know that the technology is not available to all their competitors.

Newman does, of course, have tremendous support from numerous individuals numbering, so he says, over thirty top scientists, including Dr Roger Hastings, Principle Physicist for Sperry-Univac Corporation, and Eike Mueller, European Space Agency mission coordinator with NASA. Further, at least two congressmen have both individually filed for Congress to grant Newman his patent by congressional action, thus ending his long drawn out and expensive battle with the patent office. He has sworn affidavits (legal statements) from these and other good people, that have been reproduced in his book, attesting that his machines do work. Neither is there any hint of any fraud nor even of any reason for deceipt.

That, then, is some of the background. Joseph Newman is clearly a man of considerable charisma, as well as inventive genius, though even his friends say that he can be stubborn and arrogant, quick to anger if he senses a lack of sympathy for his ideas or if his integrity is questioned – traits common to many pioneers, scientific and otherwise. But Newman has determinedly fought legal battles long after others would have given up in resentment and bitterness, or have simply run out of money or motivation. And like many other path-beaters before him, he is a man of complex psychological make-up.

What then is the science behind Newman's Energy Machine? Dr Roger Hastings first heard of Newman's work in 1981 and conducted regular and thorough tests in subsequent years, as Newman's work progressed.

Examining Newman's C-1 model in 1981, he noted that while the power input was 1.7 watts, the motor – acting as a generator – output 4.5 watts. The following year, in 1982, he tested a Newman model B motor, hooked up to an oil pump. A conventional DC motor drew two amps of current, exhausting eight 1.5 volt alkaline batteries in about six minutes. Newman's motor, on the other hand, to Hasting's amazement, was still running happily, drawing only 0.2 amps, when he switched it off seven hours later.

Since then, Hastings has performed many other similar tests, as have other visiting scientists. All have shown the same, apparently greater than 100 percent efficiency.

The capacity of Newman's machines to draw so little power from the batteries powering his devices and even to get recharged, has not, of course, gone unnoticed! The batteries have been supplied to him by the large corporation, Rayovac. Pat Spellman, director of product development there, who has examined the batteries after their use in Newman's experiments, comments:

> Some unique stuff is going on down there in Lucedale. It's not at all clear to us how the batteries get rejuvenated when they run a Newman motor. Beyond that, I'd rather not get into it.

Again, in 1985, Newman demonstrated a 130 pound motor with battery inputs of 1000 and 2000 volts and output powers of 50 and 200 watts respectively. With input power of only 7 and 14 watts, efficiencies of 700 percent and 1,400 percent were demonstrated. In 1986, he demonstrated a rotor driving a fifteen inch fan blade, drawing a current of only 1.8 milliamps, for a total power input of 4.5 watts. A similar, conventional fan motor draws about 300 watts at a far greater current.

Newman's system clearly requires low current at high voltage. In fact, he states that the higher the voltage and the lower the current, the better. This is indicative of a massless charge at work, that is: a high electrostatic potential difference with a minimum flow of electrons, causing vacuum 'strain'.

On February 4th 1987 he demonstrated an 1800 pound car, powered by his generator, drawing current from 1810 Rayovac 9-volt transistor batteries connected in series. The car covered a half mile journey at 4 mph and also showed that it could go up slight inclines. This may not seem like much, yet it served to graphically demonstrate a new principle that needs to be developed.

Remember that in 1903, during their first four flights, the Wright brothers, Wilbur and Orville, flew the first heavier-than-air powered aircraft for flight times lasting between only twelve and fifty-nine seconds. A few days earlier, 'experts' had, of course, declared as impossible, the flight of a vehicle which was heavier than air. Yet how simple an invention is the lift-producing aerofoil shape! Simple with hindsight, that is. And look how far we have gone since then.

In fact, only nine days previously, the *New York Times* had carried an editorial predicting that "man would not fly for a thousand years." They were complaining about the "foolish dreams" of American scientist, S.P. Langley, whose experimentation with manned flight they considered a waste of government money. Langley had correctly worked out the necessary aerodynamic principles but was unable to find suitable materials for the wings and engine.

Even two years after the first successful flight, *Scientific American* magazine suggested that the flights had been a hoax. "Far more harm," said Dr Robert Wood, when director of research and development at McDonnel-Douglas, "is done to the progress of science by scepticism than by gullibility."

Actually, the comment that man cannot fly because he is heavier than air is not even observant of nature, for my garden is full of birds and insects that fly about with the greatest of ease despite their being heavier than air. Man has discovered some of the mechanisms that the birds have used for millions of years without giving it a moment's thought. Yet still, the dexterity of bird and insect flight, controlled by the mind and life force within them, is quite unmatched by any artefact that man has ever produced.

Just watch any bird or bee for only a few minutes and the secret is revealed. The life force and mental intention provide them with something that no dumb or artificially intelligent machine of man can ever do. But the materialistic scientist does not even believe in consciousness or life as anything other than material substance, so he remains in egocentric ignorance of the fundamentals of existence.

It is common knowledge that the famous bumble bee should not, according to the known 'laws' of physics, be able to fly. But this does not hinder its aerial dexterity one whit. So many of man's inventions have later been found to have been in use in nature for millions of years that one wonders if maybe some of our lesser cousins have, in some clever way, been using vacuum state propulsion and lift, all along. Why not?

Actually, the 1810 transistor batteries would be capable of powering a motor car by conventional means for a limited period of time, so critics may rest easy if they consider Newman's car alone, for the purpose of the

Lucedale demonstration was really to generate publicity.

But the heart of Newman's work lies in his less exotic electric motor demonstrations. These are not explicable without recourse to an understanding of the vacuum state energy field. Newman's machine is another permanent magnet motor, but with a difference. It consists of a stationary conducting coil, a rotating permanent magnet and a commutator which rotates with the magnet, ensuring a unidirectional current flow. But the coil is of no ordinary length. In some models, over fifty-five miles of wire have been used in thousands of turns. Energy from the electric current supplied by the batteries is fed to this coil which forms a magnetic field around and a current within the coil. This magnetic field then rotates the magnet.

The electrical current input is then cut off and the energy within the coil is fed through an electrical load. Thus, the energy of the magnetic field is reconverted to an electrical current. The remaining part of the input energy which has been transformed into the rotational energy of the magnet, induces a current in the coil, giving rise to an equal and opposite magnetic field surrounding the coil. This opposes the rotation of the magnet.

The sequence is then repeated. Under the conventional laws of physics, the system should slowly come to a halt as the input energy is drained from the battery powering the system. "Not so," says Newman, for additional energy is derived directly from the kinetic energy of particle spin creating the magnetic lines of force and is converted into electric power within the system, becoming available to perform 'work'. Driving a motor, for example.

The large number of turns in the coil results in an extraordinarily high inductance – the resistance to current (electron) flow due to an opposing electromotive force. In fact, the wire is so long that the electrons do not have time to reach the other end before the flow is reversed by the commutator as the motor turns. Once again we see that a tremendous 'strain' is being placed upon the vacuum energy as the inductance pushes against the steep voltage gradient. Perhaps it is at this point that the motion of the electrons is aligned or reorganized or reaches some threshold at which the vacuum energy is trapped as usable energy.

In technical terms, one has *gated* the energy comprising

the electron. Electronically, a gate is like a cat-flap, permitting flow in only one direction. In this case from the vacuum to the 'manifested' world.

As we have said, magnetic fields, electrical charge, electron spin and all physical phenomena are only effects of vacuum state activity. This vacuum substructure, then, is of importance, just as two equally matched, heavy trucks pushing against each other is a quite different situation to that of two trucks parked front bumper (fender) to front bumper with all engines switched off. The nett result of 'no movement' is the same, but the pressure of potential energy is vastly different in the two instances.

So like Howard Johnson's permanent magnet motor, the kinetic energy of the electron spin which is an integral part of the way a magnetic field is manifested, is converted into usable energy. Indeed, Newman's theory suggests that subatomic particles behave like tiny gyroscopes.

But why don't the electrons slow down and stop when their kinetic energy is transmuted in one of these devices? Because they would cease to exist. The question is actually quite meaningless, because, as Puthoff points out, the electron is constantly drawing on the zero point sea of vacuum energy for its very existence. Its movement and other properties *are* its existence. Bearden describes electrons as 'spray nozzles' – points or vortices at which the vacuum energy becomes stepped down into manifestation, constantly drawing upon the energy of the vacuum sea and radiating it into the manifested world.

The 'spray-nozzle' image of an electron is of interest, for it again leads to an understanding of a subatomic particle, not as a 'thing', but as a point of energy flux in relation to surrounding, as well as more inward, energy patterns. The subatomic particle is no more a static 'thing' than is the hole at the end of a hose-pipe with water pouring through it. Turn off the inward cosmic motor and the subatomic energy tapestry – and thus the entire physical creation would disappear – just like the flow of water when you turn off the tap. Neither the water flowing from the end of a hose-pipe, nor the subatomic 'particles' comprising the physical world can exist without their hidden source of power.

So the question of stopping the perpetual motion of an electron or any other subatomic particle or arresting the motion of light are about as meaningful as considering how to stop the manifestation of the entire physical creation. Not something within human power!

So the extra energy that is delivered by Newman's machine comes from the energy potential locked into the permanent magnet. And assuming that a reasonable magnet is expected to lose about five percent of its power in a hundred years due to ambient temperature effects, we can confidently predict that Newman's device will take about 1300 years to be reduced to half its power.

Perhaps I may also be forgiven for pointing out that in my book, *Subtle Energy*, mostly written in autumn 1984, I did suggest this very mechanism – harnessing the kinetic energy of particle spin, thus drawing on the great, virtually unlimited source of creative cosmic energy, since movement and manifestation are synonymous. And at that time I was quite unaware of the work of Newman and Johnson and many of the others mentioned in this book.

This is a wave that many of us are jointly riding and which is simultaneously breaking, apparently independently, in all parts of the world. The time for this kind of energy translation is clearly imminent. Our planet requires a time for openness and sharing, rather than self-seeking. And through the networking efforts of many people, including books such as this, the work is being drawn together in a clear and urgent fashion, with such visible evidence of its reality, that it can never again be brushed under the carpet by prejudice and vested interest.

Motion and Magnetism

In a conventional motor, electricity is generated from the relative motion between a conductor and a magnetic field. But Michael Faraday describes a series of experiments in his laboratory notebooks, dated December 20th 1831, in which he generated electrical potential by rotating both the magnet and the conductor *together*. He observed the results with no great surprise for at that time, over 150 years ago, there were no 'laws of electromagnetism': their originator, James Clerk Maxwell, had only just been born.

Following in the great man's footsteps, American scientists, Bruce DePalma and later, Adam Trombly, both took this recognised 'anomaly' as a basis of their vacuum energy research, producing the *N-Machine* and its cousin the *Homopolar Generator*. Both generate power by rotating a conducting disc sandwiched firmly in the middle of a stack of magnets.

DePalma also discovered that rotational motion has an effect on the inertia of an object. It had always been assumed that mechanical systems function identically whether they are stationary or spinning, so no-one had ever really bothered to check. DePalma checked, finding that a spinning object generates an *inertial field*. "Forces in a rotating object exert an effect upon the space around that object. The motion of objects in the plane of a spinning flywheel have their inertia reduced and the motion of objects on the axis of spin have their inertia increased." This is totally contrary to conventional theory which assumes that inertia remains constant.

For over more than a decade, DePalma has checked and rechecked his results. Identical ball bearings, for example, when projected in a vacuum, follow different trajectories when spinning, than when they are not, the difference being due to changes in the inertial and gravitational forces. His definitive experiment, however, is the behaviour of an electric clock which uses a special variety of electrically-oscillated tuning fork as its time keeper. The frequency of a tuning fork's natural vibration is directly related to its inertia. DePalma found that when he ran the clock above a spinning flywheel, it lost a full nine-tenths of a second in only seventeen minutes, whereas with the flywheel motionless, it gained a quarter of a second in four hours.

DePalma's research continues today and his N-machine is based upon a combination of these intertial field effects of spinning objects and Faraday's original observations. In the next chapter, therefore, we explore some of the mysteries of spins and spirals.

—— CHAPTER 10 ——

Fish, Birds, Bumble Bees and the Levitating Gyroscope

Viktor Schauberger, the Energy Spiral and the Trout Turbine

Spin and motion are the essence of creation. The universe is in constant flux. Without motion it would collapse in on itself. So it is a fundamental phenomenon worth considerable study, and our story starts during the early years of this century. It begins with the work of Austrian forester-turned-scientist, Viktor Schauberger.

Schauberger was one of those souls who can be called a true natural philosopher and natural scientist, one of nature's gentlemen. He was a deep observer of nature. Natural processes, he said, already hold all the secrets. If we wish to do anything, we should observe nature, and then quite simply, copy her. By this means alone, though he was also well-read and a self-taught scientist, understanding the scientific method too, Schauberger did some most remarkable things with air and water.

Since nature is the outward projection of the greater Mind, Schauberger's principle is based upon firm ground. For all patterns and mechanisms are already inherent in the natural creative process and will therefore exist automatically in nature. Man never creates anything new, he only learns how to rearrange and use existing natural mechanisms for his own purposes. Man is an integral part of nature and his own activities only reflect the activities within the whole.

Schauberger started his working life as a forester, soon rising to positions where he designed and organized the difficult engineering task of bringing heavy timber down from the high mountains to the valleys. The method used was one of artifical 'rivers' – ducts or flumes – which carried the logs to more accessible places for further industrial processing and transportation. The winding valleys and hillsides presented no easy engineering task and some of these log flumes covered distances of thirty miles, a tremendous distance to cover, if you think about it.

So Schauberger began by observing nature, and – in particular – water. He watched, with fascination, the trout and salmon of the mountain streams, noticing that they sought the cooler, denser water near the source. Water, he knew, had the anomalous property of expanding when it froze. It was at +4°C centigrade that it was in its most contracted and dense form. He noted, too, that water at this temperature appeared at its most lively, whilst warmer water was more sluggish.

He observed the trout and salmon spending long periods as if suspended, seemingly motionless, in the rapid current of the mountain streams. Yet, with scarcely a flick of their tails or fins they could dart upstream, again stopping motionless, instantaneously. He pondered how they could remain so still in such rapid currents.

Sitting quietly by moonlight near the deep woodland pools, he saw with surprise how some strange current in the water could lift certain egg-shaped stones to the surface and hold them there, suspended. But there was more to this, he suspected, than the forces of a whirlpool or a tornado which we know these days can deposit cars in trees and suck stones and rocks into the upper atmosphere, to fall elsewhere when the fury has passed[1].

In his work with the log flumes, he realized that the curves of mountain streams were more than coincidental.

[1] This observation is not as fantastic as it may seem. Substances float in water because of differentials in their density. The density of water increases as the temperature falls towards +4°C, making it more supportive. It also seems that water increases its apparent density, or is more concentrated in some way, when moving in a swirling motion, as in a whirlpool. Anyone can perform the following experiment. Take a large test tube about 12 inches long and 2 to 3 inches in diameter. Fill it with water and carefully insert an egg, which will sink to the bottom. By stirring in a suitable fashion with a thin rod, the egg will rise to the surface and remain there until stirring ceases. In the instance of the floating stones, the water was already at maximum concentration +4°C and in a natural setting. Schauberger is suggesting that there is more to these phenomena than simple upcurrents and suction..

They were essential to the well-being of the river habitat. The undulations of their banks created whirls and spiral flows of water which lifted silt from the river bed and deposited it on the banks. This encouraged the flora and fauna, which kept the banks in a firm and healthy condition, rarely needing help from man to maintain them. Straightening rivers and streams, he observed, resulted in their rapidly silting up, requiring dredging and maintenance, thus disturbing life upon their banks, making them even further dependent upon man.

The rivers and streams were, he felt, almost alive. They maintained themselves in perfect condition, following paths which no unimaginative engineer would ever have chosen for them. Perhaps this is an example of James Lovelock's Gaia principle, the observation that the spectrum of life forms is so well-balanced that they themselves maintain the environment in optimum conditions for their mutual existence.

But Viktor Schauberger's log flumes followed the example of these mountain streams, much to the derision of those scientists who had no perception of nature's more intricate fabric of stresses and strains, forms and motion. Yet Schauberger's flumes worked. Undulating down the mountains, following the course of streams, dumping the water as it warmed up and bringing in cooler water from the abundant streams, his methods were successful when others had declared such projects to be impossible by the 'laws of science'.

Schauberger noted how nature used these curves and undulations. Later he was to work on water flow with other scientists in well-equipped laboratories, where he showed that water developed remarkable properties when it moved in spirals, especially that of the hyperbolic spiral, a shape found frequently in nature, from DNA to the shape of galaxies, to the arrangement of leaves and petals on stems and flowers, and in the horn of the kudu antelope.

He again remembered the trout and the salmon, marvelling, too, at the flight of birds, wondering at the nature of the air flow around their so finely sculpted wings and individual feathers.

He noted that fish swim with their mouths open. A trout, hovering like a hawk in the strong current, allows the water to enter its mouth. From there the water passes over the gills, formed as delicately as any feather, and thence to the outside. But the gill-tips, he realized, are purposely sculpted and send the incoming water into a spiral motion as it leaves through the gill-slits. He suggested, too, that certain trace elements present in the gills, also have an effect upon the nature of the water.

He speculated that the spiral motion and the trace elements affect the nature of the water, altering its characteristics, which then flows out along the streamlined flank of the fish, interacting with the normal river water and creating a forward thrust. When the fish wants to move, just like a bird with its wings and feathers, it simply adjusts the shape of the gills and, almost miraculously, it shoots forward in the water, like a piece of iron in an attractive magnetic field.

So Schauberger took the idea and the observation into the laboratory and invented an energy generator which he called the 'trout turbine'. The machine was started by a small electric motor and water was forced into a spiral motion by internal shapes within the pipes. An excess of energy was then produced which Schauberger used for generating electricity. Had he unwittingly stumbled upon spiral motion as a means of extracting energy from the vacuum? He also demonstrated that water, when properly handled and forced under low pressure through fine holes, somehow exhibits electrical charge of up to 50,000 volts.

But by this time, Hitler was in power in Germany and the war years were approaching. Schauberger was summoned to the Chancellor's presence and Hitler promised him all the funding and resources he required to create an energy machine. For various reasons, including derision and antagonism from one of Hitler's scientific advisors, Schauberger declined. But when Hitler annexed Austria in 1936, Schauberger was again sent for and given both orders, (which he couldn't refuse), and the necessary research facilities. Schauberger made some little progress, this time working on the designs of a craft which would fly in the air, based upon the principles he had earlier discovered.

His thinking can be gauged from his own writings, to be found in Olof Alexandersson's excellent book, *Living Water*, a study of Schauberger and his work.

The form of movement which creates, develops, purifies and grows is the hyperbolic spiral (a helical pathway traced around a cone, see figure 10-1) which . . . is centripetal. We find it everywhere in nature where growth or movement is taking place, in the spiralling of the galaxies in space, in the movement of our planetary system, in the natural flow of water, blood and sap.

On the other hand, the destructive and dissolving form of movement is centrifugal in nature – it forces the moving medium from the centre outwards towards the periphery in straight lines. The particles of the medium appear to be forced out from the centre. The medium is first weakened, then it dissolves and breaks up. Nature uses this action to disintegrate complexes which have lost their vivacity or have died. From the broken-down fragments, new co-ordinated forms, new identities, can be created as a result of this concentrating form of movement.

The centripetal, hyperbolic spiral movement is symptomatic of falling temperature, contraction, concentration. The centrifugal movement, on the other hand, is synonymous with rising temperature, heat, extension, expansion, explosion. In nature, there is a continuous switch from one movement to the other. If the development is to occur, then the movement of growth must be predominant.

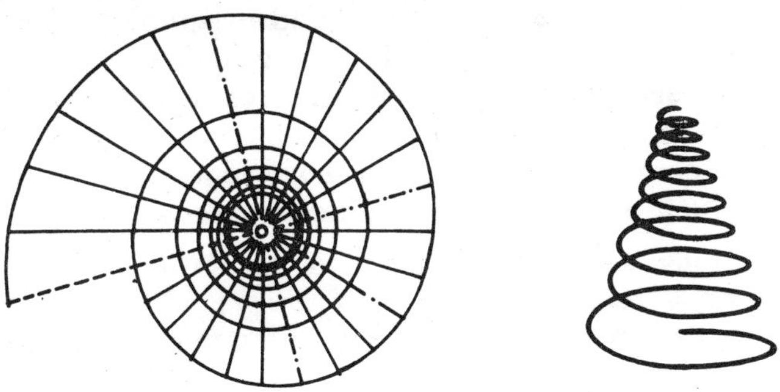

Figure 10-1. A hyperbolic spiral is characterized by its constantly changing curvature, inwardly concentrating as it moves towards the centre.

This was the philosophical basis of the thinking underlying his 'trout turbine', later to be renamed the *implosion* machine – utilizing the centripetal, cohering and life-giving positive energy of the universe rather than the expanding, *explosive* form of activity. He again wrote:

> In the case of a power generator, nine times as much energy in the form of fuel is required in its conversion to electricity or other kind of output. This system of plundering the resources of the earth's energy, is based upon the explosion motor, which operates centrifugally. The implosion motor, however, is centripetally operated. It produces its own driving source through the diamagnetic use of water and air. It does not require any other fuel such as coal, oil, uranium or energy derived from atomic splitting, since it can produce it own energy (atomic power) by biological means in unlimited amounts – almost without cost.
>
> It has been overlooked that energy is also bipolar and appears freely as part of the motion of the earth's medium – water and air, which have the effect of reviving energy.

Schauberger goes on to point out that water is also a bipolar molecule comprised of the basic elements of hydrogen and oxygen. They come together explosively to form water, this being the reaction at the basis of fuel usage in all motors. Motors are thus founded upon the explosion principle – the centrifugal, destructive force.

Interestingly, he also comments that this kind of 'centrifugal', destructive combining of hydrogen and oxygen in bodily function leads to water lacking in vitality. In this negative 'atmosphere', cancer and other pathological conditions – harmful viruses and bacteria, for example – can flourish, since this is the vibration to which they are attuned.

Schauberger, then, did create a machine, or more than one, which made use of this principle. He wrote:

> If water or air is rotated into a twisting form of oscillation known as 'colloidal', a build up of energy results, which with immense power, can cause levitation. This form of movement is able to carry with it its own means of power generation. This principle leads logically to its application in the design of the ideal airplane or submarine . . . requiring almost no motive power.'

Commenting in 1956 on this wartime research, he said:

> I preferred the first alternative (the airplane application), and about a year later, the first 'flying saucer' rose unexpectedly, at the first attempt, to the ceiling, and then was wrecked. A few days later an American group appeared, who seemed to understand what was happening, and seized every-

thing. Then, after a very thorough investigation by a high-ranking officer, I was taken into protective custody, and guarded by no less than six policemen for about six months. An important part of the apparatus was (also) found in my apartment by the Russians.

Describing the experiment in another context, he wrote:

> The apparatus functioned at the first attempt . . . and rose upwards, trailing a blue-green, and then a silver coloured glow.

At the end of the war, Schauberger's research was investigated by both the Americans and the Russians, the latter taking his models and papers with them, destroying his apartment when they left, in case anything had been left behind which might be of use to others.

After that he was confined for nearly a year by the Americans because of his knowledge, later being realeased on the proviso that he would engage in no further atomic or associated research. Confining himself to agricultural research, where again he made some fascinating discoveries, he died in 1958, aged 73. But his research is continued to this day by his son, Walter Schauberger, at the Pythagoras-Kepler School, Biotechnical Academy in Bad Ischl. Unfortunately, however, due to the war and its aftermath, much of the records of his work was lost.

His earlier, war-time work on the flying machine was by no means left unresearched, however, and other German engineers are reported to have successfully continued his work. In this respect, we have the following report from Hellmut Hoffman, translated by Callum Coats.

> It only became known after the war that aircraft resembling Schauberger's prototype had been further developed in several other production workshops. The most informative data about this is without doubt the report by Hermann Klass, an engineer from Muhlheim in the Ruhr, who had collaborated on the plans and who at the time had published a detailed report, complete with photocopies of sketches and original documents, in the Wuppertal paper, *Bergische Wochenpost* (ceased publication). He writes: "I still have drawings of a model 'flying disc' which I built in 1941; perfected by the Germans, in all truth this invention flew with almost un-

believable success. It had a diameter of 2.4 metres with a small, very fast running special electric motor, (there were no petrol-engined models at that time), which had been 'obtained' by courtesy of the Luftwaffe. It climbed straight up into the air so suddenly that unfortunately it hit the workshop ceiling and crashed to the ground in pieces.

The model which actually flew can be seen in the accompanying pictures (see figure 10-2) and also those versions begun firstly in Bohemia and later in Breslau (where the Meithe group worked), which embodies a stronger ramjet-pipe (like the V1 rocket). The three models approximate to the Ballenzo-Schriever-Habermohl prototype, even so far as the incorporation of the jet nozzles. The jets must be able to swivel in order to achieve the 'colloidal effect', which enables the 'flying disc' to climb vertically (Miethe built better models later on). On the first model, and also on the other models, the outer rim, made of high-grade metal alloys, was solid (without vents).

When this disc had gained height or had attained the desired altitude so that the thrust from the rear exhaust nozzles began to take effect, the disc transferred from vertical to horizontal flight. Naturally this control system was not simple. It was only on later designs that the 'slotted rim' was incorporated, so that the jets could be swivelled in all directions. These flying discs are today being built not only in the West, but also in the U.S.S.R.

There was, of course, a whole range of further designs, though unfortunately no entirely completed prototypes. In the beginning, neither Meithe nor Habermohl could get hold of a simple jet pipe. It could only be 'supplied' via the agency of a Luftwaffe sergeant.

The 'Schriever-Habermohl' flying disc developed between 1943 and 1945. In 1944, climbing vertically, it reached a height of 12 km in 3.12 minutes and a horizontal flying speed of 2000 km per hour.

The 'Ballenzo-Schriever-Miethe' disc. The retractable undercarriage legs terminated in inflatable rubber cushions. It carried a crew of three.

Figure 10-2. Two of the flying discs developed by war-time Germany.

The 'Flying Saucers' of the Third Reich

Years later, on the 27th July 1956, the Munich periodical *Da Neue Zeitalter* published an article headed "Hitler built Flying Saucers" . . . "The Austrian forester Viktor Schauberger was the inventor and discoverer of this new motive power – implosion, which, with the use of only air and water, generated light, heat and motion. In the implosion motor a diamagnetism was developed which made the lifting power possible. By means of a suction screw-impeller, which revolved from the outside towards the inside along a cycloid spiral space-curve, the same force is generated which creates waterspouts, typhoons, cyclones or hurricanes, through the effect of suction.

"On the 19th February 1945 near Prague, the first test of an unmanned 'flying disc' took place. In three minutes it climbed to a height of 15,000 metres and attained a horizontal speed of 2,200 kilometres per hour; it could hover motionless in the air and could fly as fast backwards as forwards. This 'flying disc' had a diameter of 50 metres."

On the 14th of August 1956, volume 31, the *Muchener Illustrierte* printed an article in which engineer Rene Couzinet's wooden model was displayed, whose external appearance was similar to Schauberger's design. Apparently, however, Couzinet was still far from achieving a working model, for Schauberger commented on the article in a letter dated 11/8/56 as follows: "One look (at the model) told me that the man is still miles away from the achievement of diamagnetic levitation power, for Couzinet has probably employed the effect of direct suction, whereas nature uses indirect, i.e. reactionary suction force. . . What various papers have published is also incorrect, namely that I might have copied typhoons, cyclones, etc., which occur in warm zones."

It should be noted in passing, that judicial circles in West Germany and abroad have posed the question as to whether Hitler was able to flee to safety in such an aircraft at the end of the war. In any case, it is a proposal put forward in Mattern's book, *UFO – the Ultimate Secret Weapons of the 2nd World War and their Further Development*, now in its fourth edition, was published in 1962 by J. F. Lehmann in Munich.

In it the author dedicated a whole chapter to the 'flying saucers' of the Third Reich, wherein it was stated: "The development, which had cost millions, was almost complete by the end of the war. No doubt the existing models were destroyed, although the plant in Breslau, where Miethe worked, fell into the hands of the Russians, who removed all the material and technical personnel to Siberia, where further work on these 'flying saucers' has been carried on with much success. Schriever just managed to get out of Prague in time. Habermohl, on the other hand, must be in the Soviet Union. The former German designer Meithe is in the USA and, as far as can be determined, is designing 'flying saucers' for A. V. Roe & Co.

"The machines, which have been observed to date, have diameters in the order of 16, 42, 45 and 75 metres and they are supposed to develop a speed of up to 7,000 kilometres per hour. Already, in 1952, 'flying saucers' had been indisputably recognized over Korea and according to press reports, were also observed and reported during NATO manoeuvres in Alsace in the spring of 1954."

The magazine *Hobby* took up the theme again in its 26th issue and quipped with the headline, "When saucers learned to fly", whereas a company newspaper made reference to "Secret Service Cases." In addition, we have been presented with many other publications on this same theme, some of which are highly interesting, in which there is no lack of amazing references to design drawings and models supposed to have fallen into Allied hands at the end of the war.

It would indeed require a hard-working and conscientious chronicler to sift through such a profusion of data. But, as the old saying goes, "There is no smoke without fire." Through the information supplied us by Walter Schauberger, which has provided us with much documentary evidence, much of the above will be made clear. We would, however, like to keep a certain distance from comments which reflect only isolated opinions. Everyone can draw his own conclusions from such views as have here been quoted.

In connection with many such reflections, a letter written by Viktor Schauberger to a friend on the 2nd August 1958 is very informative. The following are extracts:

"The 'flying saucer' which was flight-tested on the 19th February 1945 near Prague and which attained a height of 15,000 metres in 3 minutes and a horizontal speed of 2,200 kilometres per hour, was constructed according to a model I built at Mauthausen concentration camp in collaboration with the first class engineers and stress-analysts assigned to me from the prisoners there. It was only after the end of the war that I came to hear, through one of the workers under my direction, a Czech, that further intensive development was in progress: however, there was no answer to my enquiry.

"From what I understand, just before the end of the war, the machine is supposed to have been destroyed on Keitel's orders. That's the last I heard of it. In this affair, several armament specialists were also involved who appeared at the works near Prague, shortly before my return to Vienna, and asked that I demonstate the fundamental basis of it: the creation of an atomic low-pressure zone, which develops in seconds when either air or water is caused to move radially and axially under conditions of a falling temperature gradient."

Because of their many undeniably cranky associations, any mention of flying saucers tends to induce multitudinous and many-flavoured reactions, depending upon the individual. Personally, I have never seen any flying discs other than frisbees – themselves possessing some interesting aerodynamic properties – but from these and other research reports, there seems little doubt that Schauberger's work on flying discs was successful. The German research team, however, was split up when the war ended and the results were either lost, never correctly understood, or buried deep in classified governmental defence libraries.

Spin, Spirals, Shape and Motion

How does one relate the work of independent researchers such as Schauberger to what is currently considered to be the world of 'acceptable' science? In particular, is it possible to understand – in the terminology of such science – his trout turbine or the translation of one form of motion into another, even drawing in energy in the process from a more universal energy field? Such motion or energy would thus be made available for performing work in what we consider to be a purely physical manner.

Looking at things from first principles, we have to understand that motion is the essence of manifestation. Everything we perceive is an energy dance. At the physical level, this subatomic dance is spun out of the energy of space or the vacuum state energy field. And the nature of the motion of these spinning, whirling energy vortices which we call subatomic particles is of the utmost importance, for it is a pattern which gives rise to all the macroscopic forms we perceive with our senses and allied instrumentation.

So by working with these manifested effects on the vacuum surface, which we think of as our physical reality, it seems to be is possible to change the properties of the vacuum or spatial energy matrix itself. This permits a flow of energy from the vacuum into physical manifestation, as a relationship between electrical charge, magnetic polarity, mass, gravitation – and – *motion*.

As we have seen, it seems clear that the relationship between these forces and the vacuum energy state contains certain thresholds where the laws of physics as we presently understand them, become extended. And motion is one of these parameters.

Clearly, Schauberger, by observation of nature alone was able to dispense with the direct manipulation of electrical and magnetic forces, even specific attention to gravity, and by the power of shape, form and motion alone was able to mimic nature's processes.

Maybe this is one of the mechanisms by which the birds fly, the fishes swim and the bumble bee stays aloft. Perhaps the intricate weavings and travels of the blood in our veins and arteries also forms such whirls and vortices. Can the beating of our heart, the intricate mechanism of its valves, the blood flow in the capillaries, the fluids within our cells, the molecular dance of energy patterns in the DNA and all other molecules – can all these be obeying some hidden law of motion that we humans with our concrete minds and straight-edged thinking cannot comprehend? It seems very likely.

Suppose that this ever-recurrent hyperbolic spiral were an aspect of the form of motion followed by the vacuum energy as it spins – or spirals – into manifestation as the subatomic particles comprising our physical world. There could be two natural outcomes. Firstly, the forms of nature we see in the physical world, being inwardly comprised of this motion in, perhaps, clockwise and anticlockwise form, would naturally assume those shapes which bear a harmonic or even a direct relationship to the fundamental spiral or spin. At least they would be of the same 'family' of shapes, though constrained by the outworking of the inherent polarity in nature and by the patternings within the more subtle and complex energy blueprints underlying all physical forms.

Secondly, were a macroscopic object to be placed in a motion reflecting the movement of the subatomic realm which comprises it, then one can imagine that its particles, atoms and molecules might fall into an alignment related to their more inward, fundamental motion at the subatomic and vacuum state levels. And in particular, through the alignment of this energy within, the more outwardly observable properties of the molecules of, for example, *water* might be expected to exhibit unusual characteristics. Perhaps there is a resonance effect created when the outer reflects the inward condition, creating an amplification of the external effects, the 'new' energy of the system being derived from the vacuum condition.

This would be analagous to the magnetization of a piece of soft iron, or of iron filings. Each atom of iron possesses a magnetic field, but normally these tiny fields cancel each other out, leaving the nett *effect* of there appearing to be no magnetic field. By magnetizing the piece of iron, which actually means no more than *aligning* its individual atoms, the magnetic polarity of the entire material is expressed in the piece of iron itself. That is, we have created a magnet. And to do so we have done no more than create a particular kind of order amongst the *already magnetic* atoms of iron.

But magnetism is itself no more than an effect created by the clockwise or anticlockwise spin of the unpaired electrons in the *periphery* of the atom of iron. The magnetic effect caused by the spin of the other paired electrons in the atom sums to zero because the electrons are attracted to each other in these pairs, each electron spinning in the opposite direction to its partner. But note that this does not *eliminate* their inherent magnetic effect any more than two equally balanced teams in a tug or war means that the forces on the centre of the rope are non-existent. It just means that because the nett outward *effect* is zero, and we do not observe it.

Perhaps something similar happens to water when moved in Schauberger's spirals. We are aligning molecules, just as we do when we magnetize a material. And by so doing, we create outward effects which were not apparent beforehand. The effect may well be apparent if we could observe just one molecule of water, by itself. But all together, their nett effect when non-aligned is to cancel out all outward manifestation of the effect.

Indeed, the water molecule itself is polarized, magnetically and electrically, a result of its inward subatomic constitution, its own particular dance out of the vacuum state ocean, and there are many ideas amongst scientists concerning the way it behaves in both inert forms and when patterned by the life force within the bodies of living organisms. Some of these have been discussed in *The Web of Life* and *Subtle Energy*.

Professor Eric Laithwaite, Harold Aspden and the Gyroscope

As we have said, the fundamental law of all differentiated forms is polarity or duality. It arises automatically when the One is first overlain by the greater, Formative Mind and is multiplied and endlessly reflected from that point into the myriad forms familiar to us. Yet the underlying and primal polarity remains clearly identifiable in all manifestation, even amongst the manyness in which we presently find ourselves.

In our physics, whether conventional or vacuum state, the same applies. All forms are interconnected and interwoven with this law of polarity and causality. Electrostatic charge, magnetic polarity, gravitational attraction, all these produce and are a part of the *motion* which maintains things in existence. They are all aspects of patterning in the kaleidoscopic image we call our physical world and think to be so real. *And they are thus all related*. The one can be expressed as the other if only we can see how the image is projected and can see how to tweak the projection system.

So motion expressed as shape and rhythm – as differentiation in space and time – is so familiar to us that we feel that it can hold no secrets. Yet since motion is our observation of patterns in space and time – both intrinsic physical realities we do not really comprehend – one cannot say that the true nature of motion is known to us. So if certain kinds of motion produce certain unexpected results, this is no more than we should expect, for we do not understand how time and space have come into being in the first place.

It is not surprising therefore that Searl, Schauberger, Saxl and others have found intriguing and unexpected effects and relationships. Nor are such phenomena confined to the work of independent researchers, for in recent years work in our British universities has demonstrated the same effect.

Four of the principle protagonists have been Professor Eric Laithwaite, Dr Harold Aspden, Sandy Kidd and Scott Strachan. Eric Laithwaite, from London University's Imperial College, has been involved with research into magnetic levitation and gyroscope research for many years.

Harold Aspden, from the University of Southampton, describes a simple and crucial experiment[1], demonstrated for him by Professor Laithwaite.

> The facts of the experiment are so remarkable that they would be unbelievable to anyone who has not witnessed at close quarters the demonstration by Professor Laithwaite.
>
> He takes hold of a shaft with two hands, holding it horizontally at knee height. An assistant then uses a power tool to spin a 50 pound flywheel at one end of the shaft until it is rotating at several thousand revolutions per minute. A 50 pound wheel rotating at this speed and held away from, but necessarily close to, the body commands respect for the dangers involved. It is not something that one expects to manipulate with ease.
>
> However, one is aware that one could release the hold near the wheel and *expect to be able to support the full weight of the system by one's other hand, without having to exert a couple manually via one's wrist,* (ie. without needing to strain one's wrist to hold the shaft horizontal with the 50 pound weight on the other end). Indeed, it would lie outside the capacity of human strength to apply such a twist to the shaft axis.
>
> What should then happen is that the wheel will precess[2] continuously in a horizontal plane, requiring the holder to turn around with it, keeping a firm grip on the end of the shaft.
>
> What is found, however, is that the human feel for the

[1] *Ghost Mass and the Unseen Energy World as Revealed by the Anomalies of the Gyroscope,* The Tothmattian Review, 1988.

[2] Precession means that the shaft – the axis of rotation – 'fixed' at one end by one's wrist, with the flywheel on the other, will describe a shape like that of a cone – or a hyperbolic spiral.

reaction forces on the end of the shaft senses that the load can be lightened by applying a gentle pull. The wheel then precesses in a controlled manner. The surprise is that the free end of the shaft lifts with very little effort, totally incommensurate with the 50 pound weight of the wheel. By such lifting action, the wheel rises following a helical path with the shaft still horizontal. An even greater surprise is that the helix angle is 32 degrees, which also happens to be the helix angle of type A DNA, angle 32.7 degrees.

Surely, this is one of the most basic discoveries ever made? The spinning mass restrained only so as to precess freely about an axis will find it can travel around a helical path centered on that axis and do this without any particular regard for the potentials opposing its motion. *It seems that the energy needed to overcome these potentials, for example gravitation, is drawn from the spin energy. In sight, then, comes the idea that if the spin energy of an atom is sustained by sub-quantum processes that tap the energy of the universe, we can harness that energy in 'free energy' or anti-gravity applications.*

Here, we are not talking about theory, but rather reality. Professor Laithwaite's demonstration continues by him raising the flywheel effortlessly with one hand until it has precessed through 360° and is supported well above his head. The pressure exerted through the hand in the up, down and lateral sense serves to control the position of the flywheel in the helical path that is wound around the professor. The wheel cannot be held single-handed with its centre of mass at rest at any point along the helix but it can be moved up and down between such points with no apparent work being done by the person involved. Nor does that person feel the 50 pound weight of the wheel, once the manual sensing of the one-handed support has taken over whilst it is precessing.

The demonstration is not a magician's trick. Indeed, there are items of specially designed laboratory equipment that support the same findings. However, as is normal in scientific circles, those who witness these remarkable results refuse to believe that what they see can have any fundamental significance not embraced by the teachings of Newton, as modified by Einstein. A discerning evaluation, with an eye upon the tremendous technological implications of this discovery and with a willingness to see Einstein's theory overthrown if it stands in the way of technological progress, cannot fail to concede that something very fundamental and new has leapt in front of us and cannot be ignored.

Aspden then continues by describing the origin of this ghost energy in mathematical terms, concluding,

> It is submitted, therefore, that the Laithwaite gyroscope experiments give us a clear indication that energy in the vacuum or aether is involved in precessional motion. Furthermore, the energy anomaly on the precessional motion points to the existence of the gravitational 'ghost' mass produced by setting up a negative energy vacuum state by displacing energy on the vacuum itself.

Aspden then extends his argument to explain how free energy devices based upon permanent magnets can be understood as the alignment of electrons, precessing in synchrony and spacial order in their subatomic spinning motion. He writes:

> Finally, the views expressed above, in arguing that the vacuum can release its energy, particularly when primed by spinning bodies, have a natural extension to the 'free' energy devices using ferromagnetic cores. By inducing precessional motion in the spins which account for ferromagnetism and relying on these spins being maintained by environmental equilibrium, whether ambient heat or something more fundamental that determines the quantum spin states, one can hope to secure the controlled release of that energy. This is an avenue of exploration that opens up, once we face the discovery made by Professor Laithwaite.

Noting Aspden's comments on the possibility of temperature affecting the electrons' spin states, it is worth commenting that temperature is a measure of the excitability or motion of the atoms or molecules in a substance, which (along with pressure), provides the energy influencing the marked changes of state between solid, liquid, gaseous and plasmic phases of matter. Therefore, temperature will be yet another parameter for the melting pot in our search for the threshold where vacuum energy can be outwardly utilized.

Indeed; returning to Viktor Schauberger's flying disc research, (page 255), he himself comments on the creation of anomalous effects discovered, "When either air or water is caused to move radially and axially (ie. precessional or in a concentrating hyperbolic centripetal spiral) under conditions of a falling temperature gradient."

And note also, the quotation of page 249, drawing attention to the fundamental polarity of the universe as expressed in rising (expanding, centrifugal) and falling (contracting, centripetal) temperature gradients.

And remember, too, that salmon and trout seek out water at its anomaly point of greatest density, +4°C. Furthermore, Schauberger also demonstrated, by adding warm water up-stream, that at temperatures greater than this, the fish had difficulty in remaining motionless in a fast flowing current. Perhaps a more detailed study of birds, fishes and flying insects could tell us something of the secrets we would like to uncover.

So, in his conclusion, Aspden has the following to say concerning free energy devices.

> Those who look with scorn on the attempts to extract energy from mysterious sources in mysterious ways should be more cautious. It no longer suffices to rely on the laws of Newton or Einstein's philosophy. Even the law of conservation of energy has to be ready to admit that there can be energy in the vacuum itself, enough at least to match the precessional energy density content of the flywheel, and possibly vastly more.
>
> This does not mean, of course, that all 'free' energy ideas are to be considered with respect. The field is alive with proposals that cannot stand up to close scrutiny and many are clearly non-runners even from a superficial viewpoint. However, it does seem that Professor Laithwaite has found the key to one of the possible routes by which we can explore new technological opportunities in a field which takes us closer to the dream of 'free' energy or anti-gravity.

Sandy Kidd, Scott Strachan and the Levitating Gyroscope

Tying up the threads, as they are at the present moment, there are at least two inventors with gyroscope-based machines which can be demonstrated *to become lighter without any reactionary force*, when set in motion. These machines *exhibit a lifting force which has no reactionary counterpart*, as conventionally 'required' by Newton's laws of action and reaction, unless one assumes that there is a balancing pressure exerted by the vacuum. These reproducible, experimental results are inexplicable by Newtonian or Einsteinian theory.

The two inventors are both Scotsmen – Sandy Kidd from Dundee and Scott Strachan from Edinburgh. Sandy

Kidd first came to the public notice in 1987 when he demonstrated a device hovering above his workbench, balanced against a counterweight weighing almost half a pound less than the machine.

Professor Laithwaite was fascinated when the gyroscope was demonstrated to him, excitedly telling the inventor, "You have a potential space drive there. It has all the right ingredients to go forward without having to shovel material out the back as with conventional engines." Rockets are powered through space by reacting – in a forward direction – against all the material they blow out the back. A motion which requires no reaction, nothing to push against, also requires nothing to throw out the back and a host of space-drive problems are instantly solved, not the least of which is the weight of fuel which must be carried, only so that it can be shovelled out backwards!

Kidd was taken on by Dundee University as a consultant and paid a professor's salary to pursue his research. He was featured in the national press and in a TV documentary, even becoming a local folk hero with a song written about him! But scepticism and sniping from other academics slowly eroded Dundee University's enthusiasm and they finally pulled the plug on Kidd's gyroscope research. People find it hard to modify entrenched ideas – whether social, religious, philosophical or scientific. Our ignorance of the true or natural state of affairs leads us to mistake such ideas and descriptions for reality.

Rescue was at hand, however, in the shape of Noel Carroll, millionaire boss of an Australian high-technology company. Overriding the advances of a couple of merchant banks and a business consortium who were considering funding Kidd, Carroll whisked him off to Melbourne, after an official civic farewell from Dundee. There he is presently developing the technique of gyroscopic propulsion.

Meanwhile, back in Edinburgh, physicist Scott Strachan, head of the problem-solving electronics and engineering company, Syrinx Innovations, was experimenting with his own gyroscopes, demonstrating the same effect of lift without reaction. This time, British industry have been quick off the mark, with British Aerospace indicating an interest in his work.

Regarding these gyroscopes, Aspden has an apt last word. He reminds his readers in the December 1988 edition of *Electronics and Wireless World* about a photograph of Professor Laithwaite, "supporting a heavy precessing gyroscopic flywheel with his little finger and arm partially extended." This photograph was printed as supporting evidence of Alex Jones', January 1987 contribution. "Surely," he says, "Isaac Newton would have burnt out many a candle revising his laws had he been aware of this phenomenon?" So one imagines, would Einstein.

The Full Story of the Five Blind Men and an Elephant called Raj

Once upon a time, long, long ago, in a far off distant corner of Rajasthan, there lived a Maharaja. The Maharaja was a humble and pious man and did his best to rule with fairness and firmness. And he was well loved.

The Maharaja possessed a magnificent estate. As far as the eye could see from his palace, the grounds and gardens extended away on all sides. Down to a lake, squawking, quacking and squeaking with wild creatures; along rushing streams, cascading waterfalls and bubbling rivulets; to ornate flowered gardens; to a wilderness of ancient trees, thick jungle undergrowth and wild animals – all these spread out around his central dwelling. And the Maharaja was contented.

His household included many servants, as well as innumerable cousins, brothers, in-laws, salaried courtiers and even a few bureaucrats. There were also many tamed, wild animals. He was married to a charming wife, the Maharana. And they were all more or less content with their lives.

Amongst the animals was one grand old elephant named Raj, the Maharaja's favourite, who had carried him and his father before him on many ceremonial processions, as well as on frequent outings into his wide estate.

The elephant, like his master, had an observant eye and a kind heart, as well as enjoying the fuss and pomp which was invariably made of him. He lived, with his mahout, nearby to the main palace and had for company a number of less-aged elephants. They all lived together in a large paddock, while the mahouts lived in a neat collection of small Indian cottages, alongside. And they, too, were all quite contented.

One day, a group of Indians from the open plains came to visit the Maharaja. Amongst them came five blind men. The group had many things to discuss with the Maharaja, as men do, but one of their more innocent wishes was that their small number of blind brothers should be permitted to meet the great elephant, Raj. For they had never, in all their life, ever before met an elephant.

The Maharaja was, of course, delighted to be able to offer this small service to his guests and in the cool of the late afternoon, he personally conducted them to the paddock where the elephants lived.

Raj was dutifully led out by his mahout and presented to the five blind men. These five went forward, each encountering a different part of the beast.

"Ah," said one, bumping into the flank of the animal, "An elephant is large and mostly flat, like the side of a tent."

Another, who had taken hold of Raj's tusk, exclaimed, "But no, the elephant is long, hard, curved and pointed. Rather like a warped fencing post."

But the third had stumbled into one of the front legs of the great creature and proclaimed that the elephant was, "No more than a large, tall pillar – yet strangely capable of self-activated movement." This man was clearly a philosopher and observer of life.

The fourth, catching hold of the tail, decided that an elephant was a kind of snake, whilst the fifth finding himself mischievously teased by Raj's long trunk was firmly of the belief that an elephant was more like an animated, but intelligent rope. Probably self-organizing.

These five, standing around the elephant, each with his own honest yet limited perception and experience, began to debate the nature of the beast, while those who had eyes kept quiet and looked on with both affection and some considerable humour.

Being blind to the visual nature of the physical world, the five men were used to discussions concerning the nature of things they were unable to see. Indeed, this occupied much of their time. And so they happily debated the true nature of the elephant, while all the time Raj stood quietly by, whisking his tail to drive off the flies, teasing the man who was in the region of his trunk, and occasionally adjusting the weight upon his legs.

The informal parliament continued and new insights were received by this leisurely group. Suddenly, Raj, flapping his ears, brushed the top of the head of the man holding fast to one of his front legs. (He was a very tall man, I have to admit). "Ah hah," said the philosopher, "An elephant is not just a self-activating, mobile pillar but has wavy, floppy characteristics too." This gave the discussion even greater interest, as you can imagine!

Well, the Maharaja and his court watched them with amusement while he, his courtiers and the remainder of the visitors had a cup of tea. Finally, he thought that it might be kind to let the five men know where they were going wrong. Accordingly, he asked one of his entourage to gently inform them of the true situation.

But the result was not as he had expected. For while one or two of the group had begun to suspect that perhaps they were all correct and yet incomplete in their perceptions, the remainder had become so heavily entrenched in their position and so identified with their own point of view, that they rounded on the poor courtier and with one accord told him to go away. "After all", they said, "You aren't even touching the elephant, and you certainly haven't been considering the problem as long as we have So how can you know anything about it?"

And so the Maharaja and his party left both them and the long-suffering Raj, to enjoy the remainder of the afternoon and evening in what had by then become a formalized philosophical debate, with a variety of possible, yet conflicting theories.

But the Maharaja and his party had a good walk around, thoroughly enjoying both the beauties of nature and each other's companionship. And to this day, at least as far as I have been told, the five blind men are still vigorously debating the nature of elephants. Whilst those with eyes are quite contented.

—— CHAPTER 11 ——

The Nature of Nothing

Back to the Vacuum – A Summary

There have, over the ages, been many philosophers and scientists who have expressed a belief that there must be some sort of an ether. This is true of eastern philosophies, the Greek philosophers such as Plato and Aristole, and right through the centuries to our present day. I began chapter six with a discussion of some of these people and their ideas.

Aristotle, often called the father of modern reductionist science, thought of it as filling the heavens outside the earth. Early physicists thought of it as a substance filling all of space and within which light travelled as waves. They had no knowledge that most of our nicely 'solid' matter is comprised almost entirely of 'empty' space, too, permitting enlargement of the concept to that of an all enveloping spacial matrix in which substance is perceived both as vibrations and spinning vortices of energy.

Maxwell described the ether as, "A material substance of a more subtle kind than visible bodies, supposed to exist in those parts of space which are apparently empty." To Newton, the ether occupied all space, including that between the atoms. At the time, he did not know of the vast spaces *within* atoms, as well. Similarly, many modern scientists and philosophers, including Bertrand Russell, C. W. Richardson, Tydal, Carl Krafft, Sir Oliver Lodge, and Sir Arthur Eddington have confirmed their belief in the existence of an ether. Ideas concerning the nature of this ether can, however, be wrong or at least, inexact.

The controversial experiments first conducted by Michelson in 1881 and 1887 to determine whether or not the ether existed may well have been based upon incorrect assumptions concerning it. If we are uncertain whether a thing exists, we are certainly in no position to accurately predict its characteristics. Michelson's experiment was based upon the assumption that ether was 'motionless' and *filled* all of space, with the earth travelling through it. Therefore, he argued, if a beam of light is projected in the direction in which the earth is moving, it will travel faster than one which is simultaneously projected at right angles to the earth's movement. Subsequent recombinations of these two beams should therefore demonstrate that they are out of phase, this being visible as interference patterns. In his experiment, no interference patterns were detected and thus the theory of an ether was reckoned to be disproven. In fact, all it proved was that that particular theory concerning the nature of the ether was incorrect. It did not prove that ether did not exist, per se[1].

The more modern theory, however, comprehends that all material substance is just patterns on the etheric 'surface', that the ether *is* space itself, but as a real formative energy. Under these circumstances, it is clearly difficult to make definitive decisions regarding how these patterns will behave in relationship to each other. In specific mathematical terms, we just do not know how one 'piece of space' will behave as it passes 'through' other space (eg. air or water, or the space between planets and stars). After all, *what does it mean for space to pass through space?* We can make some intriguing surmises and guesses, but we have no real knowledge as yet. We certainly could not predict how the speed of the patterns which we perceive as electromagnetic energy, would be affected by the movement of their source. Yet this was at the basis of Michelson's experiment.

Einstein, himself, was aware of the mathematical problems associated with consideration of three-dimensional (spatial) objects moving (passing through) other space, whether those objects were planets, stars and oranges, or electrons and photons. His geometrically-based theory of relativity addressed itself to all these problems of space, relative motion, time, mass, gravity and speed, predicting some fascinating relationships between them. Things get

[1] See footnote on page 311.

heavier the faster they move, you cannot go faster than the speed of light because mass becomes infinite, light is bent by gravitational attraction, time passes at different rates for two observers depending upon their relative speeds, and so on.

Some of these predictions have been shown to be true or true only under certain circumstances. Others may not be true at all, for as we have pointed out, even Einstein himself acknowledged that his model was incomplete and is therefore an imperfect image of what is happening in nature. He never really relinquished his attraction towards the ether concept, nor is it really known whether he envisaged his 'space-time' as a theoretical construct or as a real existent something.

But it was Einstein who laid the foundations, along with quantum theory, for all the present day theoretical work concerning the nature of the spatial matrix and its manifested substance in which we find ourselves embedded. Whether we call that matrix the ether, space-time, space, hyperspace, zero point energy, the physical vacuum, the gravity field, the tachyon field, the Fermi-sea, an eleven dimensional superforce – or whatever – is largely irrelevant. Nature is no respecter of our concepts and terminology, but carries on regardless! Nature has no interest in who wins a Nobel prize for the best current model of how she works and – to be frank – neither should we!

These terms, no doubt, reflect different approaches or understandings of this creative fabric of vacuum, but energy fabric there most certainly is and I have plumped for the more simply understood expression of the 'vacuum state'.

In England, Sir Oliver Lodge, one of the early pioneers in the field of electricity and radio, never abandoned his belief in the ether. His book, *The Ether of Space*, published in 1909 contains many astute observations. He comments:

> We have no means of getting hold of the ether mechanically; we cannot grip it or move it in the ordinary way: *we can only get it electrically*. We are straining the ether when we charge a body with electricity; it tries to recover, it has the power of recoil.

"We can only get it electrically", he says and the theme is also taken up by modern physicist, Schaffranke, in his book, dated 1986, nearly eighty years later. The link to extracting this energy of the ether or vacuum seems to be through electricity and probably relative motion and magnetism, too, as we have seen. Certainly, those scientists who have either made experimental contributions to this area of science or who have presented useful theoretical concepts giving us ideas on how to proceed experimentally, have all involved electric, magnetic or electromagnetic energy as the key link point in experimentally connecting gravity, mass and electromagetism. In fact, since it is thought that electromagnetic energy is the only other force besides gravity outside the atom, there is no other alternative remaining. Even within the atom, we know that electromagnetism and the weak and strong forces are all interconnected, for there are mathematical models describing this. But gravity remains the elusive, yet all-pervading force that we have not yet tied in, theoretically, with electromagnetism and these other forces. Yet we know they must be connected for the universe is a manifestly integrated affair.

The reason must be that the linkage is more subtle than that of electricity and magnetism. And it seems very clear that this linkage must be within the vacuum or etheric state. But if our scientific paradigms do not include a reasonable recognition of this sea of creative energy, then clearly we will find it difficult to know just how to proceed experimentally, when attempting either to harness gravity or to produce electricity out of this zero point of vacuum energy.

So the concept of an ether in which matter or substance moves around like vegetables in a stew would seem to leave too many questions unanswered. For we would still not comprehend what material substance and forces actually *are*, in their inner constitution. We would still be left with ultimate, fundamental particles, but possess no knowledge of what makes them exist. "A tiny, spinning, charged blob of something" would not suffice as an explanation. We would have to know the details of that something.

The ether, or vacuum however, is more correctly

perceived to be the fundamental gross physical energy matrix or ocean from within which the subatomic particles and other forces manifest or dance into existence due to aspects of movement and polarity. This activity is linked in to consciousness through our unconscious mental processes and our perceptive mechanism of the five senses, with their more inward mental counterparts. From this we can understand that everything which appears to our senses and to our instrumentation is actually only patterns upon this vacuum energy, bubbles upon the ocean which exist only as an intrinsic part of that ocean. And this is the way that the Eastern philosophy describes akash. It is said to be the space within which and from which things are manifested. "From the void come a thousand things."

We still have the problem, of course, concerning the detailed nature of that vacuum or akash, but we have at least found the unified field of outward physical manifestation, the energy field of creative potential within which all energy is seen to be related. We have also realized in the process that at that point we start on a vertical energy spectrum which lies within ourselves and which includes our own mind energies, the whole of which is enlivened by consciousness.

We thus have the mechanism by which we create our own pre-programmed destinies from within our own minds and a total concept which permits an understanding of many previously ignored or little understood phenomena of everyday life, as we have previously discussed.

We have also described a mechanism of manifestation from within, which can account for all the higher levels of energies within us, and within creation. For the lower is created out of the higher and our all-important *experience* of these layers or levels depends entirely on the level to which our consciousness has attained, the point at which our attention is focused.

That is to say that the highest level of Supreme Being or Consciousness is right here, right now, but that since our point of perception or attention on this ladder is down at the bottom, we can see only the bottom rungs. If our level of attention or consciousness is raised higher or to the top, then we perceive all the lower levels as manifestations within our own consciousness and discover that all of them are within us, right here and now. In simple terms, God is everywhere and within everything. And He is also the one Source, the undifferentiated Ocean of Creative Love, from which all else springs. This is the perennial mystic perception.

Theories of Vacuum State Structure

So there are innumerable theories concerning the nature of the vacuum state, some ancient, others stemming from around the turn of the century, with new suggestions continually being presented right up to the present day. This theorization has continued because the idea is too fundamental to just go away. There are too many discrepancies and unexplained laboratory phenomena for scientists to really think that they have got it all wrapped up. If they are honest, they know that they have not. Indeed, this is why there is all the effort to find a Grand Unified Theory.

Even to this day, scientists have no real idea what keeps the subatomic world in perpetual motion and why the atom does not collapse, with the positive protons attracting the negative electrons. That the original energy in the universe came out of nowhere in a Big Bang long, long ago is the creation myth of the scientific world.

But *where* did that energy come from? Paul Davies (in *Superforce*) and others try unconvincingly to explain away the original 'free lunch'. But that still doesn't explain why electrons and protons, not to mention quarks, mesons, bosons, neutrons, neutrinos and much more, with all their various flavours and charms, go on moving so merrily and in such a constant fashion. Why don't they just slow down and stop or collapse into each other? And in particle accelerators there seems to be no end to the multitude of subatomic particles that can be created at energies high enough to break up the vacuum whirls which constitute the particles, creating mass, charge and motion in an almost endless array of variations even within our perceived dimensions.

Note, again, how motion is essential at the subatomic level to the existence of that particle (it is part of what the particle is) and how, along with that motion, such manifested and polarized properties as electrical charge, magnetic polarity and mass are produced. So we should not be surprised if in a converse manner, spinning a charged object such as Saxl and Searl have done, results in a change of mass and weight. It is quite analagous, but at a macroscopic level to what is already happening at a subatomic level, where it is simply an energy vortex which manifests to us as the mass of subatomic particles, and hence in aggregate – as the mass of an object. Once again, man has only mimicked a natural process. Nature was at it all along. This is part of the mechanism of manifestation! We only need to bring together our observations in conventional science, but in a different way. The answer must indeed be very simple and be staring us in the face.

It might be of interest to mention some of those theories that have not already been discussed. The bibliograpy will help any interested readers to track down the sources more specifically.

Harold Puthoff, for example, of the Institute for Advanced Studies in Austin, Texas thinks in terms of a zero point or background sea of electromagnetic energy that constitutes the vacuum state. It is this background energy level, which, he suggests, prevents the electrons and protons collapsing into each other in the atom. Physicists say that electrons possess an energy which prevents them from doing this. But from where does that energy arise and why dosen't it just radiate away? Nobody knows.

Puthoff suggests that the energy of electrons is in a dynamic state, continually 'absorbing' energy from the background vacuum energy and radiating it away. He has mathematically shown how this could be so, (*Physical Review D.* Vol 35, p3266). This is like Bearden's image of the electron as a spray nozzle, as we have previously noted. I would further add that the electron is an effect, perceived by the instrumental extension of our senses upon this vacuum sea. It does not so much absorb and radiate, but actually *is* this energy in manifested form. But perhaps these are two ways of saying the same thing.

Actually, the concept of zero point energy was first conceived by physicists back in the 1930's when they realized the necessity for a mathematical term arising from the calculations of quantum theory. For with the concept of an ether having lost respectability, the mathematics still required that vacuum possessed an energy. In fact, these days, theoretical calculations lead to the embarrassing conclusion that ninety-nine percent of the mass/energy of the universe is 'missing'. This energy was called zero point energy because it still remains even at temperatures of absolute zero, when all the oscillations we call thermal energy have ceased. J. A. Wheeler even calculated in 1962 that the energy density of vacuum is a prodigious 10^{94} grams per cubic centimetre. Paul Dirac actually showed theoretically how electron-positron (matter-antimatter) pairs could arise from it and its role in the manifestation of subatomic particles has been the subject of continuous speculation and theorizing over the last few decades. So the concept of an ether by another name has never really gone away.

In more recent thinking, the expression of zero point has also acquired an additional meaning, as a point of structured balance or zero as I have described earlier.

Regarding Barrett's report on the Searl generator, Mr Jan P. Roos, also of Austin, Texas, a fluid dynamicist and president of the private, Association for Pushing Gravity Research, comments that Barrett's theory, based upon the concept of an ether, is quite correct. He also points out the self-stabilizing, gyroscopic effects of a rotating ring, as used in Searls' generator. This is like a top, which spins on a pivot for as long as it is spinning, but topples over as soon as it slows down below a certain critical point. So we are once more faced with relationships between motion, stability, thresholds and change of state.

Again, Dr Arthur Cam, an American Space Scientist, after he had travelled from California especially to meet Searl and see his work, had this to say:

> I was very sceptical indeed. In the meantime, I have let myself be convinced that Searl's calculations are sound, and that he will make it. . . . Searl's propulsion system will make customary propulsion as obsolete as a mill-wheel.

Similarly, in Japan, Professor Schinichi Seiki has developed an elaborate theory of the ether, starting with the established theory of the Lorentz force which involves the *movement* of atoms in the presence of external electric and magnetic fields. Seiki has theorized on the possibility of creating "negative gravitational energies" (i.e. anti-gravity) through the application of a suitably oscillating electromagnetic field, to create resonance at an atomic level.

Nuclear Magnetic Resonance (NMR) is a phenomenon that is understood well enough to be used in medical diagnostic equipment, where the changes in spatial electron spin are observed when a high-frequency, oscillating magnetic field is applied. Depending upon the frequency, different molecules go into resonance, thereby absorbing the energy at that frequency. Since it can be calculated which molecules resonate at which frequencies, it becomes possible to monitor the composition of the substance under test. In medical diagnosis, this 'substance' is the body itself, though I do not think that I would fancy having every molecule in my body interfered with!

Seiki, however, has taken this idea further. Polar spin, he suggests, is associated directly with the gravitational field. After all, *something* in matter at the subatomic level must be creating the gravitational field of the whole body. It is the gravitational effect at the subatomic level of the whole earth which can be seen as creating the gravitational pull of the earth as a whole.

When a rotating AC electrical field is superimposed upon a DC magnetic field, the superimposition causes a summation of forces, resulting in a vacuum stress. Seiki states that at a certain resonant frequency a threshold is reached at which "negative gravitational energies" occur. At the atomic level, he calls this *Nuclear Electrical Resonance*. Seiki's work does appear to have been taken seriously even amongst some conventional scientists, for Dr Wernher von Braun made a point of discussing it personally with him on a visit to Japan. Amongst vacuum state theorists and inventors, his work is well respected.

And so the story continues. Dr Marcel J.J. Pages, a doctor of both nuclear engineering and medicine in France and founder member of C.I.R.G., an international centre for gravitational research formed in Rome during 1961, received a patent (No. 1,231.902) for an anti-gravity propulsion space vehicle. This is described and explained in his book *Le Defi De L'Antigravitation* (*The Challenge of*

Antigravitation). This is, once again, based on a theory of the ether and its energetic properties and constitution.

Dr Page's principle is also one where the electrostatic charge rotating around the body is to be 'degravitated'. As a consequence, he says, the body loses both weight and mass, or inertia. Another Frenchman, involved in this research was Professor Claude Poher, when director of the National Centre for Space Studies, the French equivalent of NASA.

Dr Poher has reportedly investigated around 35,000 UFO sightings, using computer analysis. A scale model of their anti-gravity propulsion unit is said to be a square metre in area, using both electromagnetic and nuclear energy, "to provide tremendous thrust". So says Dr Jean-Pierre Petit, a plasma physicist at the French Government's National Organization for Scientific Research.

The French, in fact, have had an official policy since 1954, as revealed by the French Minister of Defence, Monsieur Robert Galley during a radio interview in 1974, for studying UFO sightings and forwarding all such reports to French scientists for evaluation.

Again in France, Dr Marcel Pages refers to an old french manuscript from the 1800's. Quoting from a translation in Schaffranke's book, to which I am so much indebted, it says:

> We also saw in the Ducretet House, an old apparatus that has been forgotten for a long time and which merits being returned to a place of honor. As can be seen, it is a mica disk which is mobile on a point and which assumes a very rapid revolving motion when it is presented to a very powerful static machine, such as the Wimshurst machine.
>
> The rotation is then so energetic that gravity appears to be eliminated by centrifugal force although the latter seems to give only horizontal components, and the disc *flies off*. . .

Meanwhile, back in the U.S.A., as we earlier discussed, Bruce DePalma, an M.I.T. graduate and former lecturer, reports that, "We have discovered that the spinning or rotation of objects, *changes their inertia*." That is, that rapidly spinning an object changes its apparent mass. Schaffranke points out that, "The analogy between the kinematics of a spinning sphere and that of an electron in the gravitational field may cast some light on the mechanism of Searl's discs." This supports my earlier comments and relates directly to the work of Viktor Schauberger, the gyroscope experimenters and the attempt to create special magnets possessing precessing electron spin.

So these few theorists and experimenters that have been mentioned here are just a small representation of those pioneers who have risked ridicule and censure in their search for fundamental physical realities. Their work continues to this day. For the many whose work along these lines has not been mentioned, I must apologize. This is in no way a reflection upon their research, but only upon the limitations of a book of this type.

Pure Charge and Charged Mass

The scalar wave exponent, Tom Bearden, points out that in conventional electrical engineering, no difference is made between an electrically charged mass (e.g. an electron) and pure massless charge. This is because the concept of charge is always linked to a something (a mass such as an electron or proton) holding that charge. This, however, is a limited point of view and prevents us from ever considering the intrinsic nature of charge devoid of mass. For the two can be considered as separate phenomena.

Nobel laureate, Paul Dirac, was one of the first in recent years (in 1951) to reopen the ether question, by suggesting that space itself might possess such a charge but which is so ubiquitous that we cannot ordinarily notice its effects. This is like a bird sitting upon a high tension electrical cable who feels no ill effects because it is itself at the same high potential as the wire. No current, therefore, (i.e. electrons, charged masses) actually flows through it.

Similarly, all the space which we occupy is at the same high absolute potential. This we experience as zero because it all appears to be the same. We work with electricity, therefore, purely at a 'mechanical' level, pumping charged masses (electrons) up and down wires. Charge attached to mass is, however, only one aspect of its being. Using Bearden's neat and imaginative phraseology, conventional,

> Electromagnetic theory restricts us to walking along the high tension line, laboriously carrying small batteries and power units, unaware of the limitless surging power beneath our very feet.
>
> Electromagnetically, we have been rather like one of the five blind men who touched an elephant. We have only touched one small portion of the electromagnetism 'elephant', yet we thought we had grasped the entire beast.
>
> Orthodox scientists have never looked for a way to engineer the vacuum, because they have not realized that it is composed of pure massless charge.

This sea of highly charged, high energy potential can be engineered, as we have described, and one of the earliest verifications of this was in the ability of the theory to explain an effect first noted by H.B. Casimir in 1948. This Casimir effect is demonstrated by placing close together two uncharged parallel plates made of an electrically conducting material. The two plates are attracted to each other in a way which is not convincingly explained in any other way except that each plate reflects a substantial part of this zero point energy field away, creating a zone between the plates which is less energetic and therefore exerts less pressure. The result is an attractive force. A similar theory lies at the base of Dr Hans Nieper's shielding effect of gravity field energy.

Similar theorization also leads to a better understanding of surface phenomena in chemistry, including surface tension, bubble formation and surface adhesion.

Furthermore, such effects as are demonstrated by the Casimir effect could underlie all other zero point or vacuum energy, shape-related phenomena such as we find in pyramids, domes, arches and in the subtle atmosphere we feel inside or outside different buildings, and which relates to their architectural structure.

It also leads us into an understanding of beauty and aesthetics as a harmony and integration within the energies that comprise the beautiful object or scene, the painting, the sound or the idea. The harmony without resonates within our minds and we perceive whatever it is as beautiful. But the actual experience of the beauty is within ourselves, within our own minds. Others may not experience it. If we are upset emotionally, or just tired, we may even realize with one part of our mind that it is beautiful, but yet be unable to inwardly respond or resonate. If we are always disharmonized inside, then we appreciate but little of the beauties that surround us. We may never realize just what we are missing. This, too, is what all the mystics have said regarding mystic experience – that it is right here, within us, but our attention is focused in the wrong direction.

Actually, physicists are well aware that there is something odd with their calculations, for, as mentioned above, there appears to be a vast quantity of energy that has gone missing! Within the framework of modern physics the most recent answer is that this energy is in the form of a cosmic cloud of neutrinos (electrons with no charge). This is a pretty safe answer because neutrinos, carrying no charge, pass right through most substances without a trace. Only occasionally do they collide with an atomic nucleus, making their presence known only if the event happens near suitable particle detection equipment. But the theoretical necessity for suggesting this sea of neutinos can also be satisfied by the sea of zero point vacuum energy, or whatever other name one cares to call it.

These, however, are all concepts in the mind, which can put one into a mental spin and make one forget one's simple immediate experience in the here and now, where all our sensory experiences appear as just patterns upon the fabric of space. And these concepts, too, are conceived in different ways, depending upon the originator or the exponent of the concept. Which all goes to show that although understanding of this vacuum state abounds, no-one yet has very much idea how it is actually structured.

Concepts and Definitions

Just to give you an idea of how science, like any language, is a tightly-knit, locked-in language with everything defined in terms of everything else, possessing no absolute point, try looking through the following definitions and you will see what I mean. Each one is defined using terms which do themselves require further definition.

Space	The unlimited, three-dimensional expanse in which all material objects are located
Dimension	A measurement of size in a particular direction
Expanse	An uninterupted surface of something
Something	An unspecified or unknown thing
Thing	An object, a specific kind of something (!)
Object	A tangible and visible thing
Matter	Substance that occupies space and possesses mass
Position/ Location	The spacial co-ordinates of something
Motion	Change in position of something
Mass	The amount of matter in a body
Inertial Mass	A body's resistance to changes in velocity
Gravitational Mass	The force experienced by a body in a gravitational field. According to Einstein's theory of relativity, inertial mass and gravitational mass are equal
Gravity	Force of attraction between masses
Weight	Vertical force experienced by a mass due to gravity
Body	A something with three dimensions and a mass and which is distinguishable from surrounding objects
Force	Mass of a body multiplied by its acceleration
Field of Force	A region of space around a body within which it can exert a force upon another body not in contact with it
Energy	Capacity to perform work
Work	Force multiplied by the distance moved
Acceleration	Rate of change of velocity
Velocity	Rate of change of position, relative to time
Resistance	A force that tends to retard motion
Time	A quantity measuring duration
Duration	The length of time that something lasts
Point	A geometric element having no dimensions

Scalar	A quantity with magnitude but not direction (eg. temperature)
Quantity	A specified magnitude
Magnitude	A number assigned to a quantity (eg. such as weight)
Direction	Motion along spacial co-ordinates
Distance	Length of space between two points
Vector	A variable quantity that has magnitude and direction
Vector Field	A region of space under the influence of some quantity (eg. magnetic field strength) in which each point can be defined by a vector
Field	(i) A region of space under the influence of some scalar quantity (eg. temperature) (ii) A region of space that is in a vector field
Charge	An attribute of matter responsible for all electrical phenomena

These are some of the basic terms used in physics, with further definitions taken from *Collins English Dictionary*. Each is defined in terms of the other in a tightly interlocked set of concepts. This is the same in all language. My favourite pair are: *time* – "A quantity measuring duration" and *duration* – "The length of time that something lasts"... There are, of course, much more than just these few in the whole of science. Just trying to get one's head around all these definitions is enough to divorce one from the reality of what *is*. We then live just in our circular thoughts and lose sight of our experience of being. This is why science is confused between the concept and the thing itself. Meaning is different from what is.

So what can be said from an examination of the above is that science is the study of relationships, expressed conceptually, in what *is*. Relative relationships that is. Since any point of observation is already a part of the web, there is no point, in the physical universe, of absolute or non-related observation.

Please accept my apologies if reading through this lot has got your mind into a tangle. Please just look out of the window or go for a walk to know that nature knows absolutely nothing of any of the above. It just quietly gets on with it, as should we!

Effects, Causes and the Vacuum State

Bearden points out that all electrical and mechanical engineering is based upon the concept of a *force* being a real entity – a cause rather than an effect. But in engineering terms a force is actually defined as its ability to move some *mass*. That is, force is actually defined by its *effect*, not what *underlies* that effect at a fundamental level. All our present electrical and mechanical engineering, therefore, is logically or mathematically based on a perception and manipulation of *effects*, not deeper *causes*.

Our devices, of course, do work but they are extremely crude artefacts since they are not based upon any deep perception of physical fundamentals. They are a limited subset, comprised of the most obvious ways of using these electrical and mechanical effects or forces. Or in simple terms, we can make electrons move along wires and make use of the resulting *electrical current*, but we have not addressed ourselves to comprehending the fundamental nature of an electron and what keeps it in perpetual motion with properties (or effects) of charge and mass etc. We have still not understood what in essence it really *is*. In our engineering, we have rarely attempted to use a more fundamental understanding of the nature of an electron, or the complex web of energy interrelationships at the subatomic and vacuum levels. This has been previously pointed out.

Similarly with all the phenomena of science – magnetism, gravity, mass, electrical charge, force etc. They are all defined by their effects – as the effects themselves, in fact – and in terms of each other, too, and our engineering uses an understanding of these phenomena only in a strictly classical and 'obvious' manner. This creates a tight system of interlocked mathematical equations, but obscures from our mind the underlying reality of the vacuum energy matrix from within which all these effects are manifested. Indeed, *everything we perceive with our senses or physical scientific instrumentation is an effect, not a primary cause.*

Thus, our scientifically created devices, all our technology, is employing just a subset of the available possibilities. We are playing with the bubbles on the ocean and have not yet addressed ourselves to the ocean itself.

Put in another way, a force implies the presence of a mass, since force is defined as the ability to move a mass. The magnitude of a force is equal to the mass of the body multiplied by its acceleration. This is the definition we are taught at school. Force cannot, therefore, exist in a vacuum chamber, since a vacuum is defined as the absence of mass.

Electrical, magnetic and gravitational forces, therefore, which can be shown to *act* in a vacuum chamber, without the presence of any mass or any thing between the two objects, are hence only *effects*, not causes.

That means that despite all our electromagnetic inventions, conventional science still has no real idea *how* they work. To understand this requires a deeper understanding of the basic fundamentals of our physical universe.

Now, having shown that force per se does not exist in a vacuum, it also means that electromagnetic 'waves' do not exist in a vacuum either, for an electromagnetic wave is defined as an interaction of electric and magnetic 'force fields'.

Thus, electomagnetic waves are also effects, not primary. In fact, as Tesla pointed out in the 1890's and remained convinced of to his dying day in 1943, electromagnetic waves may really be longitudinal pressure waves, (like sound wave propogation), in the vacuum energy field. It is only in this way that they are transmitted through vacuum. What we think we perceive as transverse Hertzian waves (eg. oscillations of a guitar string) are only a perception of a part of the picture. Hence the problems with electromagnetic energy sometimes behaving like particles (photons) and sometimes like Hertzian waves. Physicists like Bearden suggest that it is neither, but energy variations within the vacuum state, transmitting as longitudinal pressure waves. It is only a part of these that our instrumentation perceives as either Hertzian waves or as particles. So we are back with the two-dimensional flatlanders perception of the three-dimensional orange. They see it only as an expanding and contracting circle. In

Bearden's phraseology, we have only grasped a small part of the elephant of electromagnetism, yet we thought we had got hold of the entire beast.

These problems are not unknown to physicists, of course, and it was deliberations of this kind that led Einstein to 'explain' gravity by means of 'curved' space, or the geometry of space, and its interaction with mass. Similarly, in quantum theory, the impossibility of forces acting across nothing, have led to their conception as the interactions between virtual particles – particles that come into existence, perform their function of transmitting energy (which we perceive as the 'force') and disappear again just as fast as their quantum legs can carry them, and before anyone can catch them doing it. To actually catch them at it would actually upset the 'laws' of energy conservation.

Similarly, the observable wave characteristics of photons, for example, in electromagnetic energy, are 'explained' as waves of probability in the positioning of the 'particle'. But in real terms, it is not surprising that physicists cannot agree what such a description actually means.

Stated in terms of vacuum state understanding, these are all partial truths. For all that exists are vibrating energy patterns manifesting as 'particles', 'waves', 'forces' etc. At the subatomic and vacuum state levels, they are none of these, but an interconnecting web or tapestry of energy, whose manner of interconnection we do not understand very well. It is the interplay of the three gunas (−, 0, +), weaving the fabric of the five tattwas, underlain by the inward creative power of the cosmic motor of Shabd, the Word or the Sound Current, which gives rise to all that we perceive and think, and indeed to our own consciousness as well.

As we have discussed, science recognizes the existence of only four forces – electromagnetism, gravity and the two intra-atomic forces, the weak and the strong. But these 'forces', even the intra-atomic pair, are actually mathematical *descriptions* of certain effects. Just like Newton gave a mathematic formulation to a force he called gravity and just as Einstein expanded this formulation, similarly the definition of the other 'forces' is purely a mathematical description of what they do (their effect), not what they *are*. Hence the need to describe the fundamental forces as particle interactions. But this only postpones the misery, for we still have no half-decent model of what a subatomic particle actually is. The images in our mind may be helpful, but what is happening is actually none of these. And whatever it is – we are an integral part of it, and thus can never adequately describe it as something apart from ourselves.

In the world of classical, reductionist science, scientists first observe a phenomenon. Then they attempt to describe it mathematically. When they have found a neat equation or set of equations, the phenomenon is said to have been 'discovered'. But apples drop on our heads and atoms hang together, just as they always did. The great Sir Isaac Newton himself actually made a most memorable comment regarding this:

> You sometimes speak of gravity as essential and inherent to matter. Pray do not ascribe this notion to me; for the *cause* of gravity is what I do not pretend to know, and therefore would take more time to consider it.

This classical kind of scientific description, however, is still so powerful and so practical that we have spent the last century discovering ways of using these 'forces' or effects. And this exciting chase for scientific glory and financial rewards has quite obscured from us from a knowledge of what these phenomena actually *are*.

Similarly with the 'search' for the superforce, the unified field of material substance. The 'search' is conducted mathematically by attempting to create just one interlocking set of equations in which all known phenomena can be described. And even when this is done, we will only have reached a description of vacuum state manifestation at the physical level. We will still not understand the why and wherefore of creation. It will lead to fascinating technology, no doubt, but not to final answers. For this, the mystic experience is required.

Ultimately all mathematical equations have to add up correctly. That is what the word 'equation' means. They all are based upon an intuitive understanding that cause equals effect, that there is somehow a balance in nature.

So the ultimate equation represents only this duality, thus:

$$+1 - 1 = 0$$

And while science analyzes the +1 and the −1, the mystic seeks inner experience of that which is beyond the pairs of opposites and from whom all dualism proceeds. This is the ultimate zero point, where nothing is manifested, where there is only pure creative potential and where there is no individuality.

The Inner Dimension and Mystic Experience

I have a feeling that this ultimate equation would be more correctly represented as:

$$0 \Rightarrow -1 + 1$$

Where '⇒' means 'goes to', 'becomes' or 'manifests as', rather than 'equals'. For actually, +1 −1 does *not* 'equal' 0 at all. +1 −1 is different from 0 in its essential reality, though the nett *effect* of +1 −1 *may* equal 0.

Apply this to the mechanism of vacuum manifestation, for example. If the vacuum is denoted as 0, the zero point, then manifested substance is represented as +1 and −1. This is why we perceive the pairs of opposites in all manifested existence. If we do not actually perceive the 0 or the zero point from which the +1 and −1 arise, then we will think that +1 and −1 are related only because of their *effects*, not because of any fundamental understanding of what they are, in themselves, as vibrating energies, or how they have come into physical existence.

This is exemplified by our comprehension of north and south magnetic poles, positive and negative electrical charge, for example. We use and quantify their *effects*, without ever knowing what they *are*.

This can be sketched as follows:

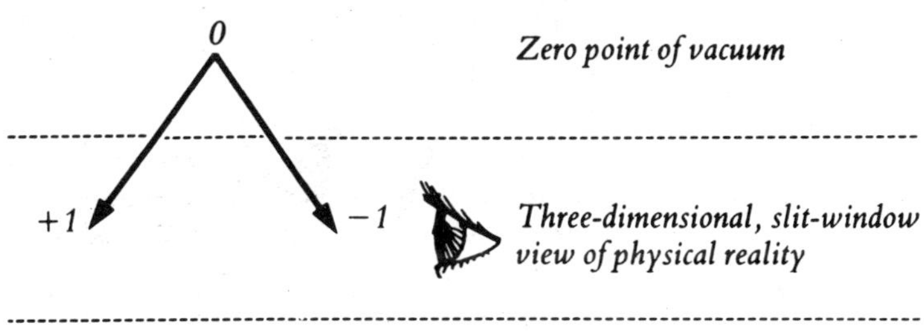

Similarly, apply this perception of effects to gravity (G) and electromagnetism (E), for example. Thus:

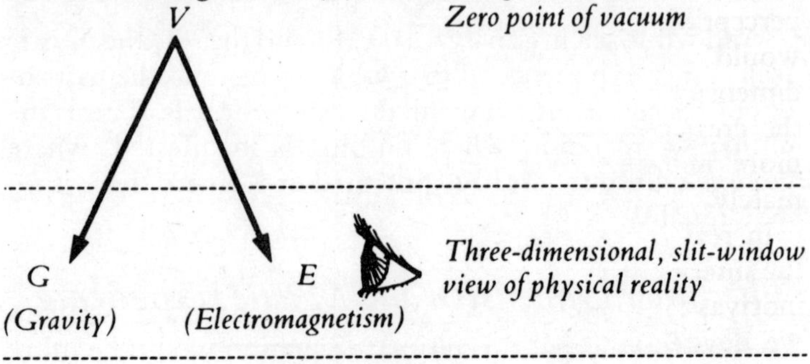

Again, we physically *observe* no connection between gravity and electromagnetism, but only because of our three-dimensional, horizontal and limited perspective and experience. In our *mind*, however, we intuitively know that there must be a connection, but this is hidden from our actual experience. And physicists are seeking it, both practically and theoretically.

It seems, therefore, as if there are actually *five* dimensions (or six if you include time) – the three spatial dimensions with which we are familiar, plus an *inward* and an *outward* dimension. *These are the pattern-forming dimensions of being, energy and mind.* If we had five-dimensional perception we would see things from both vertical, creative or formative (inward-outward), as well as horizontal points of view, thus:

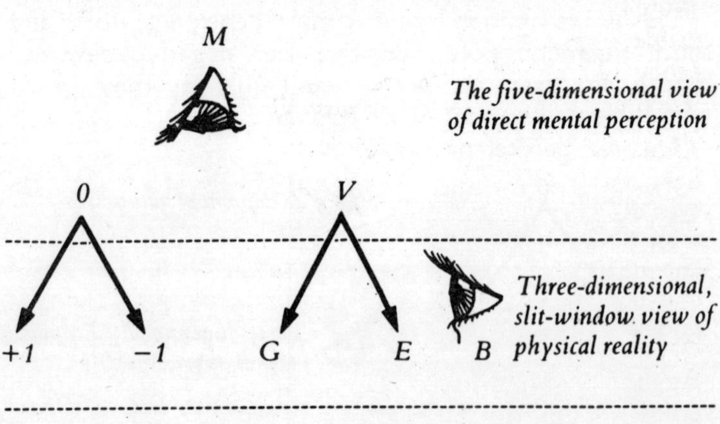

In fact, with our physical *eyes* and senses we would see three-dimensionally, from point B, while with the direct perception of our *mind* (enlivened by consciousness) we would see from point M. The two inward-outward dimensions are thus dimensions of the Formative Mind, the creative process by which patterns are formed from more inward subtle blueprints. This hierarchy is ultimately all of the greater Mind.

In reality, we never perceive anything except through the intermediary of our mind, through the mind's eye or indriya, the mental counterpart to each sense organ. And if we develop our mind through meditation it is actually possible to perceive more directly, with a finer range of mental senses, the entire structure of the physical universe. This experience has been described many times and you will find some of these quotations in *Subtle Energy*. Consider, for example, this quotation from St. Ignatius:

> As he was . . . . sitting on the banks of the Gardenera, his mind was suddenly filled with a new and strange illumination, so that in one moment, and without any sensible image, or appearance, certain things pertaining to the mysteries of the faith, together with other truths of natural science, were revealed to him, and this so abundantly and so clearly, that he himself said that if all the spiritual light which his spirit had received from God up to the time when he was more than sixty years old, could be collected into one, it seemed to him that all of this knowledge could not equal what was at that moment conveyed to his soul.

Note that it was his *mind* which was filled, "Without any sensible image or appearance" – it was not a normal sensory experience.

Then again, the quotation from St. Francis Xavier:

> After this prayer, I once found myself inundated with a vivid light; it seemed to me that a veil was lifted up from before my eyes of the spirit, and all the truths of human science, even those I had not studied, became manifest to me by an infused knowledge. This state of intuition lasted for about twenty-four hours, and then, as if the veil has fallen again, I found myself as ignorant as before.

Again, it is *within himself* that this perception is obtained, even of physical things. And these experiences lie only at the very threshold of the inner mystic ascent into more inward regions where man and his science can, oh so thankfully, never intrude.

After this experience, which – you will note – lasted for a day, St. Francis Xavier adds:

> At the same time, an interior voice said to me, 'Such is human knowledge, of what use is it? It is I, it is My love, that must be studied.'

A salutary thought for those of us involved in the pursuit of 'knowledge'.

Or take these translations of the seventeenth century Maharashtran mystic, Tukaram (1598–1650):

> Clever play of words bring you nothing
> Of no avail will poetic fancy be.
>
> God is my constant companion. . . .
> All creatures have become divine to me,
> I have transcended time and space
> And I shall never be born again. . . .
> I am even smaller than the atom,
> But I have expanded to the outer limits of space. . . .
> What is left of Tuka is only
> For the benefit of others.

Energy

Returning to our discussion of effects and causes, it is in a similar vein that the concept which physicists normally have of *energy* is of a 'capacity to do work, if and when we arrange for the work to be done at some future time'. For example, a ball held at a certain height above sea level contains a *potential energy* relative to the force of gravitation. When we let go of it, the potential energy is translated into kinetic energy (motion), plus some heat energy due to friction as it passes through the air. This energy of motion, for instance, is what is used to create electrical energy in a hydroelectric power station. The falling of water due to the force of gravitation is partially converted into electrical potential energy as a high voltage, which is then used to drive charged mass (electrons) along wires. We call it an electric current.

In fact, the same is true of all our scientific and technological inventions. They are all concerned with energy as the capacity to perform work, and that work can be transformed or transferred into some other kind of potential energy or is used up in the work done against some other force or forces. Flying against wind resistance, gravitation and the inertia of the aeroplane, for example, or driving a car against the friction of a road surface and wind resistance. And so on. We endlessly chase our tails converting one form of energy into another.

But if we look a little deeper, we find that since energy is defined in terms of work, and work involves the concept of force (work = force × distance moved), *energy is actually defined as an effect* – since force is also an effect.

Energy, as understood by conventional physics, therefore, is not related to what actually *is* but only to *effects*. In my writing, and in the common parlance of many people nowadays, energy has come to mean 'all that is' – all manifested substance – physical, subtle physical, astral and causal. Energy is the movement inherent in duality. Movement implies duality or polarity. This perception is also wrapped up in Einstein's famous equivalence of mass to energy ($e = mc^2$), but it can be interpreted in both the conventional and in the light of this more recent thinking. In mystic philosophy, the creation is said to be a movement within the Supreme Being, within God. It is His projection, a duality played out between the manifest and the eternal, self-existent Reality.

So we are back where we began in previous sections. Conventional science does not possess a structure that permits it to really see the difference between the concepts of things (in our minds) and the existence of things *in themselves*. The definition is generally considered to be identical to what the thing is. And in this way, science works only with ideas concerning effects, *not* with the thing itself, not with causes.

But, once again, by relating everything back to the vacuum or akashic state, we at least find a common causality for all manifested things. "From the void comes a thousand things," says Lao Tse. Though we still have to find out what causes that void or vacuum to exist! Plus what its structure is and what patterns it.

But we can find a more intuitive way of comprehending this, for the mind is latched in to the vacuum state. This is the outward screen upon which the karma of our destiny is played. And the mind is itself an energy, enlivened from within by soul, consciousness or the life force. So it all fits together and leads us, unwittingly at first, towards the comprehension that the only way to really understand it all is to still the endless thinking and gyrations of our mind and to develop direct mystic perception from within.

Lost and Embedded in the Energy Dance

I have pointed out many times that we do not know just what gravity actually is. The same is true of all the four basic forces. In the atomic nucleus, we observe or theorize as to what is going on and realize that something must be holding it all together. We call it the strong force. Just like we see apples falling or planets orbiting, and describe it as gravity. But to then say that mass "obeys the law of gravity" or that the strong force *holds* the neutrons and protons together is really putting things back to front! The 'law of gravity' is only our language to describe our experience, it is not an intrinsic part of nature, per se. First of all we observe an effect (gravity, strong force etc.), then we describe the effect as if it were something real and primary. Then we say that it is a causative law that the physical universe actually obeys! It is really a primary confusion. Similarly, to say that forces are 'strains upon the fabric of ether' is also incorrect.

There is only a vibrating dance of energy – 'particles', 'waves', 'forces' are really only different aspects of this same one thing, different ways in which this dance manifests itself to us. It is possible to *experience* the oneness in all things, but talking or thinking requires division, so as soon as we attempt to *express* this oneness, we have to divide it. Mostly, our minds experience only the division, therefore we describe the world in terms of division, unaware of the essential unity within 'us' and 'it'. But even mystics, when they communicate with us in human ways, have to use language. The language they use is beautiful, of course. It has a ring of truth to it. But at every step they only use language as a pointer to the higher, inner reality and experience.

Many mathematicians even believe that mathematics is not just a tightly compressed language, but is intrinsic in nature itself. But this is not strictly so. Like all our thinking, mathematics lies in our own minds. It is our minds which are divided and hence see the world as such. When we see the One within us, we also see Him everywhere. But there is a relationship between our human mind, mathematics and nature since our individual minds bear the same characteristics as the greater Mind, the real architect of all form. The better concepts of our human mind, therefore, do bear a relationship to the way in which the greater universe is constructed. But they are only reflections, not the reality itself.

So – our mind is an energy dance; our sensory perceptions are an energy dance; our actions are an energy dance; the physical world is an energy dance. We are completely immersed and embedded in our interactions or relationships to this one big multilevel, energy dance which we call the creation – and we are indivisible parts of that. The problems arise when we feel (which we do feel) that we are separate. But this is also an aspect of the energy dance – the aspect of the mind energy we call *ego*, or what in yogic terminology is known as *ahankar*.

Human identity or ego in its balanced expression tells us of our place as humans in the scheme of things. It is, like legs and knees or any other aspect of our construction, gross or subtle, an essential part of being human. But when imbalanced – as in our normal human experience – our understanding of our place in the network of energy patterns becomes distorted. This we recognize as human ego – an incorrect or illusory perception of our place in the creation.

The human mind does have a true focus within our human structure. This is known as the *Eye Centre*, behind and a little above our two physical eyes. For example, if we want to concentrate we put our hands to our forehead – we do not hold our knees or some other part of our anatomy. Our thinking centre, we instinctively know, is in our head. But the more the mind moves out or e-motes from this centre, the greater is our imbalance in our perception of the physical universe; the greater is our degree of subconscious e-motional entrapment. Our balanced sense of human identity becomes an imbalanced ego, who no longer knows who or what either he – or the universe – actually is.

Pride, for instance, which is one aspect of ego, telling a person that they are better than everybody else, is clearly an incorrect perception of the way things actually are, as is the false humility or inferiority complex which suggests that a person is worse than everybody else. The entire egocentric idea that people are better or worse than each other is an expression of an imbalanced ego or sense of identity. It is an illusion which has nothing to do the reality of our human situation.

So we experience this energy dance of creation and inwardly understand its manner of manifestation depending upon the point at which our mind energy focuses and upon the degree of consciousness we have. It is like a multi-storey department store. From the lift, from our inward centre of consciousness, we can get a good perspective as to what is going on. The higher we go, the clearer and more completely do we see into the nature of things. But if we spread our mental energy outwards through our senses – whether on this physical plane, or at higher levels of consciousness, in the higher worlds – then we get lost at those levels, on those floors. Then the goods on display have become too enticing for us.

So then we lose our perspective and become confused. And confusion on the ground floor, on the physical level, is disastrous for us, for we become so totally engrossed in the goods that we completely forget that we are even alive as conscious, vibrant beings within ourselves. We even become oblivious to the fact that there is a lift and that there are higher floors. Like in a dream, we so rapidly forget what has gone before, and where we came from.

But if anyone tries to tell us of this, we even get annoyed with them and call them dangerous mystics or misguided enthusiasts! Mystics in the past even had their heads cut off or were crucified or worse at the instigation of the priests and 'intelligentsia' of the day! Now we are, in some countries at least, a little more democratic, but the principle still applies that we do not like to be woken up from our sensory and mental slumber. Our subconscious, habit-ridden minds will do anything to keep on thinking and working in the way they have always done.

This state of affairs has arisen because the mind has become unconscious and unbalanced by leaving its true focus of being, the centre of conscious thought behind the eyes.

Mind and Manifestation

One can, in a sense, conceive of the vacuum as relatively undifferentiated, potential energy – locked-in stress awaiting manifestation. The impetus for this creation actually comes from within our own minds. Our individual human minds each contain within them the seed of our pralabdh or destiny karma. This destiny karma therefore patterns the five essences or tattwas and manifestation takes place, but *from within ourselves*. We perceive it as being outward only through our senses, and because of the outward direction of our attention, but actually our sensory appreciation is mental. This has been previously described.

But because our level of consciousness does not normally perceive directly the actual mechanisms by which even our individual minds function, we cannot see this process taking place. It is unconscious. We get intimations of it when we are faced with coincidences, connections and recurring patterns linking both our inner and outer lives, but we cannot normally watch this mechanism in action. We do not, therefore, understand why things happen in the way they do. But as we advance spiritually or mystically we do notice that the 'fittingness' of things seems to increase. Recently, I heard a beautiful way of expressing this: "Coincidence is God's way of remaining anonymous."

Serendipity, being in the right place at the right time, intuitively perceiving how things are going to work out – this aspect of our life appears to grow. The more we realize how little we really *know*, the more our consciousness expands within us and vice versa. The two go together. Man may think he has a free will, but yet we do not know what will happen to us in the next microsecond, let alone the next five minutes. We do not know what thoughts and emotions will come to us in the next instant. So where is the possibility of free will? What indeed is the 'I' that thinks it has free will?

Descartes is often quoted as saying "I think, therefore I am". He would have been more correct to say, "I am, therefore I think." Because consciousness, being or am-ness comes first. That is the life force within us. Mind – in Descartes' comment: his thinking – is enlivened by consciousness and arises because of it. So we *are* before we *think*. The real 'I' is of the soul or consciousness, while the little 'I' of ego, or ahankar, is a faculty of the human mind and grossly out of balance in most of us. The little 'I' speaks so loudly within us that it obscures the greater 'I' that gives it life, as Descartes so aptly yet unwittingly demonstrated to us with his expression of how he felt about himself[1].

Similarly, it is our ego, the *state* of our mind which prevents us from seeing how our minds are all linked together as co-creators, co-manifestors of the otherwise undifferentiated sea of vacuum or akash.

In other words, if one took the souls of all creatures out of this physical domain, our minds would no longer be present to whip it up into the endless play of illusory patterns that are spun out by our minds and apparently perceived through our senses, but are actually experienced within our own minds. Or you could say that without life and mental perception, there would be no physical world. At the most it would be a still akashic ocean.

The linkage of mind, senses and physical manifestation is so cleverly woven that – being an intimate part of this drama – we can never get outside it to perceive it *objectively* with our own mind. Our mind is a part of the process of manifestation. Trying to understand physical reality or Mind, *with* the human mind, is like a dog chasing its own tail. The subject becomes the object and vice versa. So the only way out is in – to get a higher perspective or consciousness of the whole drama.

Making the Most of your Potential

I wonder if we can really imagine the excitement that the discovery of electrical power must have generated at the end of the last century and during the early 1900's? If we

[1]Actually, I prefer the quip of actor, Nicholas Jones. His version is, "I think – therefore I've missed the point!"

look around our home, office and town and imagine how it would have been without electrical power, we can grasp some idea of the visions and dreams that must have fired those early pioneers. Some were driven by financial motivations, others were intrigued by this wonderful cosmic power they were learning to harness. But even those with the dimmest imaginations must have realized that the world was going to change in an unprecedented manner. And they were right.

But with the benefit of hindsight, one has to ask whether the direction taken in these endeavours was the best one? The harnessing of the electron, and later of the inward atomic structure, to provide a source of energy to obey man's will has been the continuing theme of our century. From lighting, to electrical motors, to the telephone, to radio and TV transmission, to valves, transistors, integrated computer circuitry and superconductivity, our scientists in electronics and electrical engineering have unravelled and made use of an amazing aspect of nature's natural driving mechanism of manifestation. We have split the atom, unleashing phenomenal amounts of energy. We have sent our own kin to the moon and brought them home again. We have peeped into the mysteries of neighbouring planets and even probed the secrets of Halley's comet. All with the power of electricity. Without a working knowledge of electromagnetism and the electron, nothing would have happened.

And all this, without understanding what an electron or a photon are, or what it is that holds the atom together. We have simply been using a knowledge of effects without being able to probe to the deeper level.

One could say that since J. J. Thompson's momentous experiment, man has had a bee in his bonnet about the electron. Or maybe an electron in his bonnet. Certainly he has made it the essential focus of his attention in the development of technology over the last century. Technological development of the electron has been extremely rapid. Will the same apply to our use of the vacuum state energy field which is creating so much excitement as we move into the twenty-first century?

One can understand how the impetus of early electrical success set the stage for all future research. To harness the electron must be seen as one of man's greatest scientific achievements. Compared to mechanical sources of power, even the earliest electrical inventions must have seemed possessed of tremendous finesse. Yet by modern standards, the valve radio of only thirty years ago seems amazingly clumsy. So what is it that will make our present day technology appear in a similar light to the scientists of the twenty-first century? For these changes are bound to happen. History tells us that man never stays in one place.

Since the days of Edison and Morgan, our use of electricity has hinged around the almost unquestioned idea that in order to use electrical potential, or charge, one has to drive charged mass (electrons) around two wire circuits. Yet the mass itself is of no value to us in most instances. What is usually important to us is its electrical charge. It is its possession of charge that enables us to make it drive motors, generate radio signals and so on. The energy expended, however, in pushing this charged mass around the place is what consumes the power. Is there not a better way of handling things? Can we re-think this aspect of energy generation?

Returning to Tesla's work, we find that his intuitive feeling that there was or is another way, did enable him to consider the use of one-wire 'circuits', utilizing potential and pure charge without expenditure of the energy required to drive mass. This was what he was doing in his Colorado Springs and Wardenclyffe Tower projects. But Tesla was overtaken by the impetus of events and man set off down the road we have come to know so well. He found himself out on a limb and within the context of the major thrust of electrical and electronic development, his work must have appeared increasingly bizarre. The new paradigms concerning electricity were taught to eager young engineers in the few universities where the new science was taught, and an army of scientific cookery-book followers moved in to expand the ground opened up by the early pioneers.

But it meant the loss of much truly original and creative insight. All new developments have evolved within the framework of those early ideas. The idea of an ether, in any shape or form, has hardly been considered by conventional engineers since those early days. The electron has been seen as a fundamental particle, a little blob of charged something, and it is no doubt quite amazing what we have been able to make it do. But there must be other ways of working with electrons.

So the result has been that we have studied just a few outward effects of electrical phenomena, while ignoring the cause of all these effects. These intriguing effects have alone been capable of occupying our full attention for almost a century. We have steadfastly studied a few aspects of the crest of a wave as it breaks, ignoring the wave and ocean itself.

Now, our thinking has become so conditioned that we find it difficult to perceive the obvious. From what we have discovered concerning the nature of the atom, it has become quite clear that the universe is comprised of energy. Even at a conventional subatomic level it appears to be in perpetual motion. Yet we adamantly refuse to believe in any device that can tap into this free, cosmic energy source.

It is Bearden, again, who explains how to perform this simple piece of magic. Imagine, he says, that we have two charged spheres, one at a higher charge than the other, like this:

After Bearden

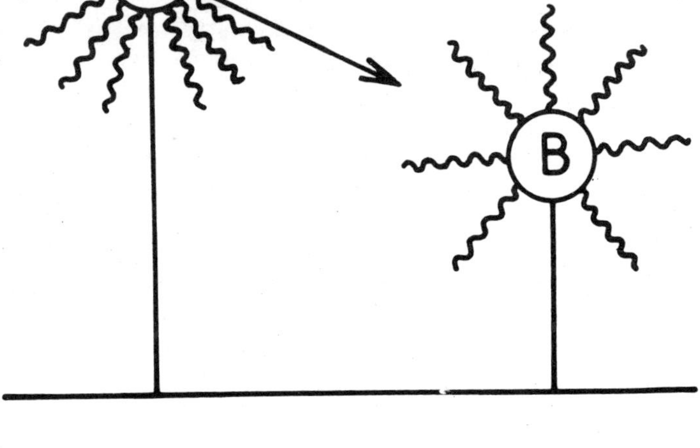

If we now connect A to B, then our higher charge of electrons within A will flow down to B. We are thus using our real energy of the vacuum state (the charge) to drive mass (the electron) down a wire. In other words, we use our charge to pump mass. Naturally, this requires work, and energy is required in the process. To maintain or recharge the system, we therefore have to 'pump' electrons back up into A, so that they can then fall down the hill again to B, thus:

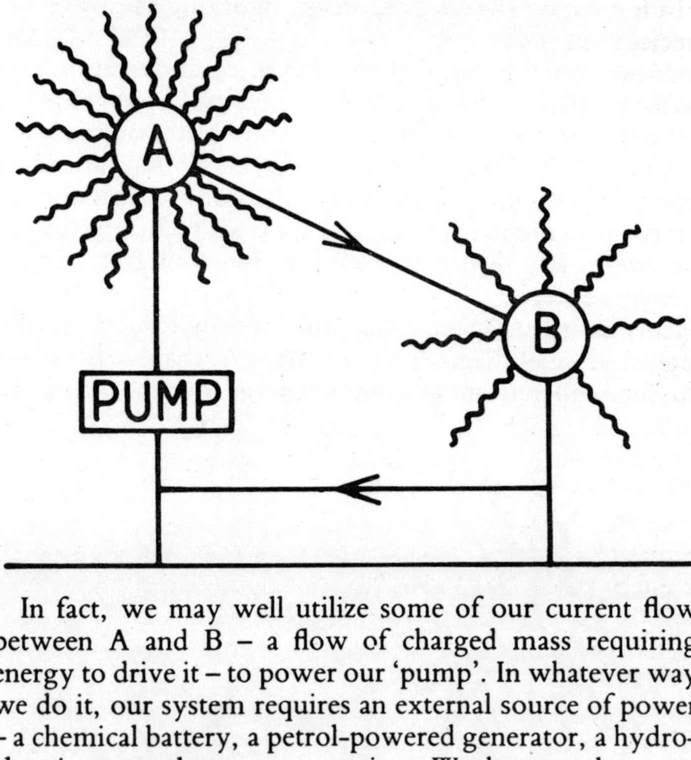

In fact, we may well utilize some of our current flow between A and B – a flow of charged mass requiring energy to drive it – to power our 'pump'. In whatever way we do it, our system requires an external source of power – a chemical battery, a petrol-powered generator, a hydroelectric or nuclear power station. We have to buy our energy, we have to get it from somewhere else.

So how do we utilize electrical charge without loss of energy, to tap into the vast reservoir of the ubiquitous vacuum? What we do, say Bearden and others, is firstly to charge up our two spheres. As is well understood, there is no flow of charged mass, no electron flow, no electrical current within these spheres, and there is no flow between them for as long as we do not connect them. There is, however, a *potential* gradient between the two, a virtual, vacuum state gradient, a scalar field.

But this potential does *not* constitute a real energy field at the physically *observable* level, because what we think of as an electrical field is actually an effect of vacuum 'stress' due to the potential difference. To be observably 'real' it would have to consist of the moving charged masses of electrons, and we have no moving charged masses in a system where the two spheres are not connected.

In free energy devices, we adamantly refuse to allow our precious potential energy, our pure massless charge, our electron spray nozzles, to drain away, giving us some usable energy in return, but being considerably less than 100 percent efficient.

When we hold a ball in our hand, it has a potential to provide us with energy, (due to gravity). Normally, we utilize this energy by dropping the ball and making it push something in the process. What we are trying to do in free energy devices is to realize that the energy held in potential is also *real* and can be tapped *without* utilizing the *effect* of that potential by actually dropping the ball. Rather than employing the heathen, loud-mouthed and obvious approach, we are trying to be more subtle about it.

So how do we proceed with such delicate finesse? It is easy, says Bearden, we oscillate 'orbiting' atomic electrons, by oscillating the charge surrounding the atom. When we increase the charge, the electron moves into a more excited or energetic state. It actually moves into a more distant shell. Its potential energy is thus increased. This is standard electrical theory and experience. For example:

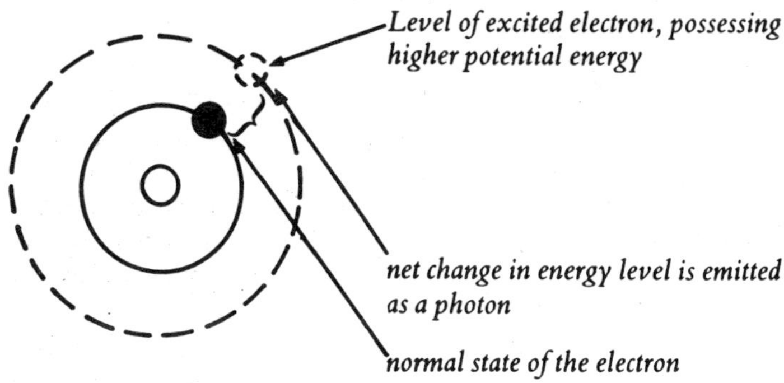

You can imagine the electron as a rubber band being stretched. The greater the stretch, the greater the energy stored in potential. But while, with our rubber band, we have to provide the energy to stretch it and so the normal laws of energy conservation apply, our electron is actually powered from within by the real potential energy of vacuum. When we change the charge, which makes the electron jump to a higher level of potential energy, the electron gathers its energy from the vacuum state. When we cut off the charge, the electron jumps back to its previous state, releasing its stored difference in energy, *not back into the vacuum state, but as a photon of electromagnetic energy*, an extremely tight and high-speed vortex of vacuum energy which can then be used to produce heat, light or more electrical charge.

In other words, we have a one way pump, a valve or a gateway permitting flow in only one direction, from the vacuum or potential realm into the physically observable realm. It is the ultimate cat-flap, that lets the pussy out, but not back in again. And as long as one does not permit the actual flow of charged masses (electrons), i.e. an electrical current, in the mechanism that drives the oscillations in charge, we have an inexhaustible supply of energy.

In fact, as Bearden points out, according to Einstein's theory of general relativity the normal laws of energy conservation as it is conventionally understood, do not apply in a region of 'curved space-time' (space-time *is* the vacuum). And a differential in charge potential without an electric field, automatically implies a curvature in space-time.

Remember that Einstein's theory is only a model or a concept that attempts to grapple with the observed *effect* of gravity, without anyone being actually able to pick up a piece of something and say, "Ah, this is a piece of gravity." Knowing that all forces (electrical or gravitational etc.) are effects of vacuum state activity gives us a better perspective on what we are dealing with.

Anyhow, the point is that even under conventional theory we know that something odd appears to be happening in such situations, when we have a charge potential without current flow.

I, however, am not a professional, all-day physicist and if your mathematics and physics can take you deeper into the intricacies of this subject than my own inclinations and expression, then as starting points, I would point you in the direction of the bibliography at the end, and to Bearden's writings in particular.

But if you are a 'conventional' physicist (do such people exist?) who is wanting to scream a little (or a lot) because you think it is all wrong, then by all means go ahead. It is supposed to be a free world. We all have as much right as each other to want to understand the universe in which we live. But do not forget that scientific and philosophical concepts do make radical shifts from time to time.

We are now in a position to understand in even greater detail what Tesla was aiming at, what Henry Moray, Townsend Brown, John Searl and all the others have been (and still are) up to. They have all unwittingly or deterministically created a valve from the universal vacuum to the world of usable physical energy. They have simply found various ways of letting it spill through, of 'gating' it, as the technical expression has it.

Searl and Townsend Brown used high electrical charge and motion (movement of large charged masses) to reach a threshold where vacuum energy flooded through into physical manifestation. Searl's machines were almost describable as enormous, spinning electrons, but at a macroscopic level. Tesla also worked with superhigh voltages, since the world of the subatomic was not so well charted then, as it is today.

Moray, Newman, Howard Johnson and others have done the same thing at a more fundamental level, dealing directly with the subatomic realm rather than the macroscopic world. This is a more subtle approach, though it is probable that depending upon the exact effect required, either (or other) approaches may be more suitable. We are talking here of free electrical power, pure scalar wave devices for communications and for energy transmission and extraction, for anti-inertial and anti-gravity devices and much more.

The Hyperactive Vacuum

Although electron spin is now a well-established fact, no-one in the early days of electromagnetism ever suspected it. This crucial piece of evidence as to what is happening at the subatomic level was therefore patched in at a later date and was never made a fundamental aspect of the theory, as it would undoubtedly have been had it been known earlier.

In conventional physics this spinning electron is considered as a bare mass with a constant flux of virtual particles "on and off the mass in all directions," (Bearden). 'Conventionally' virtual particles come into being out of nowhere and disappear again within a fraction of a time interval. This is 'allowed', indeed required, within the conceptual framework of quantum theory. On the other hand, the mass of the electron is seen as a 'kink' or curvature in Einsteinian space-time, thus locking it into three-dimensional space. But, as we know, the descriptions of physical reality provided by quantum theory and Einsteinian relativity do not interrelate too well. So it is all treated as a concept or a theory, a convenience to make the equations work out right. No-one would ever think of attempting any solid engineering based upon a knowledge of the behaviour of these 'conventional' virtual particles.

In Bearden's thinking, however, the virtual particles are definitely considered as real entities arising within the vacuum state, as does the mass itself. It is the flux of virtual particles which gives the electron its electrical charge. As we have seen, he presents the graphic picture of the electron (or any charged particle) as being something like a multi-dimensional spray nozzle. The spray being the incessant buzz of virtual particles on and off the electron. And he equates the activity of the virtual particles with the energy of the vacuum state itself.

That is, the incessant vacuum state activity not only brings the mass of the electron into being as a whirling fold of locked-in vacuum energy or as a vacuum standing wave trapped by the spinning motion of that very energy, but it also provides what we experience as electric charge by means of this virtual particle or vacuum energy activity (or flux). And all this energy is derived from the inexhaustible reservoir of the vacuum state and so is available, if we can tap, transform or translate it, as a source of free energy. The spray nozzle just keeps on spraying! Or put more simply, none of man's devices ever *create* anything. We just rearrange the energy patterns. All that this vacuum state understanding permits us to do is to tap into a deeper, more fundamental source.

The Coming and Going of Virtual Particles

Conceptual and mathematical considerations in quantum theory actually *require* these virtual particles to come into existence out of *nothing* as matter and antimatter pairs, as long as they then annihilate each other within a fraction of a time interval. But the *nature* of *where* these virtual particles come from is largely ignored, for the minds of theoretical physicists are mostly locked into *concepts*, not on experience or direct perception of what actually *is*. The difference between a thing and a description of it is not readily appreciated, as I have pointed out. Moreover, these 'conventional' virtual particles arise out of 'nothing' and cancel each other out, returning to 'nothing'. It is okay to perform this trick mathematically, but what does it actually mean, in real terms? In our vacuum state theory, the 'nothing' is actually a real energetic something.

Actually, the whole of modern physics is riddled with references and pointers to the existence of the vacuum state as a real entity, but prejudice and conditioned, classical, habituated ways of thinking are blinding screens. So is the inability to admit that we simply got it wrong – or only partially correct. But to do so is a sign of greatness, not of weakness. For ignorance of reality is our normal human condition. And the word ignorance does not mean lack of knowledge, it means ignoring what is before our eyes.

Many modern physicists will go to the most extraordinarily complex lengths, theoretically, to explain phenomena without having to invoke something that even barely resembles an ether. To do so would be to admit that since around 1900 – for almost a century – the science of physics, electricity and electromagnetism has been pretty much on a superficial track. But a hundred years is nothing in a historical context, and a new generation of more correctly educated physicists and electronic engineers will soon put paid to an outdated and limited set of concepts. Youth has scant respect for tradition, especially when it is seen to have little validity.

One of the well-documented and classic anomalies of experimental physics, something which is only explicable by vacuum state theory, is the simple experiment of the Dutch physicist, Hendrick Casimir, first performed in 1948. As we have previously described, when two plates made of a shiny, reflective material (eg. metal or mica) are placed close together in a high vacuum, they are mysteriously attracted to each other. So clearly some energetic aspect of the vacuum itself is at work, normally 'accounted' for by the activity of these virtual particles.

But the question is, since virtual particles exist only as theoretical requirements of quantum theory, and have never actually been observed experimentally, do they actually exist and what is the nature of their reality?

Certainly, something deeply significant is going on at the vacuum state level and in addition to the energy devices we have been describing, the ability to electrostatically polarize this flux of virtual particles is actually demonstrable and even measurable in the *Lamb shift* and in *Delbruck* scattering, the scattering of photons by photons.

So like 'real' subatomic particles, it seems that virtual particles are also configurations or patterns in the vacuum energy, but possessed of a far more evanescent nature.

The Big Bang, But Something Missing

One of the fundamental problems to which physicists know that they must address themselves is "Where did all this come from?" "We know that you cannot get something from nothing," they say, "But if once it did not exist, and if nothing existed before that, then it must have come out of nowhere. . . In a Big Bang, a long, long time ago, when all the energy that now exists was, for an infinitesimal fraction of a second, compressed into a point with no dimensions. Then it spread and expanded and we now have what we see today." Or what we *think* we see. . .

But even logically that makes little sense, for how can '*nothing exist*'. If it is nothing, it *does not* exist! Well, that may be playing with words, but it is another one of those pointers that keep on telling us that in conventional scientific thinking or philosophy, we have got it wrong, somewhere.

Similarly, scientists feel that for things to be the way they are, that there is a lot of matter or energy *missing*. The equations just do not add up right. Therefore, they have invented concepts such as a background sea of almost undetectable neutrinos, (electrons without electrical charge). Neutrinos are chosen because they are virtually undetectable. They are very small and since they possess no electrical charge, they pass right through most atoms without interaction or collision with the nucleus. So it would have been easy for us to have failed to spot them experimentally. The spaces between the nucleus and its surrounding electrons – relative to the size of a neutrino – are like interplanetary distances, so the chances of a neutrino actually bumping into anything are quite remote.

So this theory helps solve the missing mass (or energy) problem. And maybe the theory is partially correct. But all the same, something has to give that sea of zero-charged neutrinos (if they exist) its existence. A neutrino has to *be something*, its energy has to come from somewhere on a continuous basis, for it to continue in existence. So the neutrino solution to the missing mass equation has only been deferred by a conceptual device. The problem still remains, "Where does all this come from?" *Now!* Not long, long ago!

The Universe as a Vacuum State Fluctuation

One theory in physics suggests that the entire physical universe is actually a *vacuum fluctuation*, that it is simply something that popped out of nothing quite by chance and will one day pop back into nothing again. A sort of jumbo-sized, virtual particle. In the meantime, says the theory, all the energy (matter and antimatter) in the universe should add up to zero. But it doesn't.

Strangely enough, this idea is probably closest of all to the mystic conception of akashic or vacuum manifestation and subsequent dissolution or *pralaya*. For it is said in the Sanskrit literature of the ancient Hindu sages that pralaya of the physical universe takes place every 4,320,000,000 (4.32 billion) years. There is then a 'night', a period of cosmic recovery, possibly, before the physical universe is again re-created. At the present time we are said to be about two billion years through the present cycle, leaving something in excess of another two billion to pass before absorption back into the akash at the next dissolution.

These cycles of creation and dissolution represent the in-breathings and the out-breathings of the Universal Mind. For the entire set of mind regions – physical, astral and causal – are also dissolved and re-created at these times. Universal Mind is also known as Brahm and these rhythmic fluctuations or cycles are called a *Day of Brahm* and a *Night of Brahm*.

So the difference between the modern vacuum fluctuation theory and the description given by the ancient yogis and munis of India is really quite slight. The main difference is that modern man thinks that the vacuum is nothing, whereas the mystic insists that his personal inner experience of it is as a real something which is *meant* to look like a nothing, just to keep us more or less happily in jail.

Interestingly, the time spans of creation given in the Sanskrit literature approximate to the ever-changing scientific estimates. In recent years, estimates of the age of the universe have doubled and quadrupled until they presently stand at about fifteen billion years. No-one knows how accurate these estimates are, however, so the Hindu concept of two billion years is certainly within the same ballpark.

It is worth considering that these Sanskrit writings have been in existence for several thousand years and that not much more than a century ago, the prevailing western theory dated the origin of the universe at 4004 BC, though the intellectuals of the day debated whether creation was in the spring or autumn of that year. . .

So the Indian mystics certainly deserve to be taken seriously. Moreover, with the prevailing western creation story being based on an allegory taken from an old Jewish book, the Indian conception of creation out of akash was quite up to date, several thousand years ago. And this is not surprising, for the advanced mystic is able to see from within himself and the overall structure of creation is just the same now as it was under other cultural circumstances, millenia and more ago.

What is it about modern western man that despite the fact that we have practically destroyed our planetary garden; that we have devised weapons of war far more terrifying than anything in recorded history; that we have abandoned mutually supportive *life* in preference to a social structure which is one of mutual agression and competition for *survival*; that all the human weaknesses are so clearly manifest in our present societies – that despite all of this, we still insist that we have 'progressed' and that our understanding is better than those who have lived in past ages, or even those who simply live in other cultures? No wonder we think that we came out of nowhere. It is just the sort of crazy, mixed-up idea such an off-balance society could be expected to have come up with!

Actually, quite apart from fact that the theory more or less ignores the origin and nature of mind and consciousness, the flaw in the concept that the physical universe popped out of nowhere in a Big Bang, a long time ago, is that no-one can say what made it do that! And if it was a random occurrence, (randomness in an ocean of nothing?!), then what is stopping other 'universes' from appearing randomly out of nowhere in some nearby interstellar space? Why do we not have a multitude of Big Bangs taking place 'randomly' throughout time and space? It is all very well to think we understand what happened after the theoretical Big Bang – but what caused it and why have there not been others since? Clearly, such a situation would be chaotic, but the materialistic paradigm does not acknowledge any higher or more fundamental order underlying what we see.

Physicists have, of course, tackled this problem, suggesting on theoretical grounds that new universes cannot pop into existence in your interstellar backyard and set off expanding at a rate of knots if there is already a 'stress in space'. That is: if there is already something there. A comforting reassurance which, however, does little more than 'prove' the obvious! But the theory still does not tell us where the physical universe we experience everyday, actually came from (or comes from).

From the mystic point of view, creation is a highly ordered and structured affair, a projection of patterns from within-out. So – whatever happens – whether the creation of universes or the movement of a leaf on a tree – it is *intended* and *ordered* in the same way that the details of a projected image are entirely dependent upon the projection system and the pattern being projected.

Actually, the Big Bang theory is derived entirely from just one empirical observation – that of a red shift, an apparent Doppler Effect, in the light reaching us from distant stars. Their wavelengths appear 'stretched', which is taken to mean that they are moving away from us. From this one piece of evidence alone has arisen the idea that the universe is constantly expanding and – 'therefore' – it must have originally come out of a single ultra-dense point (a *singularity*) in a Big Bang, long, long ago.

There are, however, a multitude of other theories which adequately account for this red shift[1] and not all academic astronomers and astrophysicists, including the great American astronomer, Halton Arp, are convinced of the expanding universe explanation. The idea has caught on in the popular imagination and scientists like to see their theories selling well, so they provide no cautionary comments concerning their acceptance, but the idea is far from proven.

And if just one of these alternative theories were correct, then bang goes both the expanding universe and the Big Bang theory. So the theory is only tenuously founded.

Mystically, the creation process from within-out is all a part of activity within the patterning of the greater, Formative Mind. The primal energy of the Universal is woven into a myriad subtle and scintillating patterns, each projecting and reflecting (the process has no words in our physical language to really describe it) out of more inward patterns in a vast hierarchy of formative creation. One cannot understand the process of creation without an understanding of this inward, creative, vertical spectrum of energy.

Situated as we are now, the physical creation seems to us to be so solid, so dense and so real that we find it difficult to stretch our understanding to take in the idea that in its very beginnings it was a subtle, dancing pattern of sound

[1] See *New Ideas in Astronomy*, edited by B. F. Madore et al, Cambridge University Press, 1988.

and light and that, in fact, it is still no more that that. That it came into being as an out-breathing of the Cosmic Mind and will one day be withdrawn once again – and again re-projected. But it does very clearly demonstrate that man's perception of his universe is entirely dependent upon the level of his own mind and consciousness. Man's understanding of himself is central to his understanding of the world.

Footnote to page 269

Michelson's original experiment was designed to detect the motion of the earth through the ether of space. In this, he failed, though as we have said this may only have showed that his particular *concept* of the ether was incorrect.

However, E.W. Silvertooth reported in *Nature* magazine (1986) that under U.S. Airforce sponsorship he had repeated the experiment with far more refined instrumentation. He detected an ether-drift which related exactly to the earth's cosmic motion through free space of 378 kilometres per second.

Subsequently, S. Marinov in Austria (1987) performed the same experiment using less sophisticated instrumentation, but fully confirming Silvertooth's findings. His tests gave the earth's speed through the ether to be 386 (±38) kilometres per second.

Silvertooth and Marinov's findings therefore demonstrate yet again that Einstein's theory of relativity is not an absolute law of nature, thus opening the way to technological and theoretical research on the structure and characteristics of space itself.

CHAPTER 12

Beyond the Veil

Life Beyond The Veil

Writing a book generates a response in many ways, one of which, of course, is that people communicate with you, directly. So it is not long before one gets a feeling for the spectrum of opinion amongst those who have read one's work. Regarding the mystical parts of *Subtle Energy* I have had those who have said, "I liked it enormously, but why did you feel the necessity of putting in the first two sections on Eastern mystical philosophy?" Others, conversely, have said, "The real essence of the book lies in the first two sections. I would like to have seen more references to the mystical connections throughout the book." Many others have enjoyed it simply as a general and universal overview tying many threads together, without their feeling the need to express such opinions.

I mention this because I am about to embark on a subject area that may generate this kind of response, especially amongst honestly materially-minded people (assuming that such people got this far!). Our human mind has a built-in mechanism against countenancing ideas with which it is unfamiliar or has no inward resonance. We simply look the other way or react with negative emotion or prejudice. We rarely take things as a working hypothesis, yet to be proven to our personal experience, but worthy of study all the same. We always feel the need to have opinions, even if we have no experience or understanding upon which to base the opinion. Opinion, however, is simply a predictable reaction of our unconscious mind energies, of our own particular mind set.

But I like the wisdom of the postprandial fortune cookie:

Stiff in opinion, always in the wrong!

Dr Lawrence Crapo, medical researcher at Stanford University has it posted on his office door to remind himself, he says, "And all who enter, of the curious malady to which we in academic settings are particularly prone."

If we get hit by a bus, but do not happen to believe in buses, we are likely to come up with a multitude of possible alternative explanations, rather than accept the reality of buses.

So if what follows, does not suit you, then by all means do not wear it – but do read it with an open mind and make observations of its relevance. For many readers, this section will be light relief after chapters, some of which may have been mentally taxing.

It is of interest to note, however, that while many scientists and other people are very happy to entertain themselves with concepts of multiple universes and Big Bangs coming out of nowhere, anything remotely smacking of the spirit, consciousness or even mind and psychology are automatically disregarded as the thoughts of cranks and charlatans. Or at least they are just ignored as irrelevant.

This itself, of course, is an interesting reaction of the human mind to anything which attempts to remove its own unconscious veils. As I have inferred many times, all of science is spun out of the mind of man. To understand the nature of science, therefore, it is imperative to understand from within, the real nature of our own mind and consciousness. We are asking questions of the universe, without any understanding of the nature of the 'I' who is asking the question. If we were to study *that*, we might find that the nature of both the questions *and* the 'universe' itself would radically change. No observation of 'it' is complete without a study of the 'I' who thinks he is doing the observing.

Nowhere is the integration of mind and so called 'outside' reality expressed more clearly than in the descriptions of inner mystical experiences. In our physical world the link between mind and manifestation is hidden. We may glimpse this reality in certain expressions of quantum physics or within the intuitions of our consciousness, but the actual mechanisms by which the karmas of our destiny are stored within our minds and become an apparently outward reality are not immediately observable to an ordinary eye.

In the inner astral and causal regions, however, the situation is far clearer. Here the oneness of observer and observed is more explicitly built into the way things are seen to happen. In the physical world it is implicit, but obscured. Without mystic experience we glimpse it only through intuition, through certain logical constructs, through coincidence, serendipity and synchronicity and so on.

In the inner worlds, the linkage of mind and manifested energies is more readily apparent, while the density of vibration within the physical world means that although the same principle is at work, things take longer to manifest outwardly. It is often said that when we desire something – good or bad – it starts moving towards us. "Thoughts are things" is an old adage and similarly, "We should choose our thoughts wisely." Something which is more easily said than done. But the direct energetic linkage of mind and matter definitely underlies both physical, as well as astral and causal levels of manifestation. It just takes a little longer for the effects to become apparent at the level of our dense physical phenomena, by which time we may well have forgotton how and when we penned the invitation.

There is a beautiful section in Michael Naimy's *The Book of Mirdad* which is apropos:

> So think as if your every thought were to be etched in fire upon the sky for all and everything to see. For so in truth, it is.
>
> So do as if your every deed were to recoil upon your heads. And so, in truth, it does.

As I have said, the mind-matter linkage is hidden because of the direction of our attention. Thus, by meditation, when we change the direction of our attention from without to within, we also change our perception of the nature of 'outside' reality, and hidden connections begin to lose their veils.

When our attention stays concentrated within at the thinking centre, at the eye centre, then we continue to use our sensory perceptions and motor functions as before, but work from within ourselves. We then experience these contacts with the world, within ourselves. And since it is the cross-linkage of these sensory and motor functions that make up our feelings concerning the reality and existence of the outside world, when we find that these are within our own minds, we find that the world we thought was outside is also within our own mind, too.

More than that, in fact, for we find that in a most magical way, it is from within our own minds that the outer world has actually come into being. Aided and abetted by all the other souls with whom we share our 'reality'. This is difficult to comprehend intellectually, but it is the experience of many years of meditation and is available to all who wish to try it for themselves. There is nothing mysterious about mystical experience to the one who has it. Indeed, he feels that he is in the process of becoming more normal. Being lost in the illusory play of the mind and the senses appears abnormal. He feels that he is awakening, whilst others still slumber. And he understands, too, why others do not give credence to such experiences. It is all a built-in part of the structure of the human mind and the purposeful nature of the cosmic drama.

Whichever way we look at it, the mind most certainly is deeply involved in the second-by-second panorama of our life, and descriptions of the inner regions demonstrate the subtlety of this process. Let us take, for example, just a few extracts from Reverend Vale Owen's book, *Life Beyond the Veil*, which was impressed upon his mind by souls who had left their physical bodies and were residing in what appear to be parts of the astral region. 'Impressed' or 'transmitted' are the correct words, for he simply sat down to write and the words appeared in his mind. He was also able to ask questions, mentally, receive answers, and generally communicate with these souls.

The manuscript itself is published in four volumes with an introduction by Sir Arthur Conan Doyle. An appreciative personal note from Lord Northcliffe also points out that Vale Owen was:

> A man of sincerity and conviction. He expressed a desire for as little publicity as possible and declined any of the great emoluments that could easily have come to him as a result of the enormous interest felt by the public all over the world.

Those who would doubt the authenticity of the manuscript are thus presented with a man without the ulterior motives of fame or financial gain. The only remaining explanation for 'disbelievers', that the man was quite sincere, but that the writings are the imaginative productions of his subconscious mind, with hidden, unconscious motives, are likewise unfounded. Like all other human intellectual knowledge it is spun out in thought without any real idea of the very nature of thought itself. A shaky edifice, to say the least. For conventional psychological thinking can tell us nothing concerning the actual nature of the mind, as an energy field. Of how the energy of the mind is organized, what the mind actually is, and what consciousness is, such psychology has little to say. It is actually the mystical approach itself which makes things clear to us.

But let us have a look at some of the passages from this manuscript. This first one was taken from a session dated Wednesday, October 8th, 1913.

> Because of certain matters which are of importance to those who would understand our meaning in its inner sense, we have decided to endeavour tonight to give you some instruction which will be of help and guidance when dealing with those things which lie beneath the surface of things, and which are usually not taken into account by the ordinary mind.
>
> One of these is the aspect which thoughts wear when projected from your sphere to ours. Thoughts which are good appear with a luminance which is absent from those of a less holy kind. This luminance appears to issue from the form of the thinker, and, by means of its manifold rays of divided colours, we are able to come at some knowledge as to his spiritual state, not alone as to whether his state is of the light or of the darkness, and of what degree in light, but also of the points in which he excels or comes short in any direction. But thoughts, which are the effect of spirit action, are seen in the effect they, in their turn, *produce on the environment of the thinker*, and not only are seen, but felt, or sensed, by us in a more accurate and intense way than with you.
>
> Following on this line of reasining, you will naturally see that when we think anything very intensely our wills are able to produce an outward manifestation which is really objective to those who behold it. Thus are many beautiful effects produced.
>
> *Can you give me a particular instance by way of illustration?*

Here Vale Owen had interpolated a question, posed within his own mind and written down along with the answers.

> Yes: it will help you to see what we mean.
>
> A company of my friends and myself, who were being instructed in this knowledge, met together in order to see how far we had progressed, and resolved on an experiment to that end. We selected a glade in the midst of a beautiful wood, and, as a test, we resolved all to will one particular thing, and see if we were successful. What we selected was the producing of a phenomenon in the open space which should be so solid and permanent as to allow of us examining it afterwards. And that was to be a statue of an animal something like an elephant, but rather different; an animal which we have here, but which has ceased to inhabit your earth[1].
>
> We all sat round the open space and concentrated our wills on the object to be produced. Very quickly it appeared and stood before us. We were much surprised at the quickness of the result. But, from our point of view, there were two defects. It was much too large; for we had failed to regulate the combination of our wills in due proportion. And it was much more like a live animal than a statue, for many had thought in their minds of the live animal itself, and also of its colouring, and so the result was a mixture between stone and flesh. Also many points were disproportionate – the head too large and the body too small, and so on, showing that more power had been concentrated on some parts than on others. It is thus we learn our imperfections, and how to remedy them, in all our studies. We experiment, and then examine the result, and try again. We did so now.
>
> Taking our minds off the statue so produced, and talking together, it gradually faded away. And then we were fresh and ready for our next trial. We decided not to select the same model as before, or our minds would probably run into more or less the same grooves. So we, this time, chose a tree with fruit on it – something like an orange tree, but not quite the same.

[1]Yes, there are plants, animals and other creatures in the inner world! As described briefly in chapter four, in *The Web of Life* and in *Natural Creation* all creatures are comprised of different configurations of the five subtle essences or tattwas. These tattwas first arise at the causal level and are reflected at both the astral and physical levels. It is of these tattwas that all physical substance is comprised. You may find this difficult to comprehend or accept, but then so would the idea that physical matter is mostly comprised of vacuum, if it were presented to almost any western person more than a hundred years ago.

We were more successful this time. The chief points of failure were that some of the fruit was ripe and some unripe. The leaves were not correct in colour, nor the branches rightly proportioned. And so we tried one thing after another, and found ourselves a little more successful each time. You can imagine somewhat of the joy of such schooling as this, and the laughter and happy humour which result from our mistakes. Those among you who think that, in this life we never make jokes, and never even laugh, will have to revise their ideas some day or they will find us strange company – or perhaps we shall find them so. But they soon learn what the love of this land is, where we can be perfectly natural and unrestrained, and indeed are compelled to be so if we wish to be accepted into respectable company, as you would phrase it. I fear the obverse is rather true of earth, is it not? Ah well, live and learn, and those who live in this life – and not merely exist, or worse – learn very quickly. And the more we learn, the more we marvel at the forces at our command.

It is quite clear from these passages how the inner mind and outer substance of these realms are so closely linked, and how it is not a matter of strangeness to the inhabitants that this should be so. To an increasing number of people upon our planet earth, this perception and consciousness is an aspect of their inner life and moment-by-moment understanding which is continually growing. And we must remember that both the mind and the substance of these higher realms is of a far finer quality than we see in this world.

Note also how it is said that thoughts not only, "produce an effect upon the environment of the thinker," but are also, "felt or sensed by others." This is the natural telepathic mode of communicating or 'talking' in these regions. When, in this world, people talk of vibrations or atmosphere, it is a dim awareness of this which is being referenced.

Similarly, the statue was manifested by the "combination of the wills," or minds, of those present. This is how all the regions of the mind – physical, astral and causal – are produced. But the full mechanism is hidden until the soul has passed beyond the causal realm, the region of the Universal Mind. We observe the results, are aware to some degree of the causal relationship of 'outer' events to our inner mind, but are unable to perceive the whole story.

Certain thoughts concerning the familiarity of these scenes with earthly ones may arise in the reader's mind. This is not really the place to discuss them, but let me quote from Paramhansa Yogananda's, *Autobiography of a Yogi*. Yogananda has been conveying what his master had told him of the inner regions, and realizing that his readers may feel doubtful of his description, he adds:

> There can be no foundation for the oft-heard fear that God, having perhaps exhausted His ingenuity in organizing *this* world, has reserved for the *next* nothing more challenging to our interest than the strumming of harps!

Or one can refer to the Bible, where Christ is reported to have said, (in Hebrew):

> Let not your hearts be troubled. . . . In my Father's house are many mansions. (St. John, Ch. 14, v. 1,2).

And of course, there is the ancient Hermetic axiom, "As above, so below."

Again, there is a similar passage demonstrating the linkage of the within and the without. It is also of interest because it refers to a previous passage where the souls had come to a hall of learning. Here, as in our own world, there are artefacts or instruments, made by the inhabitants to aid them in the control and focusing of their minds, as well as in understanding the nature of their world. Such activity also makes it clear that just as we are mystified by the way our world is constructed, so too are souls in these inner regions. Although considerably more enlightened than us as to how the creation is put together, they are still – like us – exploring that part of creation in which they find themselves.

> It seems that before the students are able to progress much in the science of creation as studied in this region, they have to get a thorough knowledge of the fundamental elements with which they have to deal. This is, of course, quite natural. As the learners progress they are able gradually to achieve the result they wish without the scientific apparatus which at first is necessary. One instrument after another is left out until at length they are able to depend solely on their will. We asked our guide to what practical purpose the knowledge was put when acquired. He replied that the first use was the training of the mind and will of the student. That training was very excellent and very strenuous.

In our physical world, biofeedback instruments would come into this same category, though the point should be made that for the creation of greater awareness or focusing of the mind, the ultimate aim – as with our astral friends – should be to relinquish the use of such outer props. But note that the above was written more than half a century before anyone ever conceived the idea of biofeedback.

Interestingly, too, the personality of the individual impressing the above upon Vale Owen's mind was clearly of a particular nature, especially when we compare the style and content with information given to him in later communications, by different individuals.

Talking about the inner regions, another soul had much to say concerning the condition of science in our world. Remember, once again, while reading this, that these things were said in 1913, during the formative years of present day theoretical physics.

> Space must be enlarged in meaning when applied to these spheres; for distance has not the same obstructive sense to us, as it has to you. . .
>
> Nothing is still, all moves continuously[1]. This movement is controlled and orderly, and that is a warrant of the constant energizing. . .

Talking about the rocks of our earth, the communication continues:

> The chemical composition has been, more or less, ascertained. But the more subtle influences proceeding from the ever-vibrating particles have been neglected. . . And these characteristics are worthy of deeper study than they have hitherto received. . . Yet when it is remembered that no piece of rock or stone is still, but that all its particles are in movement orderly and constant, it is only one step onward then to realize that, in order that his movement be maintained, there must be present some great force.

The communicator has considerably more to say concerning the process of creation underlying our suns, stars and planets and the hierarchy of souls that are involved in the administration of this system. Yogic writers have termed them the *devas*, or the lesser 'gods' and 'godesses'.

[1] This was before the discovery of particle 'spin' etc.

But I believe that if I quoted these passages, that the credulity[1] of many readers could be stretched beyond bounds, if that is not already so!

We do not know how anything comes into being, but when suggestions or answers *are* given, we disbelieve them unless they are already familiar to us. And so we remain in ignorance until we are forcibly evicted from our body at death and have to learn to live in those realms until, sooner or later, we take another birth. Anyhow, *Life Beyond The Veil* is a classic and has been reprinted many times since the first edition in 1922. So it is available to all who wish to peruse its pages. After all, one is presented with so much trash on television and in the media, so why should there be a reaction to reading something more fundamental to the inner reality? Why is it that we will divert our minds with the inconsequential or even the mentally damaging, whilst running away from the truth whenever we can.

In the words of the Persian mystic, Rumi:

> Oh Man – from whom do you run?
> From yourself – Oh foolishness!
> From God – Oh crime!

Also relevant to our study of science is a transmission dated October 9th 1913:

> Perhaps if we endeavour to enlighten you on the chemistry of the heavenly bodies it may be both interesting and helpful to you. We do not mean the physical aspect of the science, as understood by modern astronomical scientists, but the deeper study of their constitution. Every star, as you know, is itself a centre of a system which comprises in itself not only the planets in revolution round the star, but also the particles of matter which suffuse that system, but are too sublimated to be cognized by any system of chemistry which is possible to those who dwell in physical bodies, and in their research are compelled to use both material instruments and material brains. These particles are between the purely material and spiritual, and indeed may be used both in the physical and the spiritual economies. For the two are merely two of many

[1] I did once get a review from one of the 'institutions' which stated that reading one of my books would stretch the 'credibility' of the reader. An interesting Freudian slip! I took it as a compliment!

phases of one progressive economy, and act and react each on the other, like a sun and his planet.

Gravitation is applicable to these particles also on both sides, and it is by means of this force – as we call it, as being a name you know, and also a very little understand – that we cohere these particles together and are able, from time to time, so to clothe our spiritual bodies as to become visible to the photographic plate, and sometimes to the human eye. But we do more than this, and over a wider range. Were it not for these particles all space would be dark; that is, no light would be able to be transmitted from planet or sun or star to the earth.

Your scientists have much to learn yet on this subject, and it is not our business to impart much which men can learn by the powers they possess.

The 'particles' being referred to here are focuses of energy at the physical or etheric level, "between the purely material and spiritual." By spiritual, here, is actually meant astral, which strictly speaking is not really the same. It is indicated, however, that the spiritual and physical are part of a continuous spectrum, "one progressive economy". Remember, too, how some of the vacuum state theories mentioned earlier perceive that space is made up of a matrix of tiny 'space particles', quanta of focused spacial, vacuum or etheric energy, far smaller than the tiniest subatomic particles presently known to us.

In addition, note how gravity is identified as a force between these subtle particles as well, both physically and in these inner regions. It is the power of coherence and relationship which exists wherever there is energy in manifestation, its most subtle essence or source being the inward creative power of the Shabd, the One manifesting itself as the many.

Finally, this most revealing of passages points out that these particles are necessary for the progagation of light, of electromagnetic vibration or energy. That is to say that light is not a something passing through nothing, but is itself a vibration within what we call 'nothing' or vacuum.

There is, in fact, one theory of the vacuum state structure which considers that a photon of light is actually a hole amongst these space particles[1], left behind after the passage of an electron or other subatomic particle; a

[1] 'Particle' is not really the right word, but what is the alternative?

subatomic particle being a whirling vortex of these spatial quanta of energy.

Now it is a postulate of Einstein's theory of special relativity that objects increase in mass, the faster they go, and this has been shown conclusively to be fact in experiments involving accelerating subatomic particles. According to the spacial matrix theory, this increase in mass is due entirely to the accretion by the electron of space particles as it travels through them, rather like a comet collecting cosmic debris from outer space.

This means that whilst these spatial quanta, and therefore electrons, have both mass *and* energy, photons possess energy, but not mass. They have no mass because they are a hole in the spatial lattice. They have energy because the hole moves and vibrates, that is to say that it travels and possesses frequency.

The problem still remains, of course, "Of what do the holes in the spatial matrix consist? . . ." For we have decided long ago that you cannot have 'pure nothing'!

Interestingly, it has been shown experimentally that electrons, as well as 'orbiting', also exhibit a perturbation or jiggling effect. One should think of the 'orbit' being more like this:

than like this:

This is analagous to *Brownian Movement* observed in small particles, such as pollen, within a 'stationary' fluid. The particles are constantly bombarded from all sides by the moving molecules of the liquid and are thus kept constantly jiggling about.

If we think of space as being comprised of 'space particles', then we can see how an electron oscillates in this way due to the incessant vibrations of the surrounding space particles or spacial matrix of energy. Conventional physics has no satisfactory answer as to why electrons should be so constantly agitated.

Mass, in the absence of gravitational attraction, is actually the same phenomenon as inertia – the reluctance of something to change its state of motion. So if our spinning, dancing whirls on the 'vacuum' surface – our subatomic particles – demonstrate a resistance to being moved, spacially, due to the drag of the vacuum energy density, (the 'space particles'), then our subatomic particles will exhibit the phenomenon we call mass. And hence any atoms and molecules comprised of them (ie. all matter), will also have mass even in the absence of gravitational attraction.

Mystically, looking from within-out, gravitation, as well as electrical charge, magnetism and the strong and weak forces, represent the cohesive power of the Creative Word, the Shabd, the primal creative current in creation, still present even in diffuse form holding inert matter in manifested existence.

In terms of physics, looking from without-in, these forces are indicative of a structured polarization of the vacuum ocean, manifesting outwardly as attraction and repulsion between the bubbles and ripples upon its surface.

Really, physical reality is manifested in the same manner as a kaleidoscopic image. Hidden patterns are picked up and reflected in a multifaceted manner. All we can see is a composite image but the mechanism by which it comes into being is hidden from us. So when we can only see the image, we are baffled by the cleverness of its construction and the intricate sequence of apparent coincidences and repeating patterns or 'laws' which make up its reality. By an analysis of the image alone, without an understanding of the formative mechanisms, we can never come to an understanding of how it comes into being. But when we see how, at heart, we are only looking at a web of manyness spun out of and across the face of the primordial intelligence, consciousness and being of the One, then 'coincidence' and 'order' are realized to be no more than one would expect. We are only seeing that one integrating light shining out from all the interstices of the tapestry covering it.

And this interwoven tapestry of manyness is the greater Mind itself, and although later in this chapter we discuss the concept of the *Formative Mind* as the great pattern maker in creation, it is a topic which is expanded upon considerably and runs throughout the next book in this series, *Natural Creation*. For being the means by which the physical creation as we know it comes into being, we cannot really understand the nature of our universe and the origin of its laws without a deep understanding of this great divider of the One which we call the Mind. And, as we have previously commented, our human mind is just one aspect of this greater Mind.

So all aspects of science and human existence become enlivened when we begin to grasp the nature of the multilevel, multireflectional, multidimensional hierarchy by which what we call nature is manifested

But returning to our theme, and concerning energy and its transmutation, on December 2nd, 1913 came the following message, from another soul:

> Dear friend and ward, I will tonight speak to you of certain matters which connect with the question of transmutation of energy. Energy, as I now employ the word, is to be understood as that intermediary which couples up the motion of will with the effect as displayed to the minds of men. We here are trained to this end that we may, by the motion of our wills, transmit, by what we may call vibration, our thoughts through the intervening spheres, or states, into the earth plane. It is this movement in vibration which I call energy.
>
> Now, you must understand that in using earth-phrasing I am employing a medium which is not adequate to express, either exactly or fully, the science of these spheres and realms. It is necessary, therefore, that I qualify my terms, and when I use the term vibration I do not speak merely of oscillation to and fro alone, but of movements which are sometimes elliptical, sometimes spiral, and sometimes a combination of these and other qualities.
>
> From this point of view the atomic system of vibration, which has but of late been revealed to men of science, is to us one with the movements of the planets of this solar sphere, and of other systems far away in space.

It is being pointed out that energy in the atom and the energetic movement of the planets and stars are all simply vibrations or energy patterns, possessing common features That there is a relationship between all forms of energy which is inherent in their movement

> But transmutation brings into any such system a change of movement, and the quality of movement being changed, there is also, and of necessity, a change of result. Thus we, acting always in perfect obedience to laws laid down by those higher and wiser than ourselves, concentrate our wills on the movement of certain vibrations, which become deflected and transmuted into other qualities of vibrations, and thus change is wrought.
>
> Usually we do this work slowly and gradually, in order to obtain the exact quantity of divergence from the original quality of vibration intended, and not less or more.
>
> It is by this method that we deal with the actions of men, and the course of nature in all its parts. There are manifold classes and companies who have in charge the various departments of creation – mineral, vegetable, animal, human, terrestrial, solar and stellar. Beyond this, also, the stars are grouped together and dealt with by hierarchies qualified for that great task.

It is by this means that souls in higher regions are involved in the administration of our physical affairs. This may be difficult for some to countenance, but at least one should approach such things with an open mind. In other words, the administration and evolution of our physical world, both in regard to its life forms as well as its inert substance, is under the control of consciousness, focused as individual souls, from within. This is indeed the case in this world alone, where affairs are dealt with by a remarkable and complex social hierarchy, the outward reflection and sum of the minds within us all.

The transmission continues:

> It is by this same method, then, of the transmutation of energy that systems are gradually developed into worlds, and these worlds furnished with form, and then enabled to produce vegetation and animal life. But, this being so, you will note that all life, and all development, is consequent upon the operation of spiritual energy, obeying the dictates of the will of spiritual beings. This once grasped, blind force disappears, and intention takes its place – intention of intelligent and powerful spiritual workers of various grades, operating according to certain fixed laws but, within the bounds of those laws, free and mighty.
>
> Moreover, matter itself is the result of the transmutation of spiritual vibrations into those of grosser sort, and these latter are now being analysed by scientists who have come to the

knowledge that matter is indeed the result of vibrations, and that no particle of matter is still, but in ceaseless movement. That is correct but not conclusive. For it does not pursue the matter to the end of it. It were truer to say, not that matter is in vibration, but that matter *is* vibration, the result of vibration of a quality more refined, which is found, not in the phenomenon of material things, but in those spheres proper to its quality.

Thus you will see how little it matters that, when the time comes for you to cast off the body of earth, you stand discarnate. Your earth body was a body of vibrations and no more. Very well, you now have a body of vibrations more substantial and enduring, because of a higher quality, and nearer to the energizing Will which brought it into existence, and so sustains it. The body will serve you while you sojourn in the lower spheres and, when you have progressed, that body will be transmuted into one still more permanent, and of quality more sublime. This process will be repeated as the ages go by and you proceed from glory to higher glory in the infinite reaches of progress before you.

It follows also that, as those in the lower spheres in this spiritual realm are normally not visible in the earth sphere, so those of the higher spheres are not normally visible in those lower spheres, and so on in like order as we rise from sphere to sphere and pursue our way along this glorious road of light and endeavour.

So it is then, friend and ward, and when you come hither one day you will be the better able to understand. For although you do now employ this same method of which I have spoken, in your own daily life, and so does every man, yet you little understand the manner of its working. Did you so, it were well that all men be of one mind with us who try to use our powers for the glory and worship of God; for the weapon, to be used for good or evil, which man would then find to his hand would pass in might and strength all his present knowledge; as that exceeds the mental endowment of the fly or the ant.

It is well that we are able to coordinate the progress in knowledge and in holiness that they journey together. For this is so – not perfectly, but within certain boundary lines, wide but sure. Were it otherwise the world would not be what it is today; nor order rule comparatively.

This, however, is one aspect of our care for the human race: and what the future holds I cannot say. For I cannot see so far as to conjecture how far men will go in this new knowledge, the threshold of which they now have crossed. But things will be well ordered by those who watch with jealous care, and wisdom very great, and all will be well while this is so.

The next day, December 3rd, 1913, the communication was continued.

I once observed a very beautiful instance of the transmutation of energy here in my own land.

There was a company of visitors from another sphere, and they were about to return to their own, their mission having been finished. A part of our own, of whom I was one, went with them to the large lake over which they had come to us. Here they embarked in boats and were giving us their parting words of thanks and goodwill, when one of our Princes, was seen approaching with a company of attendants behind us. They came through the air and hovered above us and the boats while we, knowing their habits, but not their present intention, waited to see what manner or thing they – or rather, he, had in his mind to do. For it is a delight in these realms to give pleasure, each to other, by exercising such powers as we possess, and that in varying combinations by which effects are differently produced.

Far up in the heavens we saw them, as they moved slowly, circling about the Prince from whom to those in circle went threads of vibrations of different quality, and so of different colour. These, he of his will sent forth, and those his subordinates wove them into a network of curious designs and very beautiful; and where two threads crossed, there the intensified light shone like a stone of brilliant hue. And the knots were of many colours owing to the varying combination of threads entering into their construction.

When this was complete the circle widened out and drew away and left their Prince alone in the midst. And he held the net by its middle in his hand and it floated out around him like a many-coloured spider web. It was very beautiful.

Now, that net was really a system of many qualities of vibrations woven together. He loosed it out of his hand and it began slowly to sink as he rose through it, until it was level with his feet. Then he raised his hands and descended with it. And as he came he looked through the net at the boats below; and he made slow movements with his hands in their direction.

Then they began to move on the water as of themselves, and so continued until they floated in a circle. Then the net descended and settled over them, and we saw that they were all within its circumference, and also that, as it lighted on them, they passed through it and it sank and rested upon the water. Then the Prince, standing on the net and on the water, in the midst of the boats, waved his hand in greeting to them. And the net slowly arose from the water, lifting the boats with it, and floated upward into the air.

So away over the lake they went together and the company of our sphere closed in around them, and sent up a song of Godspeed as they floated away towards the horizon over the lake.

It was merely one of those little tokens of love which we here delight to show our brethren of other spheres of labour – nothing more. My reason for relating this – which was, in display, much more beautiful than I am able to show you in writing – was to illustrate the effect of the will of a powerful Angel Lord concentrated on the forces to hand and transmuting them in quality.

Beauty is not alone the minister of pleasure to the sight. It is rather a characteristic of these realms. For beauty and utility go together here. And the more useful a man becomes the more beautiful is he in person. The beauty of holiness is literal and real, friend; and it were well if all men could accept that truth.

The Seed of Truth

Being naturally intrigued by life in there inner regions, the question is often asked, "How do souls pass their time?" From the similar book, *The Seed of Truth,* comes the reply:

> That has been answered many, many times. The question of time is one of interest because we are not dependent on your definition of time.
>
> Yours is a demarcation for purposes of convenience. That is, you have charted certain passages as minutes or hours, or seconds or days, and all that is based upon the rotation of the earth and its relationship to the sun. We do not have night and day. Our source of light is not the same as yours. Therefore, we do not have time in the sense that you have it. Our measurement of time depends upon our spiritual state, that is, we feel time in the sense of enjoyment. Time, to us, is a mental experience.
>
> The difficulty the questioner has is in understanding spiritual experiences in terms of physical measurement, but there are wide and boundless pursuits of the mind and spirit, cultural, educational, purposive, actual in their effect on your physical world, to engage us and occupy us for as long as we wish to be so occupied.

This reply then led to the question:

If you want to book something ahead, how do you do it, if time has no meaning as it has here?

Do you mean, if I wished to meet someone? Then I send a thought and if it is convenient we meet. There are no letters to be written.

What if you wanted to arrange to meet somebody at some specified time?

It does not happen in that way. The only kind of engagement like that is the perpetuation of the earthly custom of festivals. . . If I am desired to attend some group, the request is sent to me mentally, I receive it and I go. It would not be sent to me now because it would be known that I am at this moment speaking with you. There are no diaries; it is a world of the mind and of the spirit.

Are there any trains in the spirit world?

There are no trains unless you think you have a train to catch and then there is a train for you to catch. It is hard to understand, isn't it? But it is like a dream. If you think you have a train to catch, there is your train.

Even in your dreams you think you have to go on a ship. The ship is there because you make the ship, and it is real to you. You people it and it travels. It has got the necessary attendants, hasn't it? It is very real on its own plane of sensation. You must remember that reality is a relative term.

I have heard and read of these things frequently, but I must say it is very difficult for me to appreciate.

It is. But even in your world you have the illusion of time. One hour is not always the same to you; and five minutes can sometimes seem as long as one hour. That is the mental aspect of it. If you appreciate that in our world that mental aspect is the reality, you will see that we are divorced from the purely mechanical aspect of time as it affects you. I think that is the best way to express it.

In chapter six, I briefly mentioned the idea of natural law and reading through *The Seed of Truth*, I was interested to come across the following:

There is no 'parliament' in the spirit world because there is no need to make laws to regulate the lives of the people who dwell there. The natural law takes care of people in the spirit world because they are confronted with it in a form which is inescapable. They no longer have physical bodies; the problem of physical life does not concern them. They are now

> expressing themselves in spiritual form and the natural law is in operation. There is no need for any intermediary.

This interesting response demonstrates one of the fundamental differences between our physical world and the astral world which is being described. Here we all have dense physical bodies and are mostly locked in to our five physical senses. The result is that we are unable to perceive directly the mental and spiritual stature either of ourselves and certainly not of others. Souls of all levels of attainment are all locked into outwardly similar physical bodies.

In these inner mind regions, however, we go exactly to that place – spiritually and mentally – to which our inner condition is suited. The higher and more spiritualized the individual, the higher the region to which we automatically float. Or conversely, if our mind and emotional content during physical life has been hellish, where else could we go after death when deprived of a physical body but to a mind world where this kind of mental activity is expressed? They have been called the hellish regions. If our mind is already a hell while in this life, where alse can it go after death?

We create our own reality out of our own mind substance, just as we have done in this world. Our sojourn in such regions, however, is fortunately not permanent, but only for as long as these intense negative tendencies remain present within us. After that we will take another birth, though it may not be as a human. Justice is automatic in the Mind worlds. We go where our inward mind takes us. This is also a part of the law of causality, of karma. There is no question of a vindictive God, bent upon eternal punishment of the wicked, despatching us to hell forever, as some uninformed religious preachers proclaim. That is endowing Him with our human emotions and demonstates where *we* stand, inwardly, not the way He conducts His affairs. We make the bed we lie in. We punish or reward ourselves without ever knowing it.

Again from the *The Seed of Truth*, someone asked whether there were any newspapers and radio in the inner worlds. The response again demonstrated the mental nature of these inner realms.

> No, we do not have radio because communication is differently used. Telepathy is the common method of reaching one

> another. But it is possible for those who know how, to address vast numbers and to reach them, even when they are not themselves present. But it does not work on the principle of your radio.
>
> There are no newspapers in your earthly sense, because there is no necessity to chronicle happenings as you do. Information is constantly being dispensed to those who should have it by the ones whose occupation it is to spread these facts. This is difficult for you to understand.
>
> When it is necessary for me to be told something that I do not know, the thought is sent to me by the one who thinks I ought to know it. There are people engaged on the task of disseminating these thoughts. They are specially trained for it.
>
> In our life we are constantly receiving and transmitting thoughts. Those who are on our spiritual wavelength, that is, of like spiritual mentality, receive thoughts that we send them and transmit thoughts to us. The wavelength is determined by spiritual attainment.

Well, one could continue with these and similar passages, but as well as providing some wonderfully inspirational material, it must be very clear that in these inner astral regions described in this chapter, the linkage of mind to substance is the essence of their reality.

But if you have difficulty believing in any of this, it is not so very important. Experience is of vastly more value than belief, but we must put ourselves in the way of obtaining that experience. And then make our own assessment as we go along. The most important thing is to live our present life at its highest possible level, spiritually speaking, to always place our search for its meaning before all other goals. Then we must follow wherever our seeking star may lead us.

The Hidden Presence

One of the factors which always strikes me concerning descriptions of the inner regions is that the presence and existence of God, as the highest inward essence of life, is never questioned. It is immediately apparent. His presence runs and flows through all things, and the inhabitants are all aware of it.

In our physical world, unless we have become highly spiritualized within, we do not perceive this presence. We get only intimations of the infinite, immortal and immanent power. Our human minds have become too engrossed in the show of physical substance which we experience through our senses. Our attention is outward, not inward. Therefore, like Plato's story of the men in the cave, we see only the shadows playing on the wall and fail to notice the source of light which gives them existence. Yet this source pervades all things, else nothing would exist.

In our minds, we appreciate this presence as logic, causality, connection and relationship. This is the integrating power of the One within the many. This is what holds the many together, as one whole. Some of these relationships are clear to us as unquestionably those of cause and effect: I push something and it moves; I say something kind and it warm's a person's heart; I am unkind and they are hurt or angry.

These kinds of connections are clear to us, though – as we have seen – when we analyze it scientifically, we still find that we do not understand the mechanisms. But for many things in life, we can see no rhyme or reason. How do we choose our relatives? Or our children, our parents, brothers and sisters? Clearly we have no choice over such far-reaching events in our lives. The nature of the causality underlying all such things is hidden to us. This is part of the extended law of causality. The Indian mystics call it karma and it is the law which operates wholly from within the hidden dimensions of our own minds and yet creates the seemingly outward reality.

After all, why do things happen in the way they do? Disasters or pleasant happenings – in fact, all events of life. Someone oversleeps and misses an aeroplane that crashes, killing all on board. Another person may have thought himself lucky to have caught that same plane, until it crashed.

The Persian mystic, Rumi, tells a tale to illustrate the hidden force of destiny underlying the phenomena which make up our daily life.

He relates that a favourite minister of the king while walking in the bazaar one morning, met the Angel of Death, who looked at him in an odd kind of way. The terrified minister rushed to the king, crying, "Transfer me at once to Baghdad. I saw the Angel of Death and I didn't like the way he was looking at me!"

The kindly king at once transferred him to his palace in Baghdad, lending him his fastest horse for transport. The terrified minister set out immediately.

Later that day, the Angel of Death dropped in the see the king on a purely social visit. The king took the opportunity to ask what it was that the Angel of Death had done to so frighten his minister.

"I did nothing," said the Angel, "I was just surprised to see him here, for I have an Appointment with him this very afternoon in Baghdad!"

This law of karma, of causality, includes our own mind. Indeed, the mind is its real architect, for it is through the divided screen of the mind that we perceive the oneness of the whole and thus come to interpret that oneness as cause and effect within a world we think consists of a myriad parts.

Some connections we are aware of, but most, like the third spacial dimension to our mythical Flatlanders, are lost to view. We may intuitively feel that such relationships are there, but we cannot understand why we feel that way. Francis Thompson put it most succinctly:

> All things, by immortal power,
> Near or far,
> Hiddenly
> To each other linked are,
> Thou canst not stir a flower
> Without troubling a star

During our lives, all events, thoughts, desires, words and all the rest, leave a greater or lesser impression upon our mind energies, within us, as in the flight recorder of an aeroplane. When we die, our physical body is left behind, but not so this little black box, full to the brim with the recordings of a lifetime. From this box, interwoven with those of all other creatures, our future destiny is written. These are the boundary conditions upon our 'free will'. This is what gives us our wives, our husbands, our children, our talents, our disposition, our health and sickness, the events of a day, our jobs – everything.

How often does one hear, "It was just by chance that I

am doing what I am doing." What we call chance is a recognition that we do not understand the mechanism by which things happen. When chance is too much, we call it coincidence or serendipity. Then our mind is shaken into a realization that there must be hidden connections of which we are unaware. "Coincidence is God's way of remaining anonymous." We do not perceive His hidden hand in all things. And yet it is there, and by raising our level of consciousness, we can experience it, in greater and greater splendour. This, indeed, is the inherent meaning and purpose in life. This is true evolution, but of our consciousness.

Attunement or at-one-ment to this inner power also gives us the power of faith, which makes things happen. True faith, as opposed to a blind belief in the intellectual expression of a philosophy or religion, is a condition or attitude of mind focused upon the inner presence in all things. It is faith because it is an awareness of the higher power who manages all things. It is a precursor to mystical experience and is increased thereby. It is a deep intuition which underlies all that a person does. It is a focused and concentrated mind, full of increasing understanding. Faith makes things happen around us just as much in this world as it does in the more subtle astral and causal realms. It is the power of a delayed miracle. The manifestation may take a little time, but things most assuredly do happen due to the power of faith. It is also being in tune with one's destiny – going along with what is meant to be happening, not fighting to impose one's own egocentric will upon events at every step. And all this within a context of the interstitial law of karma or extended causality.

We are so blind and ignorant in our normal human condition, that what should be crystal clear to us is clouded over by our minds, our emotions, by our sensory involvement, and by the consequent loss of natural focus at our inward centre of being. To rise from this morass, we need the power of some hidden helper. This indeed is being raised from the dead.

The Formative Mind

It is very clear that this world is a Mind world. Wherever you look, people move about only because they have some thought or emotion motivating them. Without a thought or mental process, however momentary, we will not act. The actions, too, are controlled by the mind: if we become unconscious, we fall over!

Look about you in the street one day, or amongst your own family in the house, or just observe yourself. Every person has an active mind, dictating what that individual is doing. This is partially conscious, but really represents only the surface activity on a vast and surging sea of unconscious thought and emotion. All our artefacts, too, all the things we or someone else has made, have been created with the help of our mind. But do we know from where our thoughts and emotions arise? Mostly, we do not, for it is from this ocean of the unconscious that our thoughts and emotions come, patterned and shaped by the events of both our present, as well as past, lives.

So we have our 'conscious' mind and our subconscious mind. But there is a third aspect to our mind, which I would call the *Formative Mind*. Not only do we experience our conscious mind and are aware to some degree of our unconscious processes, but behind all this lies the mechanism by which our minds have actually created this physical reality, which can appear to us to be so real.

It is the fusion of our apparently individual minds at this deeply unconscious, FORMATIVE level which creates our reality. Both inward and apparently outer.

This physical world is therefore a mind world. Everything which happens here, happens under the creative influence of the minds of all involved.

On the astral and causal levels, the immediate interaction between mind and substance makes it apparent right away that they are mind worlds. But in this world, the mental causality underlying all that happens, is perhaps more than ninety-nine percent hidden. Even the emotional and psychological motivation behind our own and other people's activities is mostly unrevealed.

When I push an object on my desk, I feel that I understand the causal nature of why it moves. Similarly, with the planets in their orbits, with the construction of a motor car or electronic equipment or even with the relationship between a mental plan and its physical manifestation.

But the wholeness of the causality underlying why I was born to certain parents, how I came to speak in a certain language, how we meet our friends, our wife or husband, how our particular children come to us – how all this and all the other events of life, great or small, come to pass is beyond our ken. We can certainly see a mental involvement in much of it, but not the whole picture.

We are mentally and emotionally attracted to our husband or wife to be – this is a part of the way in which the inner mental skein of karma is worked out. But how did we come to meet in the first place? And where children come from, for example, complete with their individual temperaments and personalities is an even greater mystery. Again, our mind and emotions were surely involved when we made love, setting the whole process of birth in motion, but there is more to the apparent miracle of birth than just that.

The causality is mostly hidden from our view. Even in physics, when we trace the causality to finer and finer degrees of minuteness, it finally eludes our grasp, as we have seen. We can make neither head nor tail of what on earth is going on.

So we recognize the existence of causality and determinism, yet we cannot observe the mind mechanism by which things happen. We automatically use logical processes in our minds without comprehending where our intuitive reliance upon such logic arises.

So, in this world, as in the astral and causal domains, we drift through the dream, completely under the influence of our hidden mind processes. And the same is true of the lower species, too. They also possess an unconscious mind structure, around their inner spark of life or consciousness, which gives them the outer form they exhibit and makes them instinctively do the things they do.

Similarly, many of my friends have confirmed my own experience that when one's mind is concentrated and focused within, people and things come to us. But when the mind loses its centre and becomes scattered, then we find that we have to run about hectically in the world collecting things and going to see people, here and there. There is an obvious side to this, that when the mind is scattered and overactive, we automatically have a tendency to behave in an overactive manner, to jump the gun and, as it were, get ahead of the natural order of things which we would experience were the mind quiet.

But there is a more hidden side, too, for when the mind is quiet and within, we actually pattern the so-called 'outer' reality in a different fashion to when we are scattered. Our reality actually manifests to us in a different manner, automatically reflecting the content of our minds. This is the activity of the deeper layer of our mind, the Formative Mind, which actually makes things happen the way they do and makes us think the way we do – both aspects being an integral part of each other.

So when our mind is within, the world, in a sense, comes to us. When we are out, then out we go to run around everywhere to fulfil our destiny.

But the fact is, that inward or outward – it is all in our mind. Where we *feel* it to be depends upon where our attention is focused.

If we want chairs in our house, we can go out looking for chairs. Alternatively, we can bring a carpenter home, care for him and give him our attention. Then there will be no dearth of chairs! The Carpenter is the One central power within us, the Lord, the Creator. If we genuinely concentrate our minds upon the inward Creator, then there is no lack of His creation for us to use as required!

Everything in this world is controlled by the Mind, that which divides the One into the many. The One is still present in the many, in His creation, else it could not exist. But its divided nature provides us with a panorama of activity in which we are thoroughly enmeshed. Only with the loving help of one who can go beyond the maze, who has fully awoken from the dream, who no longer dances to the tune of the mind – physical, astral or causal – can we ourselves escape into the true freedom of the soul. And that one is a perfect master.

The Weaver of the Web

So the Mind is the formative principle. This is its intrinsic nature. To divide is to create patterns. To form patterns is formative, per se. Whether we are formulating plans in our 'conscious' mind for the things we desire or wish to do, or whether we realize the influence of our own subconscious mind upon these 'conscious' thought and emotional patterns – the patterning, Formative Mind mechanism is always at work. First we have the mental idea, the blueprint, then the action takes place. Remove this blueprint or thought process, as in unconsciousness, and we fall over in a heap, or slump in our chair.

But our human thoughts, however mysterious they may be are only a part of the totality of Mind, and the same formative process continues throughout all Mind worlds. Our destiny – the events of this life – are a part of our physical mind structure. It is from here that past mental impressions form the destiny of the present life and that patterns of the present are later formed into the destiny of future existences.

The powerhouse of the astral region, the *Sahasra*, the *Thousand Petalled Lotus*, is the formative energy crossroads for all lower creation. But it is itself only a pattern of energy, reflected from the more inward, causal realm. This causal region, the world of the Universal Mind itself, is the primal pattern maker, the originator of Maya, the weaver of the web of illusion, the spinner of the beguiling tapestry of forms which we are led – by our human minds – into considering so real.

But Mind itself only exists due to the power of consciousness, the Ocean of Being, of God. The life-giving light within this magical box of forms is the Divine itself. All Mind patterns whether of Universal Mind, of our human thoughts or of anything within the causal, astral and physical universes are only bubbles of form upon this great Creative Ocean. Mind is also a creation of the Supreme Consciousness.

So, as we have seen, what we call energy is thus only patterns in the Creative Life Stream induced by the Formative Mind. And since consciousness is One, so all energy patterns are related to each other, a phenomenon we experience as causality. So it is actually the divisions of the Formative Mind which we experience as the divisions of the physical world, the differentiation of material substance into pattern and form. This division is expressed at all levels of mind function: emotional, 'conscious', conceptual, subconscious and formative or causal. Or as the Eastern yogic aphorism puts it: *"Mind is the slayer of the Real"*.

In the physical, and indeed astral and causal worlds, the differing configuration of these forms or energies gives rise to souls encapsulated in different mind structures or patterns, which project outwardly as bodies. When we see only the bodies, we are confused. When we begin to understand the hidden laws of Mind function, then we begin to see things differently. When, at last, the soul stands naked in the spiritual regions, beyond the realm of the Universal Mind, then we know our real selves.

But this is beyond the reach of most forms of yoga. Only a perfect mystic can lift a soul to this height. The mystic experiences of most souls in this physical universe, however illuminating, blissful and unifying they may be are usually only experiences within the subtle area in the 'sky' of our physical constitution, just below or occasionally penetrating into the subastral domains. This does not demean such experiences, for they are of tremendous importance to the individual, but it does tell us of the sheer immensity of the creation and of the great 'journey' the soul must travel upon to reach its original Home. Such experiences are only the beginning.

Energy and the Formative Mind

We often hear people speak of body, mind and soul and the words are used to convey many shades of meaning. But what is really meant by these 'entities'? And what is energy? What are substance and matter? Well, we have been discussing this throughout, but since it is of such fundamental importance let us summarize it once again. Our soul is our consciousness, the innermost spark of life within us. It is a part of the Formless One, the One Ocean of Being. Consciousness is therefore One and *undivided*. No division means that it is form-*less*. That there is no difference within it, no pattern, no duality or polarity. All is One, an Ocean of Love and Life. This is the Source, the Uncreated God, Absolute Reality. It lies at the heart of what we are.

"Mind is the slayer of the Real." Mind is a part of the process of creation. In the region of Universal Mind first arises duality or polarity – difference. From duality arises *division*, *form* or *pattern* and, simultaneously, as a part of the same thing, *space* and *time*. Space, time and pattern all imply division or difference, they are patterns of separation.

The Reality of pure consciousness is now overlain by Mind, though Mind has no independent existence, but arises due to the creative urge of Consciousness. This creative urge we call the Word, the Logos, the Creative Life Stream. It is also called the Shabd, the Sound Current or Audible Life Stream, for this vibration of life can be *heard* within in mystic practice. It is actually the central pivot of the highest mystic teaching. The gospel of St John even starts out with this, "In the beginning was the Word." And we find the same central position given to this power of Life in the teachings of all mystics of the highest order, though there are also many imitations, too, which use the same language to describe a lower order of reality.

Through the causal, astral and physical worlds, the Formative Mind patterns become increasingly complex. All forms are woven by the Mind across the face of the One, of Consciousness. Mind is empowered to perform this task by the creative power of the One itself. Without this maintaining presence of the One, Mind and all its forms would evaporate, leaving only the Uncreated One.

All forms are thus of the Mind and we can look at our physical body as an image projected by consciousness though the multilayered screen of the Formative Mind. Consciousness shines through the Mind patterns and we perceive a physical body.

But actually, in the fuller sense, the physical body is really a part of this ever-increasing complexity in the Mind's activity. *The physical body is thus a part of the Formative Mind, itself.* The physical body does not give rise to mind; rather the Formative Mind gives rise to the body.

Similarly, the thoughts, emotions, intuitions and instincts which comprise what we normally think of as our human mind are only a small part of the totality of Mind. Mind is far more than our human experience of it, and is comprised of *everything* within our experience and much more besides.

Now we can begin to see how everything fits together so fittingly, for everything is a part of the same Universal Formative Mind. Mind is more holistic, holographic, whole and integrated than one could ever imagine. And the underlying, cohering reality is of the One, of consciousness. Thus, all aspects of the Formative Mind patterns are related, because their substratum is One. This relationship amongst the many, we call causality. It is the law of karma. It is the natural result of the creative presence of the One within the many. It is what happens automatically when the One gives rise to the many.

What we perceive as energy is nothing more than difference or pattern within the One. The creation is itself energy. Even above the level of the Universal Mind, there are spiritual regions created by the first, primal outpouring of the Creative Essence. These are also *created* regions. Only the undifferentiated One is beyond creation. So these primal, spiritual regions represent the first manifestation of creation, of difference within the One, that is – of energy patterns.

The simplicity of these primal energy currents or forms is multiplied as the Mind comes into action – or, more correctly – Mind is formed as the natural outcome of the multiplication of the primal energy currents, the primal creative urge, the primal form or difference.

In this physical universe and from a pragmatic point of view, considering our complete involvement with Mind, this appears to be true, though, as we have seen, there are even primal energy patterns, beyond the Formative Mind, in the purely spiritual realms of creation. But the true spark of consciousness, of life, is the primal undifferentiated energy or life force itself.

It is because energy as we experience it is no more than these patterns of the Formative Mind spun across the inward power of the One, that so many people feel instinctively that the *energy paradigm* is so fundamental and all-embracing. "Everything is energy" is a saying one hears so very frequently.

Similarly, holism is intuitively appealing because it reflects the very structure of the creative process. All parts *are* integrated into one whole. The holistic perception relates directly to the way things are put together.

So within the Mind worlds, we perceive energy as the patterns of creation, of differentiation. So fine and tenuous a net is woven, that the Mind seems so much to be the creator and the prime cause that some mystics have mistaken the Universal Mind to be the Supreme Being Himself. Then they talk of the Divine Mind, describing the primal 'divine' law as that of justice, karma or causality. This is what tells us just which region and which 'Lord' it is that is being described. For the law of the Supreme is that of Love, merging and Oneness. The 'god of justice' is the Universal Mind.

Consciousness, when seen in its purified essence, is One, undivided. It is the sustainer and creator of pattern, of energy, like the ocean supports the waves, and the waves are never separate from the ocean. But fundamentally and in essence, consciousness is formless and uncreated, a drop of the Supreme Being.

Energy is thus both the Creator and creation. In the Mind worlds, energy is the same as pattern plus primal power, and all patterns are of the Mind. But the power within it, which gives it existence, is the One Ocean of Consciousness, the Creative Life Stream.

Or in simple terms: there is just one Big Thing going on!

The Wholeness of the Energy Dance

This process of forming increasingly complex patterns from within-out gives us a most amazingly breathtaking and beguiling spectacle of integration and wholeness, for the One is always present within everything. The more inward patterns, the more inward energies, are formed into the more outward and more diverse patterns, but the laws governing this multireflective, multifaceted, multilayered, multidimensional process are way beyond the wit of our human intellect to grasp. Our human mind and intellect are themselves only a part of the total pattern of the Formative Mind.

But with this vision or understanding of the symphonic, multilevel wholeness of the Mind, we can begin to glimpse how our physical universe and physical body are constructed. But still we are only looking at the outer layers of this cosmic onion. So we see only effects.

We can intuitively perceive the relevance in coming to grips with the fact that all sensory experience is subjective, incommunicable and in our own minds – that the apparently outward world is thus within our own mind structure. With the body as only an outer shell of the Formative Mind's patterning process, we can understand the integral blueprinting mechanisms by which it is formed or patterned and how our whole existence is really psychosomatic – mind and body are part and parcel of the same process of Mind.

We can see how the body-emotion-mind structure can be seen as patterns and relationships of energy, for pattern and relationship are all that the creation is – this is the nature of form. We can see, too, how the same language is as applicable to the world of physics and science as it is to human psychology and the healing arts. They are all dealing with a web of relationships, of patterns, of energy. They are dealing with different aspects and levels of this energy, but the instrinsic laws remain the same.

We can see how spiritual evolution entails the shifting of one's point of perception ever higher or more inward within the integrated patternings of the Mind. And it becomes clear why spiritual progress requires meditation, control of the mind. And why the highest form of meditation is to ride on the backbone, the spine, the substratum, the Creative Essence of all the Mind's diversity, that is, to contact the underlying Creative and Audible Life Stream itself.

With the physical universe being described as no larger than a hair in an ocean when seen within the context of the more inward realms of the Mind, one can see too why there are so many schools of meditation. For meditation has come to mean developing contact with any part of our existence other than the gross physical, shutting one's physical eyes and doing almost anything within oneself. This includes contacting the subtle patterns or energies of our physical covering – the pranas, chakras and physical tattwas – or enlarging consciousness of our human mind structure. Even just sitting and cogitating has come to be called meditation. There is no lack of inward things to be explored.

Automatically, too, as they realize the inherent subtlety of their own mind, practitioners of meditation become more aware of the subtle patterns of existence. Clairvoyance, psychism, telepathy, even the ability to heal or perform miracles automatically comes to such practitioners as they begin to perceive, intuitively and almost unconsciously at first, how the patterns are put together, related and integrated.

But then the mind energy patterns of egotism can come into play and the soul can remain entranced with such phenomena for a long while, while further progress ceases. The attention may be playing on the higher floors of this multilevel department store of the Mind, but in so doing, it forgets the central lift shaft of the Creative Word and the One who dwells in the Penthouse Suite!

So it is all one big dance of creation, of energy, of pattern, spun out by the Formative Mind. In this, we have danced for innumerable lives and in many forms, sometimes even as a temporary denizen of the astral, perhaps even the causal, realms. But always we have danced to the tune of the Mind, and will continue to do so, evolving and devolving on the inward ladder of consciousness, until we get the message and wish to be released from this great 'jailhouse' of creation.

Mathematics, the Laws of Nature and the Formative Mind

Geometry and mathematics, even statistics, are essentially only a language or a terminology for the expression of relationships in space and time. Space and time being fundamental attributes of the Universal or Formative Mind, it is easy to see how some mathematicians feel that mathematics and the 'laws' of statistical probability are fundamental attributes of nature. Actually, the ordered relationships within the many do indeed make up that of which nature consists, but the concepts of mathematics lie within man's intellectual mind. So one can say that our human mind is thus perceiving the greater, Formative Mind – the small part is looking at the whole and automatically finds an affinity between itself, its own manner of functioning, and that of the greater universe, 'outside'.

The ordered structure of this whole egg of manyness, this great womb of pattern forming, is thus partially expressible by geometry and mathematics, as indeed by any terminology or language which describes repeating relationships, such as statistics. But, for their highest expression, geometry and mathematics really need to describe the way in which the One actually *becomes* the many in our multireflective, multidimensional, multilevel, integrated system of Mind, though in reality the laws of the higher aspects of Mind cannot be understood by the human intellectual mind. And this attempt to portray the creative process of the One giving rise to the many underlies the ancient science of *Sacred Geometry*, a subject considered in some detail in the next book in this series, *Natural Creation*. It was the essential study in the ancient mystical Pythagorean School.

With regard to the apparent paradox between the more obviously *deterministic* and mathematically described 'laws of nature', such as gravitational, optical or electromagnetic 'laws' and the *statistical* basis of quantum theory and many other descriptions of physical events, there is really no paradox at all. For we neither understand the fundamental basis underlying the deterministic, mathematically defined 'laws' nor those describable by 'laws of chance', or statistics. Since both represent our observation of patterns, relationships and causality, the real origin of which is beyond our normal human perception, there is really no conflict between the two. Mathematics, geometry, statistics and the 'laws of nature' defined by them do no more than describe or identify patterns. But the manner by which these patterns are manifested to us is beyond our normal ken.

So nature is only an aspect of the Formative Mind. And this subject of nature and the role played by the Formative Mind is most fascinating and fundamental, for one cannot understand the nature of form without understanding the role of the form-maker, the greater, Formative Mind. This is also discussed more fully in *Natural Creation*.

—— CHAPTER 13 ——

Quantum Riddles and the Dance of Relationship

Mystics and Physicists

Let us, for a while, address ourselves directly to quantum theory, but from the point of view of mysticism, and see what arises. This, by the way, is different from a physicist noting parallels between the manner in which he perceives the universe and what he has read, heard and understood about things mystics have said or written.

Very few physicists even 'believe' in the existence of mystic experience, fewer still have ever discussed matters with those who both have had experience of the mystical and who may also have some sort of a grasp of physics, so that a reasonable dialogue can take place. Even fewer physicists have ever experienced true and deep mystic experience. And if they have, they may never mention it, but remain incognito and continue on within the context of their times.

Not a few physicists are quite antithetical to anything that smacks of metaphysics, let alone mysticism. True mystics are *not* theoretical philosophers, spinning out intellectual abstractions. They are not pantheists or monists, nor do they belong to any other category of mysticism which academically trained scholars may ascribe to them. They deal only with experience and, if they are teachers, they are interested only in teaching others how to enjoy that experience themselves.

Whether people in general *believe* in what they say, is quite irrelevant to them. They are here only for those who want to experience inner life beyond the outer show. They are not out to start a religion or a cult or generate fame for themselves. Their minds and emotions are fully under control, so they do not feel hurt or offended by disbelief or worse. What is important to them is providing those who *want* to experience that state, and are drawn to them, with the wherewithal – the technique – to actually go ahead and experience it. There is little point, they say, in discussing the possible flavour of an untasted strawberry. The thing to do is to eat it. Right now. That puts an end to all discussion.

In a way, it is strange that people do not believe in the existence or validity of mystic experience. For even though it is our *experience* of being alive which is of the greatest importance to us, yet we know that we cannot describe or convey that experience to anyone else. Similarly, mystic experience is actually no more than a super-enlargement of our day-to-day, subjective experience of being alive. And just as no-one can convince a live person of sound mind that he is not alive, similarly the inward force of mystic experience is self-revealing. Just like awakening from a dream, it needs no-one else to convince you of its relevance and reality. For life is the same as consciousness, and mystic experience is 'only' an expanded awareness of the true nature of that life or consciousness.

But few physicists, or any other humans, are drawn to a wholely mystic perception of life, though a recent survey amongst our general British population showed that over a third were 'inwardly directed' in their approach to life. Cambridge University scientist, Stephen Hawking, acknowledged by his colleagues as one of the greatest theoretical physicists of our times, comments[1] that:

> Eastern mysticism is an illusion. A physicist who attempts to link it with his own work has abandoned physics.

Quite a statement for a scientist who has never really studied eastern mysticism nor practiced any of its techniques. Not, in fact, a scientific statement at all. And to write off the philosophy of one of our planet's most ancient and wisest of cultures simply by saying that, "they got it wrong," seems facile in the extreme. I worked in the same university department as Stephen for seventeen years and have a great respect and liking for him and his quest

[1] *Beyond the Black Hole, Stephen Hawking's Universe,* John Bosclough.

for understanding, but I would good-naturedly respond to his comment by saying:

> It is an illusion to take the conceptions of the intellect as absolute reality. A living human being who attempts to find the ultimate answer to life's puzzle outside the sphere of his own inner consciousness has forgotten that he is truly alive. He has abandoned life.

Actually, it is these limitations we place upon ourselves – "I am a physicist," "I am a doctor," "I am a follower of this or that belief system or ideology," which are the illusions. To mistake a belief system, a religion or a concept for Reality is the illusion of the intellect. Within ourselves, we are all automatically universal human beings with the capacity to find God, the Supreme Being or Consciousness within our own souls. Then our consciousness and knowledge encompasses everything. But this is beyond all divisions of the mind and intellect. Certainly, it is beyond physics! Even the vacuum state!

Some physicists have been described as a 'physicists' physicist', which I suppose means that such a person is one who believes that all the answers to life's mysteries and experiences will be found in mathematical formulations and intellectual constructs. It would be the same, I imagine, as a 'soldier's soldier' – one who considers that the answer to all problems lies in well-executed, agressive, mutually destructive competition with one's fellow humans.

But such phrases only show how great knowledge or ability can result in severe limitation in our perception. You must have heard Bernard Shaw's definition of a specialist:

> A specialist is one
> Who gets to know more and more,
> About less and less,
> Until finally he knows everything about nothing!

The fact is that we are "Children of the Universe," as the poem goes. It is within the universal substrate of existence – consciousness – that the answers will be experientially found, beyond all self-imposed mental constraints.

A Certain Strangeness

It is often said that the fundamental strangeness in quantum theory can be summarized in the *two-hole experiment.* This experiment is considered to contain within it the only real mystery, because it is impossible to understand what happens using any of the classical 'laws' describing physical phenomena. All other quantum oddities are of a similar nature, logically. The two-hole experiment is a real experiment and has been performed in a number of different ways. The results are always the same. This experiment has been described in every popular book on modern physics, but briefly put, it goes like this.

Supposing we have a source of waves in a water tank and in it we place a barrier with one hole in it. Diagrammatically, what we get can be seen in figure 13-1.

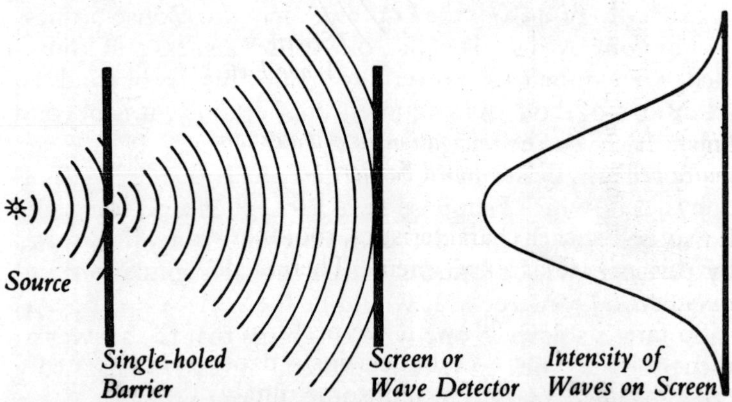

Figure 13-1. Wave propagation in a water tank with one wave source behind a single-holed barrier.

If we now replace our barrier with another containing two holes, we obtain the result shown in figure 13-2.

The two holes act as two new sources and the waves now add and subtract to form what are naturally called, *interference* patterns. There is nothing mysterious about that.

Now, if you redo the experiment using a source of light the result is identical. We get interference patterns. This is light, behaving as waves and when Young first performed the experiment in 1803 it was thought to be conclusive evidence that light has a wave formation. Actually, all that can be deduced from the experiment (with the benefit of hindsight) is that light exhibits characteristics that can, under suitable experimental conditions, appear as waves.

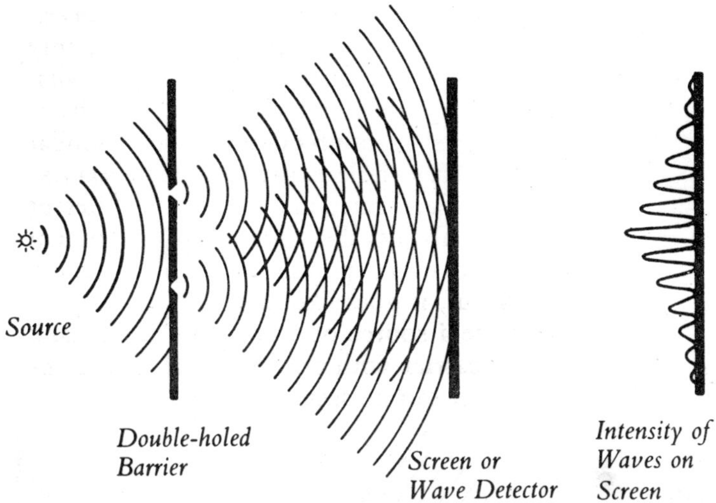

Figure 13-2. Wave propagation in a water tank with one wave source behind a double-holed barrier.

It may have other characteristics, too, that are *not* observed by this particular experiment. Therein lies a key to the mystery.

So far, so good. Now, if we perform a similar experiment with a source of bullets instead of waves and we catch the bullets on a screen of some suitable sticky goo (an ultra-dense jelly or plasticene would do nicely), we will observe the distribution of bullet positions shown overleaf. Most are in the centre, with a tail-off on either side. There is no interference, because bullets are not waves. And we need to use two sources in order to get bullets to go through both holes. What we get is a simple distribution curve, (see figure 13-3).

Now, supposing we conduct the single-source, double-hole version of this experiment with electrons instead of light. The double-hole version with light can, of course, be done in every school physics laboratory. The equivalent experiment with electrons is a little more difficult and is usually accomplished by scattering beams of electrons from the atoms in an ordered, crystalline substance. But we can speak of it here as if it were done with holes in a barrier.

Under these experimental circumstances, electrons

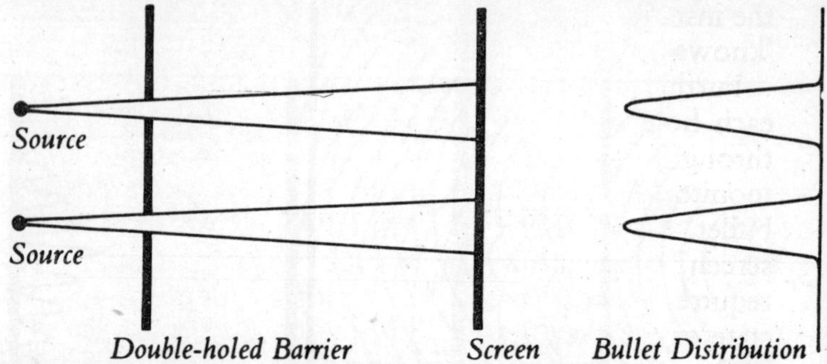

Figure 13-3. Bullets passing through a double-holed barrier from two sources.

demonstrate wave-like characteristics. We get interference patterns, as in figure 13-2.

However, unlike water waves and bullets, electrons exhibit characteristics of bullets in a single-hole experiment, and of waves in the double hole (or multi-hole) experiments! Why the difference? Simply blocking off *one* hole makes the electrons going through the *other* hole behave as bullets. It is as if the electron *knows whether the other hole* is open and modifies its behaviour accordingly. In fact, this wave pattern with two holes is still observed if electrons are shot through each of two holes, one at a time, with a long time delay between firings. Indeed, even if a thousand individual experiments are set up with just one electron fired by each experiment, five hundred through one hole and five hundred through the other, the pattern resulting from the addition of all these results still gives us an overall pattern demonstrating wave behaviour – as long as the barriers had two holes in them.

The fact that the electron's behaviour can be described by the statistical laws, *only if it 'knows' whether or not the other hole is open at the moment at which it passes through* is the central mystery of quantum theory. The statistics and the theory *require* this 'knowledge' in order that they may describe the result. Not *explain*, mind you, just *model or describe* it. The theory, of course, originated from such empirical observations, in an attempt to understand what was going on.

Even if we try to trick the electron and shut off one hole *before* it reaches the barrier, but *after* it has left the source, at the instant it passes through the hole it still behaves as if it 'knows' whether the other hole is open.

Furthermore, if we put an experimental watchman on each hole and look to see *which* hole the electrons pass through, that very act of watching, of experimentally monitoring the electron, makes it behave like a particle, a bullet. No interference patterns are then detected on the screen. Note, however, that no watching is passive. It requires an interaction, which itself changes the energetic state of the electron.

Quantum theory draws the following conclusions from these apparently bizarre observations:

1. Nature keeps its options open. Unobserved electrons behave as *waves of probability*. Nature herself does not know which hole individual electrons are going through. But when we conduct an experiment to observe the electron as a particle, it behaves as a particle. This is what is called the 'collapse of the wave function'. And it only happens when we make an experimental observation. Until then, say the theoretical physicists, nature herself does not know what is going on. One might add, as an aside, that it seems to be us humans, not nature, who do not know what is going on! Nature keeps on going quite happily, quite unmoved by what our latest theories are concerning her!
2. Probability or the potential to become something specific, is inherent in nature, but only when we observe/interact with it. The implication of probability is intrinsic to quantum theory. The theory is based upon the supposition that if there is more than one possible way in which an event can occur, then *unless we actually observe the details of the event itself, the outcome we observe will be the sum of the probabilities of all the various possibilities having actually* occurred. That is, our electrons behave as waves.

   In terms of our electron experiment, it means that once one electron leaves the source, it disappears into a cloud of potential or 'ghost' electrons, each pursuing its own path to the detector screen. There, all probabilities interface, producing our interference pattern. But as soon as we observe the electron, it crystallizes as one solid particle and all the 'ghosts' disappear.

Now the basic mathematics for all of this, though complex, can be readily understood, taught and used to describe and devise technology in the real world, just like Newton's classical 'laws'. Quantum theory can therefore be used as a cookbook, without recourse to metaphysical speculation. This is the way the majority of physicists use it and it lets them off the hook of considering the deeper implications of the recipes they are using. And this cookery can be both theoretical – expanding the range of applications of the theory – as well as practical. Indeed, from a purely practical point of view, it has been a remarkably successful description of physical reality. But it is also a 'law' (like all others) based upon empirical observation and, if our observations are incomplete or limited, such limitation will be reflected in the theory. The trouble is that although there are a number of possible models of reality describable by quantum theory, the 'realities' they suggest are all bizarre, seeming to run counter to common sense.

So the fact that the theory 'works' to some degree does not prove that it is completely true. It was, indeed, *designed* to 'work' – to describe the observed phenomena. But that does not tell us how the phenomena arise in the first place. In fact, the limitations of its truth, will also be directly reflected in the limitations of the technology resulting from it. Just as Newton's descriptions of gravity and motion could never have resulted in the development of nuclear power, (just apple power, maybe – a wonderful Heath Robinson energy source!)

An Alternative Point of View

So how does this fit in with our understanding of the vacuum state and also with the mystical perception of things. Well, the experimental observations can be understood, but in a different way. These may be summarized as follows:

1. A subatomic 'particle' is a vibrating energetic complex. It is a moving energy. Its movement and its

varying polarities of electrical charge, magnetic polarity and so on are a part of the vacuum energy pattern we observe as its being. So it is neither a bullet nor a wave. It is what it is, a slithy tove, vibrating and dancing, a pattern within the energetic fabric of space. We have said all this before.

2. In our experiment, when it arrives at the barrier, it passes through *both* holes, because its movement or vibration *encompasses* both holes. When we shut off one hole, it can only pass through one hole and we are effectively either stripping off some of the 'wavy parts' or forcing it to reconfigure itself as a 'particle' (a very tight, inwardly as well as outwardly, vibrating thing), in order for it to get through. The electron passing through the hole in the barrier is also an energetic event, remember. The electron *interacts* with the barrier and its holes in order to get through or otherwise, as the case may be. Really, the experiment should *also* monitor what happens to the energetic constitution of the *barrier* in both the one-hole and the two-hole circumstances. They would, I imagine, be different.

   In essence, whatever an electron is, our two experiments constitute two different ways of looking at it. And like the blind men and the elephant, we see different aspects of the same thing, depending on how we look. There is really nothing mysterious about it except that we need to admit to a fundamental ignorance of exactly what it is we are observing.

3. There is a confusion in quantum theory between the concept and the thing itself, as there is between determinism and probability. Even the more enlightened writers still speak of "electrons *obeying* the laws of quantum theory." As I have pointed out before, these laws are more in our minds, than in nature. Though in the final analysis nature is only an aspect of the Formative Mind and hence there is bound to be an affinity between our individual mind and nature.

   But electrons do not *obey* the laws of probability any more than people do. If we are unaware of all the determining factors, then the use of statistics may be our only recourse. But statistics or probabilities assume that there is an underlying order, otherwise there could be no 'law' of probability. One cannot describe the behaviour of something in detail, statistically or even determinstically, and then say that the something *obeys* that description!

Consider a common expression from physicists. This is a quotation from Fritjof Capra's evolutionary book, *The Tao of Physics.* He says, "Rather than particles circling around the nucleus, we have to imagine probability waves arranged in different orbits." This comment succinctly demonstrates the source of the confusion. For it would be better to say that we have to imagine a dynamic, vibrating, web of interconnecting energy relationships which at the present time we have only been able to *model* by involving ideas of probability. Probability is our mental concept, arising because we cannot see the hidden causes of things. To then insist that nature behaves like our limited and confused concepts of her is putting the cart before the horse.

'Probability waves' are an uncomfortable hybrid of 'things' (waves) and mental concepts (probability). Clearly a concoction devised by the human mind, not something one can actually put in a jam jar. We are simply using concepts of probability to describe the energy patterns and relationships, part of which we are observing/interacting with as electrons. What we call an electron is that aspect of the web for which we have designed an experiment to observe. And different experiments will see different aspects.

This is due to the interaction of the observer and the observed both at the experimental level, as well as in the logical, theoretical constructs. This is not an intellectual quibble, but demonstrates even more clearly the interaction of the observer and the observed, for in statements such as Capra's the thing itself and our conception of it are being confused.

And this is quite understandable, for even when we perform an experiment, all we ever observe are our *interactions*. We cannot escape from this. We become like a dog chasing its own tail. So really, statements such as Capra's are confusing the *interaction*, with *ideas concerning the interaction*. But again, we have to realize that both of these are only parts in one big whole.

4. So the interaction of the experimenter with the experiment is fundamental to the source of the confusion, but it must not be assumed that until this takes place, all that exists is a *web of probability*, an uncollapsed wave function. These are just concepts in our minds, which do not exist 'outside'. If we could devise an experiment to look for an electron as something other than a particle or a wave, then the experimental results would be different from anything yet observed. But yet we would, at best, only measure our *interaction* with what we are calling the electron. In a very real way, our interaction does change things, but only because nothing is static in nature, everything is interactive, everything participates. We only have a *whole* situation – a uni-verse, not a lot of little parts or a multi-verse. The more our mental conception and theories think of things in terms of little parts, the more these kinds of paradox arise.
5. It seems more likely that what exists is a dynamic web of relationships, an interconnected energy dance, and our experiments are only ever able to see a part of these relationships, which we then call subatomic particles, waves and so on. In fact, it is *we* who have created electrons in the sense that we have defined experiments to look for certain characteristics of this cosmic energy mosaic. Each experiment looks at different characteristics which we then call electrons or protons and so on. Different experimental factors will allow us to perceive different aspects of this dance or tapestry, this ultra-fine lattice of relationships of the One appearing as the many. But two *similar* points of view, two similar experiments, are not identical. Each experiment, therefore, sees something different.
6. We confuse ourselves by insisting that there really is a little solid blob of something called an 'electron',

and then in feeling surprise when the 'electron' turns out to have conflicting properties depending upon how we observe it. Nature knows nothing of little solid blobs. No doubt, there are focuses in the web that we have called electrons, but these focuses are not independent of the total web. Nature certainly does not 'see' them that way. Depending upon how *we* observe that focus, we see different facets of it. We are back with the five blind men observing the elephant. Each one caught hold of a different part and thought he had grasped the entire beast.

7. All divisions, of whatever kind, are in our minds. In fact, nature is just a dynamic web of interrelated energy patterns with which we can interact, experimentally, in a host of different ways and in which we are already embedded through the sheer process of existing in the physical world. But *we* are the ones who keep changing the colour of our glasses with each experiment we perform. And then we insist that it is *nature* who keeps changing colour!

   If we want to understand what is going on, we must study the nature of *all* the relationships within this multilayered energy dance. This includes our own minds. So we have to study the energy structure of our own minds, too.

8. It is possible that statistical calculations will be as far as mathematics and physics will ever be able to go in dealing with the fundamental determinism underlying our physical world. This is because, firstly, the causal determinism comes ultimately from within, from the Universal Mind. Secondly, the physical universe 'exists' because of our destiny karmas. This latter is the same thing as saying that we are 'participators'. But we have to understand what *we* are, to get any further with the real *nature* of that participation. The *we* includes our minds.

   The human mind is deeply and intrinsically implicated. This is how our destiny takes shape. But to explain this in deterministic detail is impossible – it would require a complete deterministic description of the entire energy of the universe and all the living creatures in it – what they are doing and their karmas, past and future – and such a thing is clearly beyond the capabilities of the intellect and logic. It is the ultimate infinite regression of reductionist thinking, because there is no end to analysis and division.

So, faced with this tremendous wealth of data concerning energetic interchange, plus the fact that we are ourselves a part of this picture, that there is probably no objective place upon which we can stand in order to survey the scene, we are left with no alternative but to approach the data statistically. But it should be *with* an understanding of the determinism underlying it, with a knowledge that we cannot have statistics and probability without a deterministic substrate.

In simple terms, if I toss a coin, I can determine statistically how many times it will come down heads or tails. But the underlying order is firstly that it can *only* be heads or tails, and secondly that I could actually calculate exactly whether it would be heads or tails if I knew the full mechanical details of each toss

In many respects, it comes back to the age-old debate concerning free will. If I have free will, at every split moment in time I would need to have an infinite number of possibilities open to me. Anything less than that and I would at best have a conditioned free will. The greater the constraints or boundary conditions, the less free will I have. This is quantum theory applied to our individual lives. And at every moment we collapse the wave functions by behaving in one particular way. But if, like Schrodinger's cat, we were in a box and nobody else could observe us, that represents a 'wave of probability' only for the external observers who cannot tell what we are up to in there. It does not mean that our actions are like the array of 'ghost' electrons before we 'observe them'.

And the regression is infinite, for even if there were a window in the box and the observers in the same room could see what we were doing, thereby collapsing their wave function, the wave function of probability would still not be collapsed for those in the next room, behind a closed door, or for those outside the house. And so on, ad infinitum. But we will be tangling with Schrodinger's pussy a few pages further on.

So quantum theory as a description of physical reality is still highly imperfect, because we are forgetting:

1. The involvement of the mind and karmas of all living creatures – whether man, animals, plants or bacteria. We have yet to realize that there are hidden causal relationships between our own minds, and the things and people who surround us.
2. We have yet to unravel the more holistic and probably holographic nature of non-local causality and relationship, inherent in the vacuum and more subtle states.
3. We are thinking of subatomic particles as little, solid, independent somethings, when actually they are only our partial observation of certain focuses or aspects in the dance of interconnected vacuum energy patterns.
4. We have yet to determine the inward, vibrational structure of subatomic 'particles' as expressions of energy within and upon the vacuum sea.
5. There is a causal link between mind and the vacuum state which is part of the process by which what is within our minds manifests itself outwardly as our destiny and by which new karmas are etched into our minds for outward enactment in a future scene of the drama.
6. That the use of statistics presupposes determinism and order. Statistics and 'laws' of probability should be applied with this understanding of their limitations. This means that there is fundamental order, not chaos, in the universe.
7. That, actually, the so-called 'outside' reality is also within our own minds. But to comprehend this requires a deeper understanding of the nature of the mind. It is clear to us that our thoughts and concepts are a part of the mind, but the fact that the apparently so solid physical universe is also a mind world is not so obvious. In a sense, therefore, one could say that there are two levels of illusion concerning physical 'reality'. Firstly, our ideas and theories concerning physical 'reality'. Secondly, physical 'reality' itself. But both of these lie within our own minds. Thinking that either our concepts are real, in an absolute sense, or that our sensory perceptions are real are both indicative of our human state of illusion.

8. That the superb, seemingly coincidental, ordering of the universe, as identified by the *anthropic principle* or the *Gaia hypothesis*, arises in a manner that in some respects parallels the creation of an image in a kaleidoscope[1]. What we are taking as absolute physical reality is a projected image, built up within the projection mechanism of the Formative Mind and reflected-projected-manifested outwardly, through the medium of our individual minds.

   Therefore, like the kaleidoscopic image or a mirage in the desert, it can never be grasped in the hand for it has no reality separate from its projection mechanism. Furthermore, like the ordered patterning of the kaleidoscope image, however much you shake it, whatever the patterning produced, order is intrinsic because of the nature of the whole creative mechanism.

   The fundamental order is inherent in the undifferentiated and coherent nature of the One, which we are perceiving as the many. Whatever the patterns of the many, it is always pervaded by the underlying, integrated Oneness.

   Furthermore, the difference between the kaleidoscope analogy and the reality of the Formative Mind projection system is that we are ourselves an integral part of the process. Our sense of being and our own mind are a part of the very process of manifestation itself. Therefore there is no objective, 'high ground', upon which we can stand to view things, other than rising up the formative ladder or inward dimension within ourself.

Slithy Toves Again

The wave aspect of an electron confined in a nuclear orbit is actually described as a standing wave – ie. a complex oscillation within fixed constraints, like a guitar string, with a likelihood or probability of 'it' being at any particular point at any particular time. But the electron is

[1] You can never physically grasp a kaleidoscope image because it is only a pattern of light created by prisms and mirrors.

not a wave, neither is it a little solid something moving along that wave pattern. It is a slithy tove, an energy vibration. In fact, 'it' doesn't really exist as an independent entity. It is a focus, a point of confluence and polarity in the web of relationship.

When we directly interact with it in an experiment we not only change the shape of its energy pattern, but we only interact – or observe – a small part of that pattern, anyway. It is *that* which we observe or interact with, which we call an electron. And depending upon the experiment, we interact or observe in a variety of ways. So in that sense only, have we created the electron. The "it only exists when you observe it" school of thinking is incorrect, if they suggest that nothing specific exists until we observe it. There is thus confusion between what it is presently possible for us to experimentally observe or interact with, a lack of appreciation that all divisions and categories are in our minds, and the inability of present mathematical language or formulation to model this interrelated web of energy.

This inability is because it is not appreciated that energy has both horizontal and inward, or vertical, relationships, as a natural part of the creative process. Ultimately, the One is always present within the many. We have not yet designed any experiment to observe directly the vacuum oscillations of an electron. We can only surmise as to what is happening when we note effects which we call electrons going through two holes simultaneously or when we observe distant photons affecting each other without any energetic connection on 'this side' of the vacuum. But to interpret these experiments as nature being essentially probabalistic is incorrect. It does not really mean anything. It is just a teasing intellectual conundrum, like the sound of one hand clapping. The correct interpretation is to realize that we still have our work cut out to determine the relationships of this inward dimension of the creation process, in a purely deterministic way. Though we may then have to handle this knowledge in a statistical fashion.

Just in case you have an idea that the subatomic world is in any way a world of lazy vibration, you might be interested to know that inasmuch as electrons can be said to be particles, when these highly energetic fellows are tightly confined into an atom, they express their internal energy and frustration by zooming about at around 600 miles per second! In the atomic nucleus, the neutrons and protons, being even more tightly confined, express their vibration and energetic exuberance by moving at velocities approaching 40,000 miles per second. And that motion is a part of the total energy of what they are. They are not 'somethings' that move. The movement is a part of their being.

Wholeness and the Divided Mind

When I look out of my window, I see things that I have come to call trees, plants, stones, birds and so on. I might think that I could describe a bird in exact detail. At least I feel that I could define some of its physical dimensions and characteristics. But does that really describe the bird? In the whole garden scene, the bird has a myriad relationships with the trees and bushes, with the insects and other living organisms it eats, with other birds, with its mate, with its family, with neighbourhood cats who come on the prowl, with the wind and weather, with myself and the food I put out – with so many things. Can I describe a bird without describing these relationships? Of course not. Without them it would be only a partial description.

But where does this description end? What about the similar relationships of all the other creatures and things with which my bird is associated? Do I describe those as well? And what about the mind of the bird? It is an infinite regress of analysis which becomes more and more meaningless.

Nature is a whole, our indivisible, integrated web of relationship. For convenience and to achieve practical ends we apply our minds in analysis to certain parts and aspects of this lattice. But if we then think that these parts have an independent existence from the whole, we have become a victim to our thinking process, to our intellect. Intellect, by nature divides. It was never meant to understand the whole. This is the function of consciousness – to know the whole in mystic experience.

But this is what has happened to us. Our own mind, clouded by unconscious emotion and scattered into uncontrolled thoughts, running far away from its natural inward centre, is divided. So it sees division everywhere. Wherever it looks it sees pieces, not a whole. It has forgotten the true nature of perception. Yet:

> If the doors of perception were cleansed,
> Everything would appear as it is – infinite.

So wrote William Blake. And for infinite, we could also substitute the word 'whole'. Everything would appear whole if the windows of our mind were whole. Then we would use our analytical minds and intellects purely as a practical means of accomplishing things in this world and as stepping stones towards the mystical. We would never lose consciousness of the underlying whole. The reality would be apparent to our inward selves.

So in just the same way, we have to understand that when we look through the coloured glasses of a particular experimental procedure, we are only observing a part of the whole. With another pair of glasses, we perceive another part. If those two parts are dissimilar, even apparently contradictory, is that so strange? I think not. It is just what we would expect.

Three Points of Observation

In a sense, there are three points of observer-observed interaction. One is the obvious one of when we experimentally measure something, we change the process we wish to measure. We have to interact, and hence the uncertainty principle of Heisenberg comes into being. This is the yang mode of outward, motivated action.

Then there is the sensory perception of things. Here we feel we are passive observers. The mind is involved, but we are not changing the things we observe. This is the yin mode of sensory input. Unfortunately, with our normal physical perceptions, we cannot directly perceive electrons and the subatomic world for what it is. If we could, all the fuss would be over!

Moreover, it is clear that logic has led us astray when, by confusing the yin with the yang, it tells us that a thing only exists when we observe or interact with it. Fortunately, this is not so. It would be surprising to find our house disappear (not to mention one's own body) every time we went to sleep at night or went into town to do the shopping. This is clearly absurd – and yet this line of argument leads us back to the proposition that there really is an objective, outside reality.

So where is the link? The link lies in the third and more primary interaction of observer and observed. The passive observer is the mind, the observer who interacts is the mind. In the mind is stored the potential, the impressions which – interacting with the impressions in the mind energy of others – patterns the physical world. This is the karma of our destiny.

But because of the downward and outward direction of our mental attention, we have become unconscious of the primary way in which our joint mind energies have actually created this physical creation. So we are aware only of the yin and yang modes of observation, of receptivity and action. We do not see their point of origin in the inward processes of mind energy. That is all unconscious or subconscious.

We can refer to our familiar diagram once again:

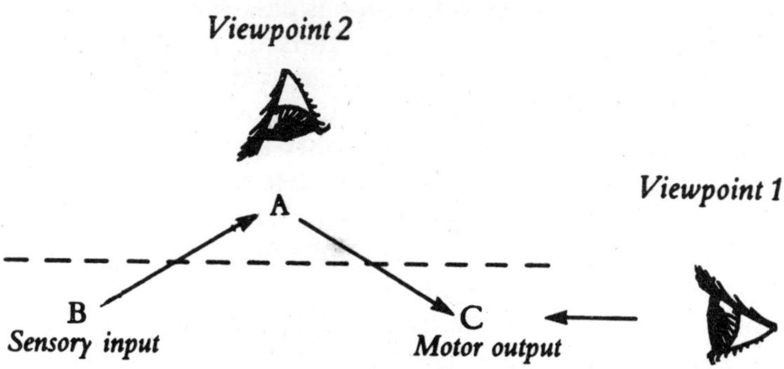

Now, B and C represent the yin and yang modes of mind function, of observation, while the vertical scale is that of our level of attention. The point of origin lies in our unconscious mind energies. So we intuitively realize that the mind is involved in the creation of outward phenomena, but we do not know how. Our logical, intellectual aspect of that same mind ends up with conundrums like, "It only exists when we observe it." This is true, but not in its obvious meaning. For we need to expand our understanding of what is meant by *observation*, to include the all-important unconscious creative activity of the mind energy domains – an energy more primary, and hence more real, than anything we can observe with our senses.

How to get this perception? Train the mind, using the right type of meditation. It is the only answer. Intellect cannot take us to that point. Rather its divisive nature keeps us away.

Schrodinger's Famous Participating Pussy

A few pages back, I mentioned Schrodinger's cat. Erwin Schrodinger was responsible for first formulating the wave function – the set of equations describing the realm of quantum probabilities – and his everyday tale of the cat encapsulates the apparent quantum strangeness when applied to the 'real' world.

Schrodinger considered what would happen if one took a box and placed within it a source of lightly radioactive material, a detector of radioactivity connected to a glass phial containing cyanide, and a live cat. The frequency and nature of the radioactive emission is described by quantum theory, but only within the realms of probability, not absolutely. Using this theory, therefore, we cannot say *exactly* when radioactive emission will occur. We can only present a statistical evaluation of when it *might*. So choosing a short enough time interval, the detector is switched on and off for just long enough that there is a 50-50 *chance* whether there will be a radioactive emission.

If there is, the detector activates the mechanism to break the phial of cyanide and the pussy dies. If there is no emission, the cat lives, (see figure 13-4).

However, the box is sealed and until it is opened, the outside observer still does not know the outcome. The 'laws' of quantum theory state that in fact *the cat has neither died nor is it still alive*. It is simultaneously both alive and dead. Until the box is opened, the probability is still 50-50 and each possibility possesses equal 'reality'. The probability wave function holds supreme. It is only when we collapse the wave function by looking into the box that one or other of the possibilities actually occurs.

Now this is clearly absurd. However, it is a logical outcome of the theory, and neatly demonstrates how

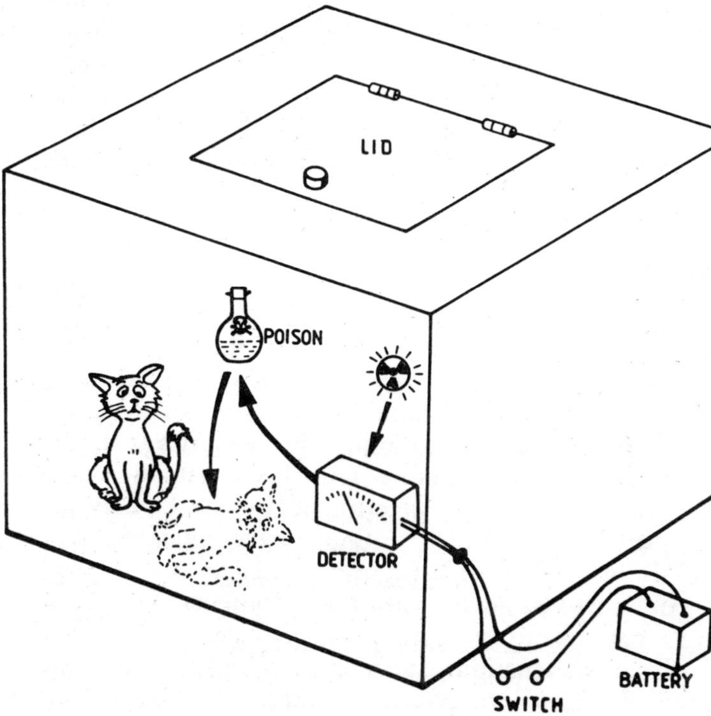

Figure 13-4. The Strange Case of Schrodinger's Probable Pussy

concepts and physical reality have become confused. Clearly, therefore, the theory is at least partially incomplete, or dare I say, incorrect. This is, after all, why physicists go on looking for more complete theories. But what is missing?

From the mystical point of view, the answer is clear. We are ignoring the karmas of the cat! And karmas means the *mind* of the cat. The outcome was already predetermined. It was even determined who would perform the experiment, and where. The cat, the experimenter, the carpenter who built the box, the owner of the cat, the little girl who brought flowers for the pussy, all are involved through their karmas. That is the interstitial law of causality that made the whole thing happen in the first place. And the karmas are stored as potential and worked out through the minds of the cat and all the people involved.

Some physicists do point out that the consciousness of the cat would be sufficient to collapse the wave function, that the cat would know whether it were dead or not! This is partially true, but we also have to understand what is meant by consciousness. Actually, we experience our consciousness and mind .tangled together as our *attention*. The same is true of the cat. Though a pussy's mind structure is somewhat different from our own, he (or she) still has its mind and its karmas. It is its karmas which give it that particular mind structure and hence body structure.

So in a very real sense it is our karmas, our minds, which conjointly collapse every possible wave fuction. The whole set-up is determined by the joint collapsing and determinings of all the minds and karmas involved. Thus the infinite regress due to infinite probabilities at all points is avoided. The plenum of potentiality within the akash or vacuum is completely determined by the karmas of all involved. Its potentially infinite wave functions are all tightly pre-processed and pre-collapsed.

And while we act out the karmic contents of our minds, we repattern our own minds to provide the causal seeds for future incarnations, for future collapsing of the akashic wave function into physical reality. Thus there are no infinite parallel universes taking off from each and every point in space and time to maintain the full range of probabilities, as Everett has proposed and for which he has even derived the mathematics and quantum theoretical basis. These are just intellectual games, though understandable when one takes only logic and intellect as one's guides.

So there is confusion in quantum theory between the acknowledgement that the observer is an integral part of the observations, and that we are only partially observing the electron or any aspect of the subatomic world. *Partial* observation of a thing is neither equatable with probability nor, in the metaphysical sense, with the interplay of observer and observed.

Observation, per se, even when correct, may always require the use of statistics for further prediction, because we cannot capture all the necessary factors governing physical manifestation in mathematical symbols. But it does not mean that the fundamentals are probabalistic or non-causal. It just means that it is too deep for us to unravel with intellectual constructs. And then, too, the part (the observer) cannot comprehend the whole (the observed) because, in fact, there only is one whole, one uni-verse. And that *includes* the observer.

So, when physicist, John Wheeler, suggests that the universe only exists as something 'real' because it is observed by intelligent beings, he is right, according to the mystic viewpoint. But there is much, much more to it than that, because the whole deterministic mechanism of manifestation, mind and karma needs to be understood, too. And Wheeler himself is said to have a personal antipathy to metaphysical speculation and anything smacking of psychism or mysticism. They call him a physicist's physicist. But that, of course, is only his personal, mind structure (and karmas) speaking. His own probabilty wave function has already been collapsed, determining that he possess just this very attitude and point of view.

Quantum Riddles

Before leaving this subject, let me try one again to summarize and clarify these quantum riddles. We have been through the details before, so a quick reference is all that is required.

1. *Heisenberg's Uncertainty Principle.* Both experimentally and theoretically it is impossible to know the values of both sides of two interrelated things – eg. momentum and position – because we are participators in the event. By entering into the arena, we change the circumstances. Observation means interaction, and that changes what is being observed. It is impossible to do otherwise.
2. This uncertainty leads to the use of probabalistic logic and mathematics in order to describe events.
3. Subatomic particles do not appear to be either waves or particles, but in conventional science we do not have any good description of what they really are, other than as one or other of these two. When combined with 1 and 2 above, this third factor creates even greater strangeness.

4. Both quantum theory and certain experiments based upon the theory show non-local connection, as predicted by the probabalistic rules of quantum theory. This is taken as 'proof' of the probabalistic structure of nature. The existence of any fundamental causality is thus called into question by quantum theory.

These, then, are the fundamental conundrums. How am I suggesting that they are resolved?

The Reasons for the Riddle

1. The logical structure of physical analysis has itself reached a point where it cannot cope. Logic supposes a separation between the observed and the observer which does not in fact really exist. Therefore, when you apply logic to the physical universe in order to try and understand it, you ultimately reach the point where the lack of real differentiation between the observer and the observed, between the part and the whole, can no longer be neglected. Logic and intellect then become insufficient. We are a part of the picture. How can the part understand or claim freedom from the whole?

   This lack of real objectivity is expressed both within the mathematical or even philosophical theory as the principles of uncertainty and complementarity, *as well as* at the experimental level when we are forced to interact and thereby change the very thing we thought we could observe objectively.
2. The extended nature of causality itself is not understood. The observation of non-local connection *does not* imply an intrinsic acausality at the basis of physical manifestation. It just means that we do not understand the inward mechanisms of creation, of causality, of connectedness within the whole. Logic, in fact, is a mostly unconscious mental appreciation of the connectedness of things, of causality. To use logic or causality to prove acausality is clearly incorrect. Whichever way we turn, we are embedded in logic and causality. After all, why do we unknowingly consider logic to be of value, of being the way to proceed? It is because logic is our appreciation

of the inherently causal nature of relationships within the whole, of which we are a part.

3. As described elsewhere, the apparent non-locality of connections occurs due to our point of vision. We need to re-understand what we mean by 'non-local'.

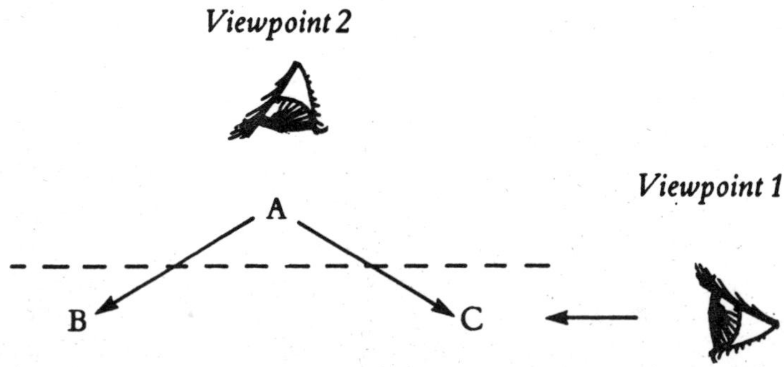

4. Referring to our familiar sketch, three further factors may be noted.
   (i) The actual reality of B and C lies at A. However, B and C are separated in space, whilst their point of origin is one. At least it is deeper than the kind of space existent in the world of B and C. So to perceive from viewpoint 2, would be to transcend the space separating B and C.
   (ii) Changes to B will *automatically* influence C, but through the invisible A, because A *manifests* as B + C. The change may also be both non-local and instantaneous, *without anything passing 'between' B and C*. So the question of faster than light communication becomes irrelevant, because the relationship of B and C is through A. It is not a question of anything travelling, but of relationship.
   (iii) The change in C will be exactly equivalent to that of B, because of the extended conservation of energy principle. (ii) and (iii) are actually observed in the various experiments demonstrating non-local causality at faster than the speed of light.

5. Experimentally, we are only making partial observations of our web of dancing energy relationships, depending upon the nature of the experiment. In the two-hole experiment, our electron is simply doing its best to get through whatever holes are offered to it. However many holes are offered, it will quite happily go 'through' all of them. Our energetic, vibrating vacuum pattern simply adjusts itself or interacts, given the circumstances. This can be shown by experiments with multiple holes. If you block up only one out of three, you still get interference patterns. As long as there is more than one hole, we still observe wave characteristics. When only one hole is left, our little oscillating pattern has no option but to 'draw in his wings' and zoom through as a 'particle'. At least there is no opportunity for wave interference. The nature of energy relationships which make up a wave can no longer be expressed.

   Each variation of the experiment is a separate energetic situation and our web of energy behaves differently under different circumstances. We have made the mistake of thinking that we really do have independent things which we can call electrons or photons or any other subatomic particle. So when, due to a change in circumstances, 'their' characteristics appear to conflict, we are confused. As in human relationships, we have made the mistake of imposing unconscious expectations on the situation and then interpreting events in that light. When these expectations are not met, we sit like Snoopy, with a big question mark coming out of our heads.

   But in fact it is our own preconceptions which we find difficult to relinquish, which are causing the confusion. Nature is not confused as to what is happening. We are!

   So there is nothing mysterious about the two-hole experiment if we see it in the correct light.

6. From our limited point of consciousness we see only the 'many', not the One from which they spring. We glimpse the interconnections as causality, but understand neither its true nature, nor its extent. We discover that laws of probability work in predicting

certain things, but do not understand that this is because of the inward, holistic causality. We therefore make the mistake of thinking that fundamental causality does not exist. But this is only because we cannot see how it operates.

7. We still *feel*, however, that despite our theory and thinking telling us that there is nothing objective, that the outer world really is objective, 'out there'. This is due to the direction of attention of the mind, as we have discussed. Change the direction of attention by meditation and we change our perception and experience of the world.
8. The condition of the mind is such that we are inwardly divided. We have no inward awareness of how our minds and personality are put together with consciousness. Inwardly, we are legion, and we automatically reflect that lack of personal, spiritual integration onto the logical intellectual constructs which the mind presents to us as our view of reality. That is why the mystical and holistic perceptions go together. The higher our consciousness rises, the more whole and integrated we are within and the more we perceive the universe as one whole. The changeover from a reductionist to a holistic view of the world and of science is thus directly related to our level of consciousness, to the degree of universality in our spiritual awareness, to our personal inner development or evolution. And the way to expand one's consciousness is through meditation, leading ultimately to the mystic experience of personal union with the One within the many. Then we know exactly what is going on! Thought is then used as a necessary part of human existence, but it is not the primary means of our understanding the cosmic mysteries.

Well, this chapter has been somewhat intellectually tortuous, and I have probably said quite enough. I have inserted it for those physicists and others who have struggled with the implications of quantum theory and who are used to dealing with these kinds of conception. If you did not follow a word of it, it does not really matter. You have probably saved yourself a headache!

Reflective Patterns and Hidden Relationships

So – to summarize yet again – what we have is a web or a network of interconnected energy in which we are ourselves deeply involved. Some of the relationships within this dance are clear to us, but others are not.

Electrons, protons, gravity, magnetism, oranges, planets, stars, galaxies and all the rest are all our own mental analyses and sensory observations of certain aspects of this web of energy relationship. None of them exist per se, as independent entities. Nothing is independent of the whole. They exist only as concepts in our minds and as partial observations. Therefore, this web can appear in many different ways, depending upon how we look at it or interact with it. And the degree of consciousness enlivening our minds will directly affect the way we perceive things. The less divided our inner minds, the less we perceive division in the 'outside' world. So by refining our instrument of perception, the mind – by practising good techniques of meditation – we change our understanding of the universe in which we live. It is this that represents our real evolution, the evolution of the soul, its slow disentanglement from substance. This is the meaning of life – to find out what life is, within ourselves.

So within this dance of energy, depending upon our point of vision, some relationships appear obvious to us, while others do not. Moreover, the higher the point of inward vision, the more do these previously hidden relationships come into view, until ultimately we see everything as one.

The more heavily enmeshed in the dance we are, then the less do we observe of the hidden relationships and the more confused we are, whether we know it or not.

But at this level of physical observation, are there patterns or relationships which tell us of these hidden connections? Well, we have already discussed many of these – the connections between electricity, magnetism and gravity, for example, not to mention 'coincidences' and the mysterious linkage of our inward personality to events which come our way and the amazing manner in which the mind and life force pattern bodily processes.

Indeed, everything we experience and observe is evidence of hidden relationships.

But let us momentarily take the limited view and assume that we do understand the causal relationships involved in dropping a stone and seeing it fall, or in flying an aeroplane, or eating an apple. Are there other such patterns or processes in nature in which we are failing to observe the relationships because they are not so obviously causal, in a linear sense.

Well, in the not so distant past and in many places of the world today, man has looked for such patterns to help him live his life. What else is the search for omens and hidden meanings? Do we not intuitively feel that these connections do abound in nature? Fear and ignorance may overlay these intuitions, resulting in superstition and ritual, but have we not all at one time or another felt the excitement of meaningful 'coincidence'? When we knew that there was some hidden process at work to make things happen in the way they did? Do we not feel at such times that the veil between the invisible and the visible has almost been shattered? These may be times of crisis in our lives or times of great inner peace. Often the one follows the other.

So yes, there are ways of reading one pattern to gain understanding of another, without our knowing fully or even at all how the two are inwardly related. Astrology is one such science. The Chinese I-Ching, much beloved of Carl Jung, is another, and there are many more. At this point, (having mentioned astrology), some people may switch off, while others become immediately energized. But science is only a study of energy relationships, of causal patterns. Advancement of science means uncovering hidden relationships. So why the negative reaction?

The great Johan Kepler (1571–1630) was a court astrologer, though today he is heralded as one of the fathers of modern astronomy for his work on planetary motions. Sir Isaac Newton (1642–1727) spent much of his time in the study of alchemy and only took time off to write *Principia Mathematica* (1687) and *Optiks* (1704).

We select from an individual's work what we consider to be relevant and ignore the rest as if it were an insignificant aberration, not a major part of the person's thinking.

Astrology is a science of reading patterns. It is not that the stars and planets actually control our destinies and our psychology, though there will most probably be some energetic connection at a physical level. The heavenly configurations represent a part of the web of relationships within the whole, and like the part of a hologram, the nature of the whole is reflected therein and can be read by a skilled person. Just like a part of a hologram can be used to project an image of the whole.

Much popular astrology, of course, can hardly be considered as a true science, but I have met a few people in my life in both India and the West who have a thorough grasp of the highly scientific principles, as well as the art, and can make the most interesting and accurate assessment of people and situations.

Similarly, in the healing arts, all the reflex energy techniques are based upon the principle of hidden connection. The hand, the foot, the iris of the eye, the ear – all these have been used for centuries, if not millenia, as valuable diagnostic and therapeutic points from which to approach the total, holographically structured energy system of the body.

So the study of pattern and relationship covers far more than we presently conceive through the restricted view of classical, reductionist logic. And interestingly, it is physics – the most analytical of all avenues of thought – which has led us back to this point of greater holism in our understanding of the world in which we live.

Piscean and Aquarian Ages

While on the subject of astrology, it is interesting to note that we have now entered upon what astrologers have called the Aquarian age. Previously, we were passing through the Piscean age. These ages, of course, just like the Hindu yugas, are our own classification or delineation of periods in our history, but Pisces is a water sign, generally indicative of the deep and surging sea of unconscious emotion which has dominated world history during the last two millenia.

Aquarius, on the other hand, is an airy sign. The airy tattwa is the energy field underlying the fleetness and intricate cleverness of the mind and intellect. The Aquarian age is said therefore to be an age of the mind, and of reason. This we can see in the trend towards rational science which has overwhelmed the twentieth century with its influence. Though science still has a long way to go before it can call itself truly rational, as we have seen. But this has been the lead in to an age when the tremendous power of the mind will become far more fully understood than it is at present, and when mind, rather than body, is the factor we are aware of dealing with in each other. It is also demonstrated in the advances of psychology, as well as the rationality behind considerations of political and religious freedom and democracy. It is through deep emotional, watery feelings that people suppress the human right of others to express themselves in harmless ways. This is alleviated by the airy intellect.

The weakness of this airy nature is a tendency to lose contact with the natural environment, as the individual mind gets wrapped up in itself, in its own desires, goals and ideals. But it will also lead to a time when the human mind and the nature of the physical universe as a mind world will come to be more fully comprehended. It is this trend which leads to books such as this being written and finding a sympathetic readership. It is this trend which can be seen manifesting itself in all the 'New Age' activities – whether meditational, healing, social, environmental, scientific or whatever.

Concepts, Mental Habits and Personal Graphics

Although physicists may talk of subatomic particles being neither wave nor particle, it is difficult for anyone to *imagine* what they actually are. We all have our own personal, mental, graphics that give us an idea of what we think these particles are up to. But it is fair to say that none of these images are, strictly speaking, correct.

Given an image of all manifested phenomena – particles, forces and everything – as being no more than our interpretation of and interaction with the energy movements and patterns upon the vacuum 'surface', it is easy to conceive of subatomic 'particles' as more or less any combination of these patterns. The pattern would be able to 'go through' two holes at once, for example (like a wave), if given the option, or would be happy to just pass through one if that is all that were available, and thus end up looking like a particle. If we insist that we really do have a 'particle with wave characteristics' (or whatever), then our friend the 'particle' would appear as quite the ultra-adaptable chameleon.

But the classical idea persists, even within much of the theoretical physics fraternity, that particles are indeed real and individually identifiable little fellows. Experimental observation and theoretical constructs concerning them are therefore based upon this assumption with the result that at times the particles appear to be doing unreasonable things. A sense of reasonable personal, mental graphics as well as mathematics, therefore suffers a serious set back. So the personal graphics of many physicists need to be reorientated before they can seriously consider the possibility of vacuum patterning, either generally, or at a mathematical level.

But the 'reality' of the physical world and its particles has become the mental habit of a lifetime and is not easily discarded, any more than any other habit or way of looking at things. Social, personal, religious, philosophical or ideological habits are just the same as scientific ones. They are grooves within the mind energy fields and to change these habits requires a tremendous effort of will and may not, in fact, be within the capability of the individual, however intelligent he or she may be.

But when once we do realize that any manifested object in our real world is just a vacuum patterning, an energy dance in space, a set of relationships, then our options available for explanation as well as personal, mental graphics, expand considerably. For each 'particle' or focus of energy will have both explicit or outward characteristics which we may observe (with difficulty) and depending upon the design of the experiment, as well as patterns that *only* exist within the vacuum state and which are thus lost to the view provided by conventional experimentation.

So we need to devise a entirely new range of equipment that outwardly portrays to us the state of those vacuum patterns which are not yet observably manifested to us.

Then we will no doubt find that what we thought were non-local connections without a causal basis at the manifest level, do in fact possess a causal basis within the more subtle and holistic patternings of the vacuum state.

Man's Uncertainty

The theory that describes the continual emission and absorption of virtual photons by an electron is a good example of the confusion between theory and nature. First of all, no-one has ever seen this cloud of virtual photons – they are a theoretical construct. Secondly, their *theoretical* lifetime is 'allowed for' by the uncertainty principle, which *theoretically* presents us with an indeterminacy between time and energy. That is to say that since the theory gives these virtual particles a lifetime of 10^{-15} of a second, or less, which – by the *theory* – is 'accurately' determined, the *energy* of the event is uncertain.

'Because' of this uncertainity, it is therefore 'permitted' for a virtual particle to violate the law of conservation of mass/energy by coming spontaneously into existence and then disappearing again just as fast as its legs can carry it. An alternative virtual particle theory, put forward by Sarfatti, is that space or vacuum is an infinite sea of energy. The virtual particles therefore, according to this *theory*, are momentary organizations of some of this energy.

This is more or less the same idea as the theme of this book. But note that the uncertainty principle upon which all this theory is based arises as the result of the fundamental limitations of both logic and experimentation – of dividing our experience into separate observers and observed. *It is our intellectual/perceptual limitations that underlie what we call the uncertainty principle.* To then say that nature (which includes ourselves) *obeys* this 'law', is absurd. We are again putting the cart before the horse.

It is *we* who are uncertain about what is going on – not the nature in which we are so deeply enmeshed! A realization of this intrinsic intellectual and observational *limitation* provides tremendous relief, a Zen-like, "Ah. . ." It also gives us a platform of simplicity, once again.

Mystics have said throughout all the ages that the intellect can *never* solve the mysteries of the universe and of life. To understand these things you have to become one with the inner Source. It removes the duality of the observer and the observed. This removes the uncertainty and gives one direct perception. This is where true understanding of all aspects of life are merged – and this includes understanding of the human mind and body as a complete multilayered energy structure. This is where true human psychology, physical healing and physics are merged.

Mystics often talk of the *certainty* of mystical realization and experience. This is beautiful, for it contrasts exactly with the *uncertainty* that is inherent in logical, intellectual ideas concerning the universe, where the observer and the observed are forced into assuming illusory separate identities. Wherever there is the intellect, there will be division, and wherever there is division there will be a sense of uncertainty, for there is never an end to analysis and division. One can never reach the end of the story in this way, so the outcome will always remain uncertain. One can always look at a situation from another point of view and begin the analysis all over again. And one can go on and on analysing 'parts' and their relationships to each other, there is never an end.

Some physicists may think that they are close to unravelling the secrets of the universe, and yet no book on such physics has anything to say about human life as we all experience it, day-by-day. On life, death, human emotion – nothing of any convincing depth concerning daily experience of life is ever said. Neither is the very nature of the scientists essential tool of the trade – the intellect itself – ever mentioned. What is that? In books written entirely by intellect, not one word is given as to what intellect is. . .

So the intellect or logic, and sensory or instrumental observation are quite simply, limited. This is the understanding which will actually permit us to use our intellect and technology to its fullest extent. If we expect to be able to do things with our knees, for which knees are quite unsuited, we will be forever tying ourselves into knots. Once we realize the inherent limitations of knees, we can use them to their fullest, yet limited, extent.

We cannot expect to arrive, intellectually, at the ultimate answer. The part can never know the whole by remaining separate. We can, however, understand these underlying limitations. We can observe and intellectually consider the structure of both ourselves and of the physical universe. Our scientific approach bears witness to that. But to confuse *our* uncertainty with uncertainty in the whole will most certainly result in tremendous mathematical complexities, and intellectual contortions without end.

The Complementarity of Relativity and Quantum Theory

This chapter has addressed itself largely to quantum theory, so let us for a final moment concern ourselves with Einsteinian relativity theory and its relationship to quantum theory.

The scientific definition of momentum is mass times velocity. That is, the faster and/or heavier a thing is, the more difficult it is to stop it. It is easier to stop a marble than a cricket ball, for example, but not if the marble is travelling with the velocity of a bullet. So the concept of momentum seems reasonable from our everyday experience. We do not, however, understand the intrinsic nature of mass. What is mass and why should an electron possess mass, and a photon, not, for instance?

Einstein took this to be of fundamental importance and further considered the implications of velocity being a relationship between time and space. He realized that we can never talk about space without implicating time, and vice versa. Velocity or speed is the rate of change of spatial displacement. Rate of change means time. But yet we do not understand the nature of time or space.

So once again, when we reach into fundamentals, we realize that the rug of a concrete reality is pulled out from under us. In fact, Einstein actually demonstrated that we cannot speak of space without implicating time, and vice versa. He realized that there is no absolute frame of reference by which to judge space and time, because everything, including the observer, is within space and time. This is the observer and the observed conundrum once again. The observer cannot get outside space and time in order to be a truly independent observer. So the quantum and relativistic theories are in accord, at this point.

Following through this line of thought, the Einsteinian concept of space and time results in the concept of a 'space-time continuum" while the redefinition of time and space leads to the understanding that mass is simply a form of energy. Following on from this, he suggested that gravitation is actually due to a 'curvature' of space-time and thus the concept of 'empty space' also loses its meaning. It also gives us a theory of gravity that takes into account the interdependence of the observer and the observed. Since these factors cannot be ignored at high velocities, quantum theory is itself forced to use the Einsteinian model when considering subatomic particles, because the subatomic particles are travelling at such enormous velocities.

The marriage of the two theories or models, is, however, an unhappy one. For while Einstein thought of his space-time continuum as something firmly 'out there' and objective, the quantum world recognizes the participatory integration of the observer and the observed. But relativity theory also recognizes the non-absolute nature of any space-time coordinates. What we observe of space and time are relative to where we *are* in space and time – relative to what we are observing.

So both relativity and quantum theory attempt to deal with the fact *there is only one big thing going on*, and which includes (in fact, stems from) our own consciousness, without being fully aware that this is what they are really trying to do. The problem of integrating the two models lies in the fact that while quantum theory's recognition of this conundrum results in the explicit use of indeterminism and probability, Einstein's theory was firmly rooted in the realm of determinism and good old objective (but relative) reality.

The fact is, of course, that both points of view are correct, but limited. Each one in itself represents an incomplete perception, because neither takes into account the invisible or hidden aspects of the creative process; of how the One becomes the many, and of how we end up experiencing it as such. Neither theory can tell us how space, time, mind, matter and the laws of nature actually arise.

Space, time and all the energy patterns of the physical world lie *within* us. There is no 'out there'. The point where space, time and the energy patterns which are integral to their existence are linked is within the mind. It is *there* that everything exists. Time still exists even for a person who is deprived of all sensory perception, so it means that it is within us. Mystics have always spoken of the physical world as actually being a Mind world. The extended or mystical understanding of causality does not require an independent, 'objective' reality. In fact, causality, duality, differentiation, participation, integration, relatedness – all these are inherent in all the mind worlds. They are the same thing. Causality is the nature of the Universal Mind, the law of the Universal egg of Brahm, Humpty Dumpty as one divided, yet undivided, egg of energy, pattern and relationship.

—— INTERLUDE ——

The Way of Wyrd

There is a fascinating novel written by Brian Bates: *The Way of Wyrd – Tales of an Anglo-Saxon Sorcerer.* The story centres around a young Christian missionary, Wat Brand, sent (as he thought) to convert and re-educate the anglo-saxon 'pagans'. But at the very outset, he is met by the sorcerer, Wulf, who sweeps him into another world and proceeds to expand the mind and understanding of the erstwhile converter.

In one incident, while cooling themselves in a river, they witness the flight of two ravens. Wulf makes a prediction of future events from an observation of their flight. The tale is told in the first person by the young missionary:

> I snorted with derision, . . . "How can the mere flight of birds tell us about events distant in time and place?". . .
>
> I turned to wade ashore, but Wulf suddenly gripped me by the arm and I looked at him in alarm; he was looking at me piercingly, his eyes clear azure blue through lashes sparkling with river water. He spoke with conviction: "It is a mistake to assume that events far apart in time are thereby separate. All things are connected as in the finest web of a spider. The slightest movement on any thread can be discerned from all points in the web. The flight of those ravens trembled the threads that connect invisibly with the affairs of men."
>
> My scepticism must have been plainly visible in my expression. . . . With the hint of a smile, Wulf released his grip on my arm and splashed on to the river bank. I stood in the water watching him. "Imagine you were to witness a raven swooping from the sky to peck out the eye of a warrior," he said, stretching out on the grass. "You would say that the flight of the bird was connected directly with the wound. But if you had observed the flight of the same raven half a day before the attack, you would see no connection with the warrior's injury. Nevertheless the pattern of a raven's flight at noon is bound to the pattern of its flight at dusk, just as surely as the progression of

day and night. One can read the pattern and thus see what the future has in store."

He sat up and stared at me intently. "You are labelling pieces of the world with words, then confusing your word-hoard for the totality of life. You see life as if you were viewing a room by the light of a single moving candle; then you make the error of assuming that the small areas you are seeing one at a time are separate and cannot be seen as one. Since the small areas of your life are thus seen as separate, you have to invent ways of connecting them. This is the fallacy of the ordinary person's view of life, for everything is already connected. Middle-Earth is one room, lit by a thousand candles."

. . .

Wulf leaned closer to me and spoke into my ear as if sharing a secret: "You are strangling your life-force with words. Do not live your life searching around for answers in your word-hoard. You will find only words to rationalize your experience. Allow yourself to open up to wyrd and it will cleanse, renew, change and develop your casket of reason. Your word-hoard should serve your experience, not the reverse."

He smiled gently. "Words can be potent magic indeed, but they can also enslave us. We grasp from wyrd tiny puffs of wind and store them in our lungs as words. But we have not thereby captured a piece of reality, to be pored over and examined as if it were a glimpse of wyrd. We may as well mistake our fistfuls of air for wind itself, or a pitcher of water for the stream from which it was dipped. That is the way we are enslaved by our own power to name things."

—— CHAPTER 14 ——

Man, Science and the 21st Century

21st Century Technology

Our scanty knowledge of the vacuum state is presently in roughly the same condition as was our understanding of electricity at the turn of the last century. Major breakthroughs, they say, come only once every hundred years. The next one is due and it seems that the next major upheaval to our technology and social structure will come about through the understanding and harnessing of this vacuum energy.

The changes to our way of life will perhaps be as radical as those ushered in by the advent of electricity. And most importantly, the discovery is so 'coincidently' timely – for our planet desperately needs a source of clean energy. Socially, politically and spiritually, the conditions could hardly be more opportune.

Just as the presently known laws of energy conservation need to be expanded to include vacuum state and higher (eg. mental and emotional) energies and thus the processes of manifestation and even de-manifestation, so must the laws of action and reaction (Newton's third law) be extended to include reaction *at a distance* from the 'original' action. Nor need the reaction be precisely *opposite*, just equivalent. That is, *if we do something here*, through connections within the vacuum state, *the reaction can be somewhere else.*

In specific terms, it means that we can engineer electrical charge at one place and produce, for example, gravitational or inertial changes at another. The total energy of the system remains the same (an extended law of energy conservation) and the reaction (gravitational/inertial) has been translated in 'type' from our original electric or electromagnetic action. The reaction also appears at a different place, that is: with different spatial parameters.

Note, therefore, that with a comprehension of this equivalencing of all energies, *all manifested effects become interchangable, both mathematically or theoretically, as well as in real engineering.*

Mass, inertia, gravity, electrical charge, the pure massless potential of vacuum – all these, being effects, can be manipulated relative to each other and can be interchanged. They can be transformed, the one into the other. One kind of vacuum patterning becomes another kind of vacuum patterning. The implications for the construction of free energy transformers (providing free electrical energy out of the vacuum), inertia and gravity-free transport, even perhaps that dream of science fiction writers, the teleport – all these and more become understandable possibilities.

Because of our present dependence upon and exploitation of electrical energy and the range of devices that are already in common usage, I imagine that the first domestic vacuum energy transformers will simply create electrical current to run existing domestic appliances, power electric motor cars and so on. But as vacuum energy technology is developed, one can readily conceive of a range of small, quiet, motion-free devices translating the vacuum energy into light, heat, motive power, communications and so on.

One of the more obvious changes will be that all the wires strung around our homes, not to mention our planet, will become obsolete. With the power source becoming vacuum or space itself, we can use that power wherever we are. It does not need to be pumped to us. Just like our bird sitting on the electric cable, we can take the energy from right under our feet. We do not need to pay someone else to send us what we already have. We just need to buy a device that will extract or translate vacuum energy.

Just as the transistor which is capable of amplifying electrical power, transformed the electronics industry, so will the advent of vacuum state translators usher in a new age of clean energy. At present, these devices are large and unwieldy, like the old valves replaced by the transistor, but when they are refined and miniaturized using a neat understanding of the vacuum structure to gently translate the cosmic physical energy field of space, then the new range of technology will come into its own.

Similarly, communication energies will be transferred through the vacuum itself, picked up by resonance or tuning translators, just as we tune our radios and TV's to the grosser form of electromagnetic radiation used in communications today. The speed of transmission or, more correctly, transference, may even be instantaneous, just as our thoughts and emotional energy can travel, perhaps immediately, to distant places and be felt by those people with whom we have a connection and to whom such telepathic messages have unconsciously or consciously been directed. The speed of mind is far faster than any physical energy, due to the structure of subtle energy relationships.

An understanding of the energy relationships and interconnections between what now appears to us as 'non-local' connection will become clear when we understand more of the nature of the vacuum structure, permitting instant, wire-less communication through the vacuum matrix rather than electromagnetic energy, as at present.

Energy patterns of physical reality at one place could thus be encoded into vacuum state modulations and transmitted quite readily. With suitable screens or even by a process of light *kindling*[1] – producing patterns of light in three dimensional space out of the vacuum by scalar wave interference – we could receive audio and visual signals, perhaps even tastes and smells.

Computer technology would become that of programming the vacuum matrix, in *Vacuum State Computers*. A universally transmitted database or matrix containing all relevant information could perhaps be established which would be available to anyone with the correct receiving and decoding equipment.

Locomotion would be fuelless and clean, based on inertia-free and gravity-free technology. The need to move about so much for business or other purposes would be reduced by the advent of powerful communications networks, as is already happening. When we do need to go places, the same kind of vehicles could be used for surface,

[1] A term coined, I believe, by T. E. Bearden.

air or even space travel. This would no doubt result in a move away from commercial centres, such as towns, to a more rural existence. Man needs to live with nature to maintain his sense of harmony with her or else he destroys his environment and himself to boot. Technology should be man's servant, not his master. Used if and when required, relinquished when not.

Our physical needs in this world are really very few. Food, clothing, shelter and companionship – that is about all. Now we can expand on these or keep them to a minimum, that is up to us. And the fewer the needs, the happier the man. This has always been the advice of wise men. My own guru was once asked if it was acceptable to pray to the Lord for our 'daily bread', or should we leave everything in His hands? He replied, "It is all right if we only want bread. But we also want jam and butter on it!" I think that most of our technology can be seen as jam and butter!

But human nature, being what it is and the impetus of our scientific culture being too great to stop unless there is some great planetary disaster, these devices and inventions will come. So it is as well to be prepared.

No doubt there will also be those who wish to use such energy for the destruction of other human beings, for gaining power over them or who just want to make a fat profit out of them. The desire for power over others is probably one of the greatest illusions of all time. It is simply a rampant inner ego, feeding man's other passions. What, after all, does one get out of power? Everbody dies in the end. What happens after that is more important. Is life to be played like some fascinating but mindless game of monopoly, where the only aim is to 'win', at whatever the cost? And what is actually won? Nothing. Just loss of human spirituality and ignorance of the inward meaning, purpose and experience of life.

Those humans who are given jobs of leadership on this planet should consider themselves the servants of all. They do, after all, pay themselves out of money they have taken from the rest of us and they purport to represent our interests. So we have a right to expect that they act in the best interests of the community, not in the pursuit of their own self-seeking interests, to indulge personal motivations of ego, pride, greed, anger and general empire building. But this is not a perfect world, though it would be good to see humanity act as a decent caring community of creatures, with some inkling of the mystic and spiritual reality linking us all into one family with each other and all other creatures. We inflict so much unnecessary suffering upon others and thus upon ourselves, too, automatically and instantaneously. Our own mind is always the first to suffer when we hurt or exploit others, or even consider doing so. We suffer an immediate lessening of consciousness and inner life. It is always our inward life and being which should be given precedence over outward material considerations.

But we digress, though these inward realities are so important that they should not be neglected or ignored, as is the scientific custom. For if science ignores life and consciousness, what meaning or use has it?

So there will, no doubt, be those who make weapons out of this understanding. Bearden states quite explicitly that the Russians have already done this and are capable of destroying any part of the planet they care to. These are the *scalar wave interferometers* that create 'cold explosions' at a distance from the weapon, with the energy being transmitted through the vacuum state.

He also says that criminal elements have been experimenting with such vacuum beam weapons. Fortunately, the inventor is supposed to have stepped into the beam of one of his own weapons and nearly been killed. This was discovered when one of Bearden's friends, who "moves in underground circles" (sounds like a disoriented mole!) was attempting to purchase such a weapon for Bearden's analysis. In fact, again according to Bearden, since inertia can be decreased by this kind of technology, it can also be increased, making things difficult or impossible to move. Apparently, this was demonstrated back in 1969 to the Chief of the Homicide Squad in Toronto, Canada, when the mechanism of his own pistol was jammed by increasing its inertia with a suitable intertia-plus, vacuum energy beam weapon.

In the realm of health, the subtle healing sciences of homoeopathy, radionics, acupuncture and others can all be understood as vacuum or more subtle state energy sciences. So a knowledge of vacuum and subtle state structure will have great value for the healing arts. Healing of mental and emotional imbalance may also be possible by manipulation of vacuum energies. But the possibilities are endless and I have already discussed many of these here and in *Subtle Energy*. This technology has tremendous power for both good and ill. So let us do our best to use it only for harmonious purposes.

A Man-Made Vacuum State Computer

The problem with the scalar wave model and indeed with all mathematical expression or description is that it is still, in the widest sense, linear. It cannot contain within its model a picture of the multitude of energy relationships present within the universe – within and without.

Nature itself is non-linear. It operates at a multitude of levels and in a myriad forms, *simultaneously* and as a *whole*. It is our logical, conceptual minds which are linear, perceiving only linear cause and effect pathways, rather than the actually self-existent, holistic, holographic and simultaneously active relationships within the whole. Even our most modern computing technology still has only one central processing or logical unit. We may combine many processors into one system, but these central parallel processors function *separately*, not in an *automatically* integrated fashion, where each *simultaneously* knows what the other is doing and acts accordingly and in harmony. The integration is provided by linear software, not automatic relationship.

What is required is still a logical system, but one which is based upon the holographic principle in which the parts are automatically 'aware' of the other parts and of the total functioning of the whole. Such a system would operate primarily as a whole. Note that the holographic model is still logical in nature, still functioning under the primary law of cause and effect, of interconnectedness, of karma.

As described in *The Web of Life*, this is most probably how the whole body operates, with its autonomous cells each linked by resonance and holographic relationship to each other and to the whole. This is reflected in the vibrating pattern of energy we call the molecule of DNA.

It is also the structure of the whole uni-verse.

In the brain and central nervous system, the complexity of this linkage is immense, with each of the 10^{12} brain neurons connected by up to 100,000 others in non-linear, avalanche discharge, energetic relationships.

The more primary patterner and organizer of this effect lies quite clearly in the more subtle realms of energy where the laws of energetic relationship are *inherently* holographic and holistic.

To make an advanced computing system which would model brain function is actually quite impossible for we could never endow it with a soul or with consciousness. It is in consciousness where the fundamental capacity for wholeness actually resides. It is there that the individual can become the Universal.

Put quite simply, we cannot make a machine and endow it with life. The best we can do is to copy the patterning of life's processes as best we may, but employing only the energies of inert matter. The complexities woven by the life force out of inert matter, even at the subatomic level, is quite unattainable in any artifical way. Man's machines have always been only conscious or unconscious copies or artefacts of nature's superbly constructed processes. Without the life force of consciousness, nature's individual holographic units – souls and minds entrapped in physical bodies, living creatures – cannot be even remotely constructed by man. With all our analytical thinking and experimental probing, we are still no nearer constructing the most simple cell, or the most 'primitive' life form. In fact, there are relatively few molecules, even, that we actually know how to build without the aid of living creatures.

But to begin to even try to copy just the barest outline of this natural patterning process, we need first of all to have a technology which provides for integrated relationships of all parts to the whole. This does not exist at the level of electromagnetics, as we presently understand it. Here, we are dealing with effects rather than a more primary cause, with the bubbles not the ocean.

The level of energy in which this kind of relatedness is inherent lies in the vacuum state. Our primary matrix, therefore, needs to be located in the patterning of the vacuum state. This would be our quasi-intelligent database which *automatically adjusts itself as a whole*, whenever the value of any part is changed. But to implement this, we need to understand the detailed constitution and construction of the vacuum and the way physical manifestation takes place. The holographic model gives us a good starting point, but the details are not known to us, though a number of people are currently working on this, with considerable success. Dr Jim Said is one of them, whose work is mentioned briefly in *The Web of Life*.

Having designed such a matrix within the vacuum state, so that we may modulate it at will, we then need to connect it to both input (yin), quasi-sensory aspects of the total system and output (yang) capabilities or quasi-motor functions. This would include a range of output devices capable of handling and presenting data within the holographic and holistic paradigm. These would, no doubt, include three-dimensional, optically-projected holographics, replacing our present-day screen displays of linearly-conceived computer graphics.

The vacuum matrix for such a system would most probably be contained within a perfect crystal. The uniqueness of a crystal, is that it is an *ordered* structure at the atomic level. One assumes, therefore, that this is a reflection of order at the vacuum level. And, of course, what makes a crystal a crystal is the relationship of each part to the whole, the positioning of each atom within the whole. This is inherent in their ordering. As we have previously described, however, there are an infinity of vacuum substructures which can all result in the same external materialization. It is this substructure which will constitute the vacuum matrix for the memory and processing capability of our new kind of computer, through an advanced understanding of how physical substance is manifested from the vacuum state.

So our man-made, vacuum state computer is based upon real energy fields which relate automatically in a dynamically holographic manner. The next step, then, is to connect into this matrix, devices which are automatically *both input and output*. This is necessary so that the machine can react to its own impressions or input, from without. This mirrors our own human sensory input and intimately associated motor output.

But there very rapidly comes a point where the encoding, assimilation and logical structuring of data with even such a powerful computer would be quite unable to mirror the integrating role of the mind and consciousness within our own selves. Learning, meaning, memory, recall, experience, intuition, feeling, preference – all these faculties and many more can never be copied by a computer to any degree even remotely comparable to that of a real live human being. And copying some of the things performed by a living creature does not constitute life and intelligence.

A man-made computer can never possess life and consciousness. It can never even possess a mind or emotions. It cannot fall in love, get angry or enjoy a beautiful sunset. It could never have lucid moments and mystical experiences. It could never even be aware of itself. All these are the province of life itself and it is a reflection of our how far from our inner life we have moved that many of the scientists involved in artifical intelligence really believe that if they could make a machine that did all that humans do that it would really be alive. It is a reflection of the way such people see not only themselves, but also those around them and humanity in general. It shows how little do we understand the nature of life, if we think that by imitating some of the outward show, we have actually created inward life and consciousness. The outer shell is mistaken for the life and mind within.

Returning to the imaginary design of our supercomputer. Stretching one's thinking somewhat, it may be possible for a holographically presented, three-dimensional optical projection to be engineered in such a way that it could receive a stimulus from without. Feeding this data back to the matrix which controls its presentation, the hologram could then, perhaps, be programmed to respond automatically in an apparently intelligent fashion. If this holographic projection were of a humanoid form, for example, an optical input to the eyes or any other part of this projection could possibly be engineered to result in appropriate activity of the whole humanoid.

If this holographic projection were then translated into a

robot, based upon the same holographic and holistic principles (this is all based on some enormous 'if's!), we would possess a powerful instrument. The robot could conceivably be actually engineered into existence by vacuum state manifestation with all the manipulation of gravity, mass, electrical charge and so on which we have discussed. In other words, its existence would be continuously manifested and controlled out of the central vacuum matrix and would disappear the moment this central machine was turned off! It may sound like science fiction, but so would all of our present day technology to those living even so recently as the nineteenth century.

Man has, I feel sure, discovered such technology in previous cycles of his existence upon this planet. It would seem only reasonable. Our western history goes back no further than a few thousand years, and the last ice-age only receded about ten thousand years ago.

The legends of Atlantis and Mu are probably based upon fact and were only one of many adventures man has made into technology. There are supposed to be certain crystals found in South America, for instance, of a clearly man-made design and which were possibly the basis of a previous technological culture. Perhaps they were left as a permanent record, high in the Andes, for future ages to decipher, much as we leave sealed libraries of information and encoded data for future ages to find or which we send out into space for civilizations on other planets to decode.

Such records would naturally be based upon fundamental physical principles which those who left them assumed that future ages would unravel. We are on the threshold of being able to do just that.

The records of our entire planetary history may even be encoded quite naturally and automatically into the physical vacuum itself awaiting only to be deciphered. This is the akashic record spoken of by theosophical and other writers, though whether this planetary information is vibrationally patterned into the physical akash or into one of the higher, more inward 'skies', I do not know. But certainly some imprint must be there, for this is what we feel when we experience the atmosphere of places. This is what psychically sensitive folk pick up when they psychometrize articles and are able to know something of their past history. This is the vibration we can perceive in all objects that reflect the vibrations within the minds of the users or the owner. This I have previously discussed in chapter five.

Consider, for example, the dreadful atmosphere of those concrete and steel, multi-storey and basement car parks which have such a grim vibration that they are frequently chosen by film and TV directors for unpleasant and violent transactions.

Or, on the other hand, think of the peaceful and healing vibration that extends around spiritually-minded people, in their homes, their presence and in the objects they use. There are even a few such centres or communities in the world where such loving and harmonious vibrations abound and surround one. This is all encoded within the vacuum and subtle states and may one day be decipherable by advanced scientific instrumentation, in addition to that already possible by the sensitive minds of living creatures, human and otherwise. We may consider that this is unlikely, but then – just a few decades ago – so would the genetic fingerprinting techniques recently introduced into forensic science for establishing the identity of blood and other bodily tissues and cells.

In fact, nearly all our present technology was still science fiction when Queen Victoria reigned in England less than a century ago. Man's technology *will* advance if he does not blow himself to bits or completely disrupt his environment!

The Catch 22 of Novel Scientific Research

It is a common fallacy that any new and beneficial scientific research or discovery will automatically come to the fore. This just is not the way things happen. One of the major difficulties encountered by any new idea in science is the very system of academic science itself. Scientific work only becomes known and academically acceptable if the findings are published in orthodox scientific journals or magazines. These journals therefore play a key role in which research and ideas are publicized and which are not.

But the journals themselves are tied by commercial considerations of what is acceptable to the majority of their conventional readers. They cannot afford to lose their readership. They also have to maintain a reputation, and thus cannot afford to risk publishing material which is too controversial.

With hundreds of thousands of scientists worldwide, the number of papers submitted to journals is enormous. These papers are vetted by unnamed experts in those fields, who are therefore given the advantage of previewing their colleagues work and passing judgement upon it. And human nature is no doubt involved in their decision-making. What 'expert' would like to see his lifetime's work and opinion seriously challenged?

But the nett result is that anything which challenges orthodoxy, even with experimental data, is rejected. It never gets published. The data is presumed to be flawed. And without publication it may never become known, or at best develops the atmosphere of a 'fringe' status.

Such scientists then have two options open to them. Firstly, they can plod on, hoping one day that their work will receive some acceptable corroboration. Or they can go public – write a book or contact the media. This only works if there are sensational aspects to the research and, in any event, media attention lasts for a very short while. The negative result of this, however, is that the work is now cheapened in the eyes of conventional academia. Certainly the avenues for publication in learned journals is then closed.

The scientist is then out on a limb and may drift into obscurity, maybe even losing his academic position. Scientists have seen this happen so many times that they are naturally apprehensive of it happening to them. Fear, therefore, helps reinforce the established view of things. To be unconventional is dangerous and can lead to scientific excommunication.

The other avenue by which new ideas can gain credence is from the independent scientist, though they are few in number and almost always lack resources. Such work is often acceptable to large numbers of the general public – and in the field of health and natural medicine may often prove to be of great value. And even though it often proves of great interest to many scientists, read in the privacy of their own homes, it is rarely accepted by the 'system'. The reasons all lies in the psychology of the situation.

Radically new and valuable ideas therefore rarely get the financial backing or sheer manpower they require, and they fall by the wayside. Faced wth the necessity of earning a living, there is little that the discoverer can do and his discovery is either discarded, becomes a part-time hobby, or he becomes so obsessed and unbalanced by his rejection that no-one wants to have anything to do with him. To find a wealthy backer, like Sandy Kidd has done, and like Nicola Tesla at the turn of the century, is a rare and fortunate occurence.

This state of affairs continues until man finds himself in a in a natural or man-made crisis – war, lack of energy resources, social upheaval, or – in the present instance – a heavily polluted environment and the urgent need to do things differently.

There is no doubt, for example, that the two world wars unhinged the balance of the previous social order allowing – rather demanding – that new ideas and technology were developed. Neither side wanted the other to get the edge on them, so all options, however apparently bizarre, had to be explored. With many positive avenues of research being opened up.

This pattern has been played out for almost all the researchers mentioned in this book. Even Professor Laithwaite is considered something of a heretic for countenancing the possibility that a cranky old seventeenth century scientist (Newton) may not have been infallible.

So let us hope that the work of some of these unsung heroes is taken up and more thoroughly researched. With the full support of some major corporation or government I feel sure that unequivocal experimental results could be forthcoming in even less than one year. Such technology might help to make a better world – surely the ideal of all science? So why wait until the pioneers have died?

> Through which the living Homer begged his bread,
> Seven cities claimed great Homer – dead.

Man, Mind and Spirit

The vast majority of mankind has no idea what life is or what its inner purpose might be. History does not encourage us to think that we will improve in the near future. Man, alone amongst all creatures, uses his greater ability, his capacity for higher consciousness, his supposedly higher intelligence to destroy himself and his planet. He plays a game of selfishness with his fellow humans and other creatures to an extreme degree. His ego is insatiable. He chases chimeras and phantoms in his mind, playing out his internal subconscious emotional chaos in games involving deliberate acts of violence to his fellow humans and fellow living creatures. We all do it to one degree or another. We have the capacity to be an angel or a devil.

On the other hand, there is an increasing awareness, an expanding consciousness amongst some of the people's of our planet at this time. The fundamental questions are no longer being swept under the carpet by the pressures of daily life. This is a rising tide which must be encouraged and developed, not suppressed by bureaucracy, power, politics and sheer inertia. There is an increasing core of people who see through the shallowness of governmental politics and political leaders (of whatever persuasion) and who know that human leaders should primarily be wise men, not self-seekers – those who unite, not those who create enmity and division. And these people are quietly taking their place in the fabric of life, creating change from within. People genuinely want peace; the machismo and romantic attitudes towards war, as well as the restrictive partisan and divisive nature of loyalty to one's 'country' are being seen in their true light.

Regarding scientific study and technology, there is nothing wrong with it, per se. It is man's emotional nature, the negative tendencies of our own minds, our attitude and approach to science which have caused the present troubles. We desperately need to understand the universal substrate of existence, the basic spirituality – devoid of any religious dogma – that is naturally present within all of us. Within this context and with this understanding, we would know how to make the right decisions concerning our affairs upon this planet. *Such philosophy should be an essential part of all science courses*. No knowledge should be given without some basic education in its use for human betterment and its harmonious integration with the planetary ecosystem. *Basic scientific and human ethics, devoid* of any particular religious doctrine, should be taught in all universities and colleges. But we are lost in spiritual ignorance, a prey to the weakness of our own minds without even realizing that this is so. We even take pride in our weaknesses.

It is now essential that our world 'leaders' do their best to drop the masks and the games of politics and to work together in a spirit of genuine cooperation and harmony, to bring some measure of balance back into man's outward activities. And all this, without suppressing the natural right of humans to personal freedom of expression and action, within the natural laws of reasonable harmony.

Despite all the apparently self-inflicted negativity, however, one should not forget that this universe is a continuous creation or a projection of the Supreme Being. It is by His design that we are the way we are. By withdrawing knowledge of Himself from us, thereby leaving us in darkness and ignorance, we are made to struggle back towards the light. This would seem to be His purpose in 'chastising' us in this way, so that our greatest effort and longing ultimately becomes that of seeking the highest Reality, within ourselves. "If you do not experience the darkness, you cannot fully appreciate the light," my own spiritual teacher once commented. And to find that innermost light of Reality is the Divine purpose in the creation of human life.

—— CHAPTER 15 ——

The Greatest Experiment in the World

Mysticism and Science

It seems quite clear that an understanding or intuitive recognition of the mystical is of paramount importance if the full implications of the vacuum state are to be grasped. Indeed, almost all the really great scientists over the ages have, to a greater or lesser extent, been visionaries with mystical intuition. Einstein, Max Planck and Neils Bohr all acknowledged the importance of the mystical approach to life, in their work. Bohr even incorporated the Chinese sign of the implicate yin and yang of the universe into his family crest. Einstein, Planck and many others all made mention of their appreciation of the inward side of life.

> The finding of the truth can only be secured by a determined step into the realm of metaphysics.
>
> *Max Planck*

> The most beautiful and most profound emotion we can experience is the sensation of the mystical. It is the power of all true science. To know what is impenetrable to us really exists, manifesting itself as the highest wisdom and the most radiant beauty which our dull faculties can comprehend only in their most primitive forms – this knowledge, this feeling is at the centre of true religiousness.
>
> *Albert Einstein*

In fact, it is from the higher Mind that all physical intuitions are derived. Concentration of mind is of primary importance in both mystic meditation as well as in scientific endeavour. All of these scientific pioneers were creative and concentrated thinkers who realized certain things within themselves and then expressed this realization in outward terms – as mathematical and physical concepts, and so on. All deep thought takes place at the centre behind the eyes. This is where the higher paths of yoga and meditation actually *start*. But they begin by *stilling* the mind, not by activating it. And into this stillness, the intuitions of the higher Mind can flood, often when we least expect them.

The purpose of real mystic meditation is to reach within to higher levels of expanded consciousness, superconsciousness, to reach towards the Supreme Creator or God. But in the process, the mind becomes so concentrated that it automatically comes to understand the structure of the physical universe. Then, within the limitations imposed by prevailing concepts, and the nature of the human mind and words themselves, as well as his particular personality, the individual is able to express these realizations, to communicate them. However mystically evolved a person may be, we are all karmically involved with the times in which we have presently taken birth. This is our current idiom, and within this context we express ourselves. The pioneers push forward this frontier of idiom, often to the dismay of their contemporaries, but yet are heralded by posterity, by future generations of young people with fresher minds and in a changing world.

But all things happen as they are meant to happen. We, in a sense, are just puppets. We dance according to some higher strings. But as long as we feel that we are individuals, apart from the great Ocean, we feel we have free-will. So we should attempt to discriminate and make the best possible decisions based upon the highest aspirations and endeavours, in all aspects of this amazing experience we call our life.

The Proof of the Pudding

The accepted methodology of classical science is that a theory or hypothesis remains no more than a possibility unless repeatable experiments can be performed which demonstrate its validity. So let me suggest an experiment which anyone can perform to check on the validity of just one claim made in this book.

The claim is *that the practice of meditation changes a person's perception of life and the universe*. The longer the practice, though it varies with the individual, the greater this change. The change comes about through a shift or expansion in consciousness, not simply as a result of seeing the world through the coloured glasses of a different intellectual philosophy. It broadens one's outlook on all aspects of life and involves a radical, inward change.

And the experiment? *To practise meditation assiduously, every day, for a minimum period of twelve months, and see what happens*. The laboratory is that of your own body, in the quietness of your own home, so no expensive equipment or funding is required. However, just as one only learns to swim with the aid of a qualified teacher, it is imperative that anyone embarking upon the discipline of meditation should first find a suitable teacher of this ancient technique for inner expansion. After all, if you are about to perform an experiment within your own mind and soul, where you may have had no previous experience of what you will uncover, guidance is required in such an undertaking. So do make a thorough research before making a decision, for there are many kinds of meditation and spiritual or yogic practice.

Without performing this simple experiment, no-one is qualified to make any final judgement upon the validity of the understanding which comes through meditation, though even such a step is only the first upon a million mile journey. But, says Confucius, "A journey of a thousand miles starts with the first step."

In Search of the Mystic Reality

Reality and Opinion

There is a charming tale told by script writer Allen Boone in his book, *Kinship With All Life*, concerning his association with the filmstar dog, Strongheart. Strongheart was by all accounts a dog of considerable character and presence and when his owners took an extended trip abroad they left the dog in Boone's good care. This turned out to be an event which evidently changed the writer's outlook upon life in general and other creatures, in particular. For Strongheart quite clearly had an inner life of his own. He read Boone's mind on a regular basis, even when they were not in the same room and communicated his needs, requirements and moods in a simple and forthright manner. And it did not take long for Strongheart to make Boone realize this.

Boone tells the tale of how, one fine spring morning, he was seated at his typewriter struggling with a desire to leave his writing and escape with Strongheart into the sunny world outside which beckoned him. He had no sooner made up his mind to take off into the hills for the rest of the day, when an excited Strongheart burst into the room. Skidding to halt only brief enough to dab the back of Boone's hand with his tongue, he dashed into the bedroom, returning with the old sweater his human friend always wore upon their outings. Then followed the blue-jeans, one walking boot, its partner, and the walking stick. In five rapid trips, the entire walking paraphernalia had been assembled.

After a continuous stream of such events, Boone found himself increasingly perplexed. He devoted much mental energy and intellectual thought to figuring out what was going on, but without any satisfaction.

Eventually, he remembered his old friend, Mogave

Dan, who lived in the desert surrounded by a family of dogs and burros and frequently wild animals, too, that took shelter with him. "If anyone can explain this mystery to me," thought Boone, "it will be Mogave Dan." For Dan was the only human he had ever known who could carry on a two-way communication with animals. So off he went to find Dan in the Mogave desert.

As luck would have it, he had little difficulty in locating him and at great length he set out to explain to his friend the problems he was having in understanding the dog. Mogave Dan clearly understood animals for they were his constant companions and Boone waited in anticipation for an explanatory, "This is the way it is with dogs." But none came.

Dan remained mostly silent. Boone was unable to stay very long and finally, Dan did at last attempt to communicate to his friend where he was going wrong.

"There's facts about dogs," he said, "and there's opinions about them. The dogs have the facts, and the humans have the opinions. If you want facts about dogs, always get them straight from the dog. If you want opinions, get them from the human."

Then a ray of light entered Boone's mind. He realized that he had been going about things in the wrong way.

So he set off home with the seeds of a new direction implanted in his mind and his intriguing tale tells the story of how he came to really know Strongheart.

Similarly, when man wishes to understand the nature of the world about him, he usually looks in the wrong direction for the answers. We ask our own intellectual minds for the answers – we fail to ask nature herself. The trouble is that we do not actually know how to put the question.

Nature is what she is, man has many ideas about her. And we get so involved in these ideas that we lose our perspective. We fail to see how by *quieting* our minds and being *with* nature, her secrets will slowly be revealed to us. But the language of this revelation is not that of words and formulae. Though words and mathematics may come afterwards, if we are inclined to express things in that way. It is in the quietness of a meditative state of mind that intuitions and understanding arise.

We cannot grasp the nature of reality by chasing after it with an active mind. The greater our personal egocentric desire for knowledge, the more it eludes us. For our inner ego is the source of all our human illusion, confusion and ignorance. Our scattered human mind, with its compexities of subconscious thought and emotional processes is our own worst enemy and its desire to grasp knowledge with which to impress our fellows, precludes it from finding any real understanding at all.

We cannot have our cake and eat it. We must sit down before life and nature in a humble spirit, realizing our state of ignorance. Then, maybe, we will receive some glimmerings.

Finding the Way

I took to meditation during my last year at Cambridge University in 1965-66, after a childhood and adolescence in which intimations of the mystical were frequent companions. I was twenty-one. Actually, meditation took me and I went along with it, because it seemed the most practical way of penetrating the innermost secrets of life. It was also blissful and entrancing, revealing a reality quite different from the biochemistry, physiology and other aspects of biological science I was supposed to be studying.

I had gone to Cambridge to study medicine with the intention of specializing in psychiatry. I was interested in the mind and consciousness, thinking that psychiatry would offer some answers. But when I had a closer look, I realized that mostly, it did not, and I ended up just doing a straight natural sciences degree.

Graduating, without any worldly direction in mind and intent only upon understanding the nature of consciousness and life, I supported myself for a short while by playing the guitar. But very soon I found myself deeply attracted by the philosophy of a mystic adept who lived in India. There were a few books available, printed privately in India, and the friend of one of my college friends had actually been to India and met this master. Well, the whole story is a fascinating tale though not appropriate for these pages, but in October 1967, I found myself in India, tucked away in a quiet corner of the Punjab, with a guru whose spiritual radiance and wisdom took my breath away.

He taught, and still teaches, a simple and beautiful, universal mystic philosophy that is as old as man and as natural as life. And more importantly, he taught a highly specific technique of meditation for opening up the inner well-springs of spiritual consciousness within man, if he applies himself with a will. The philosophy of mysticism is useful only if it leads to a practical method of developing experience.

This was actually what I was looking for and I stayed in India for four months, returning again the next winter for a further three months. The temperature in the summer reached to over 120°F and westerners were not advised to stay. Since then, I have visited him many times in India and on four occasions he has been to England. His spiritual radiance is quite unique and the atmosphere surrounding him seems permeated with a blissful vibration that uplifts the soul and quietens the mind.

I have yet to find a higher master; indeed, I am no longer searching for one. I am convinced with an increasing certainty that he has reached the summit of mystic experience and consciousness. He himself makes no such claims, knowing that normal humans have no way of verifying or disproving them. He only says that he is doing the duty his own spiritual preceptor requested him to perform. That is, to teach those who honestly seek to know how to meditate and to reach within themselves to the highest levels of consciousness. He takes no money or gifts from his students, but is always the giver. In a world of financial greed and power seekers, this is a hallmark of the highest spirituality.

Over the years, my own perception of the world has thus become increasingly universal, deeper, more refined and mystic, and it is from this basis of understanding that I write. It is because it is useful to understand a person's background that I tell you of the above. It is not a part of nature's pattern that all people should share the same way of looking at things.

Needing some honest and simple occupation that would permit me plenty of time for the meditation practices, I worked for seventeen and a half years at Cambridge

University's famous Department of Applied Mathematics and Theoretical Physics, not as a physicist, but in the world of computers. A world where, in those days, everyone was self-taught.

My main emphasis in life, however, has always been, and still is, on the side of mystic experience. This is the experience of life consciousness itself. Its unfoldment is the meaning and purpose in human life.

But my love of nature and a desire for a deeper understanding of biological and healing processes always remained a part of my mind patterns. Then, around 1984, shortly after leaving the university to run my own small business, I found myself writing *Subtle Energy*, really as an attempt to clarify my own intuitive perception, as well as to bring an understanding of the mystical appreciation of life into a science that was entrenched in a materialistic world view and yet showed signs of wishing to escape. The time was right and the words came easily.

Subtle Energy was published in the spring of 1987 and within a year was being reprinted and translated into five major languages. The book seemed to have struck a chord and by that time, my second book on these topics *The Web of Life* was nearly in print and has been very well received. This present book is the third in the series and there is one more, (*Natural Creation*), in the pipeline. After that, I think it may be time to call a halt, for too many words obscure the issue. Such statements have been made before, however, and I am not able to foretell the future.

I mention all of this because I want to underline that my primary perception and inner understanding of the universe is mystical. You had probably already noticed!

The Mystic Reality

Like the tale of Allen Boone and Strongheart, or like man and his outward science, the inward nature of God and His creation is the way it is and the only way to know it, is to experience it for oneself. Man's ideas about it are different from the reality itself and what a man personally believes makes not the slightest difference to the nature of that mystic reality. Indeed, his beliefs are only another part of the cosmic drama. We are meant to be and to think just the way we do!

Man's outward science is simply a study of one small part of the full mystic cosmos and if man does not realize this, then that changes the reality not one whit. It simply makes man feel confused! When one reads the scientific journals, the philosophical writings of academic scholars, and even much of the 'New Age' semi-mystical philosophy, one notices this confusion.

All these writings, including this book, actually exist *because* of our confusion. If everyone could see the way things are, then there would be no need for all these words and contrary points of view. When people write their thoughts, not understanding the forces which drive them, the ancient human weakness of wanting to be the expert and to be thought highly of by one's fellows immediately arises. Add to this the fact that we are all conditioned by the thought patterns of our era, and the result is that human writings are heavily impregnated with 'hidden' aspects of the writer's human personality, and this most certainly includes those of an apparently objective scientific nature.

Some may use long words and convoluted phraseology in an attempted to be seen as intelligent. Much scientific literature is written in a style that bores the pants off most people, even if they can get behind the amazing complexity of language in which it is often quite indulgently and unnecessarily couched! The societies that promote the use of plain English should address themselves to more than just the legal profession and government documents! In others, lies the urge to disagree with everyone else. Some fill their pages with an amazing plethora of facts. The modes of expression are as many as the writers themselves, each reflecting the thought processes, the personality, and the degree of consciousness of the writer. Myself included, of course.

Why? Well, like Mogave Dan's comment about dogs: there are facts and there are opinions concerning the nature of Reality. If you want opinions ask man. If you want the facts, find a way of asking the Reality itself, 'ask' God. Our ideas – our thoughts – are even a part of His cosmic structure. For reasons best known to Himself, it is clearly a part of the Divine plan that we should be so confused, for there is also a law or plan which governs our thought processes.

Someone once wrote to me that they did not see the necessity of including the mystic cosmology at the start of *Subtle Energy*. They thought that it was too complex. Well, there are simple ways and more complex ways of expressing this naturally existent cosmological structure, depending upon whom you are addressing and what you have in mind to accomplish. But it does not in any way change the nature of the reality. We could, on similar grounds, complain that we do not like the structure of a living organism – why could it not be built in a simpler way, so that we could more readily understand it?

The question and the complaint are in many ways irrelevant, for things are what they are. There are those who say that there is no mystic hierarchy of physical, astral, causal and spiritual worlds. That there is no God or Universal Ocean of Being within which these worlds are created, projected or manifested. From our limited point of view, we have a right to our opinion. But opinions do not change the nature of life and death. Someone may not believe in reincarnation, but it does not prevent them taking birth after birth in this world. Shutting one's eyes to something does not make it go away.

We must come to understand the degree of our ignorance. At least that should become clear to us as a starting point. We must attempt to find a way to control the inward clammer of our thoughts and emotions. They run on habituated tracks and are not usually a source of real wisdom for us, but obscure the very thing we are seeking to find. Mostly they are so intense and have wrapped us up in a such bundle of confused unconscious emotion that we do not even know that we are seeking anything.

What I am calling God is beyond all intellectual complexity. He is beyond all differentiation. He is here, within everything, right now, and yet there is a vast hierarchy of worlds 'between' the physical and the Universal. God is not to be found in the unified field of physics. In the hierarchical sense, He is not to be found just beyond the atom. He is far deeper within. And yet the perfect mystic can be with the Lord in the twinkling of an eye and be back with us simultaneously. For him, everything is collapsed into one – but not into a unified field!

God is one, undifferentiated. He is the centre within all things. From within Him arises the Creative Word, the Holy Ghost, the Shabd, the Primal Life Stream. This is the first division, but yet this Creative Power is still within Him, carrying His characteristics into creation. As the vibration, motion and differentiation increases, the purely spiritual worlds are formed. Here, the primary law is that of Love and the souls inhabiting these regions radiate an intense light and are steeped in the Love of the Supreme Consciousness.

This Shabd or Word is the central part of the highest mystic practice, for it can be heard as sound and seen as light. The soul possesses these two faculties of hearing and seeing, for we experience the source of our own inner life through these two faculties. For this reason, the Shabd is also known as the Audible Life Stream. We are drops of this mighty creative river and to merge into that river is to find our way back to its source.

The Indian Vedas, which describe the inner cosmology only up to the realm of *Brahm*, the Universal or Divine Mind, call this creative current, *Om* or *Aum*, the reverberating cosmic motor. The mental or outward repetition of the word, Om, is sometimes practiced as a mantra, to help concentrate or focus the mind, but it is quite different from the true unwritten and unspoken Word of the Creator. This Sound Current is the rope let down from God, up which – with the help of a qualified teacher – we may climb. This is a far better practice than following the pranas or the astral light, for any current into which we absorb ourselves will take us only as far as its own source and no further. Such practices may be stepping stones or byways leading to the highway, but as soon as we can find that main highway, we should travel upon it.

As creation continues outward, duality becomes explicit and the vast computer of the Universal Mind is formed. It is here that time, space, causality and the duality or polarity of life as we know it are first expressed. Time and space arise as experiences of the soul when it separates from that which it is experiencing. Here the soul takes on the first fine essence of mental covering. This is far more subtle than our human mind, but the same essential qualities are reflected therein. In this vast realm of the Universal Mind, the soul, surrounded by its first vibrational, energetic covering (the causal body and the causal mind) is still engrossed in bliss and in love. But the one primal energy current of the Shabd is now beginning to multiply and to cross-interrelate, one current with another.

Passing through a valve or a threshold in their vibrational activity, an inner vacuum or akashic condition, these currents merge and connect with each other forming the central powerhouse of the next lower region, the astral zone. This energy crossroads is known as the Thousand Petalled Lotus, the Sahasra, and sometimes as the crown chakra. But it is deep within the central creative focus of the astral realm. The soul is engaged in the pursuit of bliss and inward pleasure, but here there is greater activity. The astral mind and astral body are formed naturally around the soul in this region for its existence and expression at this level.

The tendency of the mind is now moving towards activity and outwardness. The increased vibratory activity around the astral mind begins to confuse, to captivate and to charm it. Space and time, which first manifested in the realm of the Universal Mind, appear to be smaller and to move faster as the mind's complexity and the degree of multiplicity increases. But time and space most definitely exist in all the regions governed by the Universal Mind. They do not cease as soon as the physical realm is transcended. They exist for as long as there remains the duality of mind – Universal or human. They arise as a natural outcome of the soul being separated from its source by the mind. In terms of our physical experience, they arise due to the illusory duality of observer and observed.

The one thousand energy currents of the Sahasra then weave themselves into even greater energetic complexities until the next downward phase jump is made and the physical universe is formed with both subtle and gross aspects. Here the complexities of the outer world, our physical bodies and our human, physical minds are so great that time appears to rush by, in comparison to the extended time experience of the astral and causal realms. Similarly, space appears to be contracted and smaller.

Some understanding of this may be derived from our subjective experience of time which varies depending upon our mental state – what we are doing and the rapidity of our thought sequence, for example. Similarly, those in altered states of physical consciousness report changes in their perception of time. A friend of mine once told me that when playing a complex piece of piano music, rather than rushing his fingers through its intricate requirements and losing style and expression, he expands his mental appreciation of time so that he has 'plenty of time' in which to play.

Similarly, to some people, a minute feels like a long time span, while to others it is of no consequence. Time, and space too, are thus mental experiences, not objective realities. And since everything arises in space and time, we can readily see once again how our minds are the creators, at our physical level, of our physical world.

The human mind, however, is so gripped by the senses that our mental attention runs out from its centre within ourselves and gets absorbed in the play, never realizing that it is itself the projector of the movie. Our attention is actually our mind and consciousness knotted together. So we are lost and have no comprehension of our predicament. Hence we behave in the ways that we do. And it is for this reason, too, that our physical science is so superficial and has no understanding of where it stands in the overall scheme of things. It has its place, but only at a human level. It needs to be augmented by an inward study, by consciousness of the inner realms from which the physical creation is derived. This is the mystic science of real meditation which can be taught correctly only by an advanced mystic, himself. As in all matters, an expert teacher is required.

The mystic experience is no doubt our own. But even though an Olympic athlete is the one with the skills and talents, all the same, he still needs a coach to enable those abilities to be manifested. And the better the coach, the greater the expression of ability in the student.

Since all created things come out from the One Source, they all bear an imprint of the Creator's love and being.

They are, therefore, all related to each other. The Universal is said to be both one and infinite. Further, all parts relate to each other automatically because of their identical origins. The further within we travel, mystically, the clearer do these relationships appear to us. This is the basis of the changing laws of energy relationship which I have discussed throughout this book. The part contains an image of the whole.

In recent years the invention of holographic photography has been used as an analogy to express this reality, though we are dealing with a continuous creative process from within, not a crystallized, preformed pattern at a purely horizontal or physical level. It is the microcosmic-macrocosmic principle in action that ultimately permits our individual mind to merge with the Universal Mind, and the drop of our individual consciousness to merge with the Universal Consciousness.

Now we only see bumper-to-bumper, linear relationships, though with our intuitive mind we may feel other more tenuous connections. This is the intuition which underlies the search for a unified field theory. It is not so much a rational as an intuitive *mental*, recognition that all things are linked. Without this mental cognition, physicists would not be searching for a model by which to express this relationship.

But as we move within to the higher realms we see or directly experience the way in which the energies of the cosmos and of our own inward structure are put together. The mystic experience is therefore more valid and more real than any mathematical or philosophical model. We actually become the master of all below us. We see and could control the structure of it all, if we wanted to, because it lies within our own mind and consciousness. This is the certainty or faith that can, quite literally, move mountains. Ultimately, beyond the Universal Mind region, we lay down the mind, thankfully, for it has been the cause of much struggle. Then we hasten onwards to our spiritual home, whence we have been separated for so long.

Bibliography and Further Reading

Miscellaneous

Gaia, J.E. Lovelock; Oxford University Press, 1979.

A Harmony of Science and Nature – Ways of Staying Healthy in A Modern World, John and Lucie Davidson; Wholistic Research Company, 1986, 1994.

The Holographic Paradigm, edited by Ken Wilbur; Shambala, 1985.

Ideas and Opinions, Albert Einstein; Souvenir Press, 1973.

Kinship With All Life, J. Allen Boone; Harper & Row, 1954.

The Life of Nikola Tesla, John J.O'Neil; Spearman, 1968.

Living Water, Olof Alexandersson; Turnstone Press, 1982.

Order Out of Chaos, Ilya Prigogine and Isobelle Stengers; Collins, 1984.

Out of My Later Years, Albert Einstein; Knopf, New York, 1948.

The Rhythm of Living Form, Dr Peter Guy Manners; Link Up, December 1987.

Self-Organization in Non-equilibrium Systems, Ilya Prigogine; Wiley and Sons, 1977.

Tesla, Man Out of Time, Margaret Cheney; Dell, 1981

Through the Looking Glass, Lewis Carrol; Macmillan, 1872.

Tuning In To Nature, Philip Callahan, Devin-Adair, 1975.

The Way of Wyrd, Brian Bates; Century Hutchinson, 1983.

Modern Physics

Directions in Physics, Paul Dirac; John Wiley and Sons, 1978.

In Search of Schrodinger's Cat, John Gribbin; Corgi, 1987.

The Particle Play, J.C. Polkinghorne; Freeman, 1979.

Superforce, Paul Davies; Unwin, 1984.

The World of Elementary Particles, K.W. Ford; Blaisdell Publishing Co., 1958.

Modern Physics and The New Energy Science

Beyond Matter, Paramahamsa Tewari; Printwell Publications (India), 1984.

Cohering The Zero-Point Energy, Moray B. King; privately published paper, 1986.

Current Physics Theories and the Life Sciences, John Davidson; Planetary Association for Clean Energy Newsletter, Vol. 5, nos. 3 & 4.

Do We Really Understand Magnetism?, Harold Aspden; Magnets in Your Future, May 1988.

Anti-Gravity Electronics, Harold Aspden; Electronics and Wireless World, January 1989.

The Emerging Energy Science, T.E. Bearden and Andrew Michrowski; Planetary Association For Clean Energy, 1985.

The Energy Machine Of Joseph Newman, Joseph Newman; Joseph Newman Publishing Co., 1987.

The Ether of Space, Sir Oliver Lodge; Harper, 1909.

Ether Technology, Rolf Schraffanke; private, 1977.

Experiments with a Kromrey and a Brandt-Tesla Converter Built by John Bedini, Eike Mueller and Tom Bearden; Tesla Book Company, 1984.

Faster Than Light Signals, H. W. Milnes; Radio Electronics, V. 54-1, 1983.

Free Energy Secrets, Dr J. Franklin Kilpatrick. Publisher and date unknown.

Fundamental Fields and Phase Information, Jack Dea; Planetary Association for Clean Energy Newsletter, Vol. 4, no. 3.

The Generation of Electric Power by Magnetic Force, Section 6-5 of the Japanese Yearbook of High Technology and Science, 1988. Translated by M. Nakada.

Ghost Mass and the Unseen Energy World as Revealed by the Anomalies of the Gyroscope, Harold Aspden; Tothmattian Review, 1988.

Ground State of Hydrogen as a Zero-Point-Fluctuation-

Determined State, H.E. Putoff; Physical Review D, Vol. 35, No. 10, May 15, 1987.

The Holistic Paradigm, Moray B. King; privately published paper, 1986.

In Search of Zero-Point Energy, Selby Anderson; Planetary Association for Clean Energy Newsletter, Vol. 5, nos. 1 & 2.

The Invention of Hans Coler Relating to an Alleged New Source of Power, British Intelligence Objectives Sub-Committee, 1946, declassified 1962.

Is the Vacuum Really Empty?, Prof. W. Greiner and Prof. J.H. Hamilton; American Scientist, March-April 1980.

The New Tesla Electromagnetics and the Secrets of Electrical Free Energy, T.E. Bearden; Tesla Book Company, 1982.

Paradigm of New Science – Principia for the Twenty-First Century, Dr Shiuji Inomata; Gijutsu-Shuppan, 1988. In Japanese, not yet translated.

Physics Unified, Harold Aspden; Sabberton Publications, 1980.

Psychotronics, Dr Shiuji Inomata; Section 6-9 of the Japanese Yearbook of High Technology and Science, 1988. Translated by M. Nakada.

Psychotronic Universe and *Paradigm of New Science*, Dr Shiuji Inomata. Translated papers.

Proof of Free Energy Devices and Supporting Data, Rolf Schaffranke; Tesla Book Company, 1982.

Revolution In Technology, Medicine And Society, Dr Hans A. Nieper; MIT Verlag, 1985.

Scientific Politics and the Future of the Earth, Christopher Bird, Planetary Association for Clean Energy Newsletter, Vol. 4, no. 3.

The Sea of Energy in Which the Earth Floats, Dr T. Henry Moray; Cosray Research Institute, 1978.

Search for the Sparking of the Vacuum, Jack S. Greenburg and Walter Greiner; Physics Today, August 1982.

Something for Nothing, Paul Davies; New Scientist, May 27, 1982.

Subtle Energy, John Davidson; C.W. Daniel & Co., 1987.

A Theory of Proton Creation, Harold Aspden; Physics Essays, vol. 1, no. 2, 1988.

Thirty-six Nanoseconds Faster Than Light, Pappas and

Obolensky; Electronics and Wireless World, December, 1988.

Toward a New Electromagnetics, Thomas Bearden; Tesla Book Company, 1983.

Towards Flight Without Stress or Strain . . . or Weight, Interavia Magazine; Spring 1956.

Vacuum as a Source of Energy, Harold Aspden; Magnets in Your Future, vol. III, April 1988.

Yearbook of High Technology and Science, 1988 Edition. Section on New Science translated by Mitsuo Nakada.

Mystic and Yogic Philosophy

Autobiography of a Yogi, Paramhamsa Yogananda; Rider, 1950

The Book of Mirdad, Mikhail Naimy; Clear Press, 1962.

Consciousness, Vacuum and the Formative Mind, John Davidson; New Humanity, October-November, 1988.

Heaven on Earth, Daryai Lal Kapur; Radha Soami Satsang Beas, 1981.

Life Beyond the Veil, Rev. G. Vale Owen; Greater World Association, 1922.

Mathnawi, Jalalu'din Rumi; translated by R.A. Nicholson, Luzac & co., 1926.

Mystic Experiences of Medieval Saints, R.P. Aug. Ponlain S.J.; Kegan Paul.

Philosophy of the Masters, Maharaj Sawan Singh Ji; Radha Soami Satsang Beas, 1964.

Poems of Kabir, Kabir Sahib, translated by Rabindranath Tagore; Macmillan, 1973.

The Seed of Truth, Silver Birch, compiled by Tony Ortzen; Psychic Press, 1987.

Spiritual Gems, Maharaj Sawan Singh Ji; Radha Soami Satsang Beas, 1958.

Tukaram, Saint of Maharastra, Chandravati Rajwade; Radha Soami Satsang Beas, 1981.

The Web of Life, John Davidson; C.W. Daniel & Co., 1988.

Physics with a Mystical Flavour

Stalking The Wild Pendulum, Isaac Bentov; Fontana, 1979.

The Tao of Physics, Fritjof Capra; Fontana, 1984.

Index